# ALARMSTART

## About the Author

Having retired after a career as a university lecturer, Professor Patrick Eriksson has devoted many years to research for this series of books. He returned to primary sources and, crucially, as an associate member of the German Air Force Veterans Association since 1974, he has interviewed and corresponded with more than a hundred former members of the *Luftwaffe*, from junior NCOs to *Geschwader* commanders. Such primary material is unavailable anywhere else and can never be gathered again.

# ALARMSTART

The German Fighter Pilot's
Experience in the Second World War

North-Western Europe from the Battle of
Britain to the Battle of Germany

Patrick G. Eriksson

AMBERLEY

First published 2017
This edition published 2019

Amberley Publishing
The Hill, Stroud
Gloucestershire, GL5 4EP

www.amberley-books.com

British Library Cataloguing in Publication Data.
A catalogue record for this book is available from the British Library.

ISBN 978 1 4456 9439 9 (paperback)
ISBN 978 1 4456 7123 9 (ebook)

Maps by Thomas Bohm, User design.
Typesetting and Origination by Amberley Publishing.
Printed in the UK.

# Contents

| | | |
|---|---|---|
| | Preface | 7 |
| | Maps | 17 |
| 1 | Poland | 22 |
| 2 | Denmark and Norway | 27 |
| 3 | The Phoney War | 31 |
| 4 | Invasion of France and the Low Countries | 40 |
| 5 | The Battle of Britain | 68 |
| 6 | The Channel Front, 1941–42 | 137 |
| 7 | The Battle of Germany, August 1942–June 1944 | 173 |
| 8 | Conclusions | 281 |
| | Notes | 285 |
| | Bibliography | 303 |
| | Acknowledgements | 309 |
| | Index | 312 |

# Preface

This book is about the German fighter pilots of the Second World War, based essentially on written and personal contacts established with veterans during the 1980s and 1990s once they were already ageing men. They belonged to a generation, not just in Germany but also in the then British Empire, Japan and the USA, that was special in what it was able to achieve and live through. Hanns Trübenbach of *JG 52*, writing in 1993, put it well: 'The soldierly ethos that was given expression amongst us and which accompanied me unswervingly on all my operational flights, despite my having married in 1931 and having two children, cannot be compared with attitudes in modern times.' While many of their memories and recollections are remarkably clear, with the passing of time details have faded for many veterans, and sometimes it all seems so far away, as expressed in 1995 by Dr Max Clerico of *JG 54*: 'After all, it was 55 years ago. Sometimes it all seems like a dream, the unforgettable beautiful dream of flying! Indescribable to fly along a beach at 600 km/h and 10 m height, or to play in the cloud castles of the cumulus at 5000 m, or after a good breakfast, to enjoy half an hour's aerobatics. Ah well, all over, all gone now – but the happy memory remains inextinguishable. Now I have really relapsed into a romantic enthusiasm, in a dream world. Forgive me!' The survivors have enjoyed little respect and admiration among the following generations in Germany, a point stressed by Otto Stammberger, veteran of *JG 26*: 'We last old soldiers are always seen as though we had deliberately murdered millions of people. That many of the younger generation would not be alive if we had not risked our lives in action against an overwhelmingly powerful enemy, is rejected as mere hypothesis. The youth question why we even took part in the war at all, we should rather have "stayed at home"! That's how simple it has become today!'

Strong feelings among many Germans about the perceived injustice of the Treaty of Versailles, the loss of territory and population associated with it at the end of the First World War, and the threat of global communism played right into the hands of Hitler and the Nazis, and wittingly and unwittingly a great many citizens supported and encouraged their political activities in the lead-up to the Second World War. Friedrich Lüdecke of *JG 5* still held to such views long after the war: 'We were all convinced then, and remain so now, that this war, although admittedly begun by us Germans, was justified: it was about 1½ million Germans that were given to Poland through the Treaty of Versailles and were suppressed there culturally and racially. It was about territorial access to German East Prussia, with Danzig separated from the German Reich. And the war against Russia for we Germans was an attempt to put a stop to global communism, the goal of the Communist Internationale, before it was too late. I am familiar with Poland and Russia myself and know what was being planned there against Germany.'

Despite their youth, almost all the fighter pilots tended to become old before their time, often suffering changed personalities with the stress and relentless pace and the reality of a duty that appeared to have no achievable end in sight. They lived for the day, and most believed that disaster would never overtake them; of the few that felt that it would, most died quickly, as did the vast majority anyway, the most inexperienced almost always being the first to fall. Those who lived through the war fully appreciated the gift of their survival. To survive a war or any part thereof when you were in the front line was largely a matter of exceptional luck; certainly skill, training and, most of all, experience helped a lot, but without a lot of luck nobody survived, as Johannes Naumann of *JG 26* remembered in 1990: 'I flew only in the west, from 1940 to 1945, and am still alive due to a small miracle, when seen against the ratio of enemy aircraft numbers to our own during this four and a half years in western skies.' Most feared injury and mutilation more than dying. While almost none of them wanted war, many are honest enough to admit that they also would not have missed it, as with Wolfgang Falck, who flew in *ZG 1* and was later a night fighter pioneer and leader: 'My need for war has been covered for all time and I am happy that I came out of it in one piece, although I have to admit, that now, when it is all long past, these memories and life experiences, that form one, I wouldn't have missed it! I would certainly not have been, today, the person that I now am, without it.'

Though they have often been portrayed as staid and sensible, the German fighter pilots, like their Allied counterparts, were not lacking in humour and fun, to say nothing of their sometimes demonstrably scant respect for the ever-present National Socialist structures which dominated their world. Most German fighter pilots strove to do their duty for their country as best they could, to survive if possible, and did not glory in the demise of their opponents. One such was Gerd Wiegand of *JG 26*: 'I shot down 33 aircraft, about which I am not at all proud.' They wore the few decorations that came their way with pride and dignity, and rightfully so. Their stories deserve respect and need to be told. They remained fully aware of the context of their successes and their survival, and almost all strongly regretted the death and injury that accompanied their successful combats for the rest of their lives.

The title of this book, *Alarmstart*, is a German word which equates to 'scramble' in English – an emergency take-off of a unit of fighters on receipt of an alarm from early-warning systems. This volume examines the brief Polish campaign of 1939, the intense aerial struggle over France in 1939–40, and the succeeding and critical Battle of Britain, which in German understanding ran from July 1940 to 21 June 1941. The invasion of Russia the next day changed everything, leaving only two *Geschwadern* of fighters on the Channel Front (*JG 2* and *JG 26*, later joined by *JG 1* along the Dutch coast) from June 1941 to the end of 1942; their experiences are told here also, and those of the pilots involved in the subsequent massive aerial Battle of Germany. While the vastness of the Russian Front initially swallowed up much of the *Luftwaffe*, with stiff competition for limited German aerial resources posed also by Allied operations in the Mediterranean theatre, the onset of the American four-engined bomber campaign from August 1942 wrought a radical, and in time fatal, change. The terrible battle of attrition over greater Germany and the adjacent Channel area raged unchecked until June 1944 by which time ever-improving American escort fighters had culminated in the superb P-51 Mustang. This had the range to penetrate all of German air space and the performance to prevail over the German Messerschmitt 109s and Focke Wulf 190s; these fell in increasing numbers as American aircraft production and excellent crew training increased while *Luftwaffe* casualties drained the experienced leaders away at all levels, and serious fuel shortages curtailed training time and pilot quality dropped accordingly. By early 1944 the Allied aerial forces were winning the battle of attrition, a necessary prerequisite for a successful invasion of Normandy in June 1944. While this story of sustained and massive air war over North-West Europe is tackled here, culminating in the attainment of aerial dominance over the Invasion beaches by June 1944, the final year of the war in the West will be told in a different volume, focusing on the Mediterranean air war. Another will deal with the combat over the Russian Front, the German victory claims, and their complex and changing system of claim submission and confirmation, as well as German fighter pilot training, a major influence on the *Luftwaffe*'s Eastern Front successes.

Daily life for most pilots consisted of spending the vast majority of their time at base in anticipation of action; it was this waiting which was felt by almost all wartime pilots to be the hardest part of the war. Once the call to action sounded, and they took to the air, most feelings of apprehension vanished and were replaced by an eagerness and self-confidence in their own abilities and chances of survival. The thought that 'this cannot happen to me' spared most fighter pilots (and aircrew for that matter) any foreknowledge of their death, which normally occurred within seconds, although not always. Once action was joined, training and instinct kicked in and they were mostly too busy to worry about anything. Once back at their airfields an enormous joy, almost euphoria, would set in; this happiness, illustrated in many surviving photographs, is often mistaken for intense joy at having shot down an opponent, but in almost all cases the euphoria was due to the survival of another battle, of another day. Sadly, casualty rates in all air forces and theatres were very high, as they always are for those right in the thick of it, and so many died or were badly injured. Even those lacking physical scars carried the mental trauma inherent in war for the rest of their lives. This is not a book about unbeatable aces gaily knocking the enemy from the skies, and there is no glory in war, except the bravery shown by those who were, most of the time, very scared. This book is a serious look at the life and experiences of the German fighter pilots in the Second World War, told in their own words by over a hundred surviving witnesses, whose stories were collected by the author in the 1980s and 1990s. Now very few are left alive, and these stories need to be told or else they will be lost forever.

In the end I had responses from about 120 German fighter pilots and Me 110/Me 410 rear gunners. In view of the vastness of the subject matter I have dealt only with day fighter veterans and their experiences. The basis for this book rests on the memories, photographs and documents supplied by 108 of those veterans, ranging in seniority from *Gefreiter* (normally the lowest possible rank for a qualified pilot) right up to *Oberst* (what the Americans call a full-bird colonel), covering all the major units, or *Jagdgeschwader* as they are termed in German. A *Geschwader* is a large unit made up of three *Gruppen*, each in turn of three *Staffeln*. The latter normally comprised 12 aircraft and about 15 to 18 pilots in roughly the first two-thirds of the war, later rising to 16 aircraft and with four *Staffeln* to a *Gruppe* as well as four *Gruppen* to a *Geschwader*. Throughout the conflict, each *Geschwader* and *Gruppe* also had a *Stab*, or staff flight, of four aircraft/pilots made up of the relevant commander, his adjutant and several other pilots. In my pestering of the *Luftwaffe* veteran community I eventually managed to garner the views and memories of 35 *Staffelkapitäns*, 18 *Gruppenkommandeurs* and seven pilots who had been *Geschwader Kommodoren* (in charge of about 100–120 aircraft, hundreds of ground crew, and much equipment besides aeroplanes). To balance this core of first-person accounts from the leadership cohort, I also had testimony from a large number of ordinary pilots, from the most junior NCOs through to the lower-middle officer ranks. Among the witnesses were thus the front-line leaders at all levels up to a *Geschwader Kommodore*, pilots who had flown Messerschmitt Me 109s and Focke Wulf Fw 190s – the two main German fighters during the war – as well as crew (pilot, rear gunner/radioman) from Me 110s and the later Me 410 twin-engined fighter. In addition I had also collected a *Waffenmeister*, or master armourer; a *Luftwaffe* psychologist; one ground attack, or *Schlacht*, pilot; and 17 who had flown the revolutionary Me 262 jet fighter near the end of the war. Several of the *Kommodoren* had risen further and become fighter controllers, termed *Jagdfliegerführer*, or *Jafü* for short, in charge of large geographic areas and multiple fighter units' operational guidance, with headquarters staff running to several thousand for a large control centre in Germany.

The correct abbreviated nomenclature of the Messerschmitt 109 often encompasses some confusion: is 'Bf 109' or 'Me 109' correct? Willy Messerschmitt, the principal designer of the '109', had been the technical director of *Bayerische Flugzeugwerke A.G.* in Augsburg, which became the *Messerschmitt-Flugzeug-Werke A.G.* in 1938.[1] Despite all subsequent aircraft models being given the 'Me' prefix (e.g. Me 410, Me 262) those already extant in their early versions and including the '109' and '110' retained their initial official designation of 'Bf 109' and 'Bf 110', although unofficially often known as Me 109 and Me 110. Strictly speaking, using Bf 109 and Bf 110 would thus be correct, but this volume is grounded in the reminiscences of German fighter pilots, who from the recollections inherent in this volume referred to their aircraft affectionately, most often as 'Me' or 'Messer', and specific models had additional nicknames: Bf 109 E – 'Emil'; Bf 109 F – 'Friedrich'; Bf 109 G – 'Gustav' or often 'Beule' (a word meaning 'bump', used due to the bulges on both sides of the engine cowling resulting from enlarged breechblocks of larger-calibre nose-mounted machine guns fitted in many G-models). In *Luftwaffe* documents and original German sources, both 'Bf 109' and 'Me 109' can be found. For these reasons, the author has chosen to use the 'Me 109' nomenclature throughout this volume (the only exceptions being direct quotes from *Luftwaffe* documents). Just to complicate the scenario a bit more, there was an independent factory in Regensburg constructing the '109' among other machines, known from 1938 as *Bayerische-Flugzeug-Werke G.m.b.H.*, and with its own director.[2]

The *Luftwaffe* laid excessive emphasis on victories in the air and on the scores of pilots and units, with a complex reward system of decorations tied to an ever-changing scale of achievement. This contrasts directly with the British and American approaches, where decorations largely reflected bravery, or at least that reported to higher authority by commanders. This obviously cannot imply that the Germans were not equally brave, which they were. Many, probably a majority of pilots, were more focussed on staying alive and seeing out the war than becoming famous and highly decorated folk heroes, subject to the overwhelming battery of the German propaganda machine run by that evil genius Goebbels. The entire subject of scores and claiming, the excessively complicated and typically Germanic *Luftwaffe* system of recognising and classifying aerial successes, is one for detailed discussion in a following volume, and was also subject to a significant degree of manipulation by Göring (commander of the *Luftwaffe*) and his associates. The need at various stages of the war for heroes to be identified and made into darlings of the public also played a distinct role in all of this, and a few individuals were picked out to fill such starring roles – some to perfection and others to their distinct consternation.

The *Luftwaffe* was also different in having, from August 1941, a *General der Jagdflieger* or General of Fighters, a position within the high command responsible for the fighter arm and with direct access to Hitler. Werner Mölders, known to his pilots and throughout the *Luftwaffe* as *Vati* (daddy), and the originator with Günther Lützow of the famous and still universally applied 'finger four' fighting formation,[3] was the first incumbent of this post, till his death on 22 November 1941. He was someone who cared little for scores or even decorations, although he was not an anti-Nazi. Adolf Galland, an equally famous pilot and successor to Mölders as General of Fighters, was known as a hard and ambitious man, also neither an anti-Nazi nor a party acolyte, who strove for success to win the war rather than solely for his own renown. The third general of fighters, from 31 January 1945, Gordon Gollob, in contrast to both predecessors was a convinced Nazi who was considered as fully reliable politically by Himmler, who recommended his appointment late in the war;[4] he was an abrasive and bullying commander, the direct antithesis of *Vati* Mölders.

The *Luftwaffe* was a new German service founded after Hitler's seizure of power, although clandestine training and organisational structures were in place well before that, albeit under army control. Its First World War predecessors had been part of the navy or army, and unlike the Royal Air Force no separate 'junior service' had resulted in Germany at the end of that conflict. The *Luftwaffe* was thus strongly influenced by National Socialism[5] and subject to the whims and prejudices of its commander, Göring, who lacked many technical abilities and was often a poor manager during his building of the new air force; he remained steeped in the traditions and experiences of the First World War. The *Luftwaffe* lacked any chaplains of its own, and when such services were called for they had to rely on naval and army religious personnel from neighbouring units. Almost all of the younger pilots had been through years of compulsory Hitler Youth membership, and a large number had been well schooled in state-organised gliding clubs before their compulsory *Arbeitdienst*, comprising several months of labour service of paramilitary character, which preceded joining the armed forces. The Nazi Party also had their own flying organisation, the

NSFK (National Socialist Flying Corps), who ran a number of the gliding clubs. NSFK officers carried double ranks, with their NSFK rank always one higher than their *Luftwaffe* rank; this is analogous to servicemen who joined the SS, who were always appointed at one rank higher. However, few fighter pilots were committed Nazis, and this trend grew as the war dragged on and German hopes of victory receded. Some were actively discriminated against due to perceived anti-Nazi family connections, such as Pay Kleber of *JG 2* and *EJG 1*: 'Originally I wanted to become an officer, but as my father was seen by the National Socialists as a political reactionary, this was denied me. When officers came to be in short supply, one wanted to make me an officer through "night school". This I refused. *Obergefreite* (third lowest NCO rank in the *Luftwaffe*) can be stubborn.'

However, it is necessary to emphasize that they formed part of a totalitarian state system, and one that was responsible for the most horrific crimes against humanity recorded in history.[6] Even more than the sheer scale of these massacres, maltreatments, abject cruelty, deliberate degradation and outright murder, it was the highly organised, pre-planned and methodical way in which they were carried out that shocks one, even today, that much more. The published photographs of mass executions in the East, especially of women with babies in their arms and little children at their sides, are abhorrent. Although it is commonly claimed by German ex-servicemen, and especially those of the *Waffen-SS* (fighting formations of the SS), that the frontline services had nothing to do with these 'excesses' (a term often used by veterans, which in effect is also shockingly inadequate), the boundaries between different parts of the SS[7] and between straight fighting services and those responsible for the atrocities were distinctly blurred.[8] The brutal behaviour of the German forces, SS and regular alike, reached heights of scale and brutality on the Eastern Front, and the notorious 'Commissar Order' of Hitler and instructions issued before the Russian invasion to the armed forces down to all levels provided a formal or even legal basis for widespread and relatively uncontrolled murder in many cases. There was opposition to this, and even prevention thereof, particularly from the traditional officer caste in the army, but also in the *Luftwaffe*. The horrific photos front-line troops sent home showing massacres of Jews and of Soviet 'partisans' real and assumed (the assumed normally vastly outnumbering the real), the sheer scale of the forced labour system and its camps, the concentration camps and the death camps across Germany and its occupied and conquered territories all negate to no small degree the oft-repeated claims of ignorance of the entire genocidal system by soldiers and airmen who claim to have only fought a clean war, innocent of all knowledge of the organised degradation and slaughter – the famous ace Günther Rall provides an example in his autobiography[9] – that went on so systematically from the beginning to the very end of the war.[10]

It is fitting that we who were spared the Second World War appreciate that there were almost always real consequences to aerial actions. German fighter pilots' successes were predicated on losses to the other side. Although aerial action is often described as clean, even knightly, it is clean only due to the speed at which combat occurs, which generally makes its effects on enemy crews invisible to the attacking pilot. The remnants of man and machine that reached the ground or the sea were anything but pleasant. Romantic notions of 'knights of the air' pale against the reality of surprise attacks from superior altitude and ideally from out of the sun, the ubiquitous 'bounce' which equates with ambuscade rather than chivalrous competition. Despite this, the concept of chivalry remained a strong influence among many fighter pilots, as recalled by Gerhard Schöpfel, one-time commander of *JG 26*: 'In our day we saw the fighter pilot as the successor to the knights of old and we tried to be chivalrous and to fight fairly. Thus it was easy for us to meet our old enemies after the war, to a certain extent to become close to each other, and today we enjoy a good comradeship.'

Equally, if a reader is more attracted to the Allied side in the war, the wreck of a German fighter and the interment of its unfortunate occupant in a war cemetery in many cases (in many others pilots simply disappeared into water or the ground, entombed in the wreckage of their aircraft) is the accompanying reality to the achievement of a British, Russian or American ace.

In the final analysis, this book is the story of the German pilots and crewmen in their own words. I translated them as accurately as possible, and have tried to place the individual experiences within a broader context of the *Luftwaffe*'s overall war in the air, relying considerably on many documentary and published sources, as detailed in the bibliography, and the notes for each chapter. I hope I have been able to honour these brave men fittingly; they endured much and they sacrificed equally. In post-war Germany they were often seen by the younger generations as pariahs at worst, and as uninteresting and undeserving of respect at best. Their country went to war, and thus they did also. Although as mostly very young men they were caught up in the energy of the pre-war Nazi movement and government, few were ardent supporters. Most regret the casualties they caused in opposing air forces, and almost none gloried in their achievements; to a man they had seen more than enough of war. Despite having supported, albeit indirectly in most cases, a murderous and horrific regime through their military service, they were first and foremost patriots doing what they thought was right. They deserve the respect due to military veterans who fought with honour everywhere. In a small way, this book is their story, told in unvarnished terms and in their own, often colourful language. *Horrido!*

**Map 1:** Denmark and Norway during the German invasion.
**Map 2:** The invasion of France and the Low Countries.
**Map 3:** Battle of Britain dispositions. *JG 53* based in Rennes–Brest area and operating from forward bases of Guernsey and Cherbourg; *JG 27* in Caen region; *JG 2* in Beaumont-le-Roger–Le Havre area; remaining Me 109s concentrated in Pas de Calais region: *JG 3, JG 26, JG 51, JG 52, I/LG 2, JG 54* (less one *Gruppe* in Netherlands for some time), *I/JG 77*. In late August 1940 majority of Me 109s from *JGs 2, 27* and *53* transferred to Pas de Calais area for some weeks. Me 110 fighters based as follows (but subject to complex moves also): ZG 2 (Paris–Amiens); ZG 26 (Barly, Crecy, Abbeville); ZG 76 (minus *I/ZG 76* in Norway; based in Laval and Abbeville). *Erprobungsgruppe* 210 at Lille and Le Havre regions.
**Map 4:** *Jagddivisions* in the Battle of Germany, mid-September 1943.
**Map 5:** Ranges of Allied fighters, Battle of Germany.

# Maps

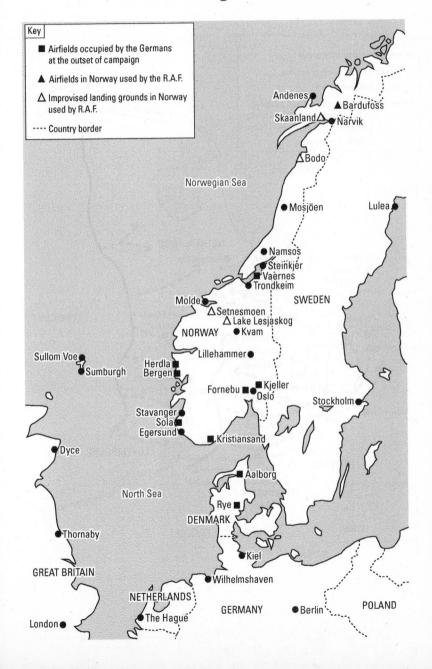

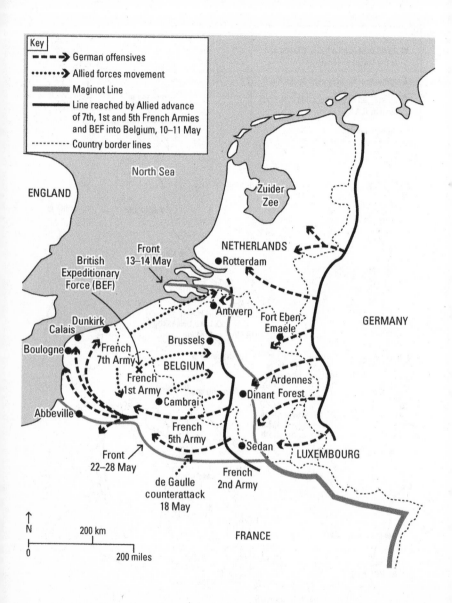

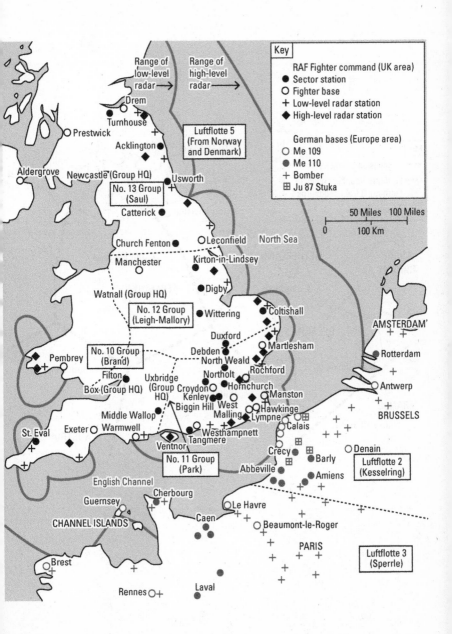

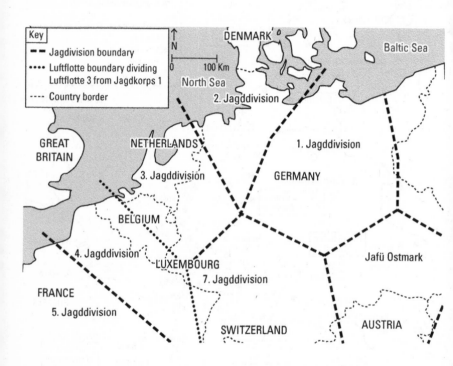

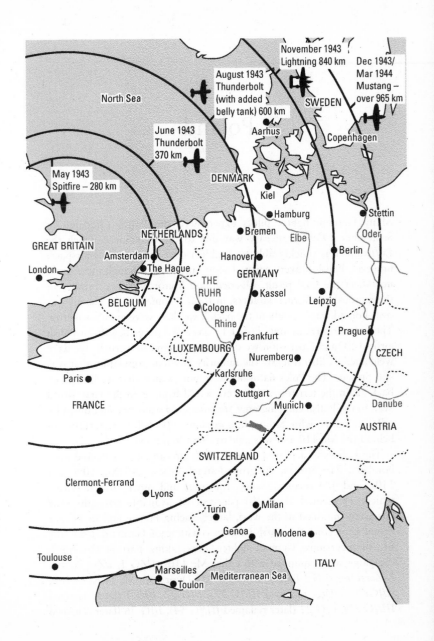

November 1943
Lightning 840 km

Dec 1943/
Mar 1944
Mustang –
over 965 km

August 1943
Thunderbolt
(with added
belly tank) 600 km

North Sea

SWEDEN

June 1943
Thunderbolt
370 km

Aarhus

Copenhagen

May 1943
Spitfire – 280 km

DENMARK

Kiel

Hamburg

Stettin

GREAT BRITAIN

NETHERLANDS

Bremen

Elbe

Oder

Amsterdam

Hanover

Berlin

London

The Hague

GERMANY

THE
RUHR

Kassel

Leipzig

BELGIUM

Cologne

Rhine

Prague

Frankfurt

CZECH

LUXEMBOURG

Nuremberg

Paris

Karlsruhe

FRANCE

Stuttgart

Munich

Danube

AUSTRIA

SWITZERLAND

Clermont-Ferrand

Lyons

Milan

Turin

Genoa

Modena

Toulouse

ITALY

Marseilles

Toulon

Mediterranean Sea

# 1

# Poland

Many German fighter pilots experienced the Polish campaign of September 1939 as an easy war due to the dominance which the *Luftwaffe* was quickly able to establish over the country's airspace; however, Polish bravery ensured some surprises, although these could not affect the final result. *Oberleutnant* Victor Mölders, brother of the famous ace Werner Mölders, in *I/ZG 1* commented: 'The air war over Poland was a "walk in the park", we fliers were greatly superior. The air war anyway only lasted 14 days. We never flew from Polish airfields. On one occasion we drove into Poland in a truck. We were welcomed as liberators by the minority German population that was still present. The Poles naturally were not excited that we had taken back again the territories that were seized from us in the First World War. In the Polish campaign my *Staffelkapitän* was even shot down by a Polish fighter, who, although more than 100 km/h slower, turned in behind the Me 110 and was able to shoot him down.'

The Luftwaffe deployed almost 1,600 aircraft against Poland (648 bombers, 219 Stukas, 30 ground-attack types, 210 Me 109s and 110s, and 474 reconnaissance, transport and other aircraft types), which represented about 40 per cent of available strength.[1] The rest were stationed in the west, largely facing France and to a lesser extent protecting the north-western coastline of Germany from any British incursions. German fighter units taking part in the Polish campaign were equipped with either Me 110s: *I/ZG 1*, *I/ZG 76* and *I (Zerstörer)/LG 1* (later renamed *V/LG 1*); or with Me 109s: *I/LG 2*, *II/JGr 186* (later renamed *III/JG 77*), *I/JG 77*, *I/JG 1* (later renamed *III/JG 27*), *I/JG 21* (later renamed *III/JG 54*), *I/JG 76* (later renamed

*II/JG 54*), *I/ZG 2* and *II/ZG 1* (both *Gruppen* flew Me 109s in Poland despite carrying *Zerstörer* unit designations; converted to Me 110s soon after the Polish campaign).[2]

The Polish campaign, and with it the Second World War, began on 1 September 1939, in the very early morning, at about quarter to five. Early operations that day were inauspicious due to widespread dense fog, but in the late afternoon Göring's planned major attack on Warsaw went ahead. It was the political and military heart of the country, and home to Poland's major aircraft manufacturers. The first major air combat occurred here.[3] *Leutnant* Hans-Ekkehard Bob, *I/JG 21* was there: 'Operations in Poland with the, for that time comparatively large aerial battles over Warsaw, brought the first experiences of war.'

Many of the 14 Me 109s lost on the first day were down to inexperienced pilots becoming disoriented after air combat and running out of fuel trying to get back home; eight were lost in this way from *I/JG 21*.[4,5] *Fähnrich* Max Clerico from this *Gruppe* made it home: 'War theatre from 1 September 1939, Poland. Mostly we flew escorts for bombers and made low-level strafing attacks on Polish troop columns. A depressing experience! Right from the first operation we had many losses: the enemy was fuel shortage, as on the way back to our airfield at Gutenfeld (south of Königsberg/East Prussia) we were surprised by a strong headwind. Many had to force-land. Together with the *Staffelkapitän* (*Oberleutnant* Scholz) I at least made it home. I only saw one Polish aircraft in the whole campaign, as it disappeared in the clouds.'

Large-scale German attacks on Polish air bases in the first few days achieved very little as the Polish air force had wisely dispersed all operational aircraft to temporary bases away from the known and well-established airfields. Obsolete and non-combatant aircraft were left on these established airfields to distract *Luftwaffe* attention.[6] *Leutnant* Gerhard Granz, *I/ZG 2* was still positive about the war: 'As a *Leutnant* in *Jagdgruppe 102* in Bernburg (renamed *I/ZG 2*), we went to war as enthusiastic soldiers and fliers, never guessing what lay ahead for Germany. I flew many missions against Poland in the Me 109 and registered three successes, when I set three Polish fighters on fire on the airfield at Lodz.'

Operational intensity was experienced as distinctly low by many pilots, including *Leutnant* Heinz Lange, *I/JG 21*: 'Operational tasks of the Me 109 pilots in the Polish campaign were bomber and Stuka escorts, fighter sweeps (free chases), and low-level attacks on troops.

I only flew a few missions, and never had any combat with Polish fliers.'
For most of the time in Poland coordination of air and ground forces
worked very well, and was a critical element of a rapid campaign.
Many fighter pilots experienced largely ground-attack missions rather
than aerial combat, among them *Oberleutnant* Erhard Braune, *I/JG 1*:
'One of the saddest memories of the Polish campaign was the low-level
attacks on Polish cavalry. The Poles had not recognised that the
pride of their army (the Poles are very proud), the cavalry, was no
longer suitable for modern war (the Marshal Pilsudski-cavalry general
syndrome). In the cockpit of every Me 109 a plate was attached with a
text banning the use of 2 cm cannon shell ammunition on live targets;
this was also followed to the letter. However, the machine guns were
efficient enough to drive the mounted troops immediately into cover –
after they had been through their first shattering experiences.'

German fighter pilots were credited with 58 confirmed aerial
victories, 29 being made by the Me 109-equipped *I/ZG 2*, and the
rest spread among *I/LG 2*, *I/JG 76*, *I/JG 77*, *I/JG 21*, *I/ZG 76* and
*I(Z)/LG 1*; Me 110 pilots were only credited with six victories.[7] As in all
air combat, especially with the lack of experience of many of the pilots
involved, over-claiming was part of the reality of the Polish campaign.
While *I(Z)/LG1*'s Me 110s claimed 30 victories, only three were
recognised and confirmed by the RLM (*Reichsluftfahrtministerium* –
Air Ministry); *Unteroffizier* Alois Dierkes was one of the radio
operator/rear gunners with this successful unit: 'The Polish operation
brought us a high score of victories, I cannot remember exactly how
many anymore, but it was probably more than 30, against only small
losses (3 killed). At the end of September we moved from Jesau/East
Prussia, from where we had flown the Polish operations, to Würzburg/
Main and were renamed as *V/(Z)LG 1*.'

Major air action took place on 3, 4, 9 and 14 September 1939.
*Hauptmann* Johannes Gentzen of *I/ZG 2* was the top scorer, with six
recognised (*anerkannte*) victories. By the middle of September 1939
aerial combat had almost ceased, and losses to both sides tailed off.
The final few days of the campaign saw violent bombing of Warsaw,
and in this period *I/JG 21* had an unusual visitor, as related by Max
Clerico: 'During the fighting around Warsaw, our *Staffel* (*1/JG 21*,
later renamed as *7/JG 54*) had the job of protecting Hitler from the air,
at a height of about 100 m. He was driving around the battle area in
his old "bucket" (*Kübelwagen*), a Rover light field vehicle. A delicate
job! Shortly after he visited our airfield and ate a meal of pea stew,

standing next to our field kitchen. We surrounded him in astonishment. It would have been easy to have shot him. One would naturally have lost your life, but made world history! After the rapid end of this war I received the Iron Cross 2nd class in September 1939. Then we moved to western Germany – remaining more or less inactive.' Interestingly, in Field Marshal Kesselring's memoirs this same meal is briefly discussed; the commanding general of the 8th German Army prepared a festive setting in the hangars at the airfield in advance, much to Hitler's disgust; he refused to eat there and instead ate at the field kitchen.[8] This illustrates also how the army's senior officer corps failed to understand that Hitler saw himself essentially as a *Frontschwein* (as he had been in the First World War; PBI, 'poor bloody infantry', or the US Marines' 'grunt' would be applicable equivalent terms) and liked to identify with the frontline soldier. Germany was a country led by an ex-NCO with many of the attitudes of such a man, including an overall contempt for general staff officers, as one would expect from frontline troops.

The views expressed above about this air war being a 'walk in the park' by Victor Mölders of *I/ZG 1* and the enthusiasm for the new war remembered by Gerhard Granz of *I/ZG 2* also reflect a certain distance from much of the reality of conflict that was common among aircrew, removed as they were from the horrors on the ground. In addition, there was also a darker side to the short-lived Polish campaign. Each of the five German armies entering Poland was followed up by an SS-led *Einsatzgruppe* (literally 'task force or 'deployment group', in reality a murder squad unit) to eliminate any threats in the newly conquered rear areas; two more were added during operations, and a massive reinforcement of 100,000 ethnic Germans enabled the 'pacification' of Poland.[9] Massacres and murder were soon common, with assistance not just from *Gestapo* personnel but also from the German army; psychiatric clinics and hospitals were cleared out, Jews were killed and the elites of Polish society (teachers, university staff, priests, government and local officials, officers, politicians, journalists, the wealthy), were simultaneously targeted.[10] Retaliatory attacks by Poles on ethnic Germans within their shrinking territory during this brief war also occurred, but these were dwarfed probably ten-fold or more by the SS and *Gestapo*-inspired actions, all carried out with the permission and hidden but enthusiastic urgings of Hitler, Himmler and Heydrich.[11] The existence of the *Einsatzgruppen* right at the beginning of the conflict shows that such measures were planned in advance.

They had the express intent of destroying not just the country but also the society of Poland, whose western reaches were anyway seen as German territories lost as part of the hated Versailles Treaty at the end of the First World War.[12] The precedent was thus set for the later invasion of the Soviet Union, when ethnic cleansing went hand in glove with military operations through expanded *Einsatzgruppen* and the use of local militias. The approach to war in the eastern and western territories was starkly contrasted. The happy air war perceived by so many witnesses over Poland must be seen in this context, as indeed touched upon by Erhard Braune of *I/JG 1* and also expressed below by Wolfgang Falck.

The Polish campaign cost the Germans 285 aircraft (around 157 of them on operations) and 413 aircrew, while the Poles lost 333 aircraft.[13] The cost to the *Luftwaffe* – around 18 per cent of the aircraft originally deployed – in the space of a couple of weeks was not trivial. The Poles fought a brave yet hopeless battle against a numerically and technically superior enemy. *Oberleutnant* Wolfgang Falck of *I/ZG 76* retained sympathy for the losing side: 'The air war over Poland was naturally – in a general sense – no problem. The *Luftwaffe* was greatly superior to the Poles in numbers and technically. Consequently, one had to admire the great courage with which they threw themselves at a superior enemy. Obviously both sides were shooting, but our losses were minimal. We also flew many low-level missions against artillery positions, marching columns, railways etc. One really had something of a sympathy for the Poles.'

## 2

# Denmark and Norway

Operations began for the invasion of Denmark and Norway on 9 April 1940 and continued until the capitulation of the Norwegian army on 10 June 1940. The British had evacuated their last forces from the Narvik area on 7 June 1940, and the next day the Royal Navy aircraft carrier *Glorious* and two escorting destroyers were sunk by the German battlecruisers *Scharnhorst* and *Gneisenau*. *Glorious* took with her the remaining aircraft of the RAF's 46 (ten Hurricanes) and 263 (ten Gladiators) Squadrons, which had miraculously landed on the ship from their Norwegian bases on 7 June; eight of the Hurricane pilots were lost and all 10 Gladiator pilots from 263 Squadron as well.[1] *Scharnhorst* was badly damaged by a torpedo hit and limped into Trondheim; British naval and land-based air attacks continued against her there and later in Stavanger until 21 June 1940, thus ending the aerial action related to what the Germans had named *Unternehmung Weserübung*.[2] This codename translates as Operation Weser (River) Exercise, which can perhaps be taken as sarcastic, bearing as it does allusions to a mere military river crossing.

German fighter units employed in this operation were limited to *I/ZG 1* (Me 110s) and one *Staffel* of *I/LG 2* (briefly) over Denmark, and *I/ZG 76* (Me 110s) and *II/JG 77* (Me 109s) in Norway; *II(J)/186* (Me 109s; later renamed *III/JG 77*) was posted into the Scandinavian theatre on 2 June 1940.[3] Despite the invasion of Denmark being generally described as bloodless, in fact two Danish fighters did get off the ground and both were shot down by Me 110s and their pilots killed;[4] one claim was awarded to *Stab I/ZG 76*'s *Hauptmann* Wolfgang Falck.

On 9 April 1940, poor weather conditions played havoc with planned German paratroop drops and airborne infantry landings over southern Norway; six of an original eight Me 110s of *1/ZG 76*, who were supposed to have landed after the initial paratroop attack to refuel at Oslo-Fornebu airfield, ended up capturing it basically single-handed as the first Ju 52 transport finally landed.[5] *1/ZG 76* had arrived first over Fornebu but were bounced by nine Norwegian Gladiators from out of the sun, losing two Me 110s and both crews; in return two of the Gladiators force-landed on the airfield and were set on fire on the ground by the remaining six *Zerstörer*. The latter had another aircraft written off when an already damaged Me 110 made a crash-landing on Fornebu. A Sunderland flying boat was also claimed by this *Staffel* during the day. Other Me 110s of *1/ZG 76* en route to cover airborne landings at Stavanger lost two of their number and both crews to the dreadful weather along the way.[6]

*1/ZG 76* (operating mostly from Stavanger and Trondheim) and *II/JG 77* (flying mainly from Kristiansand, Stavanger, Trondheim) rapidly became established on southern Norwegian airfields, and most air combat was against British bombers (including Coastal Command aircraft) flying from the UK, plus Royal Navy carrier-borne aircraft. Accredited fighter claims totalled 57: eight Wellington heavy bombers; 12 Hampden medium bombers; eight Blenheim light bombers; 14 Hudson patrol bombers; five Skua and two Roc carrier aircraft; two Sunderland flying boats; one Danish Fokker; five Gladiators (two Norwegian, three British). Most victories went to *II/JG 77* (36) and *1/ZG 76* (14), with one Hudson to *I/ZG1* over Denmark, five victories to the *Zerstörerstaffel* of *KG 30* and one to *II(J)/186*. German bombers claimed one Hudson for a grand total of 58 confirmed victories for the campaign. They also accounted for most of the aircraft of 263 Squadron RAF, flying from a frozen lake at Lesjaskog – on 25 April 1940, the day after 18 Gladiators had taken off from a carrier, 13 of them were destroyed by bombing and strafing of the German bombers on the lake, two of them after force-landing with combat damage from the bombers.[7] The remaining five Gladiators were rapidly decimated by lack of repairs and maintenance plus combat damage, and by 29 April the squadron was withdrawn. They were back on 21 May 1940 with 18 new Gladiators; of these only three were lost in aerial combat, with two pilots killed and one wounded. *1/ZG 76* claimed a Gladiator on 27 May and two more on 2 June 1940. Others were damaged in combat and two lost in crashes. The remaining 10 Gladiators flew out and landed on the carrier *Glorious* on 7 June 1940 and were lost when she was sunk next day.[8] The 18 Hurricanes of 46 Squadron RAF arrived from a carrier on 26 May and operated from Bardufoss in northern Norway.[9] They had many combats, mainly with German bombers, but also with Me 110s of *I/ZG 76*; a major action occurred on 29 May 1940, when nine Hurricanes took on 26 He 111s of *Kampfgruppe 100* and *KG 26*, escorted by elements of *I/ZG 76*. Although two He 111s and one Me 110 (crew POW) were shot down, three Hurricanes were lost and two pilots killed; at least one of the Hurricanes fell to *I/ZG 76*.[10] By the time 46 Squadron was withdrawn, eight Hurricanes had been either shot down, lost in accidents or damaged beyond repair, and the remaining 10 landed on the aircraft carrier *Glorious* on 7 June 1940, as already related.[11]

*II/JG 77* flew into Danish airfields on 9 April 1940, moving to southern Norway three days later.[12] On 13 April, in a combat against Hampdens, of which they were credited with eight against six actually lost,[13] five Me 109s were also shot down with four pilots killed, an inauspicious start to their long stay in Norway.[14] Better success attended their efforts against carrier aircraft attacking the damaged *Scharnhorst* in Trondheim harbour on 13 June 1940, when four *4/JG 77* Me 109s together with four *I/ZG 76* Me 110s fought against a formation of 15 carrier-borne Skuas, the *JG 77* pilots claiming four. Six days later, when UK-based Beaufort torpedo bombers attacked this patched-up vessel on its way from Trondheim to Stavanger, another six victories were credited to *II/JG 77*.[15] At this stage in their history, this *Gruppe* was saddled by a commander to whom it was difficult to relate; on 30 May 1940, in a drunken state, *Hauptmann* Karl Hentschel threatened some of his pilots with a drawn pistol, which they were able to take from him soon afterwards. He was replaced in September 1940 after a delegation of the *Gruppe's* officers went to higher authority.[16] An unusual '*Luftwaffe Hauptmann*' arrived in the middle of April 1940 and joined *II/JG 77* for about four to six weeks, flying operationally; he was none other than *Obergruppenführer* (SS rank of full general) Reinhard Heydrich, the chief of the Intelligence and Counterintelligence services of the SS, and later a leading organiser of the death camps and the Holocaust.[17] Soon after his arrival he wrote off his Me 109 on take-off and was lucky to get away with it.[18] Soon after this crash he is reported to have refused the award of the Iron Cross 2nd class (EK 2), awarded for combat missions flown, due to having written off his own aircraft.[19] However, many photos show him wearing both EK 2 and 1, plus the *Frontflugspange* (Front Flying Clasp) in Silver (awarded at 60 operational missions), so the refusal could not have been permanent. In June 1941, after flying briefly with *I/JG 1* over the North German coast,[20] he joined the *JG 77 Gruppe* again, this time without permission, and flew some operations on the Russian front, and after a short time was shot down by flak and crashed in no-man's land from where he was fortunate to be rescued unharmed.[21]

*II/JG 77* stayed in Norway till 9 November 1940, when they were transferred to the Channel Front.[22] After 21 June 1940 a further 45 victories were credited to them, including a notable success on 13 August 1940 as 'Eagle Day' was launched in the Battle of Britain. 12 Blenheims of 82 Squadron, thinking to take advantage of the *Luftwaffe*'s attention being elsewhere, raided Aalborg airfield in Denmark, where *5/JG 77* had just been transferred. 11 were shot down against 15 claims by the fighters and one by anti-aircraft (AA).[23] The leading ace of *II/JG 77* in Norway was *Feldwebel* Robert Menge, who was awarded 13 victory confirmations.[24] *II(J)/186* (the later *III/JG 77*), which had arrived in Denmark on 2 June 1940 and moved to Norway two days later, only claimed two victories in their time there. At the end of July 1940 they were transferred to the Berlin area, relieving *I/JG 77* who moved to the northern coastal areas of Germany. After *II/JG 77* was notified on 13 August 1940 of re-equipment with captured Curtiss P-36 fighters from France due to a shortage of Me 109s, which were reserved to replace expected losses over England, 12 P-36s were finally supplied in mid-September; they remained with the *Gruppe* till the end of October, when Me 109s were received in their place.[25]

# 3

# The Phoney War

The Phoney War, the period labelled by the British press the *Sitzkrieg*, covers the period from the British and French declarations of war on 3 September 1939 till 9 May 1940, the day preceding the unleashing of the *Blitzkrieg* against neutral Holland, Belgium and belligerent France. This period overlapped with the brief Polish campaign of September 1939 and the early part of the Norwegian campaign, and involved German fighter defence of the Western Front with France and the north German coastal areas and naval bases, as well as *Luftwaffe* bomber attacks on the British naval base at Scapa Flow. Reconnaissance activities by both sides in all these areas were ongoing and subject to interception by fighters from French, British and German air forces. Both RAF and *Luftwaffe* raids on each other's naval bases were far beyond fighter escort range, as were long-range reconnaissance operations, and all suffered heavy casualties; short-range reconnaissance missions were generally escorted and sometimes led to intense actions over the Western Front with France. Other reconnaissance missions were performed by fighter aircraft and remained relatively unmolested, as experienced by *Unteroffizier* Alois Dierkes, Me 110 radio operator/rear gunner, *V/LG 1*: 'From Wiesbaden-Erbenheim we were transferred in about February 1940 to Mannheim-Sandhofen, from where we flew our operations over France. Partly, we were employed as reconnaissance aircraft, with a large built-in camera and the two cannons removed to compensate for the weight; we flew along the front lines to be able to recognise new defensive works.'

German fighters claimed three Spitfire reconnaissance aircraft in this period, of which two can be confirmed, one flying from France and the other from the UK.[1]

Combat in general was limited for most fighter pilots and for the ground forces also, hence the description of this period as the *Sitzkrieg* or Phoney War. Many pilots, such as *Feldwebel* Fritz Oeltjen with *I/JG 21*, spent long hours at various readiness states. 'After the Polish campaign *I/JG 21* (later *III/JG 54*) was stationed at Rheine airfield, to protect the Emsland area. I was posted to the 2nd *Staffel*, *Staffelkapitän Oberleutnant* Eggers. The readiness system consisted of one *Rotte* (pair of aircraft) with pilots in the Me 109 cockpits (*Sitzbereitschaft*) and one *Rotte* waiting beside their planes (*Alarmstart-Rotte*).' *Oberfeldwebel* Artur Dau experienced a similarly boring period: 'At the beginning of the war our unit (*III/JG 51*) moved to Böningstedt near Wesel on the Rhine. Our night quarters were residences in the town area. During the day we were all on the airfield so as to be rapidly employed if needed. On the airfield, tents served as our quarters.' There were also humorous moments in the air, which *Leutnant* Hans-Theodor Grisebach still remembered: 'In early 1940 I was transferred to a front-line unit (*I/JG 2*) in Bassenheim in the region of Koblenz. The first operations against France took place soon after. The French we only heard over the radio; we hardly saw anything of them although some combats did apparently occur elsewhere. The missions took place at very high altitudes. Strangely enough we had the same radio frequency as a French fighter unit. One of our *Staffelkapitäns* spoke very good French, and had also hosted a French officers' delegation that visited Germany in 1938 and made friends with a number of them. He maintained a particularly good friendship with one of these officers and greeted these French fighter pilots at the first such radio contact with "*Bonjour* and *Guten Morgen*".'

One of the most experienced and well-trained pilots in the whole *Luftwaffe*, never mind the fighter arm, was *Hauptmann* Hanns Trübenbach, *Gruppenkommandeur* of *I/LG 2*, who had begun his flying career in 1926. His comments provide a wide-ranging perspective at the beginning of the war.

We members of the old guard who had already received a long peacetime training already also had good flying experience and were equipped with the best aircraft material. In September 1939, the German *Luftwaffe* was the best and strongest air force in Europe in terms of quantity and technology. The ranking order of the European air forces could be given as follows, based on a qualitative and quantitative evaluation: Germany had 4,300 operational aircraft, England 3,600, Italy 2,800, France 2,500, and Poland 900 operational machines. The unknown factor was Soviet Russia at that time. No nation had much experience of war at the beginning of World War Two, from which admittedly arose the fact that we were superior in shooting ability due to our outstanding reflector gun sight. One should also not forget the assistance provided by the experience which the German armed forces had picked up in the Spanish Civil War and particularly the fighter tactics, which were conceptualised by Mölders during his time in the Condor Legion. The preferred fighter squadron formation from the First World War, based on vics of three aircraft, was changed to the modern fighter squadron formation of three times four aircraft, wherein the smallest unit was no longer the vic of three aircraft, but the *Rotte* comprising two aircraft, that hunted as grouped pairs in a *Schwarm* of four machines. In this tactic, the pair-leader did the shooting while enjoying the fundamental protection of the wingman.

In spite of the inherent advantages enjoyed by the German fighter pilots and indeed the entire air force alluded to above, even at this very early stage of the war, and disregarding the shattering impact of the first *Blitzkrieg* on Poland, Göring, the commander of the *Luftwaffe* (who was also in charge of the German economy among several other high offices) was remarkably pessimistic about Germany's chances following the declarations of war by Britain and France. *Hauptmann* Hanns Trübenbach, later *Kommodore* of *JG 52* in the Battle of Britain, was a direct witness to this. 'I was already informed exactly about the true war situation shortly after the Polish campaign, by one of the best friends of Göring, *Hauptmann der Reserve* Phillipp Remtsma. And thus a few of us knew already that the war could not be won any more. A few months later, after the Battle of Britain, I heard this also directly from Göring himself, when I was permitted to attend a supper in Holland, as the only *Kommodore* of the entire *Luftwaffe* to be present amongst the *Reichsmarschall*'s guests.'

Although action on the Western Front remained limited during the Phoney War, the effects on the individual could be significant, as *Leutnant* Josef Bürschgens, *I/JG 26* experienced himself: 'On 28 September 1939, I got my first aerial victory, which was also

JG 26's first victory of the war, over or near Metz, Alsace-Lorraine, against 11 French fighter planes, American-built P-36 Curtiss machines. Because I was seriously wounded during this fight, I only came back into action again on 9 June 1940, in the last days of the war in France.' A few German fighter pilots suffered mishaps and were taken prisoner by the French, with treatment being generally harsh. One who recalled such treatment was *Feldwebel* Georg Pavenzinger, *I/JG 51* who became a prisoner in the first month of the war.

On 25 August 1939 we in *I/JG 51* moved westwards to a field base near Horb am Neckar. That we were actually going to war as a consequence of this relocation, hardly any of us believed. Even at the outbreak of the war on 1 September 1939 against Poland we did not yet think about a larger-scale war. We were generally of the opinion that the western powers would not take up arms and that negotiations would continue and another option be found. However, on 2 September 1939, General Sperrle visited us, and he gave a short talk during which he said, amongst other things: 'The *Führer* is of the opinion that the western powers will not join in the war, but we generals are of a different opinion.' On the next day, 3 September 1939, England (*sic*) and France declared war against us. Immediately thereafter began the so-called *Sitzkrieg*. The pilots sat strapped in and ready for action in the machines, the mechanics also ready next to the aircraft. In the following few days border patrols were flown, and in between there were alarms and scrambles, when enemy reconnaissance aircraft were reported. About 20 September 1939 we moved to Speyer, where we again flew border patrols, but further over the lines into France. On 28 September 1939 at about 11h30 our 2nd *Staffel* was in the air with eight machines, when my engine stopped and I had to force-land in French territory – directly on the Maginot Line. What happened thereafter, from my capture till my return after the French campaign was over, is a story all to itself; to tell it fully would take much too long. I was taken into custody at great effort and expense, even motorised units were involved in this, and with arms bound and a great swirl of drums I was brought to the fortress at Dijon, where I was kept in perpetual darkness for seven weeks. I was sentenced to seven years of forced labour and there followed a further charge of a death sentence. However, this second charge never resulted in a trial before the French fortress tribunal, as the German armoured troops were too close.

Action against the few incursions of British bombers attacking north German naval targets led to intense air battles, particularly that of 18 December 1939, described below by Rudolf Petzold, Me 110 radio operator/rear gunner in *I/ZG 76*. Very soon, these battles showed the British that unescorted bomber formations were not capable of effective defence against fighter attack during daylight raids. Major actions were as follows:[2] 4 September 1939, 15 Blenheims made low-level attacks against ships in Wilhelmshaven, five being lost, mainly to anti-aircraft fire; 4 September 1939, 14 Wellingtons flying against ships in Brunsbüttel lost two bombers to fighters; 29 September 1939, 11 Hampdens lost five aircraft to fighters while operating against ships at Heligoland; 3 December 1939, 24 four Wellingtons bombing ships at Heligoland got off scot-free and one German fighter was lost; 14 December 1939, 12 Wellingtons operating against a convoy north of Wilhelmshaven suffered five losses to fighters, one German fighter being lost in return. The climax that finally drove the lesson home came on 18 December 1939 when 24 Wellingtons went out to attack ships off Wilhelmshaven, with 12 lost to German fighters who suffered two casualties themselves. Thereafter such raids kept away from the coast, only attacking ships on the open sea, and losses in the few resultant fighter actions were much reduced.[3] *Unteroffizier* Rudolf Petzold of *I/ZG 76* was among the Me 110 crewmen who were stationed along the North German coast to intercept such raids and was an eyewitness to the combat on the big Wilhelmshaven raid.

After we had survived our baptism of fire in the Polish campaign well, with several victories in aerial combat, we moved with our Me 110s temporarily to Bönninghardt – a small grass field near Geldern – and on to the North Sea coast to Jever in Oldenburg. Here one expected incursions of British bombers into the German Bight from across the sea. Every day we flew patrols with two aircraft along the coast at Wilhelmshaven. The days passed and of English aircraft there was nothing to be seen. The crews who were not immediately at readiness passed the time playing cards or with snowball fights, which as an equalization sport provided much fun. As Christmas was approaching we had much to do to prepare for the first war Christmas. On 18 December 1939 the order for a number of crews to come to readiness and sit in the aircraft came like a bolt from the blue into the midst of these happy preparations. We did not really believe in an English attack at all, as we had experienced nothing more in the air since the end of the Polish campaign. Suddenly at 15h00 came the radioed order for a mission, course to the north. My pilot, *Oberfeldwebel* Fleischmann, an experienced flier from Spain, and I started at 15h09 and immediately took up our course towards the North Sea. In the distance we could already see the flak bursts in the sky and knew immediately that something was brewing! Right, throttles forward and off we go! We arrived at exactly the right time and saw an estimated 50 English bombers at about 2500 m altitude approaching above the coast near Wilhelmshaven. We closed in on the bomber formation – everything seemed to happen much too slowly – and recognised them as twin-engined Vickers-Wellington machines and realised that here caution was needed. These machines were equipped with 2 cm cannons[4] and machine guns to defend them that could be aimed to all sides. My pilot Fleischmann, who had already registered victories in Spain and who had gained more experience together with me in Poland, was known as a reckless daredevil and immediately went over to the attack. He placed himself behind the Wellington flying closest to him. From the rear quarter he fired several bursts from all his guns into the engine and fuselage of the Englishman. The effect was not long in coming. A smoke trail showed us that the right-hand engine was on fire and the machine flew irregularly. The pilot was probably hit. As we turned away – we had to be careful and avoid ramming the Englishman – we were able to observe how the machine spun away below and hit the sea. That was our first downing of an English bomber. This victory really got Fleischmann going and I had my hands full to change the ammunition drums of our cannons so that we could tackle the next opponent. We did not have to search; today there were enough English bombers flying all around us. I reported over the microphone: 'everything ready to shoot!' Fleischmann went into his next attack straight away. He put himself behind a Wellington and shot – like the previous attack – several bursts, exactly from behind through the rear turret into the fuselage of the enemy machine. We received strong return fire from the rear gunner. The battle swung to and fro. Our cabin was shot through by the opponent's shots and I had to report: 'no more ammunition in the drums'. So, turn away from the enemy, reload and attempt a second attack. Fleischmann turned and hung behind the Englishman, who had in the meantime dived steeply, to fly just above the water on a course homewards. But Fleischmann, the old fox, did not let himself be shaken off. Now we flew very low close behind the English machine. Around us was nothing except water and sky! There where it had bubbled and boiled in the air a few minutes ago, where friend and foe were curving amongst each other and violent aerial combats took place, now there was peace and nothing more to be seen. Only this bomber and ourselves! We now thought we would be able to do for the English aircraft at our leisure! However, when Fleischmann pressed the firing buttons for the cannons, nothing came out, absolutely nothing! Our guns had jammed. Despite all our efforts, we could not remedy this. It is beyond possibility to describe what one feels in such a moment. In a fury over this mishap Fleischmann pulled up left of the Englishman and threatened him with a clenched fist – we could see him very well. It seemed as if the entire English crew, except for the pilot, were no longer alive. This all played itself out far out over the North Sea. We flew back to our base in Jever at nought feet. At 17h15 we returned waggling our wings, to show our success, and landed as the last aircraft, with uncountable holes in the fuselage and cabin. Our ground crew received us joyously and with many macabre remarks removed the many, many small flexiglass splinters from our faces. We had gotten away with our lives! Thus ended the air battle over the German Bight of the 18 December 1939 for us. When the next incursion into the German Bight by three Wellington bombers occurred, on 2 January 1940, all three Englishmen were shot down and I unfortunately seriously wounded. I was in hospital for eight months. During this time the *Gruppe* moved to Stavanger in Norway and my pilot, with whom I had experienced so much, got a new radio operator, *Oberfähnrich* Mirke. Both were killed after an operation from Stavanger when they hit a rock while landing.

In this combat of 2 January 1940, described in detail in an overstated newspaper article, Fleischmann had again charged in to the attack without hesitation and as a result received the combined return fire of all three Wellingtons, hitting the Me 110 20 times, mostly around the cabin, and wounding his radio operator/air-gunner Rudolf Petzold with a bullet in the leg as well as metal splinters in the upper jaw, chin, nose and mouth. Fleischmann fired back and the Wellington exploded, for his seventh victory. He returned to base on one engine, as did the *Schwarmführer* of the four attacking Me 110s of I/ZG 76, whose aircraft was hit eight times.

German fighter pilot claims during the Phoney War period, as identified from the web-published lists of Tony Wood,[5] total 135 over the French front (Western Front) with a further 65 over the North German coast against British bomber incursions. The latter encompassed 47 Wellingtons, six Hudsons, two Hampdens and 10 Blenheims; of the 65 thus claimed over the German coast at least 36 can be confirmed from British bomber unit records, but some or all of the Hudsons were likely Coastal Command aircraft rather than Bomber Command losses.[6] Of the 135 claims over the Western Front, approximately 99 can be confirmed by careful post-war research,[7] an overall rate of 73 per cent. This is relatively high, as will be seen in later chapters from much more intense conflicts and air battles, and will have been strongly influenced by the limited aerial combat and relatively small individual actions of the Phoney War period. As is well known, larger numbers of aircraft in a battle always leads to higher over-claiming, for all air forces; the relevant example is of the action of German fighters *versus* 24 RAF Wellingtons over the German Bight on 18 December 1939 discussed earlier, with 12 RAF losses against 32 confirmed German claims in total. The over-claiming resulting from larger numbers is also often greater when multi-engined aircraft losses are involved, as multiple pilots often attack the same aircraft. This sort of thing is no reflection on the pilots involved but a natural outcome of rapid and intense fighting. In addition, any measure of losses is always clouded by damaged aircraft, especially those which force-land but are repairable. Interestingly, in the claims over the Western Front, one *Geschwader* stands out: JG 53, which made 76 of the 135 claims. For one *Gruppe* thereof, I/JG 53, all 27 claims can be confirmed from French and British records;[8] II/JG 53 also made 27 claims but only 13 can be confirmed with some certainty, and for III/JG 53 the figures are 16 out of 22 claims.[9] German fighter losses during the Phoney War period amounted to 36 Me 109s in aerial combat (16 pilots killed, 10 POW, four wounded) and six Me 110s (seven crew killed, one POW, four wounded). In addition, one Me 109 and pilot were lost to anti-aircraft fire.[10]

The top-scoring *Luftwaffe* fighter pilot of the Phoney War period was *Hauptmann* Werner Mölders, *Staffelkapitän* 1/JG 53 until 30 September 1939, when he was promoted to *Gruppenkommandeur* III/JG 53. He made 10 claims; of these two appear to have no confirmation in Allied records, five do, and the other three were all hit, damaged (force- or crash-landed; one pilot lightly wounded, one seriously) but were repairable.[11] This illustrates the difficulties in judging a victory – if an aircraft is hit, crash-lands and has a wounded pilot, this can be equated as a shot-down victory (in German, an *Abschuss*), but if the aircraft is later repaired, and the pilot recovers, both can serve again. The German term *Luftsieg* (literally 'air victory') implies a fully destroyed aircraft and reflects what might be termed a total victory, irrespective of whether the pilot survives or not. Mölders was acknowledged at the time, and even more so since, as one of the *Luftwaffe*'s most outstanding pilots and aces, and certainly a very honest man, but still even he was subject, like all fighter pilots of all nations, to the inevitable over-claiming bogey. On the Western Front, German claims against the Morane 406 fighter showed the highest overestimation of actual successes, with 41 claims against 22 losses to fighters.[12] This is not unusual, with fighter-*versus*-fighter claims often being thus overestimated. Interestingly, Mölders is credited with four of the nine British Hurricanes actually lost, and appears to have twice shot down the earliest famous ace of the RAF, F/O 'Cobber' Kain, with one forced-landing (Hurricane repairable) and one total destruction (Kain bailed out successfully, slightly wounded).[13]

# 4

# Invasion of France and the Low Countries

Often neglected as an aerial campaign and overshadowed by the Battle of Britain which followed, the campaign in the west, or the French campaign (10 May–24 June 1940), was in fact a major clash between large air forces, with high losses to both sides.[1] These losses were significant as they exclusively involved pre-war trained professionals who were really irreplaceable. The losses also directly impacted the Battle of Britain, as these aircrew were no longer available for that critical campaign. In addition, several German (and British) units that suffered morale problems in the fight over the UK did so as a direct result of losses suffered and combat experiences lived through over France. Despite the large scale of this campaign, the numbers of aircraft involved on both sides and the significant losses to all air forces involved, some pilots, such as *Fähnrich* Max Clerico, 7/JG 54, had only limited combat exposure:

On 10 May 1940 the French war began. We had hardly any contacts with French fliers. Mostly we flew low-level attacks against ground targets. I can clearly remember a wonderful combat (26 May 1940) over Cambrai, noted in World War One for a tank battle. My *Staffel* had a fight with the fighter escort of a Potez 63 in which a high-ranking general was sitting. The French fought bitterly, aggressively and flew elegantly. I scored two victories. Suddenly four or five Curtiss machines were behind me and shooting at me. I dived away, levelled out very low and had almost given myself up. My last thought, ridiculous and absurd: 'at least there is swampy ground here, at least you will not hit the ground hard.' Then I gathered myself together again and climbed away at a shallow angle, and they could not follow me. At the airfield after landing, General Milch (deputy to Göring) had arrived, he presented me with the Iron Cross first class. That was my only contact with French fighter pilots. I can thus not say any more about them.

The French air force (*Armée de l'Air*) could call on 1,145 combat aircraft on 10 May 1940, which included 490 modern single-engined and 67 modern twin-engined fighters; a significant part of the French bomber and reconnaissance force comprised obsolete machines.[2] The majority of the French fighters were stationed in the northern command area, facing the anticipated direction of the weight of the German attack.[3] The Belgian air force (180 serviceable aircraft including 11 modern fighters, Hurricanes) and the Dutch air force (108 serviceable military aircraft, including 28 modern indigenous fighters and 23 modern heavy fighters, plus 53 naval aircraft largely uninvolved in the brief campaign over Holland)[4] added to the Allied total. However, both these latter countries were neutral and there was no coordination nor any overall Allied war plan before the *Blitzkrieg* was unleashed on 10 May. For the RAF, when the great German attack began, a total of 400 aircraft were stationed in France, divided among 25 squadrons: eight with the terribly vulnerable Fairey Battle light bombers, six with Hurricanes (one of these was still converting from Gladiators to Hurricanes) and the balance with Blenheim bombers and Lysander reconnaissance machines.[5] The RAF had deployed the Air Component (AC; four Hurricane squadrons, reinforced in the first few days by three more) to provide cover for the British army, and the Advanced Air Striking Force (AASF; light bombers, Battles and Blenheims, with two Hurricane squadrons, soon reinforced by one more).[6] Within days, as German pressure and successes mounted, and as the British fighter units suffered increasing losses, 12 more Hurricane squadrons or flights therefrom operated for short periods in France.[7] After the Dunkirk operations, three Hurricane squadrons were sent from the UK to cover remaining British troops withdrawing from western France.[8]

The *Luftwaffe* began the French campaign on 10 May 1940 with a total of 3,689 frontline aircraft, of which 71 per cent were serviceable – 2,612 machines. Of these totals, the breakdown (total/serviceable) was: bombers (He 111, Ju 88, Do 17) 1,577/1,064; ground attack (mainly Ju 87s, a few Hs 123s) 427/356; reconnaissance 135/99; Me 110 fighters 319/209; and Me 109 fighters 1,231/884.[9] In addition there were 340 army co-operation (mainly short-range reconnaissance) aircraft, around 100 long-range reconnaissance machines, 475 transport Ju 52s and 45 gliders not directly under the active *Luftflotten*.[10] Never again would the *Luftwaffe* be able to marshal such strength against an enemy or in a campaign; this was in effect the high point of German aerial strength in any specific major campaign, and with machines manned exclusively by peacetime-trained professionals. The German fighters were divided between *Luftflotten* 2 (north) and 3 (south).

Organisation (under specific staffs) and location (arranged below in rough north-to-south geographic order) of major German fighter units on 10 May 1940[11]

## LUFTFLOTTE 2

*Jagdfliegerführer (Jafü)* 2 (opposite central – southern Holland)

        *Stab/JG 26* (II & III/JG 26; III/JG 3; II/JG 2)

        *Stab/JG 51* (I/JG 20; I/JG 26; II/JG 27; I/JG 51; I & II/ZG 1; II/JG 51 joined later, from *Fliegerkorps V*)

        *Stab/ZG 26* (I & III/ZG 26)

*Fliegerkorps IV*    II(J)/TrGr186 (I/LG 2 joined 12 May 1940) (opposite Eindhoven-Venlo, southern Holland)

*Fliegerkorps VIII*    *Stab/JG 27* (I/JG 27; I/JG 1; I/JG 21) (opposite Venlo-Maastricht, southernmost Holland)

## LUFTFLOTTE 3

*Fliegerkorps I*    *Stab/ZG 76* (II/ZG 76) (opposite Maastricht, southernmost Holland)

        *Stab/JG 77* (I/JG 77; I/JG 3; II/JG 3 joined on 19 May 1940) (opposite Dutch-Belgian border area)

        II/ZG 26 (opposite Dutch-Belgian border area)

*Jagdfliegerführer (Jafü)* 3 (opposite northern and central Luxembourg)

        *Stab/JG 2* (I & III/JG 2; I/JG 76)

        *Stab/JG 53* (I, II & III/JG 53; III/JG 52)

        *Stab/ZG 2* (I/ZG 2)

*Fliegerkorps V*    *Stab/JG 52* (I & II/JG 52) (opposite southern Luxembourg)

        V(Z)/LG 1 (opposite southern Luxembourg)

        *Stab/JG 54* (I/JG 54 & II/JG 51) (Freiburg area, southern Germany)

        I/ZG 52 (Freiburg area, southern Germany)

In the organisation tabled above, many fighter *Gruppen* were under the control of *Geschwader* staffs which were not part of their formal organic structures; this situation changed in the Battle of Britain. It is noticeable that the two German fighter concentrations were 1) in the Ardennes area where the largest panzer group debouched out of the Ardennes hills (*Jafü 3*) and proceeded on to rout the French at the Sedan–Dinant crossings of the Meuse River, and 2) further to the north, along the borders of central and southern Holland (*Jafü 2*). The concentrated punch of army support offered by the massed Stukas of VIII *Fliegerkorps* effectively lay between these two fighter masses approximately opposite the Maastricht area in southernmost Holland, also roughly opposite the British Expeditionary Force as it advanced into Belgium.

Artur Dau, with *I/JG 20* (renamed *III/JG 51* after the French battles), was part of *Jafü 2* facing Holland. He was there from the beginning on 10 May 1940, during the Dunkirk operations and through to the Armistice with France, and had the pragmatic approach to war that is typical for the experienced senior NCO.

We did not analyse or think about the war. We were soldiers and did our duty. During the advance of our troops we had to provide air cover, and this assignment we repeated enough times, as well as we could. The contacts with the French were very few to begin with. On 17 May 1940 we had the first contacts with a French squadron in the Holland–Belgium region. They were flying the Curtiss. The Curtiss was more manoeuvrable than our Me – Emil. However, we were faster. I shot down two Curtiss fighters within four minutes on 17 May; and one Hurricane on 31 May 1940. Of my own victories I can only say that these were events that happened in seconds. Suddenly the enemy was within sight and then one had to get moving. Then it was only about 'you or me'. These events remain in one's memory forever. Our daily missions were directed exclusively to the support of our advancing troops and we arranged our operational service in this sense. Our missions took place from field bases directly behind the frontline. The field bases were large meadows that served only for landings and take-offs. Our operational fields in most cases lay close to a forest. The forest gave us more cover from the prying eyes of the enemy. The pilots were all together in one large tent, to be able to scramble faster in case of danger. Our chief cook was fully responsible for our nutrition. In that regard I can only say that he took the best care of us, and we lacked nothing. He was a good organiser. Air bases in the normal sense were not available to us. An exception for me was the airfield in Breda – Holland. Our accommodations during these operations were our tents. For the nights we requisitioned a house near our field bases. Our daily experiences were determined exclusively by the behaviour of the enemy as well as our own operations directives. However, there was a good comradeship in the units and the differences in rank were hardly to be noticed. An *Oberfeldwebel* could adapt well to these conditions. We had nothing to complain about with our missions. There were up to six missions in a day. When one looked at the entire affair in hindsight, it was a gypsy's life. But one can also accustom oneself to anything. The waiting times between missions were filled by games or talks. Our chief cook sometimes surprised us also with an exceptionally pleasant feast. He often had good ideas and thereby ensured variety in our fare. In bad weather, when flying was impossible, we sometimes enjoyed a trip to the nearest town or city. One could not expect more than this.

On the opening day of the French campaign, 10 May 1940, enormous numbers of aircraft were lost in action as a vast conflagration of individual and massed aerial combats and ground-defence retaliation actions spread across large parts of France, Belgium and Holland; total direct combat losses (destroyed by air combat, flak and on the ground by strafing and bombing) can be estimated at between 697 and 706 aircraft from all combatants based on data available,[12] and these exclude accidents and indirect combat-related operational losses. The French lost 70 machines, the British 55, the Dutch 138 and the Belgians between 92 and 101 (and possibly a few more), while the *Luftwaffe* suffered 342 aircraft lost.[13] Of the Allied losses, destruction on the ground accounted for the majority: 49 French, seven British, 108 Dutch and 85–94 Belgian machines.[14] A total of 18 Allied aircraft losses can definitely be ascribed to Me 109s and 21½ (shared) to Me 110s,[15] but these are only minimum known values. The Dutch and Belgian air forces were effectively destroyed and played little role thereafter. German losses on this opening day of the campaign must have given some cause for concern at high level: the figure estimated above (342 machines in combat) included 85 bombers, of which around 60 are identified as victims of Allied fighters, with only minor losses of Me 109s (7) and Me 110s (2). Much of the combat over France was of Allied fighters against bombers lacking escort or with the latter having to leave too early due to fuel shortage. Of great concern to the Germans must have been the dispatch of no less than 212 Ju 52s either destroyed or abandoned over the Low Countries; admittedly some of those abandoned were later salvaged, but the loss of almost half of the 475 available prior to the *Blitzkrieg* on the first day of conflict illustrates a fact that was to be demonstrated fairly often: quite simply, airborne troops are very expensive to train, often have long periods of inactivity as they can rarely be wasted in normal attritional fighting, and tend to suffer large losses when employed, although they are often effective in achieving their aims. This lesson was hammered home to the *Luftwaffe* in the invasion of Crete, and large losses of transport aircraft occurred in the Demjansk airlift and subsequently at Stalingrad, both in the USSR (relative success at Demjansk provided the model for assumed success over the far larger Stalingrad pocket), and over Tunisia.

On 10 May 1940, a slaughter of air-landed troops and their ferrying Ju 52 aircraft and crews in Holland was witnessed by many members of escorting Me 110 fighter formations. *Leutnant* Jochen Schröder from *II/ZG 1* (renamed *III/ZG 76* for the Battle of Britain) described operations initially from Gelsenkirchen-Buer, including three *Staffel*-strength missions on 10 May 1940 to provide cover for the paratroopers at Vaalhaven and Rotterdam. These airborne landings went on all day, with high losses of Ju 52s, some lost in their approach flights and others after landing due to mining of the airfields. The next two days brought more missions over Holland, including four by the 6th *Staffel* led by *Oberleutnant* Kadow. There were hardly any combats with enemy fighters, and his *Staffel* did their best to help the paratroopers with low-level attacks. On 13 May a planned dawn attack on Vlissingen airfield, where RAF Hurricanes were thought to have landed the previous evening, went wrong when they got there too early, before it was properly light, and the *Staffelkapitän* of *5/ZG 1* hit the ground while making a low-level run and crashed in flames with his gunner. Jochen Schröder recalled: 'We were well suited as fighter escorts for our bomber units, and enjoyed good successes in air combat against the French fighters (Morane, Curtiss, Potez 63). It must also be said that the French air force gave no impression of fighter performance at this stage.' Another pilot with *I/ZG 1*, Victor Mölders, was also a witness to the serious losses of paratroopers and Ju 52s over Holland:

> On 10 May 1940 we took off from the Ruhr area with *ZG1*. We were flying escort for the Ju-52 *Staffels* that were carrying 40–50 [something of an exaggeration] paratroopers in each machine. They landed in Rotterdam [Holland]. We were not attacked. However, when the Ju 52s landed at the airport in Rotterdam, almost all of them, about 20 aircraft, exploded as they hit mines. Hundreds of soldiers burnt in their machines. After that the Junkers landed on the grass fields next to the airport but were shot up there by the ground defence. It was cruel to watch, as almost the entire German airborne force was totally destroyed by the Dutch ground defences. We could only attempt, through low-level attacks, to eliminate the ground defences. Not far from the airport stood very large crowds of Dutch civilians, rubber-necking and watching the cruel game being played out in their midst. The advance of the German troops then went through Holland and Belgium into France and we flew almost exclusively escort operations for the bomber formations. Often we landed at strange airfields and had to wait until our ground staff caught up with us. The flying crews had always to leave the airfields immediately, so that we did not suffer losses from enemy aircraft. For the pilots and radio operators there were always night quarters made available in a nearby settlement.

The following 10 days, from 11 to 20 May 1940, saw the continuing aerial battle steadily drain German resources, and of course even more those of the Allies. Allied losses had a much greater effect in reducing combat effectiveness as they were far fewer than the Germans to begin with. Neither of the poorly equipped Dutch or Belgian air forces, though fighting bravely, had much impact; the Dutch surrendered on 15 May and the Belgians on 28 May 1940. *Luftwaffe* combat losses were not inconsiderable, as shown in the table below. Proportional to serviceable aircraft available on 10 May, losses to Me 109s and Ju 87s (surprisingly in view of their inherent vulnerability) were lowest, but bombers and Me 110s had lost 25 per cent by the 20 May 1940. The Me 109s expended much effort in protecting the Stukas, well known to be extremely vulnerable. Of greatest concern was the 83 per cent loss of serviceable reconnaissance machines available on the first day. These statistics underline the vulnerability of lone bombers (reconnaissance aircraft), of unescorted or inadequately escorted bombers, and the inherent inability of the Me 110 to defend itself adequately against aggressive opposition flying faster and more manoeuvrable machines. However, several witnesses downplayed the effectiveness of French opposition, among them *Leutnant* Hans-Joachim Jabs, ZG 76: 'I flew the "110" from 10 May 1940 over France, Belgium and later during the Battle of Britain. We were superior to the French and Belgians with the Me 110, irrespective of whether we were opposed by Morane or Curtiss. We were inferior to the Spitfires and the Hurricanes over Dunkirk.'

*Luftwaffe* combat losses, 10–20 May 1940, based on published data[16]

| Date (May) | Me 109 | Me 110 | Recce. aircraft | Bombers | Ju 87 | Other | Total |
|---|---|---|---|---|---|---|---|
| 10 | 7 | 2 | 9 | 85 | 7 | 232 | 342 |
| 11 | 8 | 7 | 5 | 26 | 9 | 3 | 58 |
| 12 | 9 | 4 | 8 | 22 | 6 | 1 | 50 |
| 13 | 6 | 4 | 5 | 13 | 5 | 2 | 35 |
| 14 | 15 | 4 | 4 | 17 | 14 | 3 | 57 |
| 15 | 6 | 9 | 7 | 16 | 5 | 1 | 44 |
| 16 | 6 | 3 | 13 | 10 | 3 | 0 | 35 |
| 17 | 9 | 4 | 5 | 12 | 10 | 0 | 40 |
| 18 | 7 | 11 | 9 | 23 | 1 | 0 | 51 |
| 19 | 13 | 2 | 8 | 33 | 0 | 0 | 56 |
| 20 | 5 | 2 | 9 | 7 | 0 | 1 | 24 |
| Total | 91 | 52 | 82 | 264 | 60 | 243 | 792 |

British and French air forces continued the struggle as best they were able in the face of increasing losses, confusion, supply problems and, worst of all, pilot fatigue. Both air forces rapidly lost combat effectiveness after the spectacular losses caused to the Luftwaffe on 10 May 1940. The RAF made major efforts on 14 May over the Sedan breakthrough area, and from 17 to 19 May 1940, with significant Hurricane reinforcements flying in from the United Kingdom daily and mostly returning there at night for safety. By the end of 20 May 1940 the Air Component Hurricanes and these reinforcements had all been withdrawn, with only the few RAF Hurricanes of the AASF remaining to hold the field with the French air force.

While British and French fighter losses in aerial combat from 10 to 20 May 1940 were necessarily episodic, reflecting waxing and waning intensity, their trends (see chart of losses in the plate section) were opposite: RAF losses showed an overall increase while the French casualties decreased overall. This can perhaps be interpreted as a reflection of maintained fighting spirit and decrease thereof, respectively. However, not all German fighter pilots experienced low morale in their French opponents, as emphasised by *Hauptmann* Rolf Pingel, *I/JG 53*: 'The French were brave soldiers and good pilots. The Messerschmitt 109 was superior to their aircraft. For the operations over Sedan, my *Gruppe* was stationed in Kirchberg and flew many operations with good success and many victories.' Individual French pilots and units fought very hard, as remembered by *Feldwebel* Erwin Leykauf of *I/JG 21*: 'Where the air combats with, for example, French Moranes were concerned, it can only be noted that the Moranes were always aggressive and their central cannon was not much loved by us.' This is a strong positive opinion of the French fighter pilots as the Morane was not an aircraft of very good performance.

By charting victories between 10 and 20 May 1940 attributed to Me 109s and Me 110s by post-war research,[17] two different trends reveal themselves (see plate section): the combat effectiveness of the Me 110s gradually decreased, while that of the Me 109s was effectively going up. There is no doubt that the Me 109 was supreme in the skies above France in this period, equally outclassing all the French fighters and the RAF Hurricanes, even though the latter aircraft was still a success against the *Luftwaffe* generally. The inherent superiority of the Me 109, even compared to the most modern Dewoitine fighters of the *Armée de l'Air*, is underlined by *Oberleutnant* Günther Scholz, *1/JG 21*: 'The French fighters, Potez, Dewoitine or Morane, were likewise all inferior to the Me 109.'

In contrast, the Me 110 did not reign supreme over France in May 1940, although it was superior to most if not all French fighters. *Oberleutnant* Gerhard Granz of *I/ZG 2* had confidence in his mount: 'After the Polish campaign, my *Gruppe* converted onto the Me 110 and was renamed as *I/ZG 2*. Our *Kommodore* was *Oberst* Ibel, who had already participated in the First World War as a fighter pilot, and my *Gruppenkommandeur* was Major Gentzen, sadly soon to be shot down. In the campaign against France I scored two victories and received the Iron Cross first class. As to tactics: in Poland and France these were simple, as the Me 109 and Me 110 were superior flying machines to those of their enemies, so it came down only to flying ability, a good eye and shooting ability; that is what our large successes were based on at that time.' While not technically superior to the French fighters on paper, certainly the Me 110 appears to have had little trouble dealing with French aircraft, at least in the opinion of the aircrew involved. Me 110s had trouble with the RAF's Hurricanes but also caused them severe losses on occasion. *Hauptmann* Wolfgang Falck, *ZG 1* had distinct memories in this regard:

> The French fighters were hardly to be taken seriously. They were hardly to be seen and then vanished very fast. The British Hurricanes were an opponent to be taken seriously, as we provided them with a significantly large target due to the size of our aircraft, and they were naturally more manoeuvrable than us. Apart from that the British were excellent pilots and hard fighters!! The operations over France were not walks in the park for us, as when for example we had to escort bomber formations deep into enemy territory, but still basically they were problem-free. We hardly ever flew in defensive circles. At every contact with enemy aircraft the formations and units effectively broke up into single combats. I only experienced the defensive circle once over France, when we met a French fighter formation. We attacked – even though we were fewer in numbers – and to my great surprise the Frenchmen straight away formed a defensive circle.

The recollection of Wolfgang Falck quoted here suggests a morale problem in elements of the relatively poorly organised and equipped French air force, which also suffered indifferent leadership at the higher levels. This must inevitably have had an effect lower down. Some pilots, such as *Leutnant* Heinz Lange with *JG 54*, hardly saw anything of the French: 'France 1940: I only had contact once with French fighters, over Cambrai – without results.'

The Germans, with the Spanish Civil War, the Polish campaign and some with the Norwegian campaign behind them, enjoyed a critical (although small) advantage in experience and even more so in tactical formations and fighting dogma. However, inexperienced German aircrew suffered as much as their unschooled opponents, and inevitably paid the same price, as Alois Dierkes, a rear gunner in *V/LG 1*, learnt to his cost: 'From 10 May 1940, we flew *scharfe Einsätze* (operations at the 'sharp end'). In the first days we always flew three or four missions daily. At that time I had just been assigned a new pilot, who had as yet no decorations, who as a result and being a young *Leutnant* (I was only an *Unteroffizier*) flew very ambitiously. On 12 May, that is on the third day of the French operation, after a successful air combat, we were shot down by five Moranes, and ended up seriously wounded and in captivity, where we were treated very well by the doctors. Already in June 1940 we were freed by the advance of our troops. I returned to my unit, although I was not yet fit enough to fly.'

For many German fighter pilots, the French campaign was one which involved many changes of home base as the rapid advance took place, with almost comical scenes of the new *Luftwaffe* masters flying in before the last elements of the previous French owners had departed. The fighter units moved forward just behind the fighting front, comprised largely of the mobile forces, reconnaissance battalions and panzers, way ahead of the plodding mass of the infantry, struggling to move up and secure the conquered territory. *Leutnant* Theodor Grisebach of I/JG 2 describes such experiences in detail and furthermore remarks on the poor fighting formations of the French, and the low-quality armour plate fitted to the Morane fighters. He experienced the Morane as a respectable opponent but alleges fraud on the part of the supplier of its dreadful armour plate; one cannot fault poor French pilot morale with such inadequate provision of equipment on the part of the leaders of their air force.

On 10 May 1940, the war with France began, France had declared war against Germany on 3 September 1939. The first proper day of the war on 10 May I experienced as courier in a motor car, squeezed in between artillery units of the army. Only on the following day did I get to fly an operation into France. A few days later we had to relocate from Bassenheim to Bacon and then again, to Signy-le-Petit. The active fighter units were continually moving forward, actually transferring to French airfields ahead of the advancing infantry, and that had just been taken by the most advanced frontline soldiers. Thus we were often able to greet the infantry moving up behind with chocolate and mail, and who were desperately trying to reach the front lines. The front line however moved ahead faster than the marching troops could progress. Before every change to a new base an advanced party flew with

whatever old plane was available to the new airfield, in order to
ensure that the unit found quarters, that food supplies were at
hand as well as cooking facilities etc. In this regard it happened
once, that this advance party found the French still in residence,
well, in any case the fried eggs were still in the pan, the baggage
was still there and only the French aircraft had disappeared. It
was reported that our well-loved *Gruppe* sergeant major chased
the remains of the French airfield personnel into the nearest forest
with a pistol. As far as I recall, shots were never exchanged in these
changes in base ownership. Now the first enemy contacts with the
French occurred in the air that continuously played themselves out
in approximately the same way. My *Staffel*, in which I led a group
of four aircraft, regularly stalked French formations. These French
formations consisted mostly of between 20 and 40 aircraft that
from a distance already resembled a swarm of gnats. Mostly we
were able to reach an attacking position and then we dived into
the mass of aircraft and everyone tried to shoot one of them down.
However, this was not as easy as we thought, and if it succeeded,
it was also not easy to establish who the actual victor was and
who should be credited with the victory. The French Morane was
a very fast aircraft, but had the tendency to catch fire due to its
extremely light construction. We also learned that the armour
plate that was behind the pilot, apparently could not protect him
against our machine gun ammunition. The 109 had two machine
guns (MGs) that fired over the engine, and 2 cm cannons with
explosive ammunition, one beneath each wing. Due to the very
strong MG-armament of the Morane, as far as I can remember
eight MGs left and eight MGs right, it was not nearly so safe to fly
through a Morane formation. I several times received considerable
numbers of bullet strikes, on one occasion actually counting
46 bullet holes. The armour plate in the 109 was outstanding. The
French ammunition hardly left a mark on the polished steel plate.
Our ammunition in contrast punched holes in the French armour
plate which was of very poor quality, due as I heard later to fraud
on the part of the supplier. After such a long time (he was writing
in November 1989) naturally one only recalls certain individual
scenes and events that remain stuck in one's memory. For example:
a court martial where in Paris I had to defend a German soldier
charged with looting; or the impression of a town plundered by
the French themselves; or the ladies' stocking shop in which French

and Germans had searched for stockings for their wives and that was full of paper and scattered stockings; or a journey to Lyon to requisition lorries, and the journey back again when we passed through armed French groups and where we with four men armed only with pistols took an entire unit prisoner.

## Fighter Operations over Dunkirk

Operations over France from 21 May till 2 June 1940 became relatively concentrated around the Dunkirk (Calais–Ostende) area, even though the famous evacuation itself did not begin straight away. Immediately following the withdrawal of the last Air Component Hurricanes from France, the RAF began a series of fighter patrols over France from home bases. Contacts with German aircraft remained frequent, and new experiences came the way of *Luftwaffe* fighter units previously spared any contacts with RAF fighters operating from well-organised bases. *II/ZG 1* had moved to Trier on 20 May, from where operations were flown to Dunkirk, and over Arras (tank battles). It was over Dunkirk that numbers of German aircrew first met the aggressive RAF fighter pilots, as *Leutnant* Jochen Schröder, *II/ZG 1* remembered: 'Over France we felt ourselves to be superior, but had no good feelings in aerial combat with English fighters, Hurricanes and Spitfires, that we got to know over Dunkirk.'

The British army commanders in France began to seriously consider an evacuation by 23 May 1940, and on 24 May the Royal Navy was already providing considerable support to troops trapped in Calais and Boulogne; evacuation of troops from the latter town was carried out on the night of 24 May and it fell to the Germans the next day. The Dunkirk evacuation proper began on 26 May and continued till just before midnight on 3 June 1940, although no daylight RAF activity took place on the last day.[18] With the fighter cover required by these coastal operations, almost all the available fighter squadrons in the UK were now drawn into the maw that was the French campaign. Now it was the turn of the Spitfire squadrons to experience their baptism of fire against the marauding Me 109s, to lose precious pre-war trained professional airmen, but also to exact a high price from the *Luftwaffe*, and even more importantly to leave behind an indelible impression amongst German veterans of a determined, aggressive and dangerous foe.

Losses of German aircraft, of the RAF fighter arm and known (from post-war research) victories assigned to either Me 109s or Me 110s, over the Dunkirk region, 21 May to 2 June 1940[19]

| Date | Me 109 | Me 110 | Recce aircraft | Bombers | Ju 87 | % of total daily German losses over France | RAF fighters | RAF fighter pilots | RAF fighter losses ascribed to Me 109s | RAF fighter losses ascribed to Me 110s |
|---|---|---|---|---|---|---|---|---|---|---|
| 21 May | 0 | 0 | 2 | 2½ | 0 | 20 | 3 | 2 | 0 | 2 |
| 22 | 4 | 0 | 2 | 8 | 4 | 72 | 6 | 1 | 4 | 0 |
| 23 | 9 | 0 | 1 | 0 | 0 | 71 | 13 | 10 | 7 | 3 |
| 24 | 4 | 0 | 3 | 3 | 0 | 56 | 9 | 6 | 4 | 0 |
| 25 | 1 | 1 | 0 | 2 | 5 | 43 | 5 | 3 | 1½ | 1½ |
| 26 | 3 | 4 | 1 | 3 | 5 | 47 | 10 | 6 | 7 | 1 |
| 27 | 4 | 6 | 2 | 23 | 0 | 85 | 19 | 11 | 2 | 13 |
| 28 | 2 | 0 | 1 | 3 | 0 | 67 | 14 | 8(3G) | 12 | 1 |
| 29 | 6 | 1 | 2 | 8 | 3 | 91 | 17 | 9(1G) | 14 | 1 |
| 30 | 0 | 0 | 1 | 1 | 0 | 22 | 1 | 1 | 0 | 0 |
| 31 | 7 | 0 | 0 | 7 | 0 | 82 | 21 | 9(3G) | 16 | 2 |
| 1 June | 8 | 3 | 1 | 2 | 3 | 59 | 17 | 12 | 9½ | 5½ |
| 2 | 1 | 0 | 0 | 6 | 4 | 65 | 10 | 6 | 6 | 3 |
| Total | 49 | 15 | 16 | 68½ | 24 | 62 | 145 | 84(7G) | 83 | 33 |

German losses only for aircraft lost over greater Dunkirk–Ostende–Calais region due to anti-aircraft fire and air combat; G refers to Defiant gunners (264 Squadron).

It is evident from the above table, and especially from the percentage of daily total losses over France suffered by Germans around Dunkirk, that the air action over Dunkirk dominated the fighting over France as a whole for that 13-day period. Obviously fighting elsewhere, mainly by the French and to a lesser extent the RAF AASF, continued simultaneously, and after Dunkirk the latter operations totally dominated over France, with only minor British incursions from across the Channel. What is very important to note is the relatively limited scale of the Dunkirk losses to the *Luftwaffe* (a total of only 172½ machines from 21 May to 2 June 1940); RAF fighter losses on the other hand were high, reflecting also the long flight back home with any damaged aircraft, and the fact that any minor damage leading to a forced landing in France automatically implied the total loss of the machine and possibly pilot also. The scale of the Dunkirk fighting thus never reached that of the 10–20 May 1940 period (compare the two loss tables given above), however, and in spite of relatively limited German losses, almost all the *Luftwaffe* fighter pilots remember the Dunkirk operations as particularly bitter, hard-fought affairs, as described by *Oberleutnant* Gerhard Schöpfel of *JG 26*: 'During the evacuation by sea of the English forces at Dunkirk in 1940, our *Geschwader* had the first combats with the British fighter pilots there. We recognised the bravery and the flying abilities of the English pilots. In dogfights their Hurricanes and Spitfires appeared to us to be more manoeuvrable. We considered our armament to be superior.'

No doubt these memories of the RAF fighter opposition over Dunkirk partly reflect their first combats with the Spitfire, which was basically the equal of the Me 109. While no self-respecting *Jagdflieger* was ever going to agree fully with that, *Feldwebel* Emil Clade of *JG 27* recalls being impressed: 'Until Dunkirk we had no large combats with Spitfires. On the Channel coast this changed. The Spitfires with the Tommy pilots were almost our equals. They attacked us continuously and they could fight. However, they always had the problem of the flight home over the Channel.' This first experiences of the Spitfire and meeting numbers of British fighters flying from their home bases must have been a shock, as prior to that their entire war had been one where the Me 109 easily dominated its opponents – at last the German fighter pilots were being challenged by aircraft and pilots as good as they were. For Me 110 pilots like *Hauptmann* Wolfgang Falck, *ZG 1* Dunkirk retained bad memories: 'The operations at the end (*sic*) of the French campaign in the coastal areas (i.e. over Dunkirk) were however, not pleasant, as there we met the Hurricanes and Spitfires. The Spitfires were greatly superior to us in manoeuvrability, speed and climb and unfortunately they caused us large losses. They shot me up mightily, repeatedly, but through a miracle I made it home in one piece every time.'

However, it would be a mistake to view the Dunkirk period as comprising ongoing large-scale and violent air battles over the coastal areas of north-eastern France. With the speeds of the aircraft involved, and bearing in mind that the sky is pretty big, German fighter units often met no opposition at all. There were not enough British fighters to maintain a continuous presence over the beaches, and sensibly they resorted to strong patrols separated by periods with no RAF fighters overhead. *Hauptmann* Hanns Trübenbach supports this view, and most interestingly provides a different slant on why the German panzer units were held back at Dunkirk, and one not thus far appearing in the history books, but nevertheless based upon the personal experience of a mature leader and a very objective and honest witness to *Luftwaffe* fighter operations in the Second World War. He will reappear often in these pages and occupied very important and senior positions later in the defence of Germany against the vast Allied aerial onslaught:

I experienced Dunkirk as the *Kommandeur* of I/LG 2, but carried out only a few strafing attacks on British ship units. The loading of the British army units proceeded strangely enough without German bombardment and without action by the German ground units. Hitler had ordered all German panzer units back, to be able to swiftly take Paris. There were thus days during which enormous army formations crossed over rivers and fields in full harvest moving to the south. Naturally the fighter units were used to cover these huge advances and to keep the sky above them clean of enemy aircraft. What other fighter and bomber units experienced at Dunkirk, I cannot say; however there is an appropriate list of army reports. By the way, in my personal attacks on English warships in the harbour of Dunkirk, I never had any contacts with English fighters, not ever.

The Dunkirk fighting also was concentrated over a relatively small area and was thus intense when combat did occur, and the RAF was flying larger formations, often of two or even three (admittedly poorly coordinated) squadrons together; and this was against a background of tragic loss of men and material on the ground, never mind ships and boats at sea as well. The obvious catastrophe also affected at least some of the German pilots who were witness to the tragedy and chaos that was Dunkirk, including *Oberfeldwebel* Artur Dau, *III/JG 51* who commented perceptively on what he saw.

> On the events over Dunkirk, I can only say it was an enormous catastrophe. The entire English (*sic*) army was squeezed into a very small area right up against the coast at Dunkirk. Off the coast lay the English naval vessels to take off the troops and bring them back to England. The entire coastal strip was continuously attacked by the *Luftwaffe*, bombers and fighters. The German army added their artillery fire to this mess. Part of the British navy lay bombed and destroyed along the French coast. English soldiers rowed out to sea in a column of rowing boats in the direction of England. These boats were not attacked. The trapped army and the navy were attacked throughout each day by the German *Luftwaffe*, by bombers and fighters both. At this time aerial combats with English fighters were limited; I can only say and confirm this from the perspective of my own unit. We flew mostly as bomber escorts in this area and thus had few contacts with the English fighters. On the return flight to our field bases we almost always attacked the troops on the ground. These pictures remain fixed in one's memory. It was simply a catastrophe and one can only hope that such a thing is never repeated.

## After Dunkirk, the French Fight On

Giving an overview of the campaign up to this stage, *Leutnant* Josef Bürschgens of *JG 26* observed: 'At all times we had gained air superiority over France since 10 May 1940. We had to fight against the RAF in the North, against the Belgians and the Netherlands air forces. In the last days of the struggle, only the French still fought back. The Belgian and Netherlands air forces had capitulated, the RAF fought over Dunkirk, but was on the retreat.' Towards the middle of June 1940, western French ports were being used to evacuate remaining British forces still in France and uninvolved in the Dunkirk debacle; this involved the three original AASF Hurricane squadrons (1, 73, 501 Squadrons) plus two more sent from the UK temporarily (17 and 242 Squadrons).[20]

Intelligence had warned of a mass attack by the *Luftwaffe* on the airfields protecting the French capital as well as railways and Paris factories on 3 June 1940, and when this duly got underway the prepared and massed French fighters were ordered off too late due to poor communication systems on the ground despite more than adequate warning from shadowing French patrol aircraft.[21] The retreating bombers were attacked furiously, but the French fighters were in a poor tactical situation due to the late scramble. The 243 French fighter sorties suffered 17 fighters destroyed; four more force-landed short of their bases, and 12 pilots were killed and eight wounded, with 26 German aircraft brought down.[22] This had been the largest single battle of the entire campaign, with no less than seven bomber and five fighter *Geschwader* involved.[23] Despite the botched control of the French fighters, the *Luftwaffe* performed little better, only destroying 16 aircraft on the ground.[24]

From 6 to 8 June 1940, British fighters, often escorting bombers, attempted to support the French, operating from UK bases and even on occasion using French airfields to refuel the Hurricanes.[25] The table below, summarising operations over France from 3 to 24 June, shows how the French air forces fought as hard as their equipment and organisation allowed, destroying at least 157 and sharing two further German aircraft (against 33 and one shared by the RAF) while losing almost equal numbers of their own fighters. From about 17 June 1940, large numbers of unserviceable or damaged French aircraft were abandoned as airfields were evacuated during the French retreat before the advancing German armies (e.g., 39 out of 40 aircraft lost on 18 June, or all but one of the 86 aircraft lost between 22 and 24 June 1940; table below).[26]

German losses to French and RAF fighters (and Allied fighter losses, 3–24 June 1940[27]

| Date in June | German losses to French defence | French fighter losses | Other French aircraft losses | German losses to RAF | German losses to other or unknown causes | British fighter losses operating from France | British fighter losses operating from UK |
|---|---|---|---|---|---|---|---|
| 3 | 11½ | 21 | 3 | 1½ | 1 | 2 | 1 |
| 4 | 1 | 0 | 2 | 0 | 1 | 2 | 0 |
| 5 | 31 | 17 | 18 | 4 | 2 | 2 | 0 |
| 6 | 12 | 17 | 16 | 2 | 2 | 0 | 2 |
| 7 | 9 | 12 | 12 | 6 | 2 | 0 | 12 |
| 8 | 10.33 | 14 | 14 | 4 | 4.67 | 1 | 4 |

| Date in June | German losses to French defence | French fighter losses | Other French aircraft losses | German losses to RAF | German losses to other or unknown causes | British fighter losses operating from France | British fighter losses operating from UK |
|---|---|---|---|---|---|---|---|
| 9 | 13 | 19 | 15 | 0 | 1 | 2 | 0 |
| 10 | 8 | 5 | 7 | 1 | 2 | 1 | 0 |
| 11 | 3 | 12 | 0 | 4 | 3 | 0 | 1 |
| 12 | 2 | 1 | 10 | 4 | 3 | 0 | 0 |
| 13 | 6 | 7 | 19 | 0 | 2 | 0 | 0 |
| 14 | 7 | 2 | 8 | 3 | 3 | 3 | 0 |
| 15 | 20 | 8 | 13 | 0 | 4 | 1 | 0 |
| 16 | 12 | 4 | 9 | 0 | 4 | 0 | 0 |
| 17 | 0 | 1 | 3+ | 0 | 0 | 0 | 0 |
| 18 | 3 | 1 | 40 | 1 | 0 | 6 | 0 |
| 19 | 2 | 2 | 16 (+?) | 1 | 3 | 0 | 0 |
| 20 | 5 | 3 | 4 (+12 on 20–24 June) | 0 | 0 | 1 | 0 |
| 21 | 0 | 0 | 9 | 1 | 0 | 0 | 0 |
| 22 | 1 | 4 | 0 (+86 on 22-24 June) | 0 | 0 | 0 | 1 |
| 23 | 0 | 1 | 0 | 1 | 0 | 0 | 0 |
| 24 | 1 | 4 | 1 | 0 | 0 | 0 | 0 |
| Totals | 157.83 | 155 | 317+ | 33½ | 37.67 | 21 | 21 |

Other or unknown causes of German losses included: 3⅓ (shared) losses due to Swiss fighters on 8 June; 3 by bombs on their bases 19 June 1940 (unknown if British or French bombs).

Several Me 110 pilots had rather unusual experiences during these operations, including *Oberleutnant* Victor Mölders of *ZG 1*, who received a special assignment directly from Göring:

The French and the British fighters were absolutely superior to the Me 110, they were faster and more manoeuvrable. The good armament of the Me 110, four MGs and two cannons, helped little in this regard. The Me 110 was totally inferior to all fighter types and was only suited to attacks on bombers and ground targets. When I, despite all this, was able to shoot down two Moranes and one Hurricane in the French campaign, this was only to be ascribed to the effect of surprise. In this campaign I was given the assignment, from Göring, to test the Me 110 armed with a 3 cm cannon. In place of the usual two 2 cm cannons, this machine had a 3 cm cannon beneath the fuselage. The firepower was absolutely tremendous. In the French campaign, during the retreat of the French troops, I was able to stop every locomotive I saw in its tracks, west of Paris. With the same weapon I also shot a bomber, a Blenheim, out of a formation of six. Fact: the Me 110 is good for night fighting, attacks on bombers and for low-level ground attacks.

Even more unusual was the experience of *Leutnant* Jochen Schröder, *II/ZG1* who was one of a small group of *Luftwaffe* aircrew who found themselves fighting the German-built Me 109s of the Swiss air force. Following the end of the Dunkirk evacuation, Jochen Schröder's *Gruppe* moved far to the south, flying from Freiburg, to provide escort for bombers attacking the port of Marseilles. Just prior to this move of *II/ZG 1*, on 2 June 1940 anti-aircraft fire and French fighter action against attacking German aircraft in the Belfort area separated the *Luftwaffe* fighters from the bombers, and some of the latter were damaged also by the French fighters. These struggling bombers took the shortest route home, passing over neutral Swiss territory where some were attacked and shot down by Swiss Me 109s. This provoked the so-called Swiss incidents. The first retaliation came on 4 June, when 28 Me 110s of *II/ZG 1* and a lone decoy He 111 provoked combat by parading themselves just outside the Swiss border. They were successful in this and the hapless He 111 force-landed with wounded crew members south of the Black Forest, while two Swiss Me 109s were claimed for the loss of two missing Me 110s. Jochen Schröder recalled: 'After the combat with the Swiss fighters – they flew our Me 109 E that Germany had sold to Switzerland in 1938 – we were employed again in the further fighting in France.' For this, *II/ZG 1* were moved north again, to Lachen-Speyersdorf (north-west of Karlsruhe), and carried out bomber and Ju 87 escorts and ground-attack missions north of Paris on 5–7 June 1940. The next day it was back to Freiburg, and another mission to provoke the Swiss was flown, this time with more serious consequences for *II/ZG 1*: the Me 110s surprised and shot down a Swiss C 35, but the 6th *Staffel* was bounced by the Swiss Me 109s and Schröder had an engine shot out. His wingman was shot down and killed. In *Oberleutnant* Kadow's aircraft the gunner was killed and Kadow lightly wounded, and from 5th *Staffel* a further Me 110 was shot down and belly-landed in Swiss territory. Jochen Schröder's final memory of fighting over France was of his own likely successes: 'In total during the French campaign, I was personally able to shoot down two Morane fighters, one near Reims and one in the vicinity of Lyon. Two other claims were not confirmed, but the operational time also went by too fast, as France capitulated on 24 June 1940.'

## A Gruppenkommandeur's French Campaign

*Hauptmann* Hanns Trübenbach, *Kommandeur* of I/LG 2, provided a much more extensive overview of his experiences fighting over France:

In the whole French campaign, I only once caught an entire French squadron that was romping in our full view, and they did not notice when I shot one of them down in flames. Only when my wingman, a *Reserve Leutnant*, wanted to shoot down the next one from this Morane 406 squadron and promptly missed it did the entire company burst asunder and dive vertically away. During this mission we were escorting a Heinkel 111 bomber *Gruppe* and were returning from the Le Havre area. As usual, our fuel got used up and the red warning lights showed in the cockpits, and we had to rapidly land at our field base. All 40 of us at the same time! These fields were so big that nothing ever happened on these occasions. The Western campaign for me as a passionate pilot was a pure gentleman's war. If, as happened occasionally, there was an isolated fight near the ground and the enemy landed in a meadow due to fuel shortage, as I experienced myself, then one waited until the pilot had exited his aircraft and waved. Then we flew at grassroots level past him and greeted the enemy. It was a big fat Curtiss and the dogfight at treetop level gave neither of us a proper firing position. And thus I flew with my wingman back to base.

There were the strangest happenings in the Western campaign. One time we had a free chase mission and flew in a widely spaced formation over the Somme in 800 m height. Suddenly French flak shot a 4 cm shell into my right wing cannon, and also hit my cooling system and the right hand side of the engine. I pulled up fast to 1,200 m, radioed wingman Ihlefeld to approach and see how big the hole was. He dived rapidly beneath my right wing and pulled up again with a silly expression on his face and showed me the size of the hole with his two hands. I was immersed in a white trail of smoke, the engine started to burn and seized. I pushed the

Me's nose down, the radiator water flowed forward and put out the flames. I landed near Bapaume on the main road on my belly. Dutifully, I screwed out the secret reflector gunsight. Already a truck approached and a major from the Reconnaissance Group Kiel received me and brought me back to my field base. The next mission had already been ordered and I had to ask: 'who will lend me his Me?' Big silence. Then my oldest Staff Sergeant approached, and intimated I could take his crate.

We flew in the direction of Amiens at 4,000 m with the entire *Gruppe*, my I/LG 2. I quickly tested the weapons, they were in order. Far ahead we could see the flak bursts, apparently against a reconnaissance machine. I called the left-hand *Staffel* to attack and shoot in the air. But they could see nothing. So once again I reacted faster with my staff *Schwarm* and saw a Fairey Battle that to all appearances was taking photos. The observer was not to be seen and his machine gun could be seen standing vertically in his gun position. I thus flew a textbook approach from below upwards, shot briefly into his fuselage, and naturally flew straight into the prop-wash of the Fairy Battle and had to lower the nose sharply from very close to the enemy. The observer suddenly sat up and shot at me, as evidenced from his winking nozzle. My two cannons and my left upper MG went silent, jammed! The right upper MG gave out enough stuttering shots so that the observer crumpled up and the Battle's engine began to burn. The Battle dived nearly vertically down and slammed into the main road to Reims. What does the old proverb say? 'Full penholders, horses and aircraft, one does not lend!' (*Füllfederhalter, Pferde und Flugzeuge verpumpt man nicht!*). But in the ancient text, it is naturally somewhat different: '*Füllfederhalter, Pferde und Frauen verpumpt man nicht...*'

These few examples illustrate the character of this war. The *Kommandeur* or a *Staffelkapitän* shot down victories, while the entire *Gruppe* watched. That all changed when the English came over the Channel and we flew low-level attacks against their ships. Then every pilot got the chance to shoot. And the entire *Gruppe* stayed together. Of course in the French campaign every now and then there were also low-level strafing attacks on retreating French and English ground troops, who were raked with fire at low level and suffered serious losses as a result. In the Pas-de-Calais we also hit sleeping airfields in the early morning and destroyed the parked and almost un-camouflaged aircraft. Our tactics: two *Staffels* stayed above as protection, the third and the staff *Schwarm* flew the low-level attacks from all directions, to split the defence. But there was hardly any resistance, in contrast to the strafing attacks by the entire *Gruppe* on ships that were waiting at Dunkirk and who fired at their attackers with all available weapons. I had no losses on these missions. Our Me 109 E had after all only the two Oerlikon wing cannons with 120 rounds of 20 cm ammunition, and the two nose-mounted MG 131s. With these one always had to carefully monitor ammunition use, until one could reload the guns at the field base. The French had no chance with their obsolete machines, such as the Morane, Bloch or the most modern Dewoitine and mostly withdrew from any warlike actions. At the beginning of June 1940 the entire German fighter armada flew to Paris, but had only isolated combats with the enemy and then flew back to their bases, to prepare for the massive coming war. My victories over France: 26 May 1940 – 1 Curtiss; 29 May 1940 – 1 Morane 406; 8 June 1940 – 1 Fairey Battle. One day a Ju 52 landed at our base, and my friend *Hauptmann* von Below, Hitler's *Luftwaffe* adjutant, got out and made an important announcement to the officers. Hitler had ordered that Paris was to be taken rapidly, without it being destroyed. Subsequently all the air force units were to be concentrated on the English Channel, so that he (Hitler) could give the English a sound thrashing. Then we pricked up our ears. My fighter *Gruppe*, the I/LG 2, remained an independent unit until the beginning of the Battle of Britain, and never fell under a foreign *Geschwader*'s control nor had to stand ready to perform special missions.

Example of a fighter pilot's operational life, based on flying logbook, 19 May 1940–22 June 1940: *Hauptmann* Hanns Trübenbach, *Kommandeur I/LG 2* (field bases in bold) (Source: Hanns Trübenbach)

MAY

19: *Gruppe* moves from Essen-Mühlheim to **Tirlemont**
Operation, 11h50–13h00 (87th operational flight); evening, *Gruppe* moves to **St Aubin**
20: Free chase, 16h52–18h20 (88th op.)
Stuka escort, 19h50–21h35 (89th op.)
23: *Gruppe* moves to **Ecouvez**, via Cambrai
24: Strafing, Lille, 06h42–07h40 (90th op.)
Strafing, Lille, 13h55–15h00 (91st op.)
Strafing, Lille, 17h49–19h15 (92nd op.)

26: Scramble, 09h16–09h50 (93rd op.); Curtiss shot down at Peronne
    Operation, 18h40–19h42 (94th op.)
27: Operation, 20h00–21h15 (95th op.)
28: Free chase, 09h20–10h40 (96th op.)
29: Operation, 06h00–07h00 (97th op.)
    Bomber escort, 15h05–16h10 (98th op.)
    Air combat, 19h52–20h35 (99th op.); Morane 406 shot down
    near Chauny
31: Bomber escort, 08h45–09h15 (100th op.)
    Bomber escort, 14h10–15h30 (101st op.)
    Operation, 18h05–19h05 (102nd op.)
    Operation, 20h20–21h15 (103rd op.)

JUNE
 1: Reconnaissance flight, 11h15–12h10 (104th op.)
 3: Free chase, 14h00–15h20 (105th op.)
 4: *Gruppe* moves to **Liegescourt**
 6: He 111 escort, 16h50–18h00 (106th op.)
    Patrol, 21h40–22h35 (107th op.)
 7: Air combat, 17h10–17h43 (108th op.)
 8: Ju 88 escort, 15h48–16h45 (109th op.); Fairy Battle shot down
    near Aumale
 9: He 111 escort, 15h15–16h35 (110th op.)
10: Free chase, 07h42–08h55 (111th op.)
11: Free chase, 17h45–18h40 (112th op.)
20: *Gruppe* moves to **St Inglevert**
22: Operation, 07h50–08h20 (113th op.). This was the first operation
    for Hanns Trübenbach across the Channel and into British
    air space and the Battle of Britain ('officially' from 10 July till
    31 October 1940) had thus, in a way, begun.

## Conclusion

The assertion is often made of the ineffectiveness of the French air force,
although more serious writers state clearly the brave and prolonged
fight put up by that air force, while simultaneously remarking on an
almost total lack of data to evaluate their contribution.[28] A balanced
and objective opinion is given by *Oberleutnant* Erhard Braune of
*III/JG 27*: 'Being a fighter pilot during the German advance into
France and up to the Channel coast was an operation of limited
demands, although individual pilots of French fighters and heavy

fighters (Potez 63!) showed remarkable flying and fighting ability. The French air force, at least from my perspective, was materially too inferior to be able to ward off our attacks, especially the Stuka attacks (*VIII Fliegerkorps*) made under our escort that persistently supported the army. Only after the end of the army operations did the contacts start, exclusively of fighter against fighter that occurred with the appearance of the first British Hurricanes and Spitfires; in these contacts, however, our experience advantage was still noticeable, even though this only derived from a few weeks' worth of operations.'

Many memories of the French campaign stress the aerial combat role of the *Luftwaffe* fighter pilots, such as expressed by *Unteroffizier* Alfred Heckmann of *JG 3*: 'Main operational tasks were bomber escorts and fighting enemy aircraft.' In actuality their function was far more closely tied to German army operations, as noted by *Hauptmann* Hennig Strümpel, *I/JG 2*: 'I cannot recall any special *Gruppe* tactics used against the French fighters; there was really no such thing anyway. I only became *Gruppenkommandeur* of *I/JG 2* in the middle of June 1940, prior to that I was *Staffelkapitän* of *3/JG 2*; I thus experienced the French campaign essentially as a *Staffelkapitän*. Missions with the entire *Gruppe* together in the air at the same time were rare in France, actually only over the Dunkirk area during the British evacuation, or later as escort to the Stuka and bomber formations in the Paris area, always within a framework of army operations. In general in the French campaign only *Staffel*-strength missions were flown, and very often only *Rotte*- or *Schwarm*-strength operations, the latter for example as escorts to short-range reconnaissance aircraft.'

The French aircrews fought as best they could, despite being hindered by poor aircraft and equipment on those aircraft, indifferent top leadership and a general lack of planning and organisation. All of these things combined to affect morale, but individual units and pilots fought very hard and many lost their lives. The statistics presented here, extensive post-war research in great detail,[29] and several comments by their German opponents make this clear. The French did not have the choice to withdraw to the UK, there was no Dunkirk for the *Armée de l'Air*; they faced up to a much bigger, well-equipped, well-led opponent with a very definite plan of action, and suffered disproportionately heavy casualties.

Total losses suffered by the various air forces in the French campaign (10 May–24 June 1940)[30]

|  | RAF | French | Dutch | Belgian | *Luftwaffe* |
|---|---|---|---|---|---|
| Aircraft total losses | 1,067 | 1,403 | 246 | 304 | 1,814 |
| Aircrew losses | 1,127 | 923 | 47 | 40 | 3,278 |

Minor Italian losses = 9 aircraft and 21 personnel. Aircraft losses defined as those destroyed, missing, abandoned to enemy, and to all causes; obviously many damaged aircraft were later actually written off or abandoned and would increase these figures. Aircrew losses are those killed, missing, died of wounds or POW – many German prisoners were released at the end of the campaign by France and returned to duty, but obviously not those taken across the Channel to the UK.[31] RAF losses include also aircraft operating from UK bases which became casualties over French soil.

A total of 1,378 accredited claims awarded by the *Luftwaffe* authorities to individual pilots and units have been traced.[32] Using these data the Me 109 and Me 110 *Geschwader* performance over France and the Low Countries was as shown in the table below.

Victory claims by *Luftwaffe* fighter *Geschwadern* over France, 10 May 1940–24 June 1940

| | |
|---|---|
| JG 2 | 179 |
| JG 3 | 180 |
| JG 26 | 157 |
| JG 27 (*I* and *II Gruppen* plus *I/JG 1* which later became *III/JG 27*) | 190 |
| JG 51 (*I* and *II Gruppen* plus *I/JG 20*, later the *III/JG 51*) | 89 |
| JG 52 | 38 |
| JG 53 | 179 |
| JG 54 (*I Gruppe* plus *I/JG 76* and *I/JG 21*, later *II* and *III/JG 54*, respectively) | 133 |
| JG 77 (*I Gruppe* plus *II(J)/TrGr186*, the later *III/JG 77*) | 36 |
| I/LG 2 (a still fully independent *Gruppe*) | 44 |
| V/LG 1 (independent *Gruppe*) | 14 (+5 ASM) |
| ZG 26 (3 *Gruppen*) | 61 |
| ZG 76 (*I* and *II Gruppen* plus *II/ZG1*, later *III/ZG 76*) | 80 (+11 ASM) |

Me 110 units with few exceptions had much lower accredited claim scores (ASM = claims considered 'probable' subject to later confirmation).

Top-scoring Me 109 *Gruppen* were *I/JG 2* (125 accredited claims), *III/JG 53* (99), *I/JG 3* (88) and *I/JG 1* (82); amongst the *Zerstörergruppen*, *II/ZG 76* scored all of the successes awarded to this entire *Geschwader*, followed by *III/ZG 26* with 53 credits. The top-scoring pilots of the campaign, by accredited victories, not claims,[33] were: *Hauptmann* Wilhelm Balthasar, *Staffelkapitän 1/JG 1* – 23 victories; *Hauptmann* Werner Mölders, *Kommandeur III/JG 53* – 16 victories; *Hauptmann* Adolf Galland, *Stab/JG 27* & *Kommandeur III/JG 26* – 14 victories; *Oberleutnant* Helmut Wick, *I/JG 2* & *Staffelkapitän 3/JG 2* (from 22 June 1940) – 12 victories; *Oberleutnant* Lothar Keller, *Staffelkapitän 1/JG 3* – 10 victories; *Oberfeldwebel* Werner Machold, *1/JG 2* – 10 victories.

With the exception of Wick and Machold, most of these ace pilots were unit leaders throughout, always a preferential position from which to score victories as in combat they flew at the head of a formation, were the first to attack and had many protectors at their back. Werner Mölders was the top ace of the entire *Luftwaffe*, with a total score of 25 victories by the end of the campaign, and had been awarded the coveted *Ritterkreuz* (*RK*) on 29 May 1940 for his then 20 victories. He was the first German fighter pilot to reach 20 victories and the first from the fighter arm to receive the *RK*. He had been the leading ace in Spain (14 victories) and in the Phoney War (9 victories).[34] He was also one of the two originators of the 'finger four' fighting formation and probably the *Luftwaffe*'s most important tactical innovator. Later the first General of Fighters, he was in many ways the leading figure in the fighter arm. His nickname of *Vati* (Daddy) reflects his concern with leading all his young inexperienced pilots to success and survival. Adolf Galland, another Spanish veteran but on ground-attack aircraft, later succeeded Mölders as *General der Jagdflieger* and during the Battle of Britain and 1941 they vied with each other for the top spot on the *Luftwaffe* score list and as recipients of the top decorations. Both were awarded the highest honours and were dominant figures in Luftwaffe fighter circles during the war. Balthasar was to be seriously wounded in the Battle of Britain and was killed early on in the war, in July 1941.[35] Wick's flame burned briefly but very intensely and during the Battle of Britain he was to successfully compete with the two giants, Mölders and Galland, and to be promoted from *Staffelkapitän* to *Kommodore* in the space of just four months, only to be killed over the Channel in November 1940 in the dying days of the famous battle over southern England.[36]

Top achievers over France in the Me 110 units were perforce much fewer and had more difficulty in achieving victories. Nevertheless, the top ace, *Oberleutnant* Heinz Nacke, *Staffelkapitän* of 6/ZG 76, was able to score nine accredited victories. By the end of the subsequent fighting over England he was able to raise this to 12 and was awarded the *RK*, following which he commanded day and night fighter and ground-attack units, surviving the war.[37] *Leutnant* Hans-Joachim Jabs, also with *II/ZG 76*, scored six victories over France and *Leutnant* Siegfried Kuhrke of *III/ZG 26*, had five accredited successes.[38]

# 5

# The Battle of Britain

The Battle of Britain was the first strategic air battle to be fought and is in many ways the iconic and quintessential aerial struggle. What was at stake was clear – the *Luftwaffe* was tasked with winning air superiority over the island and the Channel as a prelude to an invasion of the British Isles. There has been a lot written since the battle about the invasion not having been seriously intended, about it being used as a bluff, and so on, but a study by a German expert commissioned by the United States Air Force Historical Division and published in 1955, and based on surviving German wartime documents, details many meetings held and directives issued during the relevant period related to the planned invasion of Britain.[1] These meetings and directives dealt with detailed activities of the *Luftwaffe* during the intended invasion, and involved close liaison with army and navy units, the setting up of combined operational planning staffs between specific army formations and their assigned air force support units.

A few examples will suffice to illustrate that the invasion was taken seriously and that all due preparation was done in time for the envisaged deadline date of 15 September 1940.[2] At the end of July 1940 and the beginning of August 1940, the various German Air Corps received preliminary information about the invasion – for the I Air Corps, conferences were held between it and the 9th Army at the end of July; the VIII Air Corps in early August received its initial general directive to get in touch with the 16th Army, and learned it was to provide close air support for this ground formation in the Dover–Folkestone area for a mid-September 1940 landing.[3] At the end of August 1940, the I Air Corps reported to *Luftflotte* 2 that all preparations for supporting the invasion were complete; a small planning staff of the VIII Air Corps had by then been attached to the 16th Army and this air corps completed all its preparations, down to the last detail, by 15 September 1940.[4] Karl Klee, the author of this detailed study of the invasion planning, stresses that the German forces were prepared to launch the invasion by 14–15 September 1940, that it was a serious preparation, albeit rapid, and involved considerable staff work, and large army, air force and navy units, plus all the transport vessels and their human and materiel cargoes.[5] The only thing that was half-hearted was Hitler's indecision on the actual signal to go; interestingly, even after an initial postponement on 14 September 1940 and a decision three days later for an indefinite postponement, detailed preparations and staff work continued at levels below the various high commands.[6]

The Battle of Britain was largely fought between Fighter Command of the RAF on the one hand, who were fully prepared and trained for just this battle, and the *Luftwaffe*, who had never really envisaged nor prepared for such a battle at all. Having crushed Polish, Norwegian, Dutch, Belgian and French air forces in the preceding Blitzkrieg campaigns of 1939–40, they were full of confidence that they could do the same to the RAF, and in a short time at that.[7] However, a critical difference in the case of the RAF was that they had a fully thought-out, scientifically based and well-functioning system of defence, which maximised use of the fighters available and put them in the right place at the right time.[8] It was the genius of Air Chief Marshal Sir Hugh Dowding, commander-in-chief of Fighter Command, that had ensured the application of science (and many eminent scientists) to the defence problem; he had envisaged, planned and put together all the complex pieces of a very effective defence system, and had ensured that it was fully tested and de-bugged by the time the Battle of Britain was upon him.[9] In his marshalling of 11 Group of Fighter Command, that responsible for the defence of south-eastern England and London, Dowding was equally superbly served by his right-hand man, Air Vice-Marshal Keith Park; Park had previously been Dowding's Senior Air Staff Officer from July 1938, and took over at 11 Group in April 1940.[10]

Park thus grew up with the fine tuning of Dowding's defence system as it matured, and understood both the system and his superior intimately; the two were in many ways of one mind as to how the battle would be run – and, in effect, *was* run.[11] 12 Group, responsible for the eastern counties and the Midlands, was led by Air Vice-Marshal Trafford Leigh-Mallory, champion of the 'big wing' approach to fighting the *Luftwaffe* raids, who was less than efficient in supporting the beleaguered Park on several occasions, and who actively worked through RAF political factions to unseat both Dowding and Park after the crisis was over.[12] Park's tactics (fully approved by Dowding) was to use single squadrons, and less often two, to intercept bomber formations before they reached their targets, and not to seek large fighter-*versus*-fighter battles as envisaged in the 'big wing' approach.[13] 10 Group, under Air Vice-Marshal Sir Quintin Brand, responsible for south-western England's defence, was a fully loyal and very effective supporter of Park, while Air Vice-Marshal Richard Saul's 13 Group had northern England and Scotland to defend.[14] 13 Group and also 12 Group acted as the main reservoirs for replacement squadrons when those in 11 Group needed to be pulled out of the line.[15]

In a recent study of this campaign,[16] it is clear that Dowding and Park planned to fight the Battle of Britain as one of attrition, and so it turned out to be; for this the *Luftwaffe* was not properly prepared, being unable to put their aircraft industry on a war production footing and lacking adequate reserves of aircraft to cover the losses inevitable in battle. The *Luftwaffe* was prepared only for a short *Blitzkrieg* type of war, confident that anything more prolonged would be avoided; their front-line strength was thus impressive, but reserves were paltry. Although the *Luftwaffe* did recognise the importance of wastage, and planned for a figure for bombers and fighters of around 50 per cent a month, they did not put in place the necessary resources or make the required organisational preparations. In distinct contrast, the RAF Air Staff in the 1930s both anticipated and prepared for this very battle and viewed it clearly as a future battle of attrition, and thus had the necessary reserves in place, an adequate and essentially civilian repair organisation ready, and their aircraft production on a proper war footing.

The contrast is very clear-cut between Fighter Command, superbly led by Dowding and the equally professional and reliable

Park (who did much of the day-to-day fighting itself), and the very over-confident *Luftwaffe*, led by Göring, the overblown, self-indulgent and easily distracted *Reichsmarschall*, whose morphine addiction waxed and waned; he was not prepared at all for this battle, and he had suffered much more serious losses over France than most realise.[17] His two principal subordinates, Field Marshals Albert Kesselring (commanded *Luftflotte* 2) and Hugo Sperrle (*Luftflotte* 3), were neither up to the Dowding/Park standard, but for very different reasons. Sperrle, son of a brewer, was a reconnaissance expert in the First World War, and was retained in the 4,000-strong officer corps, which the Treaty of Versailles allowed Germany to maintain within its army, as one of only 180 former flying personnel. After relatively unspectacular progress over the years, he ended up leading the Condor Legion, the German air force contribution to the Nationalist side in the Spanish Civil War, where he was responsible for the first terror raid in history, the bombing of Guernica.[18] Although capable enough, the increasingly corpulent Sperrle, like the bloated and decadent Göring, had a taste for luxury, and had rather lost interest in the war by 1940; on 1 September 1940, for example, at a critical stage in the battle, he was spotted enjoying himself with Field Marshal Milch (Göring's deputy) in the casinos of Deauville, in which well-known gambling establishment he had organised himself a command post.[19] Albert Kesselring, Göring's other chief subordinate, was a Bavarian professional soldier and right-wing nationalist who did well in the First World War, being promoted to the General Staff without having attended the war academy, and like Sperrle was retained in the 100,000 man post-war army; he transferred to the embryonic *Luftwaffe* in 1933, underwent pilot training and was responsible for a considerable amount of the organisation involved in building the ground establishment and parachute corps.[20] Although an extremely able organiser, staff officer and leader, Kesselring was not an experienced, professional airman.

At the beginning of the Battle of France, on 10 May 1940, the *Luftwaffe* was at the peak of its operational strength; never again would it field the numbers available at the onset of that *Blitzkrieg*[21] (see previous chapter). The *Luftwaffe* had lost 1,814 aircraft and 3,278 highly experienced pre-war professional aircrew (though several hundred POWs were returned after the Armistice) in the campaign over France,[22] and the effect of these losses on the front-line strength of the main aircraft types facing the RAF across the Channel is obvious from the table below.

Comparison of available (serviceable) *Luftwaffe* aircraft, 10 May 1940 and 3 August 1940

| Aircraft type | 10 May 1940 (beginning of Battle of France)[23] | 3 August 1940 (5 days before beginning of heavy combat, Battle of Britain)[24] |
|---|---|---|
| Bombers (He 111, Do 17, Ju 88) | 1,579 (1,064) | 1,458 (818) |
| Stukas (Ju 87) | 427 (356) | 446 (343) |
| Me 110 | 319 (209) | 310 (240**) |
| Me 109 | 1,231 (884) | 1,065 (878*) |

*the 878 serviceable Me 109s included six *Gruppen* stationed in Germany, Romania, Norway, thus reducing this number on the Channel Front to *c.* 760; **only 230 crews were available for the 240 serviceable Me 110s.[25]

An effective 760 Me 109s in northern France thus faced RAF Fighter Command, who, on 11 August 1940, fielded 1,095 single-engine fighters of which 990 were serviceable;[26] however, in battle the RAF fighters were always outnumbered effectively, as the 990 serviceable aircraft were spread across the entire British Isles in all four operational groups of Fighter Command, whereas the *Luftwaffe* fighters could be concentrated in a narrow area of only one RAF group, and were often thus sent in against 11 Group.

*Luftwaffe* units were organised into three *Luftflotten* for the battle, each comprising subordinate *Fliegerkorps* and their component *Geschwadern,* as summed up below.

Order of Battle, location and major commanders of the *Luftwaffe* for the Battle of Britain on 13 August 1940,[27] excluding reconnaissance units

LUFTFLOTTE 2 (HQ Brussels; *Generalfeldmarschall* Albert Kesselring; spread across Holland, Belgium, Northern France)

*Jagdfliegerführer (Jafü) 2:* (HQ Wissant; *Generalmajor* Theodor Osterkamp from late July)

JG 3 (*Stab, I, II, III/JG 3*; Samer, Colombert, Desvres; *Oberstleutnant* Carl Viek)

JG 26 (*Stab, I, II, III/JG 26*; Audembert, Marquise, Caffiers; *Major* Gotthard Handrick)

JG 51 (*Stab, I, II, III/JG 51*; Wissant, St. Omer; *Major* Werner Mölders)

*JG 52* (*Stab*, *I*, *II*; Coquelles, Peuplingne; *Major* von Merhart)

*I/LG 2* (still independent, when he succeeded to command of *JG 52*, placed under that unit; Calais-Marck; *Hauptmann* Hanns Trübenbach)

*JG 54* (*Stab*, *I*, *II*, *III/JG 54*; Campagne, Guines, Hermalinghen; *Major* Martin Mettig)

*ZG 26* (*Stab*, *I*, *II*, *III/ZG 26*; Lille, Yvrench, Crécy, Barley; *Oberstleutnant* Joachim Huth)

*ZG 76* (*Stab*, *II*, *III/ZG 76*; Laval, Abbeville; *Major* Walter Grabmann)

*I Fliegerkorps*: (HQ Beauvais; *General* Ulrich Grauert)

*KG 1* (*Stab*, *I*, *II*, *III/KG 1*; He 111s in *I* and *II*, and Do 17s in *III Gr.*)

*KG 76* (*Stab*, *I*, *II*, *III/KG 76*; Do 17s in *I* and *III*, and Ju 88s in *II Gr.*)

*II Fliegerkorps*: (HQ Ghent; *Generalleutnant* Bruno Lörzer)

*KG 2* (*Stab*, *I*, *II*, *III/KG 2*; all Do 17s)

*KG 3* (*Stab*, *I*, *II*, *III/KG 3*; all Do 17s)

*KG 53* (*Stab*, *I*, *II*, *III/KG 53*; all He 111s)

*II/StG 1* (Ju 87s) and *IV/LG 1* (Ju 87s)

*Erprobungsgruppe 210* (Me 110 fighter bombers except for *3/EGr 210* which was Me 109s)

*II/LG 2* (Me 109 fighter-bombers)

*IX Fliegerdivision*: (HQ Soesterberg, Holland; *Generalmajor Joachim Coeler*)

*KG 4* (*Stab*, *I*, *II*, *III/KG 4*; He 111s in *I* and *II*, Ju 88s in *III Gr.*)

*KGr 100* (Brittany; He 111s)

*KG 40* (*Stab*, *I/KG 40*; Brittany; Fw 200s)

*KGr 126* (He 111s)

*Kustenfliegergruppe 106* (He 115s, Do 18s)

*LUFTFLOTTE 3* (HQ Paris; *Generalfeldmarschall* Hugo Sperrle; spread across N and NW France)

*Jagdfliegerführer (Jafü) 3*: (HQ Cherbourg; *Oberst* Werner Junck)

*JG 2* (*Stab*, *I*, *II*, *III/JG 2*; Evreux, Beaumont-le-Roger, Le Havre; *Oberstleutnant* Harry von Bülow)

*JG 27* (*Stab*, *I*, *II*, *III/JG 27*; Cherbourg-West, Plumetot, Crépon, Carquebut; *Major* Max Ibel)

*JG 53* (*Stab*, *I*, *II*, *III/JG 53*; Cherbourg, Rennes, Dinan, Sempy, Brest; *Major* Hans-Jürgen Cramon-Taubadel)

ZG 2 (*Stab, I, II/ZG* 2; Toussée-le-Noble, Amiens, Guyancourt; *Oberstleutnant* Friedrich Vollbracht)

*IV Fliegerkorps*: (HQ Dinard; *General* Kurt Pflugbeil)

LG 1 (*Stab, I, II, III/LG1*; all Ju 88s)

KG 27 (*Stab, I, II, III/KG* 27; all He 111s)

*KGr 806* (Ju 88s)

*V Fliegerkorps*: (HQ Villacoublay; *Generalleutnant* Robert Ritter von Greim)

KG 51 (*Stab, I, II, III/KG 51*; all Ju 88s)

KG 54 (*Stab, I, II/KG* 54; all Ju 88s)

KG 55 (*Stab, I, II, III/KG* 55; all He 111s)

*VIII Fliegerkorps*: (HQ Deauville; *Generalmajor* Wolfram Freiherr von Richthofen)

StG 1 (*Stab, I, III/StG* 1; all Ju 87s)

StG 2 (*Stab, I, II/StG* 2; all Ju 87s)

StG 77 (*Stab, I, II, III/StG* 77; all Ju 87s)

*V/LG 1* (Me 110s; Caen; *Hauptmann* Liensberger)


*LUFTFLOTTE 5* (HQ Stavanger, Norway; *General* Hans-Jürgen Stumpf; spread across Norway and Denmark)

*X Fliegerkorps*: (HQ Stavanger; *Generalleutnant* Hans Geisler)

KG 26 (*Stab, I, III/KG 26*; Norway; all He 111s)

KG 30 (*Stab, I, III/KG 30*; Denmark; all Ju 88s)

*I/ZG 76* (Stavanger; *Hauptmann* Werner Restemeyer)

*II/JG 77* (Stavanger, Trondheim; *Hauptmann* Henschel)

*Küstenfliegergruppe 506* (He 115s)

Notes: *KG 26* including its *II Gruppe* moved to France at the beginning of September 1940; *KG 30* excluding its *II Gruppe* moved to Holland on 1 September 1940, the *II Gruppe* going to France on 2 September 1940 and leaving there again on 20 September 1940; *I/JG 54* moved to Holland on 23 September 1940; on 25 August 1940 *I/JG 77* moved from Denmark to France, becoming in effect the fourth *Gruppe* of *JG 51*, an assignment later formalised.[28]

Although many sources assert that the *Luftwaffe* did not relieve or rest its fighter units during the war, nor specifically in the Battle of Britain, this is not quite true. *JG 52* is a case in point: its *III Gruppe* was stationed very briefly on the Channel coast (22 July 1940–1 August

1940) but suffered catastrophic losses within a few days, including its *Gruppenkommandeur*, the *Staffelkapitän* of 8/JG 52, while 7/JG 52 lost two *Staffelkapitäns* and an acting one within the space of just two days.[29] Following this it was relocated to Germany for home defence, surely a safe billet during the Battle of Britain; II/JG 52 was pulled out of the battle on 18 August 1940 (to Holland and North Germany) and only returned on 20 September 1940.[30] An equally exhausted II/JG 51 was posted away from the Channel Front on 30 August 1940 and returned on 5 October 1940; in its place, I/JG 77 was posted in from Denmark/Germany.[31]

The majority of *Luftwaffe* survivors from the Battle of Britain strongly maintain that there was no British victory and that the battle was essentially a draw, and that it dragged on into the first few months of 1941 until the Russian campaign drew off the majority of the German formations. As an example of this widely held view (which bears no relation to the reality of the defeat of the *Luftwaffe's* primary task, which was obvious in the German documents alluded to above), *Leutnant* Max Clerico of 7/JG 54, later a medical doctor who specialised in sports medicine, not only gives a vivid description of what it was like to be there – and for the entire battle at that – but feels the struggle had a 50:50 result:

> Then, from July 1940, came 'The Battle of England'. It was very hard and there the serious aerial combat really began! Several times a day we flew escorts or, which was much more enjoyable, free chases. I scored a few victories and was very pleased when everything was over in October! Some years ago (writing in 1994) I visited my old field base near Calais, it was now a clover field and that was a better use of the ground! Besides the English and we were exhausted by the end of the battle. However, they did not win the 'Battle of England'. The Germans did not achieve their aim, to obtain air superiority over England! We did not achieve this, the situation was always 50-50. The English were tough boys. Sometimes there were combats until the red warning lights in the Me 109s lit up (fuel almost gone!) and one had to get home straight away. After some time the English avoided further combat of fighter against fighter, being interested naturally in shooting down bombers, thus we flew always with a couple of bombers as bait. On large missions with bombers we rendezvoused with them over the French coast. In the first place it was a stupid order for us to fly close to the bombers – one flew often

with the wing slots out and could hardly manoeuvre as a fighter. Many bomber aircraft were shot down by diving Englishmen.

I recall a funny story from this time as an aside. On a free day of rest I was duty officer in our small headquarters barracks. When my comrades left they mocked me and told me all the things they were going to get up to in Lille or Calais. Finally it got quieter and I lay down to rest. Then there was a knock again. I was furious and made a very basic, internationally known comment. A senior officer then appeared who told me I had just said something impossible to perform to *Herrn Generaloberst* Kesselring (later Field Marshal). Kesselring had really just landed and was looking around, he did not take my comment amiss! He talked to me about my experiences that I shared with him without hiding anything. Something else about the English: they called us 'Bandits' over the radio (we used the code word 'Indians' to denote enemies amongst ourselves), but I never had the impression that they were enemies, but rather something like colleagues, but just from the other faculty. Sometimes they showed a sense of humour. Once, I saw a Spitfire doing an upward roll right through a chaotic mix-up of fighting aircraft, and other such pranks. Sometimes when the He 111s were flying along so slowly, I could look at London; my thoughts: so many young girls must now be sitting in air raid shelters, instead of one being able to take a walk with them in Hyde Park. I swore to myself then that after the war I would take a ship in holiday spirit across the Channel towards the chalk cliffs and go walking in London. The wish became reality, in 1956, under the sponsorship of the British Council; I was able to spend several weeks on a study visit in London. However, there was also a downside to the English operations: probably due to a crazy order from above, the English fighters attacked the German air-sea rescue floatplanes. The floatplanes – clearly marked with the Red Cross – had the task of fishing shot-down fliers from the water, irrespective of whether they were English or German. We took turns to fly escort for these aircraft. My own victories over England: four Hurricanes/Spitfires. On one occasion we again had the task to escort bombers. They flew very far over London and beyond and on the return we had too little fuel. Many did not return home, and had to belly land on the French coast, on the beach. I just made it, with a standing propeller, landing dead-stick on the airfield at Dieppe. When the entire *Geschwader* was given an escort mission over England, as far as I remember, one *Gruppe* (three *Staffeln*) flew directly with the bomber formation – rather ineffective! One *Gruppe* flew indirect escort – the most effective – and one *Gruppe* flew a free chase. I must say, however, that I no longer remember such details that well; it was, after all, 55 years ago.

*Oberleutnant* Josef Bürschgens, who flew in 7/JG 26, in the famous *III Gruppe* led initially by Adolf Galland and succeeded during August 1940 by Gerhard Schöpfel, also provided a somewhat biased appraisal of the battle, and even after the war still saw no decisive victory for the RAF:

The Battle of Britain was different. The German air force, also we as fighter pilots, fought for the first time over water (the English Channel) and then over England. Water and sea were unknown elements for us, all of us. Our planes were not built for this purpose. The endurance of the Me 109 was too short – a bit more than one hour. The bombers – there were no long-range bombers – were too slow. Fighter protection for the bombers was improvised – a task absolutely contrary to the original role of the Me 109, the intentions of its designer Messerschmitt, and our training. The numbers and manoeuvrability of the Me 110, like its cruising speed, were all too low. It happened that Me 109s, escorting bomber formations, were lost and sometimes their pilots also, because they ran out of fuel and had to bail out over the English Channel. On the British side, within the ranks of the RAF, many experienced pilots from France, Belgium, Netherlands, Norway and Poland fought extremely bravely, often brutally and with a deep hatred against us – they had the advantage of fighting over their own territory. Their numbers were increased very rapidly by Commonwealth and US volunteers. The RAF had all the advantages of the air war. But we brought the RAF very close to defeat in the days at the height of the battle. But the German *Luftwaffe* high command (Göring and Hitler, who constantly interfered) spoiled the near-victory in the air over the RAF! After that time the preparation of the attack on Russia saved the RAF and it went over to the attack on the continent.

This viewpoint totally ignores the well-known shortage of pilots in the RAF, and as so many others have stated post-war, blames Hitler for high command failures.

*Feldwebel* Emil Clade flew with *III/JG 27* over England and rather surprisingly saw the *Luftwaffe* as dominant over the RAF by October–November 1940, somewhat far from the true defeat that they had indeed suffered by then. 'In the Battle of Britain we always had the problem of having to fly home over the Channel after a mission. I flew about 80 missions as a fighter pilot over England, many over London. Towards the end of the "Battle of England" I had to attack targets in the Thames Estuary with a 250 kg bomb under my plane's belly. One can say that the English were then outnumbered and suffered from supply problems. Also, one can say that we were then still very motivated and believed in what we were doing.' The rather strange claims about RAF numbers and supply problems aside, he also ignores exhaustion of German fighter pilots after a long and intense campaign. A much more realistic and even stark picture was given in 1996 by *Staffelkapitän* Günther Scholz of *7/JG 54*, who though still only an *Oberleutnant* served as acting *Gruppenkommandeur* of *III/JG 54* for months during the battle before a replacement could be found from the thinned ranks of experienced and capable German fighter pilots.

After over 50 years looking back I can only say that the air war against England led to very high losses and for the individual pilots it was a great nervous strain. For example, my friend Leo Eggers, *Kapitän* of the *8/JG 54*, in the last weeks on the Channel Front developed psychosomatic conditions, insomnia, anxiety attacks. He was 'flown out' (*abgeflogen*) as we called it and should have been relieved. He was shot down and killed in September 1940 over southern England (Günther Scholz is mistaken here: Eggers was in fact removed from combat during October 1940 and became *Staffelkapitän* of the *Ergänzungsstaffel/JG 54*; he was killed on the first day of the Kursk battle in Russia in 1943 as *Gruppenkommandeur* of *III/JG 3*.)[32] On many days we flew 3–4 missions, sometimes with drop tanks to enable us to fly longer distances for bomber escorts; and after every mission 1–3 losses. The *Staffeln* sometimes had only five to seven serviceable aircraft. The *Gruppenkommandeur, Hauptmann* Ultsch, was also shot down and killed in September 1940 (on 5 September) and as I was the longest-serving officer, I became acting *Kommandeur* until *Hauptmann* Liegnitz took over the *Jagdgruppe* in November 1940. He was later killed in 1941 over Leningrad. The most unpopular missions were bomber escorts. One had to stick closely to the bomber formations, drive away enemy fighters and not let yourself be drawn away from the bomber formation. The most popular missions were free chases. Temporarily we also flew with a 250 kg bomb below the fuselage, to attack the docks along the Thames; after dropping these bombs, there was often air combat. The first time we carried bombs the surprise worked; the English did not know where the bombs were coming from. And during this time (summer/autumn 1940) when we were constantly fighting against superior numbers of English fighters, General Milch attended a fighter pilot meeting on the Channel coast and asserted that the English air force would soon be defeated. He claimed that factories had been destroyed, that the balance of fighters remaining to the RAF after deduction of all the aircraft already shot down was minimal, and thus not much more could be left in their arsenal. We had to laugh silently to ourselves about this nonsense and Galland dared to state our experiences clearly and distinctly. He fell into Göring's disfavour for a while after this.

By no means all witnesses were able to recall details and provide such expressive overviews of a titanic aerial struggle; some recall almost no details at all. *Unteroffizier* Alfred Heckmann, who flew with 5th *Staffel* of *JG 3*, had no specific memories of the war in general and few of the Battle of Britain: 'Our tactics consisted of direct escort, high escort and *Freie Jagd* (free chase) operations in the battle against the enemy fighters.' His *Staffel* was fortunate to suffer only one fatality in this entire time, and that due to an accident; one pilot was wounded in action and six Me 109s were shot down, with four pilots being fished out of the Channel.[33] In contrast, the rest of the *Gruppe* (*II/JG 3*) lost 14 pilots over England and the Channel, six as POWs and eight killed or missing.[34] *Oberleutnant* Heinz Lange of *Stab/JG 54* was even more taciturn: 'England 1940: the *JG 54* as far as I recall had no specific unique tactics in air combat.' Others, while supplying little information, gave interesting little gems, such as *Unteroffizier* Josef Neuhaus, *III/ZG 26*: 'After completing my training as a *Zerstörer* pilot, and following my transfer to the *Ergänzungsgruppe* (operational training unit) for a brief few days, I joined *ZG 26 Horst Wessel* and flew my first missions over England.' Interesting here is the very short period allocated in the *Ergänzungsgruppe*; clearly, casualties were leading to inexperienced Me 110 crews being exposed to combat without adequate preparation. The RAF was not the only one with a similar problem, as is so often claimed in the many books on the battle.

*Hauptmann* Rolf Pingel of *I/JG 53* was among those pilots with the longest Channel crossing: 'We were stationed in Rennes, from where we flew to Cherbourg to refuel. Missions were to escort bombers and dive bombers, as well as free chases over the English coast.' It is indeed somewhat surprising that *I/JG 53* was stationed in Rennes and thus needed to land and refuel before tackling the long cross-Channel flight from the Cherbourg peninsula to the English coast in the Isle of Wight region; presumably they also had a defence function to cover Brittany.

Several pilots remember the Battle of Britain primarily because wounds suffered in that campaign put an end to their combat careers; Feldwebel Fritz Oeltjen of *7/JG 54* was one. 'On 20 June 1940 I became part of the aerial defence of Holland. In the meantime I had been transferred to the 1st *Staffel* of *I/JG 21* (soon to become *7/JG 54*, part of *III/JG 54*); the *Staffelkapitän* was *Oberleutnant* Scholz. In July 1940 we transferred to Guines in France, south of Calais, for operations against England. The *Geschwader* was designated as *JG 54*, under the leadership of *Major* Trautloft. In October 1940 I had to force-land and was wounded. After recovery I was sent to the *Jagdfliegerschule* at Zerbst/Anhalt in 1941 as an instructor.'

## Organisation of Fighter Geschwader, Command Functions

In 1940, the RAF seldom flew formations larger than a squadron (12 fighters), with wings of two and occasionally more squadrons being used rarely. In contrast, the *Luftwaffe* in the Battle of Britain often used entire *Geschwaders* to escort a large bombing raid, but almost always split up into its component *Gruppen*, which tended to be the dominant tactical unit. Once a *Geschwader Kommodore* had split up his *Gruppen*, normally into close escort, indirect escort and free chase assignments, further tactical reactions to combat situations lay essentially with the *Gruppenkommandeur*. *Hauptmann* Hennig Strümpell was appointed to command *I/JG 2* from mid-June 1940 and offered interesting insights into the realities of this responsible position. 'In order to explain the role of a *Gruppenkommandeur* properly, I must briefly detail the organisational structure of the German fighter units, which was distinctly different to that of the RAF. A *Jagdgruppe* consisted of the *Stab* (Staff) and *Stabschwarm* (4 aircraft) and then three *Staffeln* each of 12 or 15 aircraft, so a *Gruppe* thus had between 40 and 50 aircraft altogether. In addition to the three *Staffeln*, a *Stabskompanie* also belonged to each *Gruppe* that comprised flight control, communications, technical and maintenance personnel and relevant equipment, such that the *Gruppe* could be maintained on a field base and kept operational from a ground technical aspect. The *Staffeln* themselves were provided with enough technical equipment and personnel to handle their own maintenance and light repairs. The vehicle park of a *Gruppe* was adequate enough to enable the transfer of the entire unit with all equipment and men by road to a new airbase. The *Gruppe* was also able, with their own resources, to operate from an unprepared field base and to move to another when necessary. The *Gruppenkommandeur* had to lead this unit in the air and on the ground and carried the responsibility for leadership, training, maintenance and refurbishment, and supplies in respect of his *Gruppe*. The next higher authority was the *Geschwader*.'

Very insightful commentary on leadership during the Battle of Britain, particularly from the perspective of a *Geschwader Kommodore*, is provided by the next witness. An early arrival on the Channel coast was *I/LG 2* under their *Gruppenkommandeur Hauptmann* Hanns Trübenbach. This unit, which had included the German pre-war aerobatic team which he led, had a special status in the *Luftwaffe*:

My *Jagdgruppe*, the *I.* (light fighter *Gruppe)/Lehrgeschwader 2* was treated and employed as an independent fighter unit up till it's inclusion in *Jagdgeschwader 77* at the beginning of 1942. As visible evidence of this independence we carried the golden L on our shoulder straps in war, as we had already during peacetime. And in peacetime already as the one and only *Kommandeur* in I/LG 2 I was able to enjoy a privileged position, right up to Hitler himself; I accordingly had, in every theatre I was posted to, special rights and also special duties which I had to carry out and guarantee personally. As an example, before I became *Kommodore JG 52*, I was concerned with efforts in Brussels to free my old Belgian aerobatic flying friends from their prisoner of war camp, to which I felt myself still bound, even in war, as a member of the Royal Belgian Order. Because I came originally from the *Lehrgeschwader*, I later received, as the only *Kommodore*, the latest machines, with the newest improvements. At the end of the England operations I for example received the first Messerschmitt fitted with the so-called high altitude engine with water/methanol injection. These few high altitude engines from Daimler Benz were fitted to the Me 109 E; however, this was no solution for the fighter formations in general!

*I/LG* 2 began flying over England long before the official start of the Battle of Britain, as Trübenbach explains further:

> I transferred with the entire *Jagdgruppe* to Calais-Marck, an excellently appointed field base (another source suggests the move was to St. Inglevert/Pihen, and on 20 June 1940).[35] West of Calais and also further inland, but chiefly on the Channel coast, the other *Geschwader* were stationed. The tactical leadership of all the *Jagdgeschwader* stationed in this area fell under the *Jagdfliegerführer*, *Oberst* Osterkamp, a First World War pilot decorated with the *Pour le Mérite*. The *Zerstörergruppen* also lay on the Channel coast; these were equipped with the Me 110 and became an easy prey for the English fighters. The bomber units lay further inland. On their flights to the Channel coast from these inland bases they reached about 6,000 to 7,000 m altitudes with their bomb loads, where they were met by us, as escorts for London and other targets. The *Gruppenkommandeurs* were also responsible for meeting and protecting the returning bomber units, but they often mixed it up with the English fighter units, in order to defend themselves from their attacks. However, this behaviour could not always be justified, as it led to losses in the returning bomber *Gruppen*.

The appointment of younger *Geschwader* commanders with recent and extensive combat experience began with *Major* Werner Mölders, posted early in the Battle of Britain (on 27 July 1940) to lead *JG* 51. Hanns Trübenbach, *JG* 52, was the second on 19 August 1940, followed by *Major* Adolf Galland (*JG* 26) and *Major* Günther Lützow (*JG* 3), both on 21 August 1940.[36] *Major* Hannes Trautloft took over *JG* 54 soon after (25 August).[37] Changes in *JG* 2 and *JG* 27 were more complicated: *Major* Wolfgang Schellmann was given command of the former on 2 September 1940, but was replaced by the young and rapidly rising Helmut Wick on 20 October (killed in action 28 November 1940); Schellmann was shifted to lead *JG* 27 on 22 October, replacing *Major* Bernhard Woldenga, who had been acting *Kommodore* from 11 October 1940.[38] *Major* Günther Freiherr von Maltzahn was appointed to take over *JG* 53 on 9 October 1940.[39] Hanns Trübenbach recalls his elevation to *Geschwader* command:

> Here I should briefly digress. The personal leadership of the *Jagdgeschwader* was in the hands of ex-First World War officers.

At the beginning of the Battle of Britain these old gentlemen led their *Geschwadern* from the ground; an impossibility that Göring took strong action to correct. The replacement of these *Geschwader Kommodores* followed hastily and the following assignments were made: Mölders to *JG 51*, Galland to *JG 26*, Trübenbach to *JG 52* with the justification that *Kommodores* had to fly at the head of every mission with their staff *Schwarm* and thereby also continually be the first to contact the enemy. With my appointment to *Kommodore* I organised my old peacetime *Gruppe, I/LG 2* in my *Geschwader JG 52* and thus had, on paper at least, four *Jagdgruppen* at my disposal. However, in the entire war they never operated together on operations; one *Gruppe* or the other was always flying in a different war theatre.

Being the *Kommodore* of a *Jagdgeschwader* while implying leadership of the entire unit from the air was often in reality a rather lonely position, and sometimes the leader even lacked a complete *Stabschwarm* of his own and had to borrow pilots from his subordinate units. Once again, Hanns Trübenbach clarifies this not uncommon state of affairs. 'My *Geschwaderstab* consisted of World War One veteran officers, or reservist officers. My personal wingman (*Rottenknecht*) in my *Stabsschwarm* was a *Leutnant* of the *Reserve*, a textile engineer in civilian life from Vaihingen near Stuttgart. A genuine Swabian, who could fly the Me 109 well enough, but could never hit anything with his guns (*Leutnant* Lenz, killed 15 October 1940).[40] In the middle of October, flying next to me in an attack on a Hurricane squadron at 10,500 m altitude, he was shot down by a Spitfire from above and crashed to his death over southern England. On the copy of the painting I received from the war artist Taylor, showing the *Stabsschwarm* of *Jagdgeschwader 52* over southern England, this worthy *Reserve* officer is shown flying next to me for posterity. The pilots of my second *Rotte* I had to find either from *I/LG 2* or from one of the two other *Gruppen* of *JG 52* operating on the Channel (*I* and *II/JG 52*).' An authoritative account of the changing tactics and realities of leading fighter units in the Battle of Britain is given by *Major* Trübenbach, who commanded both at the *Gruppe* level and the *Geschwader* level.

My *Couleurgeschwader* (the word *couleur* refers to European student societies, brotherhoods, etc.) was bomber *Geschwader KG 77*, which we had to escort on an almost permanent basis. However, before examining the escort missions for bomber *Geschwader* and *Gruppen*, one has to know how the first fighter missions over England went. It was only natural that we fighters were burning to finally get to know the Spitfires and Hurricanes. On the English side there were already Czech, South African and Polish pilots flying in their ranks in addition to the English pilots, and thus with the initial aerial circuses which stretched out to the middle of the Channel, and flying in *Staffels* from 6,000 m to 9,000 m we faced the 600 Spitfires and Hurricanes available. These early combats were like a film and so mixed up that in the confusion one battled to distinguish friend from foe. We managed to disengage regretfully and with massive losses, and reported to Osterkamp that this could not continue. Overnight our Me 109s received bright yellow noses and tails, the latter however not universally applied. With these brightly painted machines we could now rapidly distinguish who we had to fight against in the air. The massed aerial combat of the initial part of the battle only lasted for a short time (here referring to the period 11 to 18 August 1940); thereafter, mass against mass was not needed any more.

Increasingly it came down to small formations, mostly only in *Staffel* strength, and this aided the English, as for them it was all about separating the German escort formations from the bomber *Geschwader*, so that they could then shoot down the bombers with little trouble (referring here to the period 24 August 1940–6 September 1940). Osterkamp was not capable of enforcing the principle that the protection of the bombers must always be considered as the critical factor. Thus it only took a few months, or weeks rather, before the German bombers were close to being wiped out. Although bomber *Gruppen* were led by experienced long-distance pilots, including some from the airlines, the escorting fighters often ended up in the water or just managed to reach the French coast with dead engines, due to fuel shortage and irresponsible leadership of the bomber commanders, often leading to fighter casualties (this refers mainly to the period 7–30 September 1940). This was founded on the fact that with the Me 109 we only had about an hour and 20 minutes endurance, and the bomber commanders often forgot about this, when they flew too-long routes or took too much time over England. The English fighter squadrons never had to come across the Channel to our side, but instead waited happily until we flew over to them, with our *Couleurgeschwader*.

Cunningly, they escorted our formations from mid-Channel and caused the first disturbances amongst our escort fighters. Then the hitherto higher-flying Spitfires, at 9,000 to 11,000 m altitudes, dove down and started the circus that immediately devolved into individual dogfights and removed the fighters from the bombers. Thus it only took a few weeks until these tactics caused such heavy losses to our bombers that they could no longer be used in daylight (here again, referring to the 7–30 September 1940 period, but after the initial few raids on London). What was the result? Göring imagined that he could win the war against England within four days if every fighter *Geschwader* equipped one *Gruppe* as bomb-carriers. Field Marshal Kesselring brought over Göring's order one fine day and we all converted one *Gruppe* to fighter-bombers (actually in most cases, one *Staffel* from each of three *Gruppen* was so converted). This was easily achieved as Messerschmitt had earlier seen to it that we had the technical fittings to carry drop tanks beneath the fuselage of the Me 109, and that these could be used also for carrying a 250 kg bomb. I also had my *Stabsschwarm* converted. Then off we would go to London at 8,000 m, drop one wing to see where we were and let our bombs fall into the midday traffic. If we were intercepted by English fighters on the way in, then we immediately jettisoned the bombs wherever we happened to be and took up the fight with them. On many days we sent only two *Jabos*, or fighter-bombers across just to frustrate the crowded traffic of the Londoners when we delivered our couple of small bombs.

Returning from one such mission at a height of about 11,000 m we found a tight formation of a Hurricane squadron flying right below us. I immediately attacked the rear machine (we already had the new high-altitude engines with methanol-water injection), but at the same time from a still greater height the new Spitfires dived down and shot my wingman (*Leutnant* Lenz) down in flames, who had been flying right next to me. I myself immediately dived down under full throttle until the speedometer needle went off the clock, saw that the Spitfires were not keeping up and flew back to my field base in France. The superiority of the English now grew from day to day (referring to October 1940). Our units had heavy losses, while the English were creating new squadrons. In between with my *Geschwader* we selected air bases around London and made hair-raising low-level attacks on the lined-up English fighters. In these we still had the advantage of surprise, and we dived down like birds of prey, shooting out of all our barrels. As I was always in front in these dives I never got hit at all. The results of these attacks could not be observed clearly as the airfield defences were so strong that we got the hell out of there very quickly, and often even ended up being fired at by English naval flak as well over some areas. Thus the summer and autumn of 1940 passed and I was forbidden to continue low-level attacks on English air bases. By November 1940 we had already lost half of our pilots and the replacements from the OTUs and flying schools could not stabilise the fighting value of the fighter units any more. The two *Jagdgeschwader Nr. 26* Galland and *Nr. 52* Trübenbach were sent home (to the *Rheinland*) to rest and recoup. As I infer from my diary, *JG 27* was also transferred home, to prepare for the war in Africa. The *Geschwaders* were all housed in fixed quarters, near the Channel coast. The field bases had wooden barrack huts and also tents. My *Geschwaderstab* lived with me in an abandoned villa-like house, only a few kilometres from our base, and we had all conceivable comforts. During the day we were in the staff barracks until the last operation was complete, or we sat in deck chairs directly next to our aircraft. The food was always excellent. The workshop and intelligence platoons were also always accommodated in barracks on *Geschwader* airfields, and were to all intents stationary, as the Battle of Britain was always played out from the French coast.

A valuable command perspective at the lowest leadership level (*Staffel*) is provided by *Oberleutnant* Erhard Braune, who was the *Staffelkapitän* of 7/*JG* 27 from July 1940 through to the end of 1940 and well beyond. He emphasises the difference between leading a *Staffel* and a *Gruppe*.

The duties of the *Staffelkapitän* differed from those of the *Gruppenkommandeur* insofar as the former led a unit, a team, with close contact with the individual members of the flying and ground staff, as the leader of the unit. The *Staffelkapitän* flew on every mission where the *Staffel* flew at full strength, as did a *Gruppenkommandeur* also, where in both cases the actual tactical influence was not decisive; the sense behind many missions – particularly later in Africa – was not always apparent. However, that is a chapter on its own. In contrast on each of a limited number of missions the tactical weight exceeded the mere participation in the operation.

Duties in addition to the flying of missions and which interfered in taking part in these missions only existed as exceptions. The same applies for the *Geschwader Kommodore* also. There were only a few *Freie Jagd* missions over England, as the entire fighter arm was needed for escort duties. I cannot remember that we used any specific tactic over the island apart from the normal free actions (i.e. using own initiative at a *Staffel* level). Escort duties were either 'close' or 'indirect' (i.e. further away), where only the latter gave the possibility to utilise the specific flying characteristics of a fighter aircraft. The close escort, with increasing losses of the bombers also under these conditions, had only a slight effect against an energetically attacking enemy. This led in the end to the so-called light bomber units of bomb-carrying Messerschmitts, whose operations did more for the high command's communiques than it did damage to the enemy. My *Staffel* was the first in *JG 27* to be assigned this fighter-bomber (*Jabo*; at that stage this expression – *Jagdbomber* – was not yet in use as far as I remember) duty, after a short introduction to the new method in Valenciennes. As we needed no escort in the approach flight – so one thought – that left a much more powerful force for *Freie Jagd* assignments. After dropping the bomb a minimal disturbance of the harmony of normal properties of the aircraft was noted due to the bomb rack. As the *III/JG 27* was withdrawn from the English operations already at the end of 1940 – to prepare for the Balkan campaign – I cannot comment further on later developments.

A *9/JG 26* pilot, *Leutnant* Otto Stammberger, who began flying missions only in 1941 against the early sweeps of British fighters over northern France, in discussing the excellent fighter control in those actions, underlined that nothing of the kind was available during the Battle of Britain. 'In the offensive war, the Battle of Britain and till the end of 1940 there was no fighter control system; only the location, time and height were notified, at which the fighters were to meet the bombers, to then take on their escort. Then everything was exactly prescribed: for example the first *Staffel* was to fly in front, the second to the left and the third to the right, the *II Gruppe* was to fly behind and above the bombers, divided into specific *Staffel* locations. All fighters flew higher than the bombers. With increasing losses of our fighters, *Staffel* formations were reduced in August 1940 to only *Schwarms* or even just *Rotten*.' Operational control in the *Luftwaffe* fighter arm was thus never ideal during the Battle of Britain, and remained a clumsy system, subject to conflicting views and especially interference from the top, as recalled by *Major* Hanns Trübenbach, *Kommodore* of *JG 52*:

*Oberst* Theo Osterkamp, our *JAFÜ 2* (*Jagdfliegerführer 2*; fighter leader for *Luftflotte 2*), was responsible for the tactical operation of the fighter units under his jurisdiction on the English Channel. However, he was only the recipient of orders from the Reichsminister for Aviation and Supreme Commander of the *Luftwaffe*, as far as all combat missions were concerned – that is, these could also be ordered directly by Göring to the units themselves. In essence, though, above *Jafü 2* was the *Luftflotte* and its commander, *Generaloberst* Kesselring, whose instructions had to pass through the headquarters of *Jafü 2* to the *Geschwadern*. While the entire human-military equipment and its placement over enemy territory remained the prerogative of the Air Fleet, these matters were passed on to the flying units themselves through the *Jafü* staff and its headquarters. At the beginning of the war the medals awarded by Göring for bravery were often actually presented to the recipients by the *Luftflotte* commanders. Osterkamp was, by the way, a very critical officer, who did not hold his tongue. He did not have to ask anyone's permission when he sat himself in his aircraft and made a quick flight to Berlin to see Göring, and to tell him that one could not achieve any victory over the English by following the instructions provided. In contrast, one fine day Göring arrived in our neighbourhood and arranged to see the *Gruppenkommandeuren* and *Geschwader Kommodoren*, in order to read them the riot act. He wanted us to not fly above 8, 000 m, and if possible even only to a height of 6,000 m, because that had proven itself in the First World War! Of the new tactics forced on us by the enemy, he wanted to know nothing.

Low-level strafing attacks on RAF airfields were relatively limited during the Battle of Britain. *JG 52* was one of the few units that had experience of them, as related in 1997 by *Kommodore* Trübenbach: 'After the war the German *Kommodore* of *Jagdgeschwader Jever* in Oldenburg was for a long time also the training commander for Americans and other nations. Quite some years ago we had an evening function there which was a reunion of veteran seaplane and land plane pilots that I was also able to attend. At the end of the evening the *Kommodore* gave me some magazine articles that reported on events in the war over England. The opinion offered was that the German low-level attacks on the English airfields caused only a few losses. Given the few seconds that one had to fire during low-level strafing runs, this is a very plausible conclusion!'

## Comparing the Aircraft: Me 109, Me 110 versus Spitfire and Hurricane

While opinions of their own aircraft as against the machines of their British enemy obviously varied among *Luftwaffe* pilots, the capabilities of the Spitfires and their pilots demonstrably worried the *Jagdflieger*. A cross-section of views make for interesting reading. *Unteroffizier* Alfred Rauch, *II/JG 51* emphasised the better German tactics, which most likely reflects their much superior tactical formations of pairs and *Schwarms*: 'The English had the Hurricane and Spitfire in operation as fighters. Our Me 109 was better than the Hurricane. With the Spitfire we could take the chance to tackle them. One advantage of the Me 109 was that it was built entirely of metal and could thus take more punishment under attack. In regards to flying tactics the Germans were vastly superior to the English. The English pilots were brave and fought fairly.' Erich Rudorffer, *I/JG 2* who ended the war as a famous ace and *Major*, was then an *Oberfeldwebel* and recalled an approximate parity between the Spitfire and Me 109: 'The two aircraft, Me 109 and Spitfire, were always in their different models about equal to each other. They were both in their day very good fighters. Escort missions in the Battle of Britain constituted solely the protection and safety of bomber formations, with air combat against British fighters only in extreme situations.' Another old sweat, *Oberfeldwebel* Artur Dau, *7/JG 51* held similar views. 'Comparing the Hurricane and the Me 109 E, the Messerschmitt was a little superior to the Hurricane; with the Spitfire it was the opposite, in the beginning. Here, eventually, parity was reached, approximately, with the much later G-model, with small departures from this along the way. At high altitudes the Spitfire was better due to its wider wings. Our personal equipment in the Me 109 in the Battle of Britain was very simple: it consisted of a winter and a summer flying suit, flying helmet with microphone and earphones, Mae West (life vest) and parachute. The parachute was strapped onto our bodies and served also as a seat cushion in the aircraft. Thus everything for serious events was to hand.'

The Me 110 pilots had a much harder time of it in action against the British fighters, as witnessed by Leutnant Hans-Joachim Jabs,

*II/ZG 76*: 'I flew in the "110" from 10 May 1940 over France, Belgium, and during the Battle of Britain. In the Me 110 we were superior to the French and Belgians, whether Morane or Curtiss. But we were inferior to the Spitfire and to the Hurricane as well.'

*Oberleutnant* Ulrich Steinhilper, *3/JG 52* retained a very clear memory of the superiority given to the Spitfire Mk II, which debuted late in the battle, by its new engine with improved supercharger. He also discussed the propeller pitch system in the Me 109 E; this varied from manual change of propeller pitch to a later model with automatic pitch control. A flat pitch gave more pressure in the engine supercharger and thus higher rpm for the propeller, while a steeper pitch angle of the propeller blades gave more speed to the aircraft; at high altitude pitch was continually being changed to get maximum aircraft speed; an automatic pitch control did the job on its own, similar to the British Rotol constant speed propeller. 'Regarding the comparison between the Me 109 E and British fighters in the Battle of Britain, I can only give my personal opinions. Up to October I considered and experienced my "Emil", whether hand-pitched or automated-pitched, to be superior to either Hurricane or Spitfire. However, starting in October 1940 the British got the Merlin III engine, which provided for a higher pressure level (by supercharger) than we had with the DB 601 engine. Our supercharger gave an engine pressure equal to sea level at 4,700 m, they with the Merlin III reached that at some 5,600 m, which meant in practical terms they could climb about 600 m higher than we at the final stage of the battle.'

A final word on aircraft comparisons from that trusty *Luftwaffe* witness Hanns Trübenbach, *Kommandeur I/LG 2* and *Kommodore JG 52*, emphasises that the Me 109 E never had a centrally mounted nose cannon. 'The only pilots who were successful in fighting the Spitfire were those who had their eyes everywhere, and always attacked by surprising them from behind. Dogfights between Me 109s and Spitfires, where possible also with flaps extended, ended mostly fatally for the Me 109. There was only one artist in this respect and that was actually Marseille in the Africa campaign, who mastered this tactic. Newly joined young fighter pilots who came to units as replacements had it especially hard, as almost all of them had serious problems in their ability to control the Me 109, and then in combat drew the short straws. In the Me 109 E there was never a central cannon firing through the airscrew hub! When exactly the Me 109 F and G models with such a central cannon mounted in the engine were supplied to the *Gruppen* and *Geschwader*, I can no longer precisely recall.' It was actually in 1941, after the Battle of Britain was over.

## Opening Phases: July 1940

The official date for the onset of the Battle of Britain was 10 July 1940, with the official ending on 31 October 1940.[41] *Oberfeldwebel* Artur Dau, a senior NCO in *III/JG 51*, was there on that fateful opening day, having already spent some time on the Channel coast. Dau was an old hand who had joined the small 100,000-man army in 1931, and later transferred to the *Luftwaffe*; he was initially with the ground crews and later trained as a pilot and joined *7/JG 51* in time for the French campaign.

On 10 July 1940, after shooting down a Spitfire, a Hurricane suddenly dived on me from above and I had no other choice but to face him head-on; we thus flew at each other and each one shot at the other. In order to avoid a collision, shortly before impact, I pushed my machine beneath the Hurricane. In this moment I felt a blow in my aircraft and then concentrated on reaching the French coast. I had been hit several times, my engine was damaged and I could no longer see ahead. Then the engine gave up the ghost and I could only orientate myself by looking through the side panels of the canopy; the front of it was completely covered with oil. As I still had a lot of altitude I managed to reach the French coast by gliding. I wanted to try and reach the airfield at Boulogne but missed this by a short margin and had to land in a field; I attach a picture of this forced-landing and as can be seen my aircraft was fully burnt out. I had got away with it without any injury. *Hauptmann* Trautloft took the photo of me and my wrecked machine. This was the result of the head-on attack of the Hurricane and myself on each other. I was very glad at the time to have got away with it once again. Such events remain graven in the memory and one can just never forget them. On 28 August 1940 however my luck ran out and I became a casualty over the English coast. This event resulted in my only embarking on my journey home to Germany in February 1947. That was the end of my flying. To my sorrow I have no personal records from my active service in the *Luftwaffe*, as we were forbidden to have diaries and photos in our possession, as they could have fallen into the hands of the enemy.

I was able to tell Artur Dau that his head-on combat with the Hurricane on 10 July 1940 had been against P/O Geoffrey Page of 56 Squadron and to relate briefly Page's later history in the Battle of Britain where he was shot down and terribly burned on 12 August 1940.[42] 'I did not expect to receive such a prompt response on my former opponent; however, it made me very happy to learn the fate (survived war) of a former enemy. The subsequent history you related about Pilot Officer Geoffrey Page saddened me. What being shot down as a pilot and suffering large scale burns meant, I learnt from some of my own comrades. This example demonstrates to me once again how small the world is and how one will always be surprised. One is always overtaken by past events. I will never be able to get the name of Geoffrey Page out of my mind again; I note also that I had to do with a well-known personality in my battle of 10 July 1940.'

During July 1940, *JG 51* was initially led by First World War veteran and ace *Oberst* Theo Osterkamp, who became *Jagdfliegerführer* for *Luftflotte 2* on 23 July 1940; he was succeeded on 27 July by Werner Mölders,[43] one of the great fighter leaders and later the first General of Fighters. Early in the battle casualties from the French campaign returned from imprisonment and rejoined their units, among them *Feldwebel* Georg Pavenzinger, who was fortunate to enjoy frequent contact with his new *Geschwader Kommodore*: 'After being freed from imprisonment in France I received three weeks home leave and then returned to my old unit (*2/JG 51*) that now lay on the Channel near Calais. After a few practice flights to get my hand in again, I once more began flying operations with the 2nd *Staffel*, over England and the Channel. At this time the *Geschwader Kommodore* was *Oberst* Osterkamp, but he was soon replaced by Werner Mölders. In the 2nd *Staffel* we were very lucky that Mölders placed his headquarters in our dispersal area (every *Staffel* had its own) and thus we were for all practical purposes in his vicinity all day. I often had a personal chat with Werner Mölders, also as his brother Victor Mölders took over the 2nd *Staffel* on 12 September 1940 and I flew as his wingman. Once I had to go to the *Reichsluftfahrtministerium* (Air Ministry) in Berlin on instructions from Werner Mölders, and I made a stop in Brandenburg on the way, to visit his family, as he had asked me to do.' Another of Mölders' *Oberfeldwebels* was Artur Dau, who was one of the *III/JG 51* pilots who massacred a formation of Defiants of 141 Squadron on 19 July 1940.[44]

On one mission over the Channel our *Gruppe* shot down an entire squadron of English Defiants and three further English fighters, two Spitfires and one Hurricane, without any losses ourselves. On' this occasion, we suddenly spotted a squadron of English Defiants below us. This type of aircraft was manned by a crew of two and it had for defence a four-gun turret on board. When the *Gruppenkommandeur*, *Hauptmann* Trautloft, gave us the order to attack, this proceeded in a specific order. My 7th *Staffel* under *Oberleutnant* Oesau had to act initially as top cover during the attack by the Staff *Schwarm* while the 8th *Staffel* had to keep an eye on the airspace below, and the English unit flew on below in close formation: 12 aircraft each with four machine guns, equalling 48 barrels. Our attack followed under direction of *Hauptmann* Trautloft, in a single devastating assault. In a few minutes all 12 Defiants were shot down and fell into the Channel like burning torches. In the meantime additional English fighters had arrived in this airspace, Spitfires and Hurricanes; three of these were also claimed shot down. Our own losses in this mission amounted to two damaged aircraft without any pilot casualties. The events of this day remain engraved in my memory.

Another pilot in *III/JG 51* who also attacked these same Defiants was *Leutnant* Werner Pichon-Kalau vom Hofe: 'As far as I remember there was only one combat (on 19 July 1940) against Defiants, described by myself in the book *Volltreffer (Bullseye)* by Hermann Kohl; my account was rather exaggerated as befits an excited young fighter pilot. As I heard later from RAF circles, the Defiants were not used in daylight again.' This is not true: 264 Squadron saw a lot of action in late August 1940; however, 141 Squadron, decimated in the July action, was withdrawn from day combat and sent north.[45]

Another German fighter pilot who was in the Battle of Britain right from the start was *Leutnant* Jochen Schröder, who flew Me 110s in *III/ZG 76* and who was shot down the day after Artur Dau's head-on fight described above:

We felt at ease in the Me 110 after only a few initial flights. Naturally, we soon realised that she was much heavier and clumsier in combat than the Me 109 C and E, but despite this we had a lot of faith in the impressive armament: two 2 cm cannons and four machine guns with a high rate of fire. When practising shooting at ground targets we established that the Me 110 gave great accuracy and was also a very stable firing platform in the air. We believed that this machine was very suitable for future missions as a long range fighter to accompany bombers like the He 111, Ju 88, Dornier 17 and succeeding types. I could anticipate that the task as long range fighter in France with the Me 110 D would resolve itself well. We were well suited as escort fighters for our bomber formations and had good successes against the French fighters. After the armistice we moved to an airfield south of Paris, and, after a further move to an airfield near Laval, prepared ourselves for the forthcoming missions against England. Our morale was outstanding. We hoped for a rapid end to the war. We felt ourselves superior in the air, but worried about fighting against the English Hurricane fighters, which we had got to know over Dunkirk. On my second operation over England, the first having passed without any fighting, I was shot down in combat while escorting Ju 87 dive bombers in an attack on a convoy near the Isle of Wight.

Schröder was leading a *Schwarm* of Me 110s escorting the Ju 87s which were attacking a convoy south of Portland Bill, at 12,000–14,000 feet on 11 July 1940, when Hurricanes attacked his aircraft. His rear gunner shouted a warning that fighters were on their tail and then there was a tremendous crash in the Me 110 as the instruments were shattered and the starboard engine burst into flames. Schröder put the Me 110 into a dive and after 5,000 feet had put the fire out with the engine extinguishers, leaving only a dark smoke trail still coming out. However, they were attacked again and the port engine suddenly stopped. In the sudden calm, with no more engine roar in his ears, Jochen Schröder could actually hear his attacker's engine. He then had to ditch the aircraft in Weymouth Bay, 2 miles offshore. His gunner had been badly wounded and he managed to get him out of the sinking machine and inflated his Mae West. However, Schröder was then dragged down by his helmet, still attached by a microphone lead to the plane; he ripped off the helmet and swam to the surface. After spending what seemed like hours in the water, but was actually only 10 to 15 minutes, he was picked up by a launch and given dry clothes and some tea with rum; later on his uniform, neatly dried and still with decorations and badges intact, was returned to him. His gunner had disappeared and was never found. This account is based on a contemporary newspaper article by Harry Walton, who interviewed Schröder at the time; Schröder later obtained a copy of the article which he sent to me; the paper in which it was published is no longer known.

Early escort missions to protect bomber formations in July already revealed severe problems to come, as described by *Oberleutnant* Hans-Theodore Grisebach, 2/*JG* 2: 'After the end of the French campaign we established ourselves on the Channel coast at Fécamp for the first flights against England. After that we flew once to twice daily over to England to provide cover for the attacking He 111 bomber units. What was interesting about this was that we could not fly as slowly as the He 111s, that when fully loaded only managed to fly at 200–230 km/h. As a result we had to continually drag ourselves through the air at almost stalling speed and were in an extraordinarily unfavourable position to oppose the attacks of the English, who dove from great heights with their Spitfires right through our formations and shot down victories as they did so, while the Hurricanes approached below us before pulling up and using the dispersion of the bullets to achieve victories. My unit (2/*JG* 2) had relatively few losses in these missions but then again the number of English machines shot down remained within limits also.'

## August 1940 to 6 September 1940

From 8 August 1940, with massed Stuka attacks on a Channel convoy, the pace of the battle rapidly picked up early in the month. It was difficult enough for the old sweats, but for new arrivals a much greater chance of coming to grief was implicit. *Leutnant* Alfons Raich joined 7/*JG* 3 direct from fighter training school and found himself flying missions over England within four days of his arrival.

In the first few days of August 1940 I joined *Jagdgeschwader 3* as a young *Leutnant* straight out of the *Jagdschule*, posted to *III Gruppe*, 7th *Staffel*. The *Gruppe* was then stationed on a field base in Desvres, southeast of Boulogne. *Kommodore* of *JG 3* was *Major* Lützow, *Kommandeur* of *III/JG 3 Hauptmann* Kienitz and *Staffelkapitän* of 7/*JG 3 Oberleutnant* Neuerburg. The first day was taken up with reporting to the *Kommandeur* and then making the acquaintance of the other *Staffeln*. On my second day there was a test of my flying abilities with three landings on the field base under operational-type conditions; this was followed by getting to know the ground organisation, the quarters and the surroundings of the airfield. On the third day came my first 'operational' flight, with me assigned as number two to the *Staffelkapitän*, and with an introduction to aerial fighting. The Battle of Britain was in full swing already. On my fourth day I experienced two missions as wingman to the *Staffelkapitän*, the first an escort mission for a bomber unit and the second an indirect escort come *Freie Jagd* mission over southern England. With that my indoctrination into operational flying was considered complete and I was assigned to the second *Schwarm* in my *Staffel* as number eight; the *Schwarmführer* was *Unteroffizier* Springer and my *Rottenführer* (number seven) was *Leutnant* Troha. There followed daily two to three operational missions, and according to the weather, tasks were bomber escorts and *Freie Jagd*.

Then came my 10th *Feindflug* (defined as a flight over enemy territory or contact with enemy anywhere); the assignment was *Freie Jagd* over London and southern England. The approach flight was made at 7,000 m in wonderful weather, and over London we could see that a terrific dogfight was already in progress. My *Staffelkapitän* climbed up into the sun to be able to attack out of it, and then down we came, each behind the other, down into a pack of Spitfires. I concentrated on not falling behind and not letting myself be detached from my *Schwarm*. That was our watchword: he who fell back was eaten up. This was my very first aerial combat and I clung grimly to my *Rottenführer*. Then suddenly there was an urgent voice in my earphones: 'Marabu 8 look out, Spitfire behind you' (the 7th *Staffel* had *Marabu* as its call sign and number eight was me).

In the next second it was as if a watering can had been emptied over me, and it thumped and rattled all around me in the fuselage and the wings, and then already a white trail began to show from the left-hand radiator. A hit in the radiator, and that just south of London. In order to get out of the wild dogfight going on around me, I pushed my nose down and dived vertically, curving onto a rough course of 120 degrees on the compass, pulled her out at about 2,000 m height and flew in the direction of Dover. My engine rapidly got hot and the coolant gauge went into the red, the engine began to cough and shake, and fumes and smoke came into the cabin. Below me was Dover, and the English saw me off with a few flak bursts, almost as if they could see that they were wasting ammunition on fighting me. Then again, the voice of my *Rottenführer* in the earphones: 'Marabu 8 from 7, I am above you, fly 120 degrees.' It was very hazy, beneath me was water, and wave crests but no land was visible, and the machine shook and acrid smoke filled the cabin. Then again: '*Marabu* 8, your aircraft is burning, bail out.' I jettisoned the canopy and took a deep breath of oxygen. The shaking continued, and I held the aircraft with minimum speed horizontally above the water at about 150 m height. '*Marabu* 8 bail out, your aircraft is on fire.' In front of me the cliffs of Cap Gris Nez appeared and beneath me the fire was raging; I turned to the left along the cliffs and then I saw a valley with a clearing in the forest. With the last of my speed I turned the aircraft to the right and let it fall into the clearing. With the impact there was a terrible crashing and splintering sound and then it became very quiet; it stank and smoked but the fire was out. I looked up and saw my *Rottenführer* circling above me, he waggled his wings and flew off towards Desvres. I crawled out of the wreck and lay down on one of the wings, as I could not stand, my right knee was not working properly. However, the medics from the nearby flak position were already on their way and off I went to the hospital at Samer.

The experienced and reliable senior NCOs of the *Luftwaffe* formed the backbone of the flying units, including the fighter *Staffeln*. Amongst these stalwarts was *Feldwebel* (later *Oberfeldwebel*) Georg Pavenzinger, who was wingman to all the *Staffelkapitäns* of 2/JG 51. These included *Hauptmann* Wiggers, who shot down 13 victories between 19 July and 9 September 1940, 10 of them in the period from August to 6 September 1940,[46] and from whom Georg Pavenzinger learnt a lot: 'I can say the following about my own victories over England and the Channel. I flew as wingman to all the *Staffelkapitäns* of 2nd *Staffel*; my most important duty was to cover and protect them from attack. In this way one only very seldom had the opportunity to attack the enemy yourself, but one did receive a lot of bullets in your own aircraft. With my one *Staffelkapitän*, *Hauptmann* Wiggers, who was known as an ambitious daredevil, things were a bit different. Within a short period Wiggers scored 13 victories; Mölders reproached him repeatedly that his ambition would lead to no good in the longer term. But I learnt a lot from Wiggers. Often the two of us flew lone *Freie Jagd* sweeps over England. Now I was often able to attack enemy aircraft and to shoot some down also (first successes on 30 August 1940 and 7 September 1940).[47] In August 1940 I was shot down over the Channel and landed in the water with my parachute, and after some time I was fished out.' *Oberfeldwebel* Artur Dau, another among the ranks of *JG 51*'s senior NCOs, describes his experiences in the major raids of August 1940:

> *III/JG 51* was successful on the Channel. We flew as a *Gruppe* but divided up into Staff, 7th, 8th and 9th *Staffels* at different heights but within sight of each other. This was how we flew in for missions and as soon as 'Indians' (enemy aircraft) were spotted and reported, the attack orders came from the *Gruppenkommandeur*. Our escorts of bomber formations were carried out in the same way. For carrying out these missions one needed good eyesight and good leadership. As enemies the English were fair partners. My victories included three over France followed by one Spitfire on 7 July 1940, another on 10 July, and on each of 14 August 1940 and 18 August, a Hurricane. About these one can just add that these were events which took place in seconds. Suddenly the enemy would appear in your range of vision and then you had to work very fast. Then it was only about him or me. These events remained within one's memory for ever. The operations in the Battle of Britain were differentiated on the basis of the requirements of the mission and the enemy's attacks in retaliation. In this respect, one could define various potential operational possibilities. Firstly, there were bomber escorts; here we had the task of protecting our bomber units over enemy territory from English fighters, and here it also led to combats with the English. Then we also operated as an entire *Gruppe*, with *Gruppenstab* of four aircraft, and 12 aircraft each for 7th, 8th and 9th *Staffels*, when all these machines were serviceable. On such missions, within the *Gruppe* the components flew at different heights to better be able to counter the defensive actions of the enemy fighters.
>
> In my time in *III/JG 51* – until 28 August 1940 – the 19 July action with Defiants (of 141 Squadron) remained the biggest match we had with the RAF. All other missions followed mostly with surprise attacks in typical English weather. All our missions were flown from a field base near Lille. Our missions were mainly carried out in small formations – as a *Staffel* comprising 12 machines, a *Schwarm* of four aircraft, or as a *Rotte* of 2 aircraft. Our missions could not be of long duration; within 50 minutes of take-off we had to turn back and return to base, otherwise shortage of fuel threatened a forced landing. Up till 28 August I brought my score to seven victories. On 28 August 1940 it was a day for *Freie Jagd* missions. In this case this implied that a *Staffel* or even smaller formations – *Rotte* or

*Schwarm* – were engaged. On this day I flew with a single wingman in a *Rotte*; the operational area was the Channel and the English south coast. Over the coast we met two Hurricanes at about 5,000 m height. We followed the Hurricanes and were almost in range to open fire, when we were shot at by the flak. I maintained my attack and fired my first burst, but before I could turn the attack into a victory, I suddenly received a flak hit in my plane's belly. My reaction was to bail out followed by a good landing. I was received by a policeman and some soldiers. I was taken to an airfield near Folkestone where I was put in a cell. After a short time an officer pilot with a bandage on his head came into my cell. He shook my hand and said to me, 'You are the pilot from the Messerschmitt 109?'; I said, 'Yes.' Then he pointed to his bandaged head and said to me, 'You did this,' and I answered him, 'I am sorry.' Then we shook hands again and he left the cell. After two days I was brought to an interrogation camp in London, where the questioning began, over night and day. The questions however remained unanswered and after three weeks I was sent to a POW camp at Manchester.

It is possible that Artur Dau was shot down by Sgt George Smythe of 56 Squadron and that he was also the pilot he met in his cell, possibly at Hawkinge airfield. His reaction to this suggestion from myself was to say: 'I cannot say whether it was Sergeant George Smythe who visited me in my cell. I also did not shoot him down. He only confirmed to me that I had given him the wound on his head. Before my own demise I had an Englishman in front of me, at whom I was shooting. It is astounding after all these years to be confronted with these events once again. I recall the name of Hawkinge airfield.'

Just as many RAF pilots joined active squadrons during the Battle of Britain fresh from flying school and had to be thrown into combat totally unprepared, the *Luftwaffe* also had equally green replacement pilots coming in as losses mounted. One of these was *Gefreiter* Rudolf Miese of 4/JG 2, who was fortunate to be granted a three week reprieve to get to know the Me 109 better before entering combat. 'From the end of August 1940 until my being shot down on 15 November 1940 I was with the 4/G 2 *Richthofen*, thus only for a short while. I was a beginner and had only turned 20 on 11 January 1940. On 24 August I was posted to Beaumont-le-Roger to join *JG 2*. Together with two other comrades I joined the 4th *Staffel*. Until the end of the French campaign the *Staffel* had suffered no losses at all. Now we were the first replacements, as with the onset of the Battle of Britain losses had now begun. The *Staffelkapitän* was *Oberleutnant* Hans Hahn (known as "Assi" Hahn), then there were the *Leutnants* Meimberg and Bolze, *Oberfeldwebel* Schnell (later killed as *Major* and Knights Cross holder), and other *Staffel* members.' After his enforced wait for combat missions, Rudolf Miese had a good view of the seriousness of invasion planning: 'On the day we arrived (28 August 1940) the *Staffel* moved to Mardýck, a field base right on the coast between Dunkirk and Calais. We three new arrivals remained behind in Beaumont-le-Roger for the moment. Only three weeks later did we get three new aircraft from the aircraft park and ferry them to Mardýck. Now began the first real frontline flying for us. The first flight (a familiarisation flight, not an operational mission) I made together with *Unteroffizier* Dilthey. We had to patrol the coast between Dunkirk and Boulogne. In the harbours there lay hundreds of barges loaded with soldiers and vehicles; other barges were being towed by tugs along the coast. The invasion of England was planned, but as we all know, was not launched. This flight to test us out was satisfactorily completed, and thus I was allocated to *Leutnant* Meimberg as my *Rotte* leader.'

Me 110 crewmen were no more immune to sudden exposure to the harsh realities of combat missions over England, as related in 1989 by *Unteroffizier* Werner Ludwig, who joined *III/ZG 26* in August 1940, direct from blind flying school.

In autumn 1940 I was assigned to fly missions as escort in *III/ZG 26* for bomber units in their attacks on London, the Isle of Wight, Bristol, Plymouth etc. During the attacks of the bombers we flew a so-called defensive circle, from which we could attack and shoot at enemy fighters and then turn back into its protection. The opposition essentially consisted of flak and fighters such as Hurricanes and Spitfires. After some months our leadership realised, as our losses were too high, that the Me 110 was unsuited to its role as heavy fighter and that it could not compete with the much more manoeuvrable Spitfire. We were based on an airfield in the neighbourhood of Calais and later in Caen. Rendezvous point with the German bomber units was always Cap Gris Nez in 4,000–6,000 m height. Then we approached the targets near London (Croydon, etc.). On 18 August 1940 my right engine was shot up on my third operational mission. I then flew with one engine back over southern England and after crossing the Channel landed on the field base in France. From Caen we flew operations to drop bombs during the second part of September 1940, in lone attacks by two aircraft on targets in southern England. Once we also flew in a large formation of around 30 aircraft against Brighton. In France we lived in private quarters and had very good relations with the French, within the families whose homes we shared, or also in the cafes and restaurants, where we enjoyed our glass of wine or drank our beer. Our *Geschwader Kommodore Oberst* Huth I only saw twice, I think he later transferred to the night fighters. We always were involved rather with our *Kommandeur Oberstleutnant* Schalk, who died recently at the age of 85 in Vienna.

The struggles of freshly posted and inexperienced pilots on the Channel Front notwithstanding, the old salts were also increasingly ending up as casualties as well. Even experienced pilots such as *Leutnant* Franz Achleitner, *9/JG 3*, who had five British aircraft to his credit,[48] did not always get back home: 'During the Battle of Britain I was shot down in August (actually on the 24th) and then spent the rest of the war as a POW in Canada as the "guest of his Majesty the King".' Another old hand at combat flying who joined this unique group of 'royal guests' was *Oberleutnant* Josef Bürschgens of *7/JG 26*, who was shot down on 1 September 1940: 'My own loss after shooting down 10 enemy planes was naturally of special interest to myself; it was the feeling of a *Jagdflieger* which said, "All is over!" – I think this feeling was typical of all pilots who fell into captivity. In my 10 victories a mix-up is possible between Spitfire and Hurricane, but I think this is of minor importance.' On 1 September 1940 he took off at the head of *7/JG 26* at 13h00 from their field base at Caffiers on the Channel coast to escort a bomber formation which was to attack Kenley. Having reached the intended target as yet unmolested, at an altitude of 6,000–7,000 m they were finally engaged by the RAF, who were more interested in the bombers and Me 110s than the Me 109s. Still flying right next to the bombers, Bürschgens saw a Spitfire immediately below him attacking an Me 110, which was part of a defensive circle; he quickly pulled in behind the Spitfire. Now the rear gunner of the Me 110 was firing at the Spitfire, which was trying to silence him, and Bürschgens was able to get in a long burst at the British fighter unobserved; the latter broke away smoking in a split-S manoeuvre. Unfortunately for him, he had approached to almost ramming distance of the Me 110, whose gunner was still firing, and as he turned away he felt a bullet strike his cockpit next to his left foot and his engine stopped at the same moment. Gripped by fear at his situation, he feathered the propeller and glided towards the Channel streaming escaping fuel. As he lost altitude it became obvious he would not make the Channel and he crashed near Rye to the south of Folkestone, waking up some time afterwards in hospital with back and head injuries. About a week later he was taken to the RAF interrogation camp in London.

When I suggested to him in further correspondence that he might alternatively have been shot down by P/O Colin Gray of 54 Squadron, Bürschgens elaborated on this last mission of his during the battle: 'The combat report you mentioned of Colin Gray of 1 September 1940 is interesting – there is a certain chance that it was me. But, when I got the shot through the petrol line, the location was in the area of London City and my motor was idling until I crash-landed at Rye/Kent. At no time on my gliding path did I see an enemy plane. Time and height could match. In case you have contact with Colin Gray, give him my friendly regards.'

The increasing toll of pilots over England also included the highly experienced unit leaders who were almost impossible to replace, and whose cumulative losses seriously weakened the *Luftwaffe* for the unexpectedly long war that still lay ahead. One of the *Luftwaffe* fighter pilots lost on 5 September 1940 was the commander of *III/JG 54*, who *Fähnrich* Max Clerico, *7/JG 54* remembered long after the war. '*Hauptmann* Ultsch, *Gruppenkommandeur* of *III/JG 54* was a "Prussian", in the positive sense – if he was really one, I do not know. He was probably 30-plus, of medium build and had a full face and blond hair. He always looked as though he were angry. He was angry once, too, when we almost collided during taxying. He was very correct. We young pilots had little to do with him. I can offer no opinion on his flying abilities. I can still hear his voice today on the R/T (radio), a few seconds before he was shot down. I did not see it myself. *Oberleutnant* Scholz took over as acting *Gruppenkommandeur* for some time. I cannot remember who replaced him as *Staffelführer* – possibly *Leutnant* Lange (later the last *Kommodore* of *Jagdgeschwader 51* Mölders).'

Bomber escort tactics were a major problem, and a major cause of casualties, to both bombers and escorts throughout the battle, and the August – early September period provided unending challenges in this regard. A colleague of Max Clerico's, from *8/JG 54*, *Oberfeldwebel* Erwin Leykauf recalls the general approach of his *Gruppe* for the indirect escort. 'Bomber escorts: the tactic comprised firstly punctual rendezvous with the bombers. Then escort was taken up in a height-stepping type formation – i.e. *c.* 200 m higher than the bombers and about 1,000–1,500 m behind them.' More details on bomber escort tactics are supplied by *Hauptmann* Gerhard Schöpfel, the *Gruppenkommandeur* of *III/JG 26* since 21 August 1940: 'When escorting bomber formations we utilised our units as follows: (a) One *Gruppe* had the task of close escort, i.e. *Rotten* of fighters buzzing all around the bomber formation. (b) One *Gruppe* had the task of escorting the bombers from the side and higher, but at a distance, in *Schwarms*. (c) One *Gruppe* had the task of *Freie Jagd*, and in *Staffel* formations flying far away but within sight of the bombers, to be able to attack approaching enemy fighters before they reached the bombers.' He also described living conditions on the ground during the Battle of Britain: 'In summer 1940, after the French campaign, field bases in the Pas-de-Calais and Normandy were prepared for us. These field bases were not to be compared with normal airfields. The conditions on the ground were difficult, and accidents when landing were common. For accommodation during the day, tents and even barracks were available. Sleeping quarters were in neighbouring villages and towns. The civilian population were reserving their judgement on us still, and so we generally accepted that attitude and thus had few difficulties with them. The pilots were mostly very well accommodated in chateaux, country houses, etc.'

*Oberleutnant* Ulrich Steinhilper served in *I/JG 52*, in the 3rd *Staffel*, was shot down on 27 October 1940 and ended up as a prisoner in Canada.[49] He points out the serious disadvantages suffered by the Me 109s when performing bomber escort missions. 'The Me 109 E had only 400 litres of fuel, which lasted according to throttle applied from 70 to 110 minutes. Just to assemble a *Geschwader* (3 *Gruppen*, roughly 36 planes each) of 100 to 110 Me 109s and joining up with the bomber formations easily would take up to 30 minutes. There was no radio communication between fighters and bombers at all. Loaded bomber formations were flying slowly – sometimes still gaining height at some 300 km/h or even less – we would have preferred to go faster than 450 km/h. There was a continuous search for the better solution – stay slow and close, or swing around and about with higher speed and turning? In both cases the Spitfires and Hurricanes could dive through any formation, briefly spray out of eight guns and dive down and away. When protecting we were not permitted to follow them, but had to stay close to the bomber formations. Starting September 1940 we even had to stay with them till they reached back to the southern English coast along the Channel, in spite of fuel shortage.'

While the Me 109 pilots were becoming more and more exhausted with the almost daily missions over the hated Channel, the regular and very unpopular bomber escort duties, and the ever worsening casualties, the situation for the *Zerstörer* units was much worse. Very few crewmen from the Me 110 *Geschwadern* survived the battle and the rest of the war to give first-person accounts of their experiences. *Gefreiter* Johan Heinrich, a radio operator/air-gunner in *II/ZG 76* who figures later in this chapter, put me in touch with one of his comrades, also a gunner in this famous Me 110 *Gruppe*, known as the *Haifischgruppe* due to the shark mouth emblem painted on the noses of their aircraft. Heinrich briefly detailed his colleague's war record: 'My best flying comrade, Joachim Robel, flew as radio operator with some of the famous officers and pilots, *Oberleutnant* Wilhelm Herget and the *Staffelkapitän* of *6/ZG 76 Hauptmann* Heinz Nacke, right through the whole of the Battle of Britain in 1940 and became a highly decorated *Oberfeldwebel*, with the German Cross in Gold. He is a very nice and refined man, and a good comrade; we are inseparable flying friends and are the same age: Joachim Robel was born on 29 August 1920 in Dresden, and I on 11 August 1920 in St Josef, German Austria.' Obviously Johan Heinrich still believed in the concept of an Austrian *Anschluss* after the war! Joachim Robel himself has the following recollection of the Battle of Britain:

I flew in *Zerstörern* from 1939 to 1944. The *II/ZG 76* was set up at the end of 1939 in Garz on the island of Rügen. From the outset I was the radio operator of the then *Oberleutnant* Herget. In May 1940 we moved to Cologne and took part in the French campaign. After the end of this campaign we were stationed in Le Mans. From here in the autumn of 1940 we took part in the Battle of Britain. At the end of 1940 we transferred to Jever (north Germany). Here we took over coastal defence as well as the protection of the German shipping traffic to Norway. About my flights over England it can only be reported that every flight resulted in fierce air battles. The anti-aircraft defences affected the bombers more than us. On one occasion a Spitfire managed to place itself behind us and shot at us with all eight machine guns from a distance of *c.* 50 m. Naturally I shot back and hit its radiator. The Spitfire showed a white trail and disappeared below us. When we landed again in France I inspected our machine carefully. We had not received a single hit. Our tactics in this battle were to fly in formations of four aircraft, which was a *Schwarm*. Three *Schwarms* made up a *Staffel*, three *Staffels* a *Gruppe*. The bombers for which we had to provide close escort, we protected by flying behind them, and slightly higher. The light fighter Me 109s flew above us and protected the sky over a much greater area.

*Oberleutnant* Georg Christl was one of the very few Me 110 pilots from ZG 2 to survive the Battle of Britain. He also experienced the common practice of placing new and inexperienced pilots at the tail end of formations, where their chances of survival were reduced even more. He underlines the ineffectiveness of the Me 110 as a bomber escort, and describes the origin of the defensive circle tactic they adopted early on. Despite having begun his combat career only in the Battle of Britain, towards the end he already found himself as *Staffelkapitän*, showing just how bad their losses were in this *Geschwader*.

I took part in the Battle of Britain – this was also my introduction to operational flying – and I soon learnt that the Me 110 was not at all or at best only poorly suited to its intended purpose, escort for bombers attacking in the English hinterland. Instead we had to try and save our own hides. The actual operational assignment, to take on the escort of the bomber units, could mostly not be achieved. As a result, when we returned from a mission we were subjected to a mighty bollocking from our leadership; in my opinion this was not justifiable, and anyway it changed nothing. My first *Zerstörer* unit, with whom I flew operations over England, ZG 2 – I was *Staffelkapitän* towards the end – was dissolved at the end of the so-called Battle of Britain – there were no aircraft left anymore. The defensive circle formation was first used over England in the guise of an 'attacking circle', but this rapidly changed to the description 'defensive circle'. In single combat the Me 110 was inferior to the British fighters, which also caused the big losses. Initially the *Zerstörer* flew in loose formations, swinging from one side to the other above the bomber formation to protect them from enemy fighters. The English fighters mostly appeared in a strength of 9 to 12 machines from the rear and attacked the *Zerstörer*. A defence was then almost impossible – we were not allowed to shear out of our formation – the operational order was strictly to protect our bombers. Any circling by a single Me 110 would have been suicide. It was thus out of this situation that the defensive circle arose. The transition from the normal flying formation to the defensive circle took place through the lead machine turning in first followed by the rest of all the aircraft joining in behind. A large spiral thus formed, but this was supposed to remain strictly above our bombers under all circumstances. The call for a circle came usually through a radio message from the hindmost Me 110 to the formation leader, as soon as enemy fighters in any numbers set up their attack.

I remember one case where, as usual, I was flying as the last aircraft – according to the dictum 'the last one gets bitten by the dog' (*den hintersten beisst der Hund*) – when about 10 to 12 Hurricanes started an attack and my radio operator started to shoot with his MG 17 like a man possessed, and I gave the alarm to the lead machine, but nothing happened. When bullets slammed into my machine – I later counted 17 hits – I rammed the throttles wide open, dived beneath our formation and pulled up in front of our formation leader. Suddenly I was thus in the lead position instead of right at the back. After landing there was a terrible chewing-out by the entire flying crews, but otherwise no further consequences. However, thereafter I was never again put at the back of the formation. This occasion was a lesson for me. In my later time as *Staffelkapitän* and *Gruppenkommandeur* I always assigned the new crews to the leading *Schwarm*, and that way, in my view at least, avoided losses. Later in North Africa the English used this same defensive circle tactic, most likely because they were forced to do so by the superiority of the Me 109.

Some Me 109 pilots gave considerable attention to attacking the balloon barrages flying over many British targets, including some airbases and many ports and cities, aircraft factories, etc. Many historians have dismissed these attacks as peripheral, but they might have had some real, though indirect, impact, as detailed by a pilot from the *Richthofen Geschwader*, *Oberleutnant* Hans-Theodore Grisebach, 2/JG 2: 'I scored seven victories between 10 May 1940 and 16 August 1940, which compared to others was only a good average achievement. However, I had the idea on our return flights with our *Staffel* to shoot down the barrage balloons that the English had flying over Southampton. After the war the English reported that the balloon cables which fell across power lines did more damage than the entire bombing offensive. In retrospect I am proud of the 25 barrage balloons that I shot down. I was shot down over Portsmouth on 26 August 1940 already. The crash site of my aircraft was later found by an English flying cadet and I went on a trip with him to examine the site. In the end I spent seven years in English prisoner of war camps, five of them in Canada.'

Possibly the hardest job for a fighter pilot in the Battle of Britain was to be a unit leader, particularly of the larger *Gruppen* and *Geschwadern*. Despite his lack of surviving records and relevant logbooks, *Hauptmann* Hennig Strümpell, *Gruppenkommandeur* of *I/JG 2* recalls his time in the Battle of Britain very clearly:

Unfortunately I no longer have any records that could support my memories of the Battle of Britain. A significant number of my flying logbooks were also lost during or after the war, and just over the Battle of Britain period there is an unfortunate gap. The last entry in a surviving logbook is from 11 August 1940, a mission to Portland, and the next in another logbook, from May/June 1941. The Battle of Britain was totally different to the campaign over France. Over England the *Gruppen* were mostly operating together within a *Geschwader* formation, frequently as direct or indirect escort for Stuka or bomber units. Essentially, then, we flew in fighting formations, namely in loose groupings. The *Gruppenkommandeur* flew at the head with his *Schwarm*, the *Staffeln* following one behind the other, each according to its escort assignment at a particular height and on a specific side of the bomber formation. In direct escorts, one had to fly very close to the formation to be protected, had to take on their speed as far as possible, and we were not allowed to let ourselves be drawn off by the RAF fighters. Stuka escorts almost by definition provided large problems that could not be solved, resulting in Stuka operations being terminated after big losses. Indirect escorts gave more freedom to manoeuvre, one curved continuously above the bomber unit, without having to fly at its slow pace. The tactics of the *Gruppe* were completely determined by the mission directive: Stuka escort, indirect or direct escort of bomber formations, *Freie Jagd* in area etc. In this context I cannot go into details.

As stated above by *Gruppenkommandeur* Hennig Strümpell, Stuka missions were terminated due to massive losses, none being flown after 18 August 1940 until a few in November, against shipping in the Thames Estuary. The Stukas had a critical role to play in the planned invasion and their numbers had to be kept up for this purpose; hence they were withdrawn from combat but kept based along the Channel coast, ready for another *Blitzkrieg* in Operation Sealion.[50] By 18 August, RAF Fighter Command had already achieved a great deal: apart from taking the Stukas out of the immediate battle equation, the Me 110 had been shown up as a failure in the longer-range escort role and had also suffered appalling casualties. They were to redeem themselves on occasion, such as on 31 August and 3 September 1940, when they were sent in at height and dived down on British fighters before zoom-climbing back up again to rejoin their formations, instead of mixing it up with the much more nimble Spitfires and Hurricanes.[51] The newest Ju 88 bombers had also fared badly in the earlier August raids, especially when used en masse, such as by *KG 54* and *KG 51* on 11–13 August and by *LG 1* on 15 August 1940.[52] Later in August they were much more successful when used in small, fast hit-and-run raids which broke away from larger formations carrying out complex attacks on multiple targets.[53] Heinkel He 111 formations had shown themselves to be vulnerable and much of the August bombing fell to the venerable Dornier 17s of *KG 2* and 3, which suffered high losses (but not as bad as the other types due to their less vulnerable air-cooled engines) but kept going until 15 September 1940.[54] Due to losses suffered, difficulties with bomber escorts and to try and enforce fatal damage on Fighter Command's facilities, aircraft and pilots, from late August *Jafü 3*'s Me 109s were transferred to *Luftflotte 2* to provide a massive concentration of fighter power in the Pas-de-Calais area.[55] Only small numbers remained behind in *Luftflotte 3*. JG 2 and JG 27 moved on 28 August 1940, as did most of *JG 53*, with *Stab* and *III/JG 53* moving across on 23–24 August 1940 already; few came back to *Jafu 3*, only *I/JG 27* (30 September 1940), and all of *JG 2* over several weeks in September 1940, from the 10th to the 25th of the month.[56]

## *7–30 September 1940: Attacks on London*

A majority of published sources on the Battle of Britain emphasize that Fighter Command, very hard pressed by early September, was saved by the shift in *Luftwaffe* targets from RAF bases to London. Two German reports of unit leaders are regularly cited to support a weak RAF response during the first couple of days of September 1940: *II/KG 1*, who indicated only slight fighter attack on 1 September 1940, and *ZG 76*'s *Kommodore*, who maintained on 2 September 1940 that even the vulnerable Me 110 could once again live above England.[57] What the *II/KG 1* leader forgot to mention was that his 18 He 111s were escorted by no less than three *Geschwadern* of Me 109s;[58] one of the Heinkels was indeed hit by a Spitfire and was written off on return to France[59] – such was the genius of the Park method of using small British fighter formations which could penetrate large and clumsy German formations from on high, picking out and crippling bombers before diving on down in comparative safety. Another bad day for the British fighter defence was 3 September, when a heavily escorted raid to North Weald was effectively covered by large Me 110 formations, using the dive-and-zoom-climb tactics alluded to above, causing considerable casualties; however, once again a bomber was picked out of the formation, and seven Me 110s didn't return.[60] In direct contrast to these apparent German successes over England, the British defences disposed of 15 Me 110s with comparative ease on 4 September 1940.[61] But it was the Me 109 casualties in early September that were the real problem in limiting *Luftwaffe* power: for example, 21 lost on the 2nd, and 17 each day on 5 and 6 September;[62] due to bombers (and Me 110s) needing ever larger escorts over Britain, the lack of Me 109s would effectively limit attacking numbers no matter how many bombers were available, and this was soon to be the deciding factor. Altogether, in the first six days of September 1940, 70 Me 109s were written off;[63] this amounted to the serviceable strength of a complete *Geschwader* at this time. While Air Vice-Marshal Keith Park stated clearly that the switch to bombing London saved Fighter Command,[64] he was not aware of the staggering drop in Me 109s available to the *Luftwaffe* during September.

Total and serviceable German aircraft available on Channel Front, 17 August 1940[65] and 7 September 1940[66]

| Aircraft type | 17 August | | 7 September | |
|---|---|---|---|---|
| | Total | Serviceable | Total | Serviceable |
| Me 109 | 835 | 675 | 710 | 564 |
| Me 110 | 330 | 214 | 232 | 129 |
| Bombers | 936 | 736 | 912 | 546 |

Me 109 numbers exclude Norway-based *II* and *III/JG 77*. Bombers exclude *KG 30* – known values of 71/48 on 17 August and ?/26 on 7 September.

By the end of September, Me 109s available for operations (serviceable) had dropped to 276 plus another 130 equipped for fighter-bomber operations; this total of just over 400 Me 109s was mirrored by only 100 Me 110s available.[67] Production figures for Me 109s in August 1940 (173 only)[68] were dwarfed by British fighter production (476);[69] repairs to damaged aircraft were also much faster in the case of the RAF,[70] further exacerbating the problem. In contrast, over the course of the battle RAF fighter numbers grew, as did their serviceability rate.[71] German air staff were obviously very aware of these growing problems and the rapidly dwindling offensive power of their air force; the switch to bombing London was thus a decision predicated on the need for a rapid resolution of the battle and the destruction of what the Germans supposed was a small remaining pool of British fighters. That the latter was not the case was to be amply demonstrated in the first half of September 1940; while the cessation of airfield attacks took the pressure off the system, casualties to Fighter Command aircraft and pilots continued at the high rates of August.[72] The 'saving' of Fighter Command by the change to London as the main target is thus not tenable against this background. The battle of attrition, which was the British strategy from the beginning, had paid off; already by 20–26 August 1940, when *Luftwaffe* deputy commander Milch toured German units, significant shortfalls of both aircraft and crews were apparent.[73] Park's approach of using small, generally squadron-sized formations, fully approved by Dowding, had worked to perfection, and the 'big wing' method would not have had the same result.[74]

While RAF fighter aircraft and pilot numbers had basically been maintained up to this stage in the battle, the problem in Fighter Command was one of experience, with the lack thereof leading to excessive casualties when new squadrons were posted in from other groups to relieve exhausted units in 11 Group, which from late August 1940 faced all the Me 109s now concentrated in the Pas-de-Calais.[75] Also, by around 7 September most fresh squadrons had already been so exchanged, and there was little point in bringing back tired units depleted of experienced pilots before they were ready. Dowding thus (on this date)[76] organised his squadrons into three categories: classes A, B and C. A squadrons were all those based in 11 Group, plus others in 10 and 12 Groups which might be required to reinforce Park; B squadrons were in Groups 10, 12 and 13 and fully manned and equipped with aircraft but suffering from fatigue and/or inexperience; and C squadrons were those which were burned out from combat, resting their veterans and training the new pilots, and would be used as sources of experienced men for the A and B units once they had had some rest.[77] Dowding's timing in concentrating his resources and maintaining maximum levels of critical experience in 11 Group was pretty well perfect.

Support for the inference that Fighter Command was not at its weakest when the London bombing began is given by several of the German Me 109 pilots cited here, including one who had flown over England right through the August–early September period and then on to the end of September before being shot down in October 1940. Despite *I/JG 52* arriving on the French coast, based at Cocquelles near Calais, on 3 August 1940 and seeing action throughout August and early September in the many raids against RAF bases, convoys and so on,[78] *Oberleutnant* Günter Büsgen of 1st *Staffel JG 52* remembered in 1996 that the London raids which began on 7 September marked the real start of their tough operations:

> After my fighter school training in Werneuchen near Berlin, from the beginning of 1939, I joined *I/JG 52* which was then stationed at Lachen-Speyerdorf near Stuttgart. Only after Dunkirk did we transfer to the Channel Front to a field base in the neighbourhood of Calais. In the beginning our operations were restricted to reconnaissance flights over the Channel to Dover, limited air combats with English pilots, who in August 1940 still flew the old model Spitfires (Spitfire Mark 1) and Hurricanes. The really serious operations for us began with the bombardment of London by our bombers, which we had to escort. The total of 80 operations over London prior to my being shot down on 12 October 1940 did not make many comrades or myself very enthusiastic, as in our opinion an incorrect tactic was used. As we experienced things, after the big assembly of the massed bomber and fighter formations over Calais through to the area Boulogne was completed, one-third of our fuel had already been used up and there was always the danger that the English would cause us large losses or would force the big formation off course from the normal route over the Channel towards Calais–Boulogne during the return flight.
>
> You might have seen in the English film *The Battle of Britain*, still shown today, or read about the Tommies appearing with the new Spitfire (Mark II) on 15 September 1940, which was superior to our Me 109 E in speed and manoeuvrability. On this day we suffered high losses of bombers and also of fighters. That is when the first

signs became apparent that England could not be conquered by air attack. We found the repeated announcements of a possible invasion of England as almost ridiculous after we saw the blunt-nosed barges that were being assembled in the vicinity of Calais, and which soon disappeared from there again. The aerial combats and aerial contacts between the English and German pilots were fair and chivalrous during the months of the Battle of Britain. With only one exception known to me (not an English pilot), neither the English nor the German pilots shot enemy pilots descending in their parachutes. During the years of my imprisonment (six years POW in England and Canada) I was treated fairly and decently.

One German pilot who found out the hard way that the RAF still had plenty of defensive spirit and resources left at the beginning of the London bombing was *Oberleutnant* Gerhard Granz, who flew Me 110s in *I/ZG 2*. On 7 September 1940, Granz had taken off from his base near Le Touquet just before 16h00 and the Me 110s assembled with their He 111 charges over Calais. The Me 110s placed themselves above and behind the bombers. Battle began over the Sheerness area. Granz saw a British fighter zoom up from below and attack a He 111 and he went into a diving turn to fire at the British aircraft; he hit it, observing smoke coming from its tail, and it went down in flames. But suddenly he found himself surrounded by Hurricanes, and one opened fire from behind, the bullets passing each side of his head and out through the front of the cockpit. Gerhard Granz's Me 110 caught fire and dived vertically. He ordered *Feldwebel* Willi Schutel, his gunner, to jump, and after he had departed tried himself to follow suit. However, his chute stuck in the cockpit, so he took hold of the controls again and turned the blazing aircraft onto its back, and fell out at about 500 ft and frantically pulled the ripcord – just in time, as he almost immediately landed in a tree, to be met by two helmeted home guards who appeared from behind a hedge. His Me 110 crashed at Little Burstead close to Billericay in Essex at about 17h30. He was lucky to be alive and in one piece, one of the very few survivors of *ZG 2* from the Battle of Britain.

After many operations over England, my number came up on 7 September 1940, when my opponent, the legendary Douglas Bader (the legless pilot) set my Me 110 on fire and I was able to save myself by parachute. Six and a half years of imprisonment in Canada followed and I survived the war as one of only a few among the Me 110 fighter pilots. Not long after my being shot down ZG 2 was dissolved, due to 'lack of participation' (*Mangel an Beteiligung*), meaning too many losses suffered, and the remaining crews transferred to the night fighter arm. In this respect (only a few survivors) there is no history of ZG 2 and no veterans group to uphold its tradition. Thus I also only know a few people at the fighter pilots' meetings at Geisenheim, while in contrast at meetings of the 'Canadians' where the former inmates are present in large numbers, many are known to me.

In Poland and France tactics were simple as the Me 109 (flown by I/ZG 2 or JGr 102 as it was then known, over Poland) and Me 110 (with which the re-named I/ZG 2 were re-equipped before the French campaign) were superior to the enemy aircraft, so that combats boiled down to flying ability, and a good eye and aiming ability; this was the basis of our many successes up till then. In the Battle of Britain this picture changed completely. We flew over the Channel, and in attacks on the docks of London, the Me 109 had only enough time (i.e. fuel) for a short combat; the English of course knew this and took advantage of it. The Me 110s dispatched as escorts were in many respects inferior to the Spitfire and Hurricane and protected themselves by forming defensive circles, which was not their intended assignment. The RAF, well informed through their first-rate radar system, waited for the German formations at superior altitudes and dived through the German formations with the intention of shooting down bombers, with combats against German fighters being only a secondary purpose. One could talk a lot more about these experiences, it was a victory for the English, where shot down German pilots who managed to save themselves by parachute jumps became prisoners while the English fought on with new aircraft; it was a decisive battle of the Second World War.

Günter Büsgen's colleague in I/JG 52, *Oberleutnant* Ulrich Steinhilper of 3rd *Staffel*, was not impressed by the tactics applied by the *Luftwaffe* high command in the London attacks, and also supports a resurgent RAF in the period of the London attacks. He also makes some pointed comments on unit leaders and their personal ambitions.

As our high command was stupid enough to select continuously the same target since the middle of September – London and London again – finally nothing but London, the British fighters only had to climb and wait over London. The Allies even at their highest stage of air superiority over Germany later, never gave up the surprise or distracting effect of target changes. The British then in the final stage of the battle were smart enough to attack only out of higher altitude and in our turning curve flown over London as we began the trip home. In one extreme case, on 30 September 1940 we lost 21 Me 109s because of fuel shortage, who all fell into the channel. Because of high waves only two pilots were saved, 19 drowned (these losses reflect 21 of the total of 35 Me 109s lost in action that day for the *Luftwaffe* as a whole, not only *I/JG 52*).[79] In this mission I was leading four aircraft, we were also very short of fuel, and did not make it back to Coquelles, our base, but fortunately reached Boulogne. There were more emergency landings back in France that day also. On free chase operations we could follow enemy fighters at the will of the individual *Gruppe* or *Staffel* leaders. Some required strong discipline, not allowing individual pilots to go after the enemy on their own, but making them stay close to their leaders, others allowed total freedom, also giving chances for victories to the men flying at the tail. I was and still am today critical about the attitude and collection of decorations of those, flying ahead and shooting down the enemy, while those flying behind, protecting and being shot down themselves, were without opportunities for victories and decorations.

Although less outspoken than his subordinates, *JG 52*'s *Kommodore Major* Hanns Trübenbach felt strongly about protecting the bombers and made every effort to follow his instructions in this regard, as is normally expected of a senior combat leader. Once again, and this time from a senior German fighter leader, his recollection also supports Fighter Command being very far from defeat as the London bombing began.

Every fighter *Geschwader* had a *couleur* with a bomber *Geschwader*. My *JG 52* was assigned to the *KG 77* (*Oberst* Finck). We met the bomber *Geschwader* at 7,000 m height while still over the French coast and then flew tactically such that the bomber formation was protected from above. We had strict orders never to leave the bomber formation without adequate fighter escort, and I always carried these out. Other fighter units often in such situations entered combat with the approaching English aircraft and thereby neglected the protection of the bomber *Geschwader*. This was hard to resist, as who wanted to be shot down without fighting, without defending your own skin? The results of all this was that daylight missions with bomber formations were soon terminated, as the bomber losses had become much too great. Due to the relatively large speed difference between the bombers and the fighters, the fighters could not just fly along next to the bombers, but instead flew in ever-changing positions around them, as the German bombers like the Heinkels and Dorniers were especially vulnerable also from below. Basically, the cooperation between fighter unit and *couleur* bomber *Geschwader* proceeded without problems.

In view of the strength of the RAF fighter force, as against the dwindling German fighter arm on the other side of the Channel, the celebrated British victory on Battle of Britain Day, 15 September 1940, should not come as a surprise, or be seen as some sort of miracle resurgence. A witness to operations by the Me 110s during the first half of September, is quoted next. Having been shot down and badly wounded over France on 12 May 1940, radio operator/rear gunner *Unteroffizier* Alois Dierkes of *V/LG 1* took time to recover after being freed from his imprisonment by the French, after the armistice. He returned to his unit after recovering from his wounds, but was not yet declared fit to fly:

Therefore it was felt that it was too risky to send me on missions over England. I only flew three operations with my chief *Oberleutnant* Müller, as his own radio operator had suffered a nervous breakdown. Our losses at that time were enormous. From every mission, only half of the machines came back unscathed. And *Oberleutnant* Müller himself did not return from his next flight (shot down over Thames Estuary and killed, 15 September 1940).[80] He was posthumously promoted to *Hauptmann*, according to London radio; I was not able to check if this was correct or not. On 1 October 1940 we were withdrawn from the Channel Front and moved, after some detours, to Stuttgart. There we trained ourselves as night fighters. At the beginning of December we transferred to Vechta. From there we tried to hinder the incoming Englishmen and to achieve some victories. Our old unit designation was relinquished and we now called ourselves *I/NJG 3*, or *I. Gruppe* of *Nachtjagdgeschwader 3*.

Other Me 110 crewmen, newly arrived at their units and barely able to even fly their machines, not to mention lacking all battle survival skills, were fortunate to be protected by forward-looking commanding officers from entering combat until they had mastered actually flying their aircraft. Amongst these lucky survivors was *Gefreiter* Johan Heinrich.

I belonged to the *II/Zerstörergeschwader 76*, 4th and 6th *Staffels* (*Haifischgruppe*) only for a short time, from August till December 1940. I was radio operator for my pilot *Unteroffizier* Paul Wenke (who died flying, 20 July 1941 in Leeuwarden/Holland) and we were stationed in France at Le Mans, Abbeville and later in Jever/East Friesland, in North Germany. My highly respected officers included *Geschwader Kommodore Major* and *Ritterkreuzträger* Walter Grabmann; intelligence officer *Oberleutnant* Walter Borchers, *Ritterkreuzträger*; *Gruppenkommandeur Hauptmann* Erich Groth, *Ritterkreuzträger*; *Staffelkapitän* of the 4th *Staffel Hauptmann* Hans Hoppe; *Oberleutnant* and *Ritterkreuzträger* Hans Joachim Jabs, *Staffelkapitän* of the 6th *Staffel*; *Hauptmann* and *Ritterkreuzträger* Heinz Nacke; and *Staffel* adjutant, *Oberleutnant* Wilhelm Herget, *Ritterkreuz-* and *Eichenlaubträger*. The *Zerstörergeschwader 76* led by *Major* Walter Grabmann suffered major losses in the Battle of Britain, as the Me 110 was a heavy fighter and inferior to the British single-seat machines; however the *ZG 76* shot down over 500 enemy aircraft in 1940. *I/ZG 76* was almost destroyed in the Norwegian campaign and later operating from there over the United Kingdom, and was dissolved. The *II* and *III Gruppen* operated from 10 May 1940 in the Western campaign and thereafter in the Battle of Britain until 24 October 1940. From 24 October 1940 they were stationed in Jever/East Friesland and Aalborg/Denmark for home defence duties. I joined *II/ZG 76* on 29 August 1940 in France, flying from Dinard, later Le Mans, Abbeville/Yvrench, till 24 October. On 29 September 1940 in our Me 110 M8+YP with pilot *Unteroffizier* Paul Wenke we went into a spin for 1,000 m and, thank God, at 800 m height the aircraft recovered on its own and my pilot could regain control of the machine.

These new additions to the unit, barely in control of their aircraft, were kept busy flying wounded back to Germany in a Ju 52 and ferrying Me 110s, flying courier assignments and generally learning to fly the Me 110 properly, and did not fly any missions over England. Johan Heinrich recalled further: 'I should have flown my first mission over England on 11 September 1940, but this was cancelled as my pilot was continually employed flying shot-up Me 110s for repair to the major workshop facility at Le Mans and bringing back repaired aircraft to Abbeville in Northern France. Also, with my pilot *Unteroffizier* Paul Wenke we flew wounded airmen from our *Gruppe* from Le Mans to Munich (arrived 12 September 1940) with the *Gruppenstab* Ju 52 machine. The next day we flew to Prague in Czechoslovakia and swopped our Ju 52 and flew the new one back to Le Mans.' Living conditions on the ground during the Battle of Britain were good, even for a lowly *Gefreiter* like Johan Heinrich of II/ZG 76: 'Travelling by train in France was free for German soldiers, and part of the military occupied the finest hotels. We were quartered in a beautiful housing estate on the outskirts of Le Mans near the airfield. There in our house we had our own bathroom, kitchen and a lovely garden. The main road ran right next to our estate. But the mixed peoples in France are quite wild, one would think you were living in the Wild West!' Clearly, he was no Francophile.

*JG 52* (with *I/JG 52* and *I/LG2*, later joined by *II/JG 52*, under command) had largely carried out escorts to specialised fighter-bomber units such as *II/LG 2* and *Erprobungsgruppe 210*, as well as low-level strafing attacks on RAF airfields such as Manston during August 1940, and only experienced protecting large heavy bomber units in late September, as recalled by the *Kommodore*, Hanns Trübenbach. Here he describes a typical bomber escort mission for *KG 77*, this one occurring on 27 September 1940:

> In order to understand the so-called escort tasks one has to form a picture of the relative aerial situation at the time. For the escort of a bomber *Geschwader* there were namely no clear and unequivocal orders received. My *Geschwader* staff for example would receive a communication such as: '*Kampfgeschwader KG 77* will take off from Central France to fly to London. Rendezvous with *Jagdgeschwader JG 52* at 6,000 m height above the French coast, from where *JG 52* is to take over the protection of *KG 77*.' How to achieve this was left to the *Kommodore*, as he had to carry out the task with only two fighter *Gruppen* and the Staff *Schwarm*, seeing as the *III/JG 52* had been moved to protect Berlin (left on 1 August 1940 already).[81] And so *KG 77* flew in a widely spaced formation towards the English coast, where they were received with a massive flak barrage.

After dropping their bombs, *KG 77*, instead of going directly back to France, flew further across London and only turned back in the direction of France far too late. Even if the escorting fighters had experienced no air combat, the red fuel warning lights started to show. We were flying above the clouds and had no idea where *KG 77* would take us. Thus we had to trust to luck and dive down through the clouds and then found ourselves still far from our bases. Part of both my *Gruppen* had to force-land due to running out of fuel along the Channel coast beaches!!! Of course there were the inevitable crash-landings too! Ihlefeld, *Gruppenkommandeur* of I/LG 2 was able to land on the beach without damage, as he was no longer able to fly to Calais-Marck. In the meantime, *KG 77* flew on above the clouds alone, and was attacked viciously over England and was decimated with many losses.

This tactic of dropping bombs on London could surely not be repeated even once. Mölders flew another similar escort mission (on 30 September 1940), admittedly in good weather, with his *JG 51*, was attacked by a large number of English fighters and was forced to abandon his assigned bomber *Geschwader*. The air combats became so massive that he could no longer join up with his *Kampfgeschwader*, which then also suffered serious losses. There was one further escort case (probably also 30 September 1940) that panned out the same way, just like our previous mission, so that ended the day bombing war. Mölders was admittedly able to score a number of victories, but the bomber crewmen had to pay for them with high losses.

Somewhat later (probably November) I had to once more escort bombers, a Stuka *Gruppe*, that was supposed to attack ships in the Thames estuary, but there was such a flak barrage that I was almost shot down myself. Thank God, the Stukas had no losses, as they flew home at the lowest possible level. From 11 September 1940 till 1 October 1940 I personally with my *Schwarm* and often only with my adjutant flew escort missions of the most varied sort; thus over London, the coast of England, south-east England and south-west England. Often on these missions 'my own' (by this is meant units he often had to escort as the *Luftwaffe* encouraged such 'partnerships' at the time) fighter-bomber units were escorted, as had also happened earlier in the battle, namely the two new fighter-bomber units *II/LG 2* and *Erprobungsgruppe 210*, that always had to carry out special missions and who suffered heavy losses doing so.

As already told, after the dramatic and limited escort flights with bomber *Geschwadern* ('mine' was the *KG 77*, flying Ju 88s), that were supposed to destroy London, this tactic broke down completely and had to be abandoned. Exceptions remained purely special missions, like ship escorts in the Channel or low level attacks on English airfields with our own fighter units.

The early London raids also saw some of the aces fall, as related by *Feldwebel* Georg Pavenzinger, wingman to all the *Staffelkapitäns* of 2/*JG 51* during the battle, when *Hauptmann* Wiggers was killed:

Once more the two of us made a lone sweep to northwest of London, and here something odd happened. Above the clouds at about 6,000 m we saw a lone aircraft. We stalked it and believed, once we had identified it as a Spitfire, that we were still unobserved. We began our attack and in this moment the Spitfire dived through the clouds with us right behind. When we came out below the clouds, we found ourselves in the middle of a pack of about 30 Spitfires. Now we found ourselves in several rounds of dogfighting. Suddenly I saw how Wiggers pulled his aircraft up steeply and then disappeared vertically downwards. Now I was alone. While turning for my life in this pack of enemies, I gradually managed to get higher, until I reached the cloud base and then I was away. After landing, I found that *Hauptmann* Wiggers was not back yet. He never did come back. As we heard later, Wiggers was mortally hit in the chest and crashed. My aircraft also had many bullet holes in the rear fuselage.

*Staffelkapitän* Wiggers was lost on 11 September 1940, his aircraft crashing in flames from very low level while being chased by several Spitfires (or Hurricanes?)[82] near Lewes in Sussex; a witness saw it pass beneath telephone wires and then crash into rising ground.[83]

With such highly experienced pilots like Wiggers and Pavenzinger being killed and shot up, one can only imagine the feelings of the novices on their first operations in a battle that was now raging at full tilt; *Gefreiter* Rudolf Miese of 4/*JG 2* made his first cross-Channel operational flight in mid-September against London:

I and *II Gruppen* of *JG 2* in those days were stationed at the field base at Mardýck, directly on the coast behind the dunes, and between Dunkirk and Calais. The field telephone rang, combat mission: escort for a bomber *Geschwader* as extended escort, rendezvous 12h10 over Cap Gris Nez (near Calais), assigned altitude for us at 6,000 m. What happened next was all new for me on my first operational mission. Up till then I had only taken off and flown in either a *Rotte* of two machines or in a *Schwarm* of four machines. After a final instruction from my *Rotte* leader *Leutnant* Meimberg 'Under all circumstances always stay on my wing!' the engines were started and we taxied from the separate dispersal areas to the take-off point. On the relatively narrow meadow there was just enough space that about 10 aircraft could line up next to each other.

Now in the shortest space of time the *Geschwader Kommodore* with Staff flight and six *Staffels* had to take off, about 70 aircraft altogether. A *Staffel* taxied from left to right, the pilots next to each other, lined up and then took off in the same order one at a time. While the first *Staffel* was taking off the next *Staffel* taxied up behind them. As the last machine of the initial *Staffel*, on the right, took off so the first aircraft of the next *Staffel* followed suit simultaneously. Once airborne we climbed steeply and took up our formation and arrived punctually over Cap Gris Nez. Below us appeared the bomber *Geschwader* in perfect formation, and at our own height two further fighter *Geschwader*. All of this was confusing for a young pilot like myself but at the same time it was an overwhelming experience. Our flight path took us towards the east of London. Everything was still quiet. The white cliffs of Dover stood out on the way across the Channel. But as we neared Dover, I suddenly saw small black smoke puffs beneath us. 'Aha, that is definitely the acknowledged dangerous naval flak of Dover. Don't worry about it, stay close to your *Rottenführer*.' The flak bursts also lay 100 m too low. Now we could see the great U-bend of the Thames with the docks which were easily visible. Suddenly from all sides Spitfires and Hurricanes swarmed around us. A gigantic dogfight began. There was no question of any elegant flying: full throttle, throttle right back, grab the stick with both hands and pull into tight turns, just keep up with my leader and check behind all the time. This was flying at the highest level of concentration, there is no time to feel fear, and there is also no time to keep an eye on the bomber formation. And all this at heights that I had only experienced once in a test flight at fighter school. After 15 to 20 minutes of combat, we turned away to the south.

Past Dover we dived down almost to water level. Then our *Staffelkapitän* 'Assi' Hahn gave the order over the radio: 'Dessoy, sing!' *Unteroffizier* Dessoy, a vine grower from the Rhine and a gifted singer sang the most beautiful songs from the Rhineland. Only after landing and after parking my aircraft, did I realise what demands the operation and air combat had made on the body. Thus or similarly, the next four operations over London proceeded. From Mardýck I thus flew five missions to London. We escorted He 111 or Ju 88 bomber *Geschwader*, who were making attacks on the London docks. Mostly, three fighter *Geschwader* were assigned to protect the bombers, as direct or extended escort or through free chases. Over Dover we were greeted by the heavy flak, we were then at 6,000 to 7,000 m height. Suddenly Spitfires and Hurricanes with the cockade markings on wings and fuselages came at us, often from much greater height (visible from France already and long picked up by the radar station in Dover, our departure was known well in time). The English in the first place wanted to ward off and shoot down the bombers and we had to hinder them in this. There were hard air battles between evenly matched opponents with different machines: Spitfires were more manoeuvrable than the Me 109 and were fitted with eight machine guns, the Me 109 was faster and equipped with two machine guns and two 2-cm cannons. The losses on both sides were very high, particularly of the bombers. We could not protect them on their return flights, as our fuel was not enough for this. Due to the day attacks of the bombers being terminated because of their high losses, we moved back to Beaumont-le-Roger again at the beginning of October.

In contrast to the thorough training and rather gentle introduction into combat that Rudolf Miese was allowed, others experienced a somewhat more abrupt transition, as told by *Unteroffizier* Dr Felix Sauer of *I/JG 53*: 'At the beginning of the war, on 1 September 1939, I was teaching biology at a *Gymnasium* (high school). With around 700 other former private pilots, I was drafted at once and – in a series of rapid courses – trained as a fighter pilot. As early as September 1940 I was commissioned to fly sorties at the Channel coast, over England (roughly 90 flights over the south of England and London).'

## October 1940: Fighter-bombers

After 30 September 1940 there were no more large daylight raids over England. In their place, a rather aimless campaign of pinprick bombing by Me 109s was initiated in October, with Göring firmly believing that this would rapidly force a successful conclusion to the battle. *Kommodore* Hanns Trübenbach of *JG 52* recalls the rather pointless *Jabo* attacks of October 1940:

> Göring reacted to the 'large bomber let-down' (large raids of September) with an order to now equip the fighters with bombs of 250 kg. And indeed one *Gruppe* per *Geschwader* was supposed to be fitted to carry bombs while the two free chase fighter *Gruppen* were supposed to protect the bomb carriers. However, I flew one afternoon completely alone to the English coast and let my bomb go, to see how one could best achieve the new instruction. The Staff flight of *JG 52* then flew to London, where we dropped our bombs in the middle of the city centre, naturally without any success, as we learned after the war in English imprisonment from the 'gentlemen'. The *Reichsmarschall* Göring really believed that the rapid conversion of the individual fighter *Gruppen* to fighter-bombers would be able to finish off the war over England in a short time (four days!). When Field Marshal Kesselring expressed this philosophy of Göring to the assembled *Kommodoren*, we naturally laughed heartily at this idiocy. But that was how Göring was. In conclusion it could be said: the ideal condition for an escort task for bomber *Geschwaders* was to have one *Gruppe* as close escort, one as extended escort and one as free chase *Gruppe*. I stuck strictly to escort orders, but this was only effective in so far as the bomber unit also dutifully stuck to *their* orders. And *that* did not always work out OK.

A rather idyllic life on the ground at Beaumont-le-Roger during October 1940 contrasted with the realities of ongoing combat in the air after their return to this field base, as *Gefreiter* Rudolf Miese of *II/JG 2* recalls:

> At Beaumont-le-Roger the aircraft were dispersed under the apple trees for camouflage. The take-off and landing strips were meadows or harvested grain fields. The *Staffel* ground crew members lived in Nissan huts close to the aircraft. We pilots lived in a nice house on the outskirts of the town in full comfort. The owners had fled during the French campaign. From Beaumont-le-Roger we flew to Cherbourg or Le Havre to refuel and then from there over the 'stream' (*Bach*, i.e. the Channel) to make fighter incursions of the English south coast. Mostly the English were already up and waiting to give us a

hot reception. Hard aerial combats ensued, also dogfights at times, so that when one looked behind you could look the English in the eyes. On the 10 October 1940 I witnessed how my *Rottenführer Leutnant* Meimberg shot down a Hurricane. When outnumbered by Hurricanes we escaped being shot at by vertical dives from 8,000 m to just above the water. The Me 109 could maintain a dive, the Hurricanes could not follow. At the end of October *Reichsmarschall* Göring came to visit *JG 2* at Beaumont-le-Roger. Having by then 13 operations behind me, five of them to London, I received the Iron Cross second class from him.

During October and November, even though the height of the battle had passed, combat and flying against England remained a strain on the pilots; thus, Rudolf Miese of *4/JG 2*: 'Later, with the fighter incursions from Le Havre and Cherbourg, added to the existing pressure of flying and fighting, was the 140 km of water between England and our airfields. If your aircraft was damaged in combat or even with a run of the mill engine problem, one was in the "drink". Once, and still at high altitude over the English south coast, the red fuel warning lights showed: only fuel left for about 10 minutes. With the proverbial last drops of fuel I just made it to Cherbourg; on my final approach the "prop" stopped dead.'

The high-altitude missions of October 1940 placed an extra strain on already very tired men, the Me 109 not behaving well at these heights and being vulnerable to the Spitfires which could fly higher. *Oberleutnant* Ulrich Steinhilper, *3/JG 52* recalls wobbling around at high altitude to little purpose:

During October 1940 our "bombers", fighter-bombers in waves every 20 minutes in daylight only – 109s with 250 kg bombs beneath – were at some 9,000 m. We the covering fighters were reaching altitudes of 10,200 to 10,400 m, varying only according to atmospheric conditions. At that height we were floating around with as little as 220 km/h speed. Anything that came down from higher above, with more than double the speed, was at a great advantage and we were easy prey, losing just about one or a few experienced pilots each time in this bloody curve over London. Fuel on these missions was then no longer a problem. With fighter-bombers the return trip to London took about 55 minutes. Our *Staffelkapitän*, Kühle, in my eyes was quite a cautious pilot and leader. He managed to preserve himself, without much success, till close to the end of the war and unfortunately got killed near the end during the Battle of the Bulge.

Among the participants in the October *Jabo* attacks was Victor Mölders, brother to the famous Werner, now transferred to *JG 51* from the *Zerstörern* with whom he had served in France:

> In the Battle of Britain I flew the Me 109, as *Oberleutnant* and *Staffelkapitän* of 2/JG 51, but as *Jabo* (*Jagdbomber*, fighter-bomber) with a 250 kg bomb under the belly. We flew from the French coast over the sea, directly to the north and then into the Thames Estuary and bombed the harbour facilities of London, with the primary aim of forcing the Londoners into their bomb shelters and thereby disturbing their activities. The fate of my former comrades from my earlier unit, *Zerstörergeschwader ZG 1* saddened me when they were dispatched over England by daylight (with *III/ZG 76* and *Erprobungsgruppe 210*).[84] They were helpless prey for the Spitfires. In this context the much practiced and applied defensive circle helped not at all. The Battle of Britain was lost for the following two reasons: (1) Spitfire and Hurricane could turn better. Their superiority in speed remained within limits. Only with the Bf 109 F was equality in speed reached; (2) The British fighters allowed our fighters to penetrate far into enemy territory, while they gathered at high altitudes, partially only north of London, and dived down onto us when we had almost no fuel left for the return flight to France. In this way, I also, as fighter-bomber, was shot down. While the English pilots could save themselves with their parachutes or belly land, they were in their own territory. But we were taken prisoner and transported to Canada.

His wingman *Feldwebel* Georg Pavenzinger was with Victor Mölders when he was shot down.

> Our 2nd *Staffel*, which later became a *Jabo-Staffel*, had relatively high losses in the Battle of Britain. From July to the end of 1940 we went through four *Staffelkapitäns*. One of them, Victor Mölders, was shot down right next to me, on a *Jabo*-mission on 7 October 1940 over London, and became a prisoner. I also, as his wingman, received many bullet holes on this occasion, but managed to get home with

a lot of luck. As fighter-bombers we had a 250 kg bomb under the bellies of our Me 109s and this naturally made them slower and less manoeuvrable, but after dropping the bomb we were pure fighters again. The problem really lay in the approach flight to the target, which was mostly London. The attacks of the English fighters were made preferentially on the fighter-bombers so we had to be very careful. We also attacked airfields and convoys; these attacks were always made at low level. An attack on a convoy of 15–20 ships is, in my opinion one of the hardest assignments that can be expected from a fighter-bomber *Staffel*. In these convoy attacks one flew at low level along the length of the convoy to increase the chances of a hit with the bomb, and thereafter further low level attacks were made with our machine guns and cannons. During all this the ships flak shot like crazy and such attacks were thus seldom without loss.

RAF daylight bomber raids against the French coastal areas were rare during the Battle of Britain, but in poor weather they did fly missions. One such was intercepted in filthy weather over the Channel during late October by a *Schwarm* led by Georg Pavenzinger.

I scored six witnessed victories over England and the Channel: four Spitfires over the English mainland and one Spitfire over the Channel, and in addition a Blenheim over the sea just offshore of Dover. The destruction of the Blenheim (27 October 1940) is worth an explanation. In very bad weather four Blenheims were attempting to attack German E-boats in the Channel. I was the *Schwarm* leader of the four readiness aircraft, apart from us on this rainy day there was no other flying taking place. At about 15h00 our headquarters notified us that several English bombers were flying towards German ships in the Channel. In no time we were in the air and over the Channel, after all our airfield lay only a few kilometres away from the coast. It was raining lightly, the cloud base was at about 300 to 400 m. The twin-engined Blenheims were totally surprised, as they had not reckoned on any German fighters in this weather. Just as the Blenheims began their attack on the German ships, we appeared out of the gloom and clouds. Each of us selected a Blenheim and all four were shot down. I actually got two; my second one was already damaged and flying on only one engine, but I left this to my comrade so that each one of us had a victory (in Tony Wood's *Luftwaffe* claims lists, two Blenheims are credited to Pavenzinger, as his third and fourth victories).[85]

On the next day already two people turned up from a propaganda unit and I had to give them a story on this mission with four victories resulting. The real surprise, however, is that although these four victories were recorded in the *Geschwader*'s history, the date, take-off and landing times as well as the names of the successful pilots are missing. I am pretty sure this is only due to nobody else being around on this day of bad weather except for the readiness *Schwarm*, and so no one recorded the take-off and landing times etc., and later on nobody remembered to do it either. I also had a few other victory claims, especially in the time of flying with *Hauptmann* Wiggers, but these only counted as probable victories, as over the English mainland there were no witnesses to confirm these claims. However, I did not survive the Battle of Britain without injury. Altogether during the war I had four crashes, and twice I landed up in hospital.

## Operational Record of a Geschwader Kommodore

Flying logbooks are often seen by modern researchers as examples of relatively trustworthy original documents to reconstruct history. *Geschwader Kommodore* of *JG 52*, Major Hanns Trübenbach had some interesting comments on how his own logbook was managed:

> I took over *Jagdgeschwader 52* on 19 August 1940. The additional contexts and personnel changes related to this cannot be seen in my logbook, as long past the end of 1940 and into 1941, my flying logbook was administered from Calais-Marck. The new *Kommodore* Trübenbach cannot be identified in his logbook. I didn't even know the rank and the name of the soldier who wrote up my logbook. The mistaken entries in the period 31 August to 5 September 1940 (when the missions were entered as 'Escort free chase') typify this crazy time, during which clarity of orders issued left a lot to be desired. I can add that this remark entered on the right hand page of my logbook means nothing particular, beyond that as *Kommodore* and with my wingman, I led the escort and also the formation of the accompanying fighter *Gruppe* or even the entire *Geschwader*, and then left the formation to undertake a free chase or military observation.

Example of a fighter *Kommodore*'s operational life, based on flying logbook, 31 August 1940–27 October 1940: *Major* Hanns Trübenbach, *JG 52* (all missions flown from Calais Marck except for first mission on 27 October, flown from Jurgunblad, 10 minutes' flying time away) (Source: Hanns Trübenbach). Logbooks maintained by clerks of low rank, not by pilots themselves, hence mission descriptions are often somewhat vague or cryptic.

### AUGUST
31: Operation, 10h25–11h20 (126th operational flight); escort, *Freie Jagd*

### SEPTEMBER
3: Operation, 12h00–12h30 (127th op.); escort, *Freie Jagd*
5: Operation, 16h15–17h50 (128th op.); escort, *Freie Jagd*
6: Operation, 18h35–19h38 (129th op.); escort Me 110s
7: Operation, 17h22–18h50 (130th op.); escort for *EGr 210*
11: Operation, 16h32–17h54 (131st op.); escort He 111s to London
14: Operation, 16h15–17h13 (132nd op.); bomber escort to England
15: Operation, 14h55–16h14 (133rd op.); bomber escort to England
18: Operation, 10h07–11h31 (134th op.); bomber escort to London
    Operation, 17h28–18h49 (135th op.); bomber escort to London
20: Operation, 10h35–11h15 (136th op.); *Sperrflug* (protective patrol)
    Operation, 16h25–17h40 (137th op.); *Sperrflug*
23: Operation, 10h18–11h15 (138th op.); bomber escort
24: Operation, 09h18–10h18 (139th op.); bomber escort
27: Operation, 09h54–11h05 (140th op.); bomber escort to London
28: Operation, 10h45–11h45 (141st op.); escort to London
    Operation, 14h05–15h30 (142nd op.); escort to London
30: Operation, 11h00–11h55 (143rd op.); bomber escort to London
    Operation, 14h15–15h10 (144th op.); bomber escort to London

### OCTOBER
1: Operation, 13h45–14h45 (145th op.); escort
   Operation, 16h55–18h15 (146th op.); escort to Folkestone
6: Operation, 15h45–16h55 (147th op.).
11: Operation, 11h30–12h00 (148th op.); dropped bomb
    Operation, 12h40–13h12 (149th op.); dropped bomb
    Operation, 15h00–16h05 (150th op.); dropped bomb London
13: Operation, 14h15–15h20 (151st op.); *Freie Jagd*, London
15: Operation, 09h30–10h45 (152nd op.); *Freie Jagd*, London
    Operation, 13h10–14h15 (153rd op.); *Freie Jagd*, London

22: Operation, 17h15–18h00 (154th op.)
26: Operation, 17h25–18h00 (155th op.)
27: Operation, 10h10–11h10 (156th op.)
    Operation, 17h10–18h20 (157th op.)

## November–December 1940 and Beyond

While the official end of the Battle of Britain was placed at 31 October 1940,[86] less intense combat continued during the rest of the year before fizzling out as winter weather and transfer of many units back to Germany for a rest – and in many cases a paid skiing holiday – led to combat being wound down. For those involved in action in November, however, it was anything but desultory, and the grim round of flying, shooting down and being shot down, injured and killed continued as *Gefreiter* Rudolf Miese, *4/JG 2* found to his cost:

> My twelfth operation to the south coast, which was my seventeenth operational flight overall (on 15 November 1940), was also the last. After we had departed for England from Le Havre at midday, we flew over there again at 16h00. At 7,000–8,000 m height my *Rottenführer*, *Unteroffizier* Dessoy and I left the *Geschwader* formation and shot at a climbing Hurricane squadron. As I pulled up in the low shining sun, shots came through my cabin from left-behind, and immediately it burst into flames. I managed to climb out of the diving machine and somehow opened the parachute. Details of this experience and the related feelings I will spare myself remembering here, it would fill a page. I landed on a road right at the coast. Within five minutes I was receiving medical aid from an RAF doctor, the son of Sir Nevile Henderson, who had been the ambassador in Germany before the war. There followed three and a half months in a small private hospital in Littlehampton, with three operations – I had been shot through the left upper arm which destroyed the elbow joint and had burns on my face and hands. Then I was in the military hospital at Knutsford for five months with an operation to restore my eyelids through skin grafts. In August 1941 I arrived in POW Camp 2 in Oldham.

As had happened to so many beginners in the dangerous game of aerial battle, Rudolf Miese did not last long enough to gain the requisite experience for both survival and success in combat. He also sent me a copy of the RAF initial interrogation report (the so-called K report)[87] which provided some details on his loss. During the combat, where

British intelligence describe him as the *Rottenhund* (i.e. the wingman in a pair), in an initial enemy attack from above and behind two bullets had hit his cabin, starting a small fire and jamming the cockpit hood as he tried to bail out; a second attack was much more devastating and resulted in a blazing aircraft from which he eventually managed to escape. He came down on land badly injured as described above while the burning Me 109 (white 10, *Werkenummer 5947*) ended up in the sea off Felpham near Bognor. Miese had given the purpose of his mission as being a freelance patrol (*Freie Jagd*) and the interrogator noted Beaumont-le-Roger as his base. This does not reflect Miese giving anything away deliberately, but upon capture he was carrying two flight orders with Beaumont-le-Roger as the destination, as noted in the K report. Four further papers on his person gave evidence of visits to Rouen during September, October and November 1940; nothing much escaped the notice of the team of RAF interrogators led by the redoubtable Wing Commander S. D. Felkin, who were responsible for the K reports.[88] *Gefreiter* Miese was noted as having very high morale, despite his burns and wounds, and despite only being 20 years old at the time.

A more unusual event in November was the advent of the Italian Air Force over southern England. This small force, the *Corpo Aereo Italiano*, consisting of 80 Fiat BR 20 bombers, 50 Fiat CR 42 and 48 Fiat G 50 fighters, had begun deploying to Belgium in mid-September 1940, and after a few abortive missions flew their only large raid on 11 November 1940.[89] Once again, that excellent witness, *Major* Hanns Trübenbach, *Kommodore JG 52* was directly involved: 'At that time there were different views on the value and operational possibilities of our Italian comrades; I would never have sent them on operations as they must have been totally inferior to the English. The only Italian fighter *Gruppe* operating on the Channel that was tactically subordinated to me as *Kommodore JG 52* was definitely not capable of operating over England as their aircraft did not have even the slimmest chance of survival. When I every now and then had a talk with their *Kommandeur*, then it seemed as though they blissfully accepted that it was a risky business. When the fighter *Gruppe* of *Oberstleutnant* Bonzano flew its first mission over England on 11 November 1940 this was no longer under my command, as I had already left under orders for Germany on 5 November 1940 to recoup at home with the entire *Geschwader*, then comprising *I* and *II/JG 52* and *I/LG 2*.'

As the bloody year of 1940 closed, so did the Battle of Britain fade into the mists now gathering over the Channel, a body of water that had claimed a multitude of missing victims from both sides. *Oberfeldwebel* Georg Pavenzinger, 2/*JG 51* recalls the transition from Channel to Germany: 'In December 1940 the English operations were finished for my *Geschwader*, and the entire body of pilots was given a skiing holiday from the end of December till about 10 January 1941, in Zürs am Arlberg in Austria. Prior to that we had moved to Mannheim, for re-equipment. At the end of January 1941 I was ordered to Zerbst as a fighter instructor; the training schools urgently needed new blood, as most of the existing instructors lacked operational experience. I thus had to teach the students and the teachers about tactics and the experiences hard won in the Battle of Britain.' After their rest, *JG 52* returned to active service again, as *Kommodore* Hanns Trübenbach recalled: 'On 26 December 1940 we returned to active flying, but now to the Dutch coast and Holland itself. The *Geschwaderstab* moved to Katwyk, and only I/*LG 2* under *Hauptmann* Ihlefeld went back to France, at Calais–Marck. Already on 27 March 1941 this *Gruppe* received orders to move to Bulgaria for the Yugoslav operation.' While many Germans and battle participants insist that the Battle of Britain continued on until the invasion of Russia on 22 June 1941 put an end to it, the campaign along the Channel coast in the first half of 1941 was very different, lacking any large daylight raids on Britain and being dominated by *Luftwaffe* fighter sweeps along the coastal areas of southern England, with the first tentative RAF sweeps with small bomber formations attacking coastal targets on the other side. This will be discussed in the next chapter. Clearly the Battle of Britain had terminated with the end of 1940.

## The Great Aces: Mölders, Galland, Wick and Oesau

The top-scoring German aces for the official period of the Battle of Britain, 10 July 1940–31 October 1940,[90] are given in the table below.

The top-scoring German aces, 10 July 1940 – 31 October 1940: number of German Air Ministry-confirmed victories[91]

| | |
|---|---|
| *Major* Adolf Galland, *Stab/JG 26* | 35 |
| *Hauptmann* Walter Oesau, *Stab III/JG 51* | 32 |
| *Major* Helmut Wick, *Stab/JG 2* | 31 |
| *Major* Werner Mölders, *Stab/JG 51* | 29 |

| | |
|---|:---:|
| *Oberleutnant* Herbert Ihlefeld, *1/LG 2* | 21 |
| *Oberleutnant* Hermann-Friedrich Joppien, *Stab I/JG 51* | 19 |
| *Hauptmann* Gerhard Schöpfel, *Stab III/JG 26* | 17 |
| *Oberfeldwebel* Werner Machold, *9/JG 2* | 16 |
| *Oberleutnant* Gustav Sprick, *8/JG 26* | 15 |
| *Hauptmann* Horst Tietzen, *5/JG 51* | 15 |
| *Oberfeldwebel* Siegfried Schnell, *4/JG 2* | 15 |
| *Leutnant* Erich Schmidt, *9/JG 53* | 15 |

If one looks at the total confirmed scores at the end of October 1940, then Mölders was on top with 54, followed by Galland (49), Wick (44) and Oesau (38); by the end of 1940, the order had become: Galland (57), Wick (56), Mölders (55) and Oesau (39).[92] For the formal definition of the Battle of Britain, then, Galland was easily the top ace, with little to choose between Oesau, Mölders and Wick, all three well ahead of the rest of the pack; only five pilots claimed more than 20 victories in the campaign. The top scores were mostly posted by unit leaders, as their position brought the best opportunities for scoring; even the senior NCOs in the table above were *Schwarmführern*. The rivalry among German fighter pilots for the top scores and for the decorations that went with them remained a very powerful influence right through the war, and at this relatively early stage Mölders and Galland were the two names on everybody's lips. They rapidly accumulated the very top honours; both were *Geschwader Kommodoren* with great leadership gifts to match their large responsibilities. Helmut Wick, the 'third man', a favourite of Göring's who went from *Staffelkapitän* to *Kommodore* in only 45 days,[93] was killed on 28 November 1940; Tietzen had died much earlier, on 18 August 1940.[94] *Hauptmann* Hennig Strümpell was very well acquainted with the famous Helmut Wick:

Helmut Wick first flew in my *Staffel*, *3/JG 2* over France and then got his own *Staffel* in my *Gruppe* (*I/JG 2*), before he finally became *Geschwaderkommodore*. I knew him well and I esteemed him greatly as a person and as a comrade. He was an open and straight-up person, bright, happy and full of life, absolutely dependable, someone who never let anyone down. He was a gifted fighter pilot. He had exceptional vision and was a sure shot, and he controlled his aircraft in all situations perfectly. He always flew at full throttle, and always flew at top speed as soon as an aerial combat began. That was a great advantage, because he could hardly be surprised, but the downside of this was engine wear as no engine could take this for long. As a result, once I had his engine changed at night as a precaution, without his knowing it. I also feared that this could have been one cause of his being shot down, because he had to drag his aircraft home on a sick engine. After a combat the unit was mostly scattered so far apart that one was suddenly alone and then you had to also fly back over the Channel. Erich Leie, who I knew less well, was also a good fighter pilot and an excellent comrade. He flew for a while as the leader of the *Jabo-Staffel*, that flew along the *Knickbein* beams (a radio beam guidance system much used also by the German night bombers in the *Blitz*) in bad weather, over the Channel to make low-level attacks with bombs on RAF bases.

*Oberfeldwebel* Erich Rudorffer, then still an NCO, also flew in *I/JG 2* and was a close friend of Helmut Wick. He had qualified as an airline pilot before the war and was originally posted to a bomber unit before transferring to fighters in January 1940 – a fortunate move, as he was to go on to great things, ultimately surviving the war with 222 victory claims to his name, scored in East and West, over Africa, including four-engined bombers, and while flying the Me 262. After the war he went back to his profession, captaining airliners from 1948 to 1968. 'I knew Helmut Wick very well, we had already flown together in many air combats over France. I also flew on his final mission in his *Schwarm*. Helmut Wick was killed, not missing! I saw his aircraft hit the water. As a person and a pilot, he was outstanding.'

## The Balance Sheet
Losses during the daylight battle from 10 July 1940 to 31 October 1940 tot up as follows: 1,887 *Luftwaffe* aircraft and 2,698 airmen lost (almost all destroyed by Fighter Command), as against 1,023 fighters and 544 pilots lost to Fighter Command of the RAF; an additional 376 Bomber Command and 148 Coastal Command aircraft bring total RAF losses for the battle period to 1,547.[95] Underlining the *Luftwaffe*'s sound defeat was the decline in fighter pilots available in operational units, from 906 at the beginning of July 1940 to 735 at the beginning of September 1940; in stark contrast, British operational fighter pilot numbers grew from 1,259 on 6 July 1940 to 1,796 on 2 November 1940.[96] The 1,023 British fighters lost were balanced by 223 Me 110s

and 650 Me 109s (total German fighter loss thus 873) lost to the *Luftwaffe*.[97] Despite the opinions of several witnesses earlier in this chapter, the *Luftwaffe* had clearly lost the Battle of Britain; they did not attain air superiority in time for the planned invasion to be launched while the weather was still good. While German aircraft and crew availability declined over the battle (fighter strength by 30 per cent and bomber strength by 25 per cent from August to December 1940),[98] those of the RAF increased. It is very important here to bear in mind that the RAF was never in a position where it was unable to meet a raid in sufficient strength, nor were any major air bases non-operational for more than a few hours; only Manston and Lympne were out of action for longer, and they were not critical airfields.[99]

Assessing successes claimed (given below as totals claimed by the units and not totals confirmed by the German Air Ministry) for the various fighter *Geschwader* is difficult on a comparative basis, as reliable and relatively complete data are only available for different specific time periods:

JG 2:    307–319 victory claims (July–December 1940);[100]

JG 3:    179 victory claims (30 June 1940–31 October 1940) plus another 41 claims (1 November 1940–9 June 1941);[101]

JG 26:   285 victory claims (July–December 1940);[102]

JG 27:   147 victory claims (July–November 1940);[103]

JG 51:   588 victory claims (July 1940–May 1941) (includes 186 for I/ JG 77 which operated as a IV *Gruppe* in this *Geschwader*);[104]

JG 52:   102 victory claims by I, II, III/JG 52 (plus a few more from Stab?) (July–October 1940) plus another 39 claims for the three *Gruppen* (November 1940–21 June 1941);[105]

I/LG 2:  92 victory claims (30 June 1940–31 October 1940) plus another 24 claims (November 1940–March 1941) (operated under JG 52 command later in the battle);[106]

JG 77:   Stab, II, III *Gruppen* (November 1940–March 1941) made 14 victory claims;[107]

JG 53:   218 victory claims (8 August 1940–11 December 1940) plus another 32 claims (March–June 1941);[108]

JG 54:   238 victory claims (12 August 1940–1 November 1940).[109]

Clearly, JGs 2, 26 and 51 led the field, with the most lacklustre performance by JG 52, although their *Gruppen* were not assigned to the Channel Front for long periods of the battle.

German fighter losses were catastrophic in the longer term as most pilots lost, whether killed, missing or POW, were pre-war professionals with long training and experience behind them. They were the future leaders and senior instructors of the *Luftwaffe* and their absence in the long war that still lay ahead would become an ever more crucial factor. In addition to the dead and prisoners, many were also wounded and either never flew again or not in combat.

*Luftwaffe* fighter unit (Me 109) pilot losses over two periods: 1 July 1940–31 October 1940 and 1 November 1940–21 June 1941 (+ = killed, M = missing, POW = prisoner of war, W = wounded; all losses in action only)

| Geschwader | 1 July 1940–31 October 1940 | 1 November 1940–21 June 1941 |
|---|---|---|
| JG 2[110] | 13+, 5M, 13 POW, 4W | 6+, 1M, 3 POW, 2W |
| JG 3[111] | 18+, 6M, 26 POW, 8W | 3+, 4M, 1 POW, 3W |
| JG 26[112] | 22+, 21 POW, 4 W | 13+, 9 POW, 6W |
| JG 27[113] | 17+, 18M, 24 POW, 19W | 2 POW |
| JG 51(incl. I/JG 77)[114] | 38+, 29 POW, 1W | 20+, 1M, 4 POW |
| JG 52 (*Stab* losses excl.)[115] | 15+, 4M, 28 POW, 2W | 2+, 1 POW, 1W |
| I/LG 2[116] | 9+, 1M, 3 POW | 2+ |
| JG 53[117] | 21+, 10M, 24 POW, 7W | 1+, 4M, 6 POW, 2W |
| JG 54[118] | 18+, 13M, 10 POW | 1+, 4M, 1W |
| JG 77 (*Stab, II, III/JG 77*)[119] | 0 | 0 |
| Totals | 171+, 57M, 178 POW, 45 W | 48+, 14M, 26 POW, 15W |

At least 406 pilots were thus lost during July–October 1940, with a further 88 from November 1940 to 21 June 1941. These were indeed catastrophic losses.

While information on claims totals by German Me 109 units is available, that for the Me 110-equipped *Geschwader* and *Gruppen* is paltry. The table below provides a summary of all German Air Ministry-confirmed fighter claims made for different stages of the battle, the data being derived from Tony Wood's summaries of surviving *Luftwaffe* records, which are not necessarily complete.[120]

German fighter *Geschwader* - confirmed claims for periods during the Battle of Britain; data not necessarily complete[121]

| Geschwader | 1–9 July 1940 | 10 July–10 August 1940 | 11–31 August 1940 | September 1940 | October 1940 | Total: 10 July–31 October 1940 | Total: 1 July–31 October 1940 |
|---|---|---|---|---|---|---|---|
| JG 2 | 2 | 10 | 77 | 117 | 54 | 258 | 260 |
| JG 3 | 0 | 9 | 68 | 69 | 17 | 163 | 163 |
| JG 26 | 2 | 13 | 115 | 97 | 26 | 251 | 253 |
| JG 27 | 0 | 40 | 33 | 59 | 11 | 143 | 143 |
| JG 51 | 28 | 85 | 124 | 134 | 73 | 416 | 444 |
| JG 52 | 1 | 5 | 21 | 50 | 12 | 88 | 89 |
| JG 53 | 0 | 3 | 65 | 107 | 27 | 202 | 202 |
| JG 54 | 6 | 12 | 56 | 68 | 48 | 184 | 190 |
| II/LG 2 | 3 | 2 | 25 | 41 | 7 | 75 | 78 |
| ZG 2 | 0 | 0 | 0 | 0 | 0 | 0 | 0 |
| ZG 26 | 0 | 14 | 43 | 27 | 1 | 85 | 85 |
| ZG 76 | 0 | 0 | 42 | 25+23 ASM | 0 | 67+23 ASM | 67+23 ASM |
| EGr 210 | 0 | 1 | 3 | 0 | 0 | 4 | 4 |
| V/LG 1 | 2 | 11 | 25 | 5+5 ASM | 0 | 41+5 ASM | 43+5 ASM |
| Totals | 44 | 205 | 697 | 799+28 ASM | 276 | 1977+28 ASM | 2021+28 ASM |

JG 51 includes II/JG 77 as a fourth *Gruppe*. No confirmed claims data for ZG 2 preserved. ASM = *Anerkennung später möglich* – confirmation possible later. EGr = *Erprobungsgruppe* (experimental group).

While honours between *ZG 26* and *ZG 76* appear to have been close to equal, *V/LG 1*, with only one *Gruppe* compared to three each for these two *Geschwadern*, had a much higher confirmed claim rate. *ZG 2* was decimated early during August. *Erprobungsgruppe 210*, a specialised dive-bombing unit, understandably made few victory claims, and was also badly hit during the first half of August 1940. Interestingly, the total daytime RAF fighter loss for the period between 10 July and 31 October 1940 noted above, namely 1,023,[122] is just over half the total confirmed fighter claims made by the *Luftwaffe* fighters for the same period (1,977 + 28 ASM victory claims, table above). Bearing in mind that most British fighters were lost to the German fighters, and that the vast majority of German claims are for RAF fighters rather than bombers,[123] this reflects a confirmed victory claim rate of about twice the real RAF fighter losses. This is by no means uncommon for a long-lasting and intensively fought aerial battle. The RAF fighters claimed 2,741 German aircraft from 10 July 1940–31 October 1940, as against 1,887 German daylight aircraft losses – bearing in mind that the vast majority of *Luftwaffe* casualties were due to the RAF fighters, their claim rate was about one and a half times real German losses.[124]

The highest number of confirmed claims went to *JG 51*, and despite having a fourth *Gruppe* in *I/JG 77* attached, it was still the best on a per *Gruppe* basis. *JG 2* stands in second place with *JG 26* just behind. In contrast, *JG 52*'s performance was poor, but explained partially by much less time at the Channel fighting front for two of its *Gruppen*. In comparison, *I/LG 2* claimed almost as many victories as the entire *JG 52*. The Me 110 units were just not in it at all, their low confirmed claims totals being matched by their heavy casualties, obviously lessening effectiveness; they were best when flying in large numbers at high altitude, and making diving attacks on RAF fighters, followed by an immediate zoom back to higher altitude (as effectively used on 31 August 1940 and 3 September 1940). *JG 51* was the first full-strength *Geschwader* on the Channel in July, as reflected in their dominating the July scores. Me 110 unit claims were effectively restricted to August–September 1940, and by October they had been withdrawn from the battle, some disbanded, and most converted soon to night fighters.

# 6

# The Channel Front, 1941–42

The predominant daylight operations flown by the RAF in 1941–42, involved large fighter sweeps and complex sets of escorting wings for small bomber formations, the whole planned to entice the *Luftwaffe* fighter arm into the air under unfavourable conditions. Some of the most vivid memories of the air battles fought over the Channel Front during 1941–42 are provided by *Leutnant* Otto Stammberger, who flew first in *9/JG 26* and subsequently led *4/JG 26* as an *Oberleutnant*. He was shot down and seriously wounded in May 1943, and thereafter, although remaining in *JG 26 Schlageter*, was no longer able to fly on operations. Below he notes the fundamental change that the onset of the British 'Non-Stop Offensive', launched upon the German invasion of Russia on 22 June 1941, brought to the Channel Front.

The 'Non-Stop Offensive 1941' represented a fundamental change in the air war in the West. We no longer flew over enemy territory, but over our own, occupied territory. Those of us stationed in the West on the coast had every day to wait in full flying equipment, from early morning till evening at our aircraft, in the shade of their wings, to be able to leap into them in seconds and be ready for take-off. We had two flying suits, one for summer comprising a linen overall, and for the winter a leather suit. There were no instructions or enforced regulations to actually wear the specific suit in its foreseen season, and each pilot was allowed to wear whatever he felt most comfortable flying in; even dress uniform with collar and tie was allowed! Due to the cold at high altitudes we always wore, even in summer, our fleece-lined flying boots. Mae Wests had to be worn, as we never knew whether we would be vectored over the sea or not. Additional equipment for flying over the sea was the rubber dinghy, which when folded up served as either seat or back cushion in the aircraft, and which was attached to our bodies, as well as a flare pistol and pouch of colourant. This pouch was ripped open in the water, and produced an approximately 25 m-diameter circle of bright yellow colour that from the air was visible over quite long distances. And of course we had parachutes. These and the dinghy always lay ready in the aircraft, on the seat, and we jumped in with Mae West, flare pistol and cartridges already attached to ourselves, onto the seats where our mechanics strapped us in, also attaching 'chute and dinghy at the same time.

In summer, the continuous wearing of life jackets, flare pistol, ammunition for this, all on top of the leather suit, and wearing of flying boots on our feet, was an ordeal, but one was very glad of them all when you had it all to hand when you needed it! Yes, and on the life jacket there was also a compass attached, and in the large uniform pockets on our thighs there were the emergency rations, consisting of chocolate, biscuits and Pervitin. When we had to bail out, we did not become prisoners, but were so to say 'at home'. This reality gave us great confidence and thereby also superiority. We needed this, as, due to the massive transfer of fighter *Geschwader* to the East, we remained behind in the West with only *JG 2 Richthofen* and *JG 26 Schlageter*, to cover an area from the Atlantic coast to the mouth of the River Scheldt, in absolute numerical inferiority. This did not ever change through to 1945 and the end of the war; we were always inferior. Added to this was the tactical advantage of the attacker: they always flew higher and thus enjoyed the superior position. We as the defenders had to climb up to heights of 7,000 to 8,000 m at 220–230 km/h and once there were attacked by the Spitfires flying 1,000 m higher and at speeds 300 km/h faster than us – after all, they were flying straight and level and did not have to climb! We were always attacked from superior altitude and suffered heavy losses. We never really got at the Blenheim bombers, which also flew very fast.

Only when the relief of early English escorting fighters by later ones did not occur at the correct place and time over Northern France did our luck change and then we could indeed attack the Blenheims. We were continuously picked up above heights of 1,500 m by the English radar and then our positions were passed on to the escorting Spitfires, so that the Tommies knew exactly where we were climbing up and then they could soon see us climbing up from below and the first British machines were detailed for their attacks. Naturally we had to defend ourselves and sought to avoid the Spitfires with wily and tight turns in the opposite direction. Thus large dogfights developed covering big areas of the sky, with friend and foe being difficult to differentiate, and between 15 and 20 machines flew all over the place in an aerial volume bounded on each side by about 1,000 m. The more machines that were involved in such a dogfight, the greater did the area of sky being taken up in battle expand. The Tommies were under pressure as they had to fly back home over the Channel, 35 to 150 km wide, and thus had to choose their chances to break away and live to fight another day. The victories we achieved exceeded our own losses, but it must be said that we only counted the dead pilots as losses, and not the total of aircraft shot down. Reliable statistics of victories and losses are thus not readily available, and I believe that both sides were affected approximately equally, if there was not even some advantage to the English.

Despite Stammberger's closing comments above, these RAF operations have often been painted by post-war historians as something of a fiasco. This is especially so due to the much heavier losses suffered by the British fighters compared to their opponents. Those for 1941 and known German fighter claims[1] are summarised in the table below, bearing in mind available data sources and their reliability, as stressed by Otto Stammberger.

Combat statistics for Channel Front operations of *JG 2* and *JG 26* against RAF sweep operations, 1941[2]

| | JG 26 | | | | JG 2 | | | | JG 26 claims | JG 2 claims | RAF losses |
|---|---|---|---|---|---|---|---|---|---|---|---|
| | Aircraft lost | Aircraft damaged | P + | PW | Aircraft lost | Aircraft damaged | P + | PW | | | |
| January–June | 30 | 15 | 15 | 7 | 19 | 2 | 12 | 0 | 95 | 60 | 68 |
| July–December | 51 | 25 | 34 | 10 | 31 | 18 | 17 | 3 | 346–348 | 367 | 416–419 |
| 1941 | 81 | 40 | 49 | 17 | 50 | 20 | 29 | 3 | 441–443 | 487 | 484–487 |

P + = pilots killed, missing, POW; PW = pilots wounded. Claims data essentially claims submitted by unit. RAF losses are for destroyed aircraft (including fighters and bombers) only, and excluding those only damaged (whether crashed, force-landed, or landed at base damaged). Additional claims of RAF aircraft made by operational training units = 43; claims over Dutch and German coasts = 9 (by *JG 1*, *II/JG 53*, *II/ZG 76*). Note that *JG 2* losses are incomplete for the second half of 1941, and thus for 1941 as a whole as well.

What is noticeable from the above statistics is that fully 77 per cent of all claims made by *JG 2* and *JG 26* in 1941 were for Spitfires, and only 9.5 per cent for bombers. The German fighter pilots also claimed almost twice as many victories as are reflected in total losses for the RAF, although inclusion of damaged British aircraft would have resulted in a better picture of claims-to-losses ratios. This sort of ratio is by no means excessive and can be considered fairly typical of aerial combat generally. Far more excessive were the optimistic RAF claims for 909 victories as against total German fighter losses, to all causes, of 183 during 1941.[3] As can be seen above, *JG 2* and *26* only lost 131 aircraft in combat, with some few more from training units as well as from *JG 1* and others stationed in Holland. During 1942, summary statistics[4] show 972 German fighter claims along the Channel–Dutch Front for 272 of their own fighters lost to all causes; RAF claims this time were much fewer at around 500, largely reflecting the dominance of the Fw 190 and the slow introduction of the Spitfire IX, which could match it easily if flown well. With the very limited size of the British bomber formations on these large and often complex sweep operations, damage to ground targets was not very significant, and in thus maintaining an offensive stance over northern France the RAF lost heavily while inflicting significantly fewer losses on the enemy; they thus lost the war of attrition in this campaign. The complex arrangements of direct escort wings, target support wings, sweep-in and sweep-out wings led to confusion if timings were not held to almost perfection; when they were not, the *Luftwaffe* fighters were quick to take advantage of the situation, despite the British numbers. It is a moot point whether the loss of valuable RAF aircraft and trained aircrew in 1941–42 brought much benefit to the British war effort, and the point can be made that perhaps at least some of the modern fighter resources thus expended could have been better spent over Malta and the Western Desert, never mind in the Far East against the Japanese onslaught.

Despite these statistics (and statistics are seldom the perfect measure of anything), the almost constant forays of the British into German airspace above France, Belgium and Holland must have imposed considerable nervous strain on the *Luftwaffe* pilots concerned, who had little opportunity to relax. Despite marked success in air combat, the German pilots do not seem to recall an easy or even victorious campaign during 1941–42. Again, Otto Stammberger of *JG 26* reminds the reader: 'We were always on the defensive, had to always climb up to the high-flying Tommies flying in over our territory with about 260 km/h on the clock, and we were as a consequence regularly attacked from above by enemies flying much faster. This situation did not change for the rest of the war. The English were fair opponents; in their ranks there were also Czechs, Poles and Norwegians, who hated us due to the occupation of their homelands. These pilots gave no quarter and destroyed our aircraft with pilot and all. The English in contrast turned away from their attacks on seriously damaged aircraft to give the pilot a chance to get out of the machine.' The reality of war experience did thus not depend only on the numbers of casualties; the German obsession with victory claim statistics was thus, at least to some extent, misplaced.

The initial advantage of the German fighter pilots due to their greater experience, starting with the Spanish Civil War, and their much better tactical fighter formations adopted as a result, was largely negated by the time that the Non-Stop Offensive began as their British opponents had by then largely adopted the same tactics. *Hauptmann* Gerhard Schöpfel, *Gruppenkommandeur III/JG 26*, promoted to *Major* and *Kommodore JG 26* from 6 December 1941, and thus one of the main fighter leaders in *JG 26* on the Channel Front, emphasizes the benefits of the pair and four-aircraft ('finger four' in RAF parlance) formations as the basic unit: 'After our experiences flying operations in the Spanish Civil War (Legion Condor), we already before the war changed fighter formations from the vic of three aircraft to pairs/ fours in the fighter units; this meant that the smallest unit was two aircraft (*Rotte*), two *Rotten* made up a *Schwarm* of four aircraft, three *Schwärme* made a *Staffel* of 12 aircraft. Using these formations, pilots could see much better and more effectively protect each other, the units were more manoeuvrable, and they could cover a much larger air space with better vision. In the operations in 1941–42, there was a principle that we only took off when bombers flew in with the British fighter sweeps. The assembly of the British aircraft formations over England was detected by our radio-listening service. Upon recognition of such a mixed formation approaching, we were ordered to cockpit readiness (*Sitzbereitschaft*) and then later given the order to take off. We strove to attack the enemy formations as they flew in over the coast from the sun if possible. The fighter *Gruppen* attacked the enemy formations one after the other, first as complete *Gruppen* and then as *Rotten* in continuous attacks.' It was largely due to the very skilful leadership of the German fighter formations by men such as *Major*

Schöpfel, as well as good controlling of available fighters by radar, that the *Luftwaffe* pilots achieved a successful defence at reasonable cost along the Channel Front in 1941–42.

The other main fighter unit employed along the Channel coast, mostly to the west of *JG 26*, was the *Richthofen Geschwader*, *JG 2*. While the Spitfire remained a threat always, *JG 2* experienced few problems when they were able to get at the small bomber formations flying under protection of the sweeps, as recalled by one of their most experienced veterans, *Oberleutnant* Erich Rudorffer, *II/JG 2*: 'Until July 1943 I was with the *Richthofen Geschwader* and flew the Me 109 and Fw 190. I remember the pilots of the English units as worthy and fair opponents. In this time I served as *Staffeloffizier* of the 2nd *Staffel*, as *Gruppenadjutant* of the *II/JG 2*, as *Staffelkapitän* of the 6th *Staffel* and finally as *Gruppenkommandeur* of *II/JG 2* (acting from January to May 1943, thereafter confirmed in the post till August 1943),[5] with *Einsätze* – missions – flown in northern France. The two aircraft, Me 109 and Spitfire, were always approximately equal to each other. They were both very good fighters for their time. The operations against Blenheim, Short Stirling, Wellington and Halifax bombers were no problem, but against the four-engined American Boeings later on, they were really "Flying Fortresses".'

However, not all the action was on the Channel Front, some units (particularly of *JG 1*) being stationed further to the north-east, along the Dutch coast. Here in the beginning things were relatively quiet, but in time this became a major route for the American heavy bomber incursions, particularly from 1943 onwards. During 1941–42 opposition was mainly from the RAF, as illustrated by the following combat report or *Gefechtsbericht*, submitted by *Feldwebel* Hutter, *5/JG 1* on 9 May 1942 in support of his claim for a probable victory over a British Spitfire.[6] 'On 9 May 1942 at 17h20 the *Staffel* took off to intercept an English formation west of Vlissingen. We sighted this formation in grid square XF 3, and manoeuvred behind them. I attacked the last aircraft from above and behind. In the same instant I saw that I was in turn being attacked from the right and above and I had to turn away. I could thus no longer see what happened to the machine I attacked. *Unteroffizier* Stellfeld who was flying with me saw this aircraft spin down, on fire and pulling a strong smoke trail after it. He was also not able to see it crash.'

## 1941: Operations along the Channel Before the Non-Stop Offensive

During May 1941, the majority of the German fighter *Geschwader* departed to the East in preparation for the upcoming offensive against the Soviet Union, launched on 22 June 1941. Prior to that, the first five months along the Channel were a rather strange mixture of very early RAF sweep operations with small Blenheim formations to do the bombing, in parallel with German fighter incursions over southern England in a low-key continuation of the previous summer and autumn raids. *Oberleutnant* Günther Scholz, *Staffelkapitän 7/JG 54* succinctly summed it up thus: '1 January 1941–28 March 1941, air defence in the operational area of *Jafü 3*, based at Cherbourg. Operations against southern England.' Most of the *Geschwaders* had been given a break over Christmas 1940–41, having moved back to Germany for the purpose, where many also enjoyed skiing holidays at Göring's expense. However, very early in the new year, it was back to the serious business of an unfinished air war for many, while some units remained in Germany, particularly the Me 110-equipped formations, which now mostly converted to night fighters after their slaughter in the Battle of Britain. *Feldwebel* Joachim Robel, rear gunner/radio operator in *6/ZG 76* recalled this relative reprieve: 'At the end of 1940 we moved to Jever, northern Germany. Here we took over coastal patrols and defence as well as looking after the German shipping to Norway.' A few Me 110 crewmen still experienced missions across the Channel, even those newly posted to their units such as *Unteroffizier* Josef Neuhaus, *II/ZG 26*: 'After my transfer to the *Ergänzungsgruppe* of ZG 26, for a few days I flew my first operations over England, before moving to the Balkans.' Re-equipment of the Me 109 units with the much improved F-model also took place, providing better opportunities for success, as experienced by *Unteroffizier* Alfred Seidl, *8/JG 53*: 'January to March 1941, with the *Einsatzstaffel* at Dieppe on the Channel, flying standing patrols – with enemy contacts. In March 1941, transferred to *III/JG 53*, then in Mannheim converting on to the Bf 109 F2. Transferred back to the Channel, based at Berg sur Mer, and then to Maldegen (Belgium). Operations flown against England, and aerial combats there with Spitfires. My first victory, a Spitfire V (on 17 May 1941).'[7] Another *Pik-As Geschwader* comrade, *Feldwebel* Josef Ederer, *3/JG 53* joined his unit a few months earlier and could only notch up a few barrage balloons in missions across the Channel: 'At the beginning of 1941 I was transferred to *3/JG 53*. With the *Pik-As Geschwader* I flew missions from France to England. Victories over England were three barrage balloons over Dover.'

Another new arrival, this time in *4/JG 52*, was Adolf Glunz, who later became a major ace on the Channel Front after transfer to *JG 26*. A short extract from his logbook gives an idea of the operational life of a front-line Channel pilot at this time, shortly before his departure to fight briefly on the Russian front prior to his joining *JG 26* towards the end of July 1941. The term *Einsatz* in this logbook excerpt normally refers to a flight that did not cross over into enemy airspace (i.e. mission over the Channel, not England), so '*Englandflug*' below on 20 May 1941 is, strictly speaking, incorrect. Being over German waters, the *Frontflug*, if no enemy was met, would similarly not have been counted as a *Feindflug*, which is defined as taking place over enemy territory or having enemy contact.

Example of a fighter pilot's operational life, based on flying logbook, 20 May 1941–9 June 1941: *Unteroffizier* Adolf Glunz, *4/JG 52*; flying Me 109 E and F and based at Ostende (central Belgian coast) throughout (Source: Adolf Glunz via Lothair Vanoverbeke)

| | |
|---|---|
| 20 May: | *Einsatz*, 11h58–13h00; *Englandflug* without meeting enemy |
| | Scramble, 16h06–16h37 |
| 21 May: | Scramble, 17h02–17h23 |
| | Scramble, 17h56–19h06 |
| 22 May: | Weather reconnaissance, 11h03–11h17 |
| 24 May: | Scramble, 05h55–06h05 |
| | Convoy patrol, 17h15–18h41; *Frontflug* |
| 28 May: | Scramble, 10h24–10h46 |
| | Scramble, 19h52–20h23 |

On 9 June 1941 the *Staffel* left Ostende for Münster en route to the Eastern Front (Münster–Lüneburg–Stargard–Elbing–Suwalki; total flying time of 4 hours and 35 minutes, arrived Suwalki on 13 June 1941)

Horst Geyer, whom I met in South Africa in September 1990, was *General* Ernst Udet's adjutant, and with Udet (who was the technical and production chief of the *Luftwaffe* at the time)[8] visited many frontline units during the French and Battle of Britain campaigns as part of his regular duties. These included a visit to *JG 51*'s *Kommodore* Werner Mölders at Mardýck on the Channel during the latter battle. On a later visit to Berlin, Mölders, on hearing of *Oberleutnant* Geyer's early training as a fighter pilot, invited him to join him for some time, which Geyer did, flying as *Buzzard 2* in *JG 51*'s *Geschwaderstab*. Mölders taught him all he knew, and was blessed with phenomenal eyesight; he gradually led Horst Geyer to achieve his first victories on the Channel Front against the RAF in 1941: four Spitfires, claimed on 26 February 1941, 12 March, 8 April and 16 April 1941. Then on 8 May 1941 he shot down three without the aid of his mentor, who was then away preparing for the upcoming offensive against Russia. When *JG 51* transferred eastwards, Geyer had, reluctantly, to return to his job as Udet's adjutant.

While Horst Geyer flew in *Stab/JG 51*, where he enjoyed the personal tuition of the master in addition to his already well-developed flying skills, a much younger beginner in *JG 51*, *Oberfähnrich* Hans Strelow of *5/JG 51*, recorded in his diary[9] that he found his early operations against the British incursions across the Channel much more confusing, with haze making his life challenging and dangerous over northern France on 21 May 1941:

Many Blenheims with fighter escort are reported, some over St Omer and some over Dunkirk. To cut off those approaching from St Omer, the two of us flew in the direction of Ramsgate and then once in the middle of the Channel we flew parallel with the French coast. The English were reported at 4,200 m near Calais. We climbed to this height. Suddenly we saw beneath us – about 600 m lower down – about 18 Blenheims flying in columns, and above them on both sides a large bunch of fighter escorts. At first I couldn't believe that they could all be Tommies, without a lot of Me 109s having already joined them. But it was so. The two of us now tried to work out how to attack this formation and climbed up to 5,000–6,000 m. Every time we thought we had avoided one or the other lot of English fighters, more of them suddenly appeared above us out of the haze, so that we urgently had to avoid them again. This happened three times.

On the third occasion a mass of Spitfires was flying to our left about 300 m higher, one of which was separated from the mass and flying closer to us. When this third lot appeared we rapidly made a sharp turn to the right. Until the last minute I had kept my eyes on this separated aircraft in order to observe whether he had seen us and if he would then attack. However, he was only flying a very gentle right-hand turn. After a moment (H. had once more dived downwards, and I had followed him) I saw a Spitfire about

200 m behind me, turning away to the right again. About this I learned later that the Spitfire had turned in behind me and shot from about 200 m, but missed me. H. had told me over the radio to turn, but I did not hear him; he then dived steeply, and I as well, but without throttling up and unaware of what had been happening behind me. H., who was flying ahead of me to the right, then turned tightly into the Spitfire, which then turned even tighter past him and flew back to its formation. H. made a left turn into the haze. As I had fallen somewhat behind, I cut the corner and flew towards where I expected him to reappear. However, he did not reappear, as he suddenly saw new Tommies ahead of him and did a right turn.

I looked for him for some minutes without success. Then I flew behind the large formation for a while, continuously looking carefully in all directions and particularly behind me, until the Downs of Deal appeared below. Then I heard in my earphones something to the effect that English fighters were flying interception patrols along the English south coast. I thought to myself, there are already over 50 fighters here, when some more join them, then it will get really dangerous. Thus I turned around, as I saw directly below me the English coast. Then I appreciated how helpless one was alone, as you could not fully observe directly behind you. Thank God this did not end with something nasty happening. About 30 kilometres north of Cap Gris Nez I came out of a particularly thick patch of haze and saw about 300-400 m in front of me in 5,000 m a so-called *Idiotenreihe* (a German sarcastic description for poor and vulnerable RAF fighter formations) of seven or eight aircraft. This formation was approaching me at a sharp angle and I pulled up to avoid being caught in an unfavourable position. I let the formation fly past me and then turned in behind the last one. I shot with both machine guns, 50 rounds per gun and let him fly through the burst. He shuddered briefly and then flew on. My fire had been opened at about 100 m. As I did not press the button for the cannon, I saw no visible damage, although the tracers disappeared into the enemy aircraft. I then turned around again in order to hang onto this last aircraft in the formation, but saw nothing any more, as they had disappeared into the haze out of which I had just flown. Then I flew back home again.

Among the many fighter *Geschwader* to enjoy their Christmas 1940 break in Germany following the ordeal of the Battle of Britain was *JG 52*, led by *Major* Hanns Trübenbach. Below he tells a very interesting anecdote about a small dinner party in Holland in early January 1941, where Göring showed surprising pessimism about the war prospects at a very early stage of the conflict:

When we returned to the front at the beginning of January 1941, the entire Channel coast up to the northern tip of Holland had been divided up into defensive zones. It was often pitiful how my *Geschwader JG 52* was split up into penny packets to fill some gap in the defensive system somewhere. My Staff and one of my *Jagdgruppen* was transferred to Holland, flying from Katwijk. My old *Jagdgruppe*, I/LG 2 moved to Sofia, the capital of Bulgaria, under its *Kommandeur Hauptmann* Ihlefeld. Only *JG 26* under Galland remained in forward positions along the Channel, otherwise everything else was moving around and often to no purpose. From Belgium and Holland, *Gruppe*- and *Staffel*-sized fighter incursions were made over England. The *Kommodore* of *JG 52* often flew alone with his *Schwarm* to the other side on free chase missions. There were hardly any contacts with enemy aircraft! (Trübenbach did claim a Spitfire, however, on 14 February 1941.) In early January 1941 when I had to report to my military superior (*Wehrmacht* Commander Holland) in the Netherlands, he said to me: 'Trübenbach, you can stay over here. Göring and his party are coming to supper and that will probably be interesting.' The military commander of Holland was *General* Christiansen, a *Pour le Merite* flyer from the First World War and a friend of Göring. He was a famous seaplane pilot who insisted on being informal with us.

Göring only arrived at 21h30. We were an illustrious company: the *Reichsmarschall*, his two sisters who were both nursing sisters, Göring's doctor Dr von Ondarza, and a far-removed niece of Göring, Miss von Pilgrim, who was engaged to a Dutch Baron, was also present. In addition there was State Secretary Körner, who was a good friend of my uncle (who had started the family farm at Omaruru in Namibia), and *Oberstleutnant* Veltjens from the staff of *General* Christiansen, who was responsible for the demilitarisation of Holland. I sat next to him. Göring addressed himself first to the Baron and asked him how many Protestants and Catholics lived in Holland. He wanted to come for a walking tour here after the war and wanted to really tell off the clergy, because they were continuously agitating against the Nazis and the *Reich*. I asked

Veltjens if such arguments in the presence of the orderlies were not dangerous. He waved this aside, and said it was always like this and anyway they were all sworn to secrecy. After the meal we moved into the next room and everyone could smoke. Göring principally smoked only his Virginias with a long, thin cigarette holder that he took out ostentatiously. As the talk turned to the war situation and Göring started to talk about the final victory, *Oberstleutnant* Veltjens approached him, he was also an old *Geschwader* comrade of Göring's and also decorated with the *Pour le Merite* from the First World War, and said: 'And what happens, Hermann, if the Americans still enter the war, as they did in 1917?' At that Göring's face turned stony and he said: 'Well, then, gentlemen...' and with his free hand drew it across his throat with a cutting motion. We are talking here of the beginning of 1941 and now we few knew, who had been part of this supper, that the war was lost. Despite this knowledge none of us could release ourselves from our oath of allegiance to the flag. We had to fight to the bitter end. The fealty to the flag remained the main duty of every soldier, if he did not want to be a traitor and end on the gallows.

## The Non-Stop Offensive

With the German invasion of Russia on 22 June 1941, the British intensified their incursions into German airspace over northern France, launching what they termed the Non-Stop Offensive, a propagandistic name aimed also at boosting morale on the home front, and emphasising the importance of air operations as a way of striking back at the enemy after the ignominious departure of the British army at Dunkirk in May–June 1940. Otto Stammberger of *9/JG 26* had this to say in 1989 of the onset of the Non-Stop Offensive of the RAF:

In the period 15–21 May 1941 we had no losses; these only began in June 1941, and then seriously also, when our *Geschwader* was transferred to the Pas-de-Calais and Abbeville at the mouth of the Somme River to counter the Non-Stop Offensive of the English. That was also the time when the German fighter arm was largely moved to the Eastern Front and only the *Jagdgeschwader Richthofen*, *JG 2* and *Schlageter*, *JG 26* remained on the Channel, to protect the coastline from Brest to the mouth of the Scheldt River, with 60 to 80 aircraft each. At that time *Hauptmann*

Gerhard Schöpfel was my *Gruppenkommandeur* in the *III/JG 26*. He was a very calm and level-headed man who knew what he wanted and was loved by all his pilots. He also concerned himself with his technical and ground staff, and particularly did not put on any airs; he was a mature personality. Today he lives in Cologne; we see each other often. With the increasing attacks of the English in mid-1941, on detection of enemy aircraft on the *Würzburg* and *Freya* radar systems (respectively providing estimates of height – up to 8,000 m – and of distance – up to 150 km), we fighters would be sent up to a specified height, normally 6,000 m, and then vectored to a point, from whence the likely targets of the bombers were within interception range; these were mostly St Omer, Bethune, Lille. The positions of the bombers were continuously broadcast to us, and we received new towns to fly to, but also followed the bombers' course on our maps and determined our approach routes ourselves.

The tactics of fighting effectively against the sweeps of 1941–42 were difficult enough but much more so for the poor pilots flying the top cover; the sheer confusion of aerial combat and the speed of changing events are all recalled by Otto Stammberger.

Our tactics were planned that upon an attack from above, the top cover *Rotte* flew straight and level until the attacking enemy was within shooting distance. In the meantime the two front *Staffeln* (of *III/JG 26*) climbed steeply to right and left, while the third *Staffel*, *9/JG 26*, to which the top cover *Rotte* also belonged, divided and flew a full circle to left and to right, at the same altitude. When the enemy were within firing range of the top cover *Rotte*, these two aircraft did a steep spiral upwards and flew head-on at the attackers, turned sharply and placed themselves behind the attackers. In the meantime the other *Staffeln* had reached a higher position and from their side could now also attack the enemy. However, that was the theory; the Tommies learned quickly, and also divided themselves, one part of them attacking the left-hand climbing *Staffel*, and the other part the right-hand one. Thus within seconds a large, confused dogfight had developed in the air. Everyone against everyone else, everyone looking to himself, aiming forwards and peeking behind, so that a Spitfire did not end up behind one. It cannot be described adequately, everything that happened in a split second, what was flying through the entire mess, above, below, turns, loops, zoom climbs and tight turns downward, and in addition the screams over the radio of 'Spit behind me, help', tracer bullets flying in all directions, 10 to 20 machines in a space of 500 by 500 by 500 m, here and there a smoke trail, a parachute, a burning aircraft. And in addition to all of this, the primary rule for the inexperienced and the young pilots: 'stick to the tail of your leader, do not lose him, for the world stick to him like glue, because alone you are lost'.

That was what aerial combat was like for fighter pilots, but this soon occurred more and more seldom. We no longer took off when only enemy fighters flew in: 'leave them alone', they can do no harm. Only take off when bombers are reported. The Tommies soon noticed this: they flew with their Spits in tight formations, climbing at low speeds, like bombers approaching over the Channel, and our radar reported 'Many enemy machines approaching' and we took off and were promptly ambushed by the Spits, and in this way I was also shot down, on 13 May 1943.

The theory of planned air fighting and its rapid deterioration into chaotic reality are well illustrated above by Otto Stammberger. While British fighter losses remained significantly higher than German losses, and the British lost the battle of attrition over the Channel coasts in 1941–42, there is little of the elation of a victorious outcome in the accounts of the German fighter pilots. The higher commanders in 1941 constantly stressed the need to target the bombers rather than the very numerous British fighter escorts, no easy task as the RAF were already fully aware of all the nuances from their own experiences of 1940. *Oberleutnant* Johannes Naumann, *9/JG 26* and a comrade of Stammberger recalled: 'In fighting against the British sweeps in 1941 we were somewhat handicapped in battle by the command insisting on our shooting down the bombers, and this gave the escorting enemy fighters a measure of confidence in themselves. It was in fact almost a reverse of conditions during the 'Battle of Britain', where the English had been forced to attack the German bombers, and we on our side could then attack in turn and shoot them down while so distracted. The defensive armament of the attacking Allied bombers was admittedly stronger than that of our bombers; for example, the Short Stirling had a four-machine gun turret at the rear. The fighting against the sweeps was certainly only ever possible for short time periods, as the bombers did not penetrate far into our territory, and always then turned back and flew out again.'

While they might have won the battle of attrition over northern France, the *Luftwaffe* experienced almost continuous and hard combat in the air; casualties were commonplace, and in *JG 26* were recorded in the *Geschwader*'s *Ehrenbuch* (memorial book) volumes, which provide brief biographies of the men and of the circumstances of their deaths.[10] As has always been typical of all air combat, it was primarily the inexperienced, new pilots who made up most of the casualties. *Feldwebel* Franz Schwaiger, 26 years old and decorated with the Iron Cross second class – *EK 2* – was one such pilot, who had been with *5/JG 26* for less than three months. 'His last mission was flown on 19 August 1941. He was flying as wingman in *5 Staffel* on a scramble. In the area of Poperinghe–Cassel the *II Gruppe* was attacked from above and out of the sun by about 20 to 30 Spitfires. The *Gruppe* attempted to outclimb the Spitfires in a left turn, and in this situation *Feldwebel* Schwaiger was attacked by a Spitfire from above and hit. His aircraft showed a dark smoke trail and dived down in a right-hand turn. He was able to bail out, but when he pulled the ripcord the parachute did not open and he fell to his death. When he was found, it was seen that the left-hand shoulder belt was torn, from which it was obvious that he had tried to open the parachute too soon while he was still falling too fast.'[11] Killed on the same day was *Oberfeldwebel* Willy Vierling, at 28 already old to be a fighter pilot (he had transferred from the army), who died on only his fourth combat operation: 'He took off on 19 August 1941 from Moorsele as part of *6/JG 26*, to meet an English bomber formation approaching St Omer. After the attack was over, he was missing. Due to the wild dog fighting manoeuvres none of his comrades had been able to observe anything of his fate. It can be assumed that he was seriously wounded in air combat; witnesses on the ground saw his aircraft descend vertically from a great height and with engine still full on, slam into the ground three kilometres north of Cassel. His shattered remains were recovered at a depth of 3 m.'[12] The more experienced pilots such as Adolf Glunz (logbook detail below) were often able to carry on with operational flying and achieving victories for long periods of time, once they had survived long enough to attain that status; luck, as ever, was a potent factor in survival.

Example of a fighter pilot's operational life, based on flying logbook, 1 October 1941–6 November 1941: *Unteroffizier* Adolf Glunz, *4/JG 26* (field bases in bold); flying Fw 190 throughout (Source: Adolf Glunz via Lothair Vanoverbeke)

## OCTOBER

*Staffel* based at **Moorsele** (southwest Belgium, close to French border and Lille, France)

 1: Scramble, 13h00–14h14; (61st *Feindflug*); contact with Spitfires

 2: Scramble, 14h30–15h20
    Scramble, 18h22–19h16

 3: Scramble, 15h20–16h11; damaged main undercarriage wheel in landing

12: Scramble, 17h51–18h18

15: Scramble, 15h40–16h10

17: *Gruppe* moves from Moorsele to **Wevelghem** (close to Moorsele, Belgium)

21: Scramble, 12h40–13h40; (62nd *Feindflug*); enemy contact in St Omer area

24: Scramble, 15h53–16h38

27: Scramble, 16h00–17h03

## NOVEMBER

 1: Scramble, 11h15–12h17; land at new base, **Coxyde** (western coast of Belgium near French border)

 3: Defensive patrol, 17h11–17h42

 5: Scramble, 10h24–10h46; (63rd *Feindflug*); one Spitfire shot down (seventh victory)
    Scramble, 12h33–12h52
    Scramble, 14h36–14h48

 6: Scramble, 14h45–15h15; (64th *Feindflug*); enemy fighters attack own airfield

Notes: combat operation (*Feindflug*) on 1 October 1941 related to a *Freie Jagd* over England; *Feindflug* on 5 November 1941 versus two Spitfires on a Rhubarb (RAF term for small fighter formation operating in poor weather conditions) mission, confirmed British loss, several Rhubarb missions on this day explains the several short duration scrambles flown by Glunz; *Feindflug* on 6 November 1941 versus Hurricane fighter-bombers attacking Coxyde as target of opportunity after failing to locate set target.[13]

While the main action during 1941 was along the northern French and Belgian coasts where *JG 2* (west) and *JG 26* (east) were stationed, RAF incursions as well as German missions in the opposite direction also took place further to the north-east along the Dutch coast. *I/JG 53* flew in defence of Holland from 20 September 1941–mid November 1941.[14] *Oberfeldwebel* Josef Ederer, *3/JG 53* was one of their pilots, who remembered a sortie in October 1941: 'In Holland I shot down two bombers (Blenheims) from an attacking formation.' Only one was credited to him in the unit history.[15]

## 1942: The Battle Intensifies; the 'Channel Dash', and the Dieppe Landing

During 1942, the RAF's incursions over the Channel coast of western Europe continued apace. There were two major aerial battles: that related to the 'Channel Dash', when the German capital ships escaped from Brest to Germany by boldly sailing up the English Channel in February; and that related to the Dieppe raid in August 1942. In that same month the earliest missions of a new opponent took place, the American 8th Air Force, which was to grow into an enormous force and one that would effectively cripple the *Luftwaffe* fighter force by May 1944, just in time to ensure that the Normandy Invasion could be launched under conditions of Allied air superiority on 6 June 1944. The early US raids in 1942 will be covered under the more general topic of the Battle of Germany in the next chapter. *Oberleutnant* Theodor Lindemann, *7/JG 26* recalls the 1942 fighting as a still reasonable challenge: 'What was it like to fly against the English on the Channel Front in 1942? I can only answer that it was still within the bounds of the possible, and as far as one can say within a wartime setting, in most cases it was a sporting and fair warfare there. They were not superior to us in either aircraft or pilots, but in reality they possessed significant numerical superiority, also in the framework of their allies.' That excellent witness *Leutnant* Otto Stammberger, *9/JG 26* flew in defence of the German battleships steaming up the Channel on 12 February 1942, where he describes the fate of the six Fleet Air Arm Swordfish crews, who in hopeless bravery attacked in their ancient biplanes.

> I flew on the breakthrough of the German capital ships through the English Channel. We were then stationed in Coquelles, west of Calais. At about midday the ships were between Dover and Calais,

and the *8/JG 26* was flying escort then, on the port side, in other words left of the convoy nearer to the English coast. The weather was bad: low-lying clouds, light drizzle, poor visibility. Then coming from England about 10 Swordfish aircraft suddenly appeared, old biplanes with torpedoes under their fuselages. The 8th *Staffel* attacked immediately and shot down six or seven of them, including one victory for Paul Galland (youngest brother of Adolf Galland). Immediately after this combat of the 8th *Staffel*, we, the 9th *Staffel*, had to take off as reinforcements for the escort, as it was now clear that the Tommies had discovered the breakthrough, which until then they had been unaware of. We thus now expected a strong reaction; however, either Tommy was asleep or he could not get bombers into the air that fast, as things stayed relatively quiet.

We were flying as always in *Rotten*, also on the port side of the convoy, protecting the ships for a distance of about 50 km away from the convoy also. For us the weather was also bad; suddenly I saw in front of me, coming from the convoy's direction, a Boston appearing out of the clouds at about 30 m height above the water. I was flying practically right above the shadow he cast on the sea. I wrenched my aircraft to the left, but the Boston had disappeared again into the clouds. I had to turn back as with the violent turn my one undercarriage leg had come loose and hung down. By this time the convoy was off Dunkirk and was later attacked again by bombers and torpedo aircraft when beyond the mouth of the Scheldt River; by then we from *JG 26* were no longer involved in the escort. I flew home from over Dunkirk after I was able to retract my wheel, but it did not stay retracted and kept on falling out again. Due to the strong loading of my wing, with the sharp turn to get at the Boston bomber the wing had been deformed by a fraction of a millimetre, and thus the eye holding the pin restraining the undercarriage could no longer hold it and the right oleo leg and wheel kept falling out of the wing. *Oberfeldwebel* Koslowski from my 9th *Staffel* did not return from his escort mission on this day. As there had been no reported enemy aircraft, we assumed that in the poor weather while turning he had hit the water and crashed into the sea, despite his being an experienced and older pilot.

Much further to the north-east, and as the murky daylight faded, the Me 110-equipped units also became involved in covering the German naval units on this day, among them *Feldwebel* Joachim Robel, rear gunner/radio operator in *III/NJG 3*: 'In February 1942 the German capital ships broke out of Brest and sailed through the Channel to the North Sea, and we flew part of the escort.'

19 August 1942 would bring many more deaths in the heavily contested sky above the Dieppe landings. The *Kommodore* of *JG 26*, *Major* Gerhard Schöpfel, was in a key position, as commander of the fighter unit closest to the port being attacked, to provide an eyewitness account of fighting the RAF air umbrella above the Dieppe landings on this day. Interestingly, he makes clear that strategic surprise was not achieved, in concert with many British accounts which stress the fact that the Dieppe raid was put off after briefings had been given to the participants, before finally being launched some time later, thereby risking leaks.

From our listening service and the gathering of ships we expected an attack on the northern coast of France. As we suspected that an initial attack would be made first against our airfields, which at this time in *JG 26* were situated close to the coast, I sent the fighter *Gruppen* each to a set of inland airfields in the evenings, each *Staffel* to a different field. When the attack took place at Dieppe, many of these inland airfields were partly covered by mist/fog and thus I could initially only assign some separate *Staffeln* to the attack rather than unified *Gruppen*. I myself only got off at about 10h00, after the fighter *Gruppen* had begun flying continuous missions against Dieppe from their normal airfields (St Omer, Abbeville and Wevelghem). Operations over one's own territory are naturally less risky. We were thus able to defend effectively against the British fighter formations, who had at first to protect the troops who had been landed. During the withdrawal of the British landing boats we attacked the ships and their escorts, as well as providing escorts for our dive-bombers and bombers. In multiple missions I shot down two British fighters, but was myself chased by their fighters and once again experienced the toughness and flying ability of the British pilots.

The fighting over Dieppe, encompassing 2,604 RAF sorties met by around 945 from the German side, reflects a major air battle. Losses over Dieppe were also heavy by any standard: 62 RAF personnel killed in action (including 47 fighter pilots), 34 captured, and 97 aircraft (59 Spitfires, 20 Hurricanes, 10 Mustangs, two Typhoons, six

Blenheims/Bostons) lost and another 54 damaged in action.[16] *Luftwaffe* losses amounted to 23 fighters (16 from *JG* 2, seven from *JG* 26; 14 pilots killed) and 25 bombers (all *KG* 2) destroyed, with a further 11 aircraft damaged, to be placed against total RAF claims of 96 aircraft destroyed.[17] Naval gunner claims are not known, but should be added to this total. Some 98 German fighter claims were made (roughly 60 by *JG* 2 and the balance from *JG* 26)[18] with a further at least 30 claims from *Luftwaffe* flak gunners and four from bomber gunners, bringing total German claims to *around* 132.[19] Of the 97 RAF aircraft lost in action, an estimated 70-odd are thought to have fallen to the *Luftwaffe* fighter pilots. Once more both sides over-claimed, as is only natural in intense (and indeed all) aerial combat. As was the case over the entire 1941–42 period on the Channel coast, German over-claiming seems to have been lower than that of the RAF.

Statistics and judgements of winning or losing the battle apart, at the level of the individual pilot, personal experiences were paramount, and losses were final events, with tragic consequences for the families concerned. Amongst the German fighter losses over the Dieppe landings on 19 August 1942, was 26 year old *Feldwebel* August Golub, who had been an instructor before joining 9/*JG* 26 just over two months previous to this major aerial battle. Despite significant flying experience unlike many new boys joining the *Geschwader* in 1942, his lack of combat exposure doomed him if he lost his leader, like so many other relative innocents lost in analogous circumstances. The *Geschwader Ehrenbuch JG* 26 recorded the sad details of another pilot lost in the unforgiving sea.[20] 'On 19 August 1942 he took off on what was his 4th combat mission in the *Schwarm* led by *Oberleutnant* Neumann to intercept enemy fighter forces in the air above Dieppe. *Feldwebel* Golub did not return from this operation. His *Rottenführer*, *Unteroffizier* Niese, reported: "At about 14h45 we contacted the enemy over the sea and the two of us became separated from the *Schwarm*. My wingman, *Feldwebel* Golub and I attacked some Spitfires. Just as I was about to open fire I looked around and noticed some Spitfires behind us, and reported this to my wingman by radio. I pulled away from the Spitfires in a sharp left hand turn and ended up in an involuntary spin. From this moment on I saw no more of *Feldwebel* Golub. The combat occurred about 15–20 km northeast of Dieppe over the sea."'

Following this major event in the ongoing struggle above the Channel in 1941–42, the aerial war continued unabated. A short excerpt from

Otto Stammberger's logbook below illustrates the endless round of *Alarmstarts* – scrambles – which provided the only relief from the long days of waiting at dispersal in nervous anticipation of the next encounter with a hard enemy. Interspersed with these there were still flights over the English coast, for added possibilities of action, with success not always rewarded when no witness was available for an *Abschuss* (victory). On 9 October 1942 came an early encounter with the American four-engined bomber formations, ushering in a totally new and even more deadly aspect of the war in the West, and one which would ultimately defeat the *Jagdflieger* in that theatre once adequate escort fighters were available from the Allied side.

Example of a fighter pilot's operational life, based on flying logbook, 6 September 1942–9 October 1942: *Leutnant* Otto Stammberger, 9/JG 26, stationed at Moorsele, and flying Fw 190 throughout (Source: Otto Stammberger)

## SEPTEMBER
6: Scramble, 11h18–11h51
Scramble, 17h48–18h30
Reconnaissance of English coast, 19h44–20h25; (70th *Feindflug*); coastal reconnaissance Margate–Dover
7: Scramble, 10h40–11h16; (*Feindflug*)
Scramble, 16h40–16h55
22: Scramble, 13h00–13h43; (71st *Feindflug*)
24: Escort, 16h50–17h57; (72nd *Feindflug*)

## OCTOBER
2: Scramble, 15h17–16h05; (73rd *Feindflug*); *Abschuss* (Spitfire) east of Deal, without witnesses. Attacked from astern, included a strike in the cockpit, spun down from *c.* 1,800 m, and crashed into sea, pilot dead
Scramble, 16h28–16h55
9: Scramble, 10h25–11h00; (74th *Feindflug*); 2nd victory (*Abschuss*). B-17: Boeing. Four-engined raid in area of Lille. Attacked from astern, 4 times, stupid!

Notes: combat operation (*Feindflug*) on 2 October 1942 related to diversionary RAF fighter operations over France to cover two American four-engined bomber raids; III/JG 26 met outgoing Spitfires and shot down two, one by Stammberger, who, lacking witnesses, could not submit a claim for a confirmed success. *Feindflug* on 9 October 1942 versus large four-engined bomber raid on Lille, the escort was a mess and the bombers were attacked without cover – Stammberger shot down a B-17 of the 306th Bomb Group which his *Staffelkapitän*, *Oberleutnant* Ruppert had separated from the formation.[21] The separation (*Herausschuss*) claimed by Ruppert counted as a victory as well (as opposed to a final destruction of such a bomber, which didn't). Stammberger, not knowing of the *Herausschuss* destroyed the winged bomber and received credit for destroying a B-17. An example of honest over-claiming!

## Protecting the Dutch Coast, 1942: A Detailed Account by Unteroffizier Otto Schmid of II/JG 1

Otto Schmid, born 9 December 1920, flew in *II/JG 1* on the Channel–Dutch front in 1942. Later, in the Battle of Germany, he was grievously wounded on 21 February 1944, by three explosive bullets in his left leg, which had to be amputated. After years of correspondence I finally met Otto in May 1993 on a trip to Germany, and spent a fascinating day discussing his war experiences. He very kindly picked me up in Munich and drove me to his home in Holzkirchen, south of the city, and dropped me off again afterwards; he controlled his BMW sports coupe expertly, despite his handicap, still the quintessential fighter pilot at the controls of expensive and high-performance machinery. I stayed in touch with him until his death, on 11 September 1995.

Otto Schmid still had his logbook, plus many photographs and copies of surviving *Luftwaffe* records relevant to his time flying over Holland during 1942, and later in 1943 and 1944 over Germany. Not many of his ilk survived a long period of flying in these campaigns, and even fewer were prepared to detail their experiences frankly; Otto, flying initially with 5/JG 1, was the exception.

Our *Gruppe*, *II/JG 1*, was formed from the *I Gruppe* of *JG 3*. This *Geschwader* had been flying in Russia, and this *Gruppe* was transferred to Holland in December 1941–January 1942 and renamed as *II/JG 1*. The *Staffel* and *Gruppe* emblem on the aircraft engine hoods was inherited from *I/JG 3*: the dragon (*Lindwurm*). The *Staffeln* each had their own colour for the emblem. The 4th *Staffel* had a white dragon, and the tactical number on the fuselage of each aircraft was also white. In the 5th *Staffel* the dragon was red, but the tactical number was in black. For the 6th *Staffel* the dragon and the tactical number were both yellow. The spinner on the propellers of the aircraft was also in the individual *Staffeln* colours, white, red and yellow, as were the undersides of the engine cowlings. The white spiral on the spinners was a special wish of our *Staffelkapitän Oberleutnant* Max Buchholz. Where this *Lindwurm* emblem came from, I can no longer recall. I myself had no additional personal emblem on my aircraft. *Oberleutnant* Max Buchholz took over the *5/JG 1* about the end of January or beginning of February 1942. He was a correct commanding officer. Until the start of the operations against the four-engined bombers we only had to contend with the English, mostly Spitfires, Wellington bombers and Bristol Beauforts. Mostly, every morning and evening, sea reconnaissance missions were flown up to the English eastern coast. Other missions included escorts for German convoys and aircraft.

Examination of a chart summarising Otto Schmid's operations in the plate section (illustration number 41), makes it clear that flying the sea reconnaissance flights across the North Sea to the east coast of England was only allowed once a pilot had built up some experience of operational flying. Otto Schmid recalls these missions: 'From Holland, we flew two daily reconnaissance flights over the sea, one in the early morning and one in the evening. On the morning flight we took off at dawn, and in the evening returned in the gathering dusk. The course flown was mostly from Holland northwards to the mouth of the Thames Estuary, then further northwards for *c.* 20 minutes and then back again to Schipol, or later, to Woensdrecht. We had to locate the enemy convoys and this was then reported further to the navy, or even to bomber units. On these flights we also sometimes met the enemy, namely English or American reconnaissance units. Then, of course, there was the obligatory aerial combat. But it also happened that we had to fly escort for our own ship convoys. On these missions aerial combats also occurred. Although flying over water with a single engine aircraft was always a risky affair, these flights always brought me a lot of enjoyment.'

In the period from 30 April 1942 to the end of that year, Otto Schmid flew a total of 147 *Einsätze*. It is important to properly define such terms as well as others related to operational flying. An *Einsatz* in *Luftwaffe* usage equated to an *operational mission* in RAF parlance, a term encompassing operations in general, and which included

*Frontflüge/Feindflüge*, which are specifically *combat missions* (again, the RAF term), either over enemy territory or in contact with enemy aircraft over your own territory or the sea separating enemy and own territory.[22] Only 28 of these missions or *Einsätze* were counted as *Frontflüge* in his logbook, with *Seeaufklärung* (sea reconnaissance) missions most often being counted as combat missions. There was actually one more *Frontflug* recorded in Otto Schmid's logbook, which applied to a transfer flight undertaken in the evening on 15 July 1942; no further detail is supplied by either his logbook or the unit history.[23] The precise meaning of the term *Frontflug*, as opposed to *Einsatz*, already summarised above, is important for understanding the operational records of any *Luftwaffe* fighter pilot. To prevent any confusion, a *Frontflug* or *Feindflug* is defined as follows by one of the veterans of the Channel campaign of 1941–42, *Oberleutnant* Otto Stammberger, *Staffelkapitän* 4/JG 26: 'A *Feindflug* was recognised and counted when we flew over enemy territory, namely over England and later over the Invasion Front, or behind the lines in Russia or Africa. On flights over our own territory or over occupied areas, like France, Holland, Belgium, Denmark or wherever it was, a *Feindflug* was only counted when we experienced aerial combat.'

Of Otto Schmid's 28 *Frontflüge*, six led to contact with the enemy, termed *Feindberührung* in the *Luftwaffe*. His very first operation of all, on 30 April 1942, a scramble, also led to his first enemy contact! The next contact was many weeks later after he had moved from 5th to 4th *Staffel* of *JG 1*: 'On a mission on 22 July 1942 – while escorting a Do 24 flying boat – I flew as wingman to *Unteroffizier* Kirschner. We had an encounter with a Wellington, which Kirschner shot down. It was his first victory claim, and he received the *EK 2* (Iron Cross, second class) for it.'

A scramble from Schipol on 29 August 1942 again led to *Feindberührung*, but additional details do not appear in Schmid's logbook. Then in November, things picked up, two Spitfires being encountered on a sea reconnaissance mission on 17 November 1942, followed by another sea reconnaissance operation three days later. This time, four Bristol Beaufighters escorted by nine Spitfires were met, and *Unteroffizier* Schmid made his first victory claim. 'A correction is necessary in my logbook. My first victory (*Abschuss*) was not a Bristol Beaufort as I claimed, but in reality was a Bristol Beaufighter. I received this information from Herrn de Visser, who had obtained it from an Englishman who also wrote an account of the missions

1. Two *JG 26* pilots display what would be potentially dangerous irreverence in another unit or for another branch of the *Wehrmacht*: Günther Kelch (left) and Otto Stammberger (right) welcome Kurt Ruppert (centre) back from a mission in National Socialist style, to the amusement of the mechanic on the wing. Of the three pilots, only Stammberger would survive the war. (*JG 26* veteran via Lothair Vanoverbeke)

2. A photo of a crashed and burning Spitfire, 31 May 1942, claimed by *Hauptmann* Müncheberg of *II/JG 26* as his 80th victory, but probably his 79th in reality. This might be a Spitfire of 302 Squadron, whose pilot was killed on this day. It appears to have hit the ground at a shallow angle but rather violently, digging the heavy engine and propeller assembly into the soil. (*JG 26* veteran via Lothair Vanoverbeke)

3. Hitler poses with members of *I/JG 21* during a surprise visit to the astonished *Gruppe* during a front-line inspection tour near the Warsaw area during the Polish campaign. *Staffelkapitän* Günther Scholz of *1/JG 21* is arrowed at the back of the crowd. (Dr Max Clerico)

4. Hitler, after his vegetarian stew served from *I/JG 21*'s field kitchen, on their front-line airfield, Poland. (Dr Max Clerico)

5. *Leutnant* Bolse and *Unteroffizier* Karl Siedenbiedel (right) of *4/JG 2* get ready for a spell of *Sitzbereitschaft* (cockpit readiness) in their Me 109s, as enemy aircraft incursions have been reported. Winter 1939, at Zerbst during the Phoney War. (Karl Siedenbiedel)

6. *Unteroffiziers* Glomb, Auf dem Siepen and Karl Siedenbiedel (left to right) in the pilots' readiness room, *4/JG 2* at Nordholz, February 1940. (Karl Siedenbiedel)

7. Josef Bürschgens (left) was with *2/JG 26* when shot down and seriously wounded early in the Phoney War after scoring *JG 26*'s first victory of the war, on 28 September 1939. Pictured after his recovery, on the Channel coast, now with *7/JG 26*. He and his wingman (*Katschmarek*) examine a powerful trench periscope. The airfield boundary fence and sandbagged aircraft revetments in the background indicate a well-organised operational field. (Josef Bürschgens)

British versus French fighter victories confirmed by post-war research, 10–20 May 1940

— British fighter victories　— French fighter victories

8. For the British there were two upswings of combat effectiveness: 14 May (when a major effort was made over the Sedan breakthrough area) and 17–19 May (when large Hurricane reinforcements flew in from the UK). By 20 May the Air Component Hurricanes and reinforcements had been withdrawn and only the few RAF Hurricanes of the AASF remained with the French.

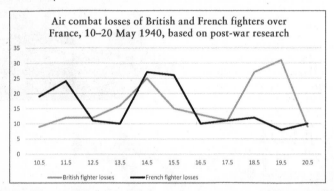

Air combat losses of British and French fighters over France, 10–20 May 1940, based on post-war research

— British fighter losses　— French fighter losses

9. Episodic Allied losses over the Sedan crossings on 14 May and those involving RAF reinforcements from 17–19 May aside, RAF casualties show an overall increase while French casualties, overall, decline.

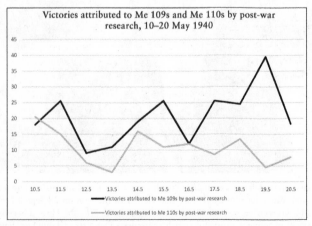

Victories attributed to Me 109s and Me 110s by post-war research, 10–20 May 1940

— Victories attributed to Me 109s by post-war research
— Victories attributed to Me 110s by post-war research

10. Two different trends are evident: the combat effectiveness of the Me 110s is gradually decreasing, but that for the Me 109s is going up. This illustrates the distinct superiority of the Me 109 over its opponents in France.

11a & 11b. RAF Hurricane which crash-landed on the Quartel family farm, just north-east of the village of Numansdorp on 11 May 1940, at about 15h30 local time, having been shot down in a combat over the Hollandisch Diep river just to the south. The son of the family who now farms the land, and who provided an eyewitness account in 1985, appears in both photos (the young boy in the top picture, standing on the port wing). The wounded pilot died despite treatment. He is buried in Numansdorp Cemetery: 23-year-old Flight Lieutenant Michael Stephen Donne of 17 Squadron. The aircraft is probably N2403, and was removed from the farm by Dutch POWs under German instruction. (Harry van der Meer of the *Nationaal Luchtvaart Museum*, Schipol, Netherlands, via the Quartel family; information also from local resident Karel Braun of Klaaswaal, and Tony Mawby of Southall, UK)

12. Blenheim from 21 Squadron RAF: L8734 burns out after being shot down by anti-aircraft fire while attacking river crossings in the Kortrijk-Menin area and crashing at Moorsele airfield in Belgium on 25 May 1940. Of the crew, Sergeant Harold Rowson (pilot) became a POW, but wireless operator Leading Aircraftsman Cleaver and observer Sergeant Keats were killed. (Lothair Vanoverbeke)

13a & 13b. Two photos of Max Clerico, 7/JG 54, from the Battle of Britain. The photo with his Dachshund shows three victory bars on the Me 109's tail, placing it earlier during the battle as he claimed two victories over France and a further four over England. The other photo has him wearing a *Leutnant*'s uniform and this promotion (from officer candidate, *Fähnrich*) took place in October 1940, so must post-date that event. (Dr Max Clerico, 7/JG 54)

14. Two old comrades from *7/JG 54* who shared fascinating memories of a battle they experienced together more than fifty years before in autumn 1940 over England. Max Clerico (right): 'September 1994 in Rosenheim, the old *Staffelkapitän* Günther Scholz, 83 and his old *Katschmarek* (wingman) Clerico, 76.' (Dr Max Clerico)

15. *Leutnant* Max Clerico: '*Oberleutnant* Scholz, *Staffelkapitän 7/JG 54,* and "Old Strauss", 42 years old, who sometimes flew operations in the Me 109 over England. He often had an enormous hangover, as he was an old student club member – $C_2H_5OH$! His face showed distinct scars from sabre duels as a student. His reactions were rather slow, also in recovering from his hangovers. However, he was not shot down, he was a charming, nice man. He visited me once after the war, in about 1957 and has certainly now passed on.' (Dr Max Clerico)

16. The *Kommodore* of the *Pik-As-Geschwader*, *JG 53* from 9 October 1940 (previously *Gruppenkommandeur II/JG 53*), *Major* Günther Freiherr von Maltzahn, seen just before taking off from a field base in France during the Battle of Britain. (Dr Felix Sauer)

*Above left*: 17. *Major* Hanns Trübenbach, *Kommodore* of *JG 52* in the Battle of Britain from 19 August 1940, in summer 1941 in Mamaia, Romania. The second pair of wings above his *Frontflugspange* (missions clasp) are from his tactical command of the Italian fighter wing during the late Battle of Britain. Trübenbach: 'On high-level orders, *Oberstleutnant* Bolzano, C/O of the Italian fighter wing, pinned the golden Italian pilot wings topped by the royal crown on my chest on 28 May 1941.' (Hanns Trübenbach)

*Above right*: 18. *Oberleutnant* Erhard Braune, *Staffelkapitän* of 7/JG 27 throughout the Battle of Britain. (Erhard Braune)

19. A *Schwarm* of four Me 109 Es from *7/JG 54*, taken by *Leutnant* Max Clerico in the nearest aircraft with the *Schwarmführer* (*Staffelkapitän* Günther Scholz?) next in line. When expecting action on a mission, the 'finger-four' formation would have been opened out quite a bit more. (Dr Max Clerico)

20. *Oberfeldwebel* Artur Dau of *7/JG 51* poses in front of his burnt-out Me 109, which he force-landed near Boulogne on 10 July 1940, after combat with P/O Geoffrey Page of 56 Squadron. The photograph was taken by his *Gruppenkommandeur, Hauptmann* Hannes Trautloft, *III/JG 51*. (Artur Dau)

21. Delighted mechanics carry *Feldwebel* Georg Pavenzinger, *2/JG 51*, on their shoulders 'after my first victory over England, August 1940'. This was scored on 30 August 1940. The mechanics were known colloquially in the *Luftwaffe* as *Schwarze Männer* (black men) from their black overalls. Note the yellow-nosed Me 109 E in the background under tree cover. (George Pavenzinger)

22. *Oberfeldwebel* Artur Dau, *7/JG 51*, standing near a Me 109 E on a *Feldflugplatz* or front-line airfield in 1940, Battle of Britain. The camouflage netting is augmented by vegetation in the foreground. (Artur Dau)

23. *Gefreiter* Rudolf Miese, a new arrival at *4/JG 2*, at Beaumont-le-Roger with 'Lori', a *Staffel* mascot, during the Battle of Britain. (Rudolf Miese)

24. *Unteroffizier* Werner Ludwig of *III/ZG 26* in a photo taken at the beginning of 1942 after his promotion to *Leutnant*, long after he had made it through the Battle of Britain. (Werner Ludwig)

25. *Oberleutnant* Josef Bürschgens, *7/JG 26* climbing out of his Me 109 E after a mission over England in 1940: 'One of me on the Channel Coast, France 1940, Battle of Britain.' (Josef Bürschgens)

26. The pilots of *7/JG 54*, taken at Soesterberg airfield near Utrecht, Holland, where they were stationed June–early August 1940. *Staffelkapitän Oberleutnant* Günther Scholz in the middle, to his right *Leutnant* Behrens (k. October 1940), to his left *Leutnant* Ostermann (later awarded the *Eichenlaub* or Oak Leaves to the *Ritterkreuz*, killed over Russia) and with white scarf, *Fähnrich* Max Clerico. (Günther Scholz)

27a & 27b. *Hauptmann*
Gerhard Schöpfel,
*Gruppenkommandeur* of
*III/JG 26* in the Battle of
Britain: 'Two photos from the
years 1942 and 1987; time has
also made some changes in me.'
(Gerhard Schöpfel)

28. Post-war amity between former Battle of Britain opponents. Gerhard Granz, veteran of I/ZG 2, made a return visit to the UK under better circumstances than when he was shot down there on 7 September 1940: 'Dinner party in Billericay in 1975. Wing Commander Bob Stanford Tuck giving a speech; from left to right: Gerhard Granz, Mrs Galland, General Adolf Galland, former *General der Jagdflieger*.' (Gerhard Granz)

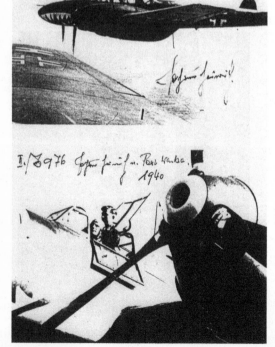

29. Photos from Paul Wenke's logbook, showing the crew (gunner Johan Heinrich, right); they are seen flying their Me 110 in September 1940 with the shark's mouth emblem of the *Haifischgruppe – II/ZG 76* – clearly visible on the nose. (Johan Heinrich)

30. A group from the 4th *Staffel* of *JG 2 Richthofen* at Beaumont-le-Roger during the Battle of Britain. The victory tally on the tail of *Oberfeldwebel* Schnell's Me 109 forms the centre piece, with from left to right: a mechanic; Schnell, the famous *Oberleutnant* Hans 'Assi' Hahn, *Staffelkapitän* (wearing his *Ritterkreuz*, awarded on 24 September 1940); and *Gefreiter* Miese (as yet without his Iron Cross second class or *EK 2*, placing the photograph before the end of October 1940). (Rudolf Miese)

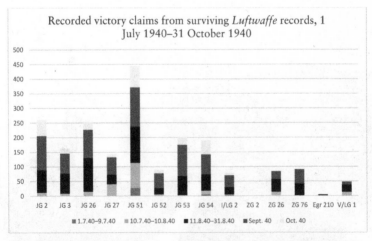

31. The performance of *JG 51* reflects its early arrival on the Channel coast in July and that it later had a fourth *Gruppe* attached; however, on a per-*Gruppe* basis it was still the top performer. In contrast, *JG 52* made few credited claims, about the same as the independent Me 109 *Gruppe I/LG 2*. Data for ZG 2 were not preserved, and those for the other Me 110 units underline the inferiority of this aircraft to the RAF fighters. Based on data contained in the lists drawn up by Tony Wood from original, mainly hand-written *Luftwaffe* records preserved on often poor-quality microfilms.

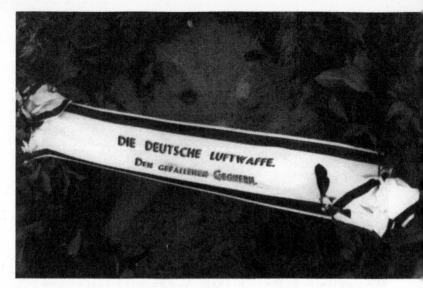

32. An all-too-common occurrence during 1941–2 along the Channel–Dutch coast was, as *Unteroffizier* Otto Schmid, *II/JG 1* recalled, 'Honouring an English fighter pilot buried in the cemetery in Woensdrecht (Holland).' The ribbon reads: 'The German Air Force. To the fallen enemy.' Due to Göring allowing no chaplains in the *Luftwaffe*, the burial services had to be performed by chaplains borrowed from close-by naval or army units. (Otto Schmid)

33. The advent of the Focke-Wulf 190 fighter on the Channel front in autumn 1941 was an unpleasant surprise for the RAF; this later example is an Fw 190 A-2 of *II/JG 1*, parked under a camouflage net at Schipol, 1942. (Otto Schmid)

34. Typical fighter pilots' pose: *Leutnant* Otto Stammberger (*9/JG 26*; right) and *Leutnant* Elmar Göcke (died of wounds inflicted in an attack on an early B-17 raid on 2 October 1942, with *4/JG 26*). (Otto Stammberger, via Lothair Vanoverbeke)

35. *Unteroffizier* Otto Schmid of *5/JG 1* at immediate readiness (*Sitzbereitschaft*) in Katwijk, Holland, in summer 1942. (Otto Schmid)

36. *Oberfeldwebel* Georg Hutter posing on the nose of his *II/JG 1* Messerschmitt Me 109 F-4 in Katwijk, May 1942. (Otto Schmid)

37. Otto Schmid, former pilot in *II/JG 1*, kindly invited the author to his home in Holzkirchen, south of Munich, in May 1993. (Else Schmid)

38a, 38b, 38c. Three photographs of members of *5/JG 1* in Holland in 1942. *Oberleutnant* Max Buchholz, the *Staffelkapitän*, sits with his dog (top left). Top right, *Leutnant* Tschire, *Oberleutnant* Buchholz and *Hauptfeldwebel* Schadow (*Staffel* sergeant major, or *Spies* in *Luftwaffe* parlance), left to right. Group photo of the *Staffel*, Schipol airfield in Holland; *Staffelkapitän* Buchholz in front-centre, with *Ritterkreuz* and dog on lap (below). (Otto Schmid)

39. While it is not certain exactly when this photograph was taken ('*Unteroffiziere* Kirschner and Schmid, right – back from an *Einsatz*') the obvious satisfaction and confident strides of both pilots suggest it may have been after a successful mission. (Otto Schmid)

40. During a coastal patrol, *Unteroffizier* Otto Schmid of *4/JG 1* had to force-land his FW 190: '[Photograph] of my water landing on 27 October 1942 just off the island of Texel (Holland), due to malfunction of the fuel pump and subsequent engine failure; the beach was mined so that I had to put the aircraft down in the water just offshore as the tide was coming in.' Otto Schmid on right, smoking a no-doubt welcome cigarette. (R. W. de Visser via Otto Schmid)

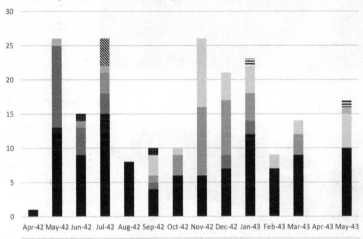

## Operational flying missions, per month, *Unteroffizier* Otto Schmid, *II/JG 1*, Holland (30 April 1942–30 May 1943)

|  | Apr-42 | May-42 | Jun-42 | Jul-42 | Aug-42 | Sep-42 | Oct-42 | Nov-42 | Dec-42 | Jan-43 | Feb-43 | Mar-43 | Apr-43 | May-43 |
|---|---|---|---|---|---|---|---|---|---|---|---|---|---|---|
| Other | 0 | 0 | 0 | 0 | 0 | 0 | 0 | 0 | 0 | 1 | 0 | 0 | 0 | 1 |
| Ueberwachungsflug | 0 | 0 | 0 | 4 | 0 | 0 | 0 | 0 | 0 | 0 | 0 | 0 | 0 | 0 |
| Sicherungsflug | 0 | 0 | 1 | 0 | 0 | 1 | 0 | 0 | 0 | 0 | 0 | 0 | 0 | 0 |
| Begleitflug | 0 | 1 | 0 | 1 | 0 | 0 | 0 | 0 | 0 | 0 | 0 | 0 | 0 | 1 |
| Seeaufklaerung | 0 | 0 | 0 | 0 | 0 | 3 | 1 | 10 | 4 | 4 | 2 | 2 | 0 | 5 |
| Sperrflug | 0 | 0 | 1 | 3 | 0 | 1 | 3 | 10 | 8 | 4 | 0 | 3 | 0 | 0 |
| Geleitflug | 0 | 12 | 4 | 3 | 0 | 1 | 0 | 0 | 2 | 2 | 0 | 0 | 0 | 0 |
| Alarmstart | 1 | 13 | 9 | 15 | 8 | 4 | 6 | 6 | 7 | 12 | 7 | 9 | 0 | 10 |

41. Schmid flew with all three *Staffeln* (*5/JG 1*: 26 April–7 July 1942; *4/JG 1*: 8 July–20 November 1942; *6/JG 1*: 24 November 1942–30 May 1943). Missions flown from Katwijk, Woensdrecht, Schipol and Leeuwarden, in Me 109 F-4 (26 April–2 June 1942) and FW 190 A (4 June onwards). *Alarmstart* = scramble; *Geleitflug* = convoy patrol; *Sperrflug* = coastal patrol; *Seeaufklärung* = sea reconnaissance; *Begleitflug* = escort for other aircraft; *Sicherungsflug* = protection flight; *Überwachungsflug* = surveillance or coastal surveillance; other = weather reconnaissance and air sea rescue search.

42a, 42b, 42c. Conversion of *5/JG 1* to the FW 190, May–early June 1942, at Katwijk, Holland. 'Factory delivered FW 190 A-2 before conversion to combat state' (top left); 'After the conversion, a test flight is carried out by the Technical Officer of the *Staffel*' (left) – note the dragon emblem has been added; the conversion team of mechanics (bottom). (Otto Schmid)

43. One of *II/JG 1*'s FW 190 A-2s after an overhaul in the workshop. Typical 1942 camouflage scheme for *JG 1*. The workshop buildings in the background are also camouflaged. (Otto Schmid)

44. *Major* Gerhard Schöpfel, *Kommodore* of *JG 26* during the period of the early American raids, August 1942–January 1943. (Gerhard Schöpfel)

45. Adolf Glunz, *II/JG 26*, who served initially and briefly on the Russian front in 1941 (in *JG 52*) at the beginning of the invasion of Russia, before joining *JG 26*, where he rose from the ranks to *Oberleutnant* and *Staffelkapitän* of 5th and later 6th *Staffeln* of the *Geschwader*. In discussion with some of his ground-crew colleagues, he is wearing the *Ritterkreuz* with *Eichenlaub* in this photo, placing it sometime after June 1944. (Adolf Glunz via Lothair Vanoverbeke)

46. Taken at Moorsele in autumn 1942: against the backdrop of a FW 190 with, left to right, *Oberleutnant* Günther Kelch (13 victory claims; killed 31 July 1943 as *Hauptmann* and *Staffelkapitän* 7/JG 26); *Oberleutnant* Otto Stammberger; and *Oberleutnant* Kurt Ruppert just promoted to *Hauptmann* (21 victories, killed 13 June 1943 as *Kommandeur* III/JG 26). (Otto Stammberger, via Lothair Vanoverbeke)

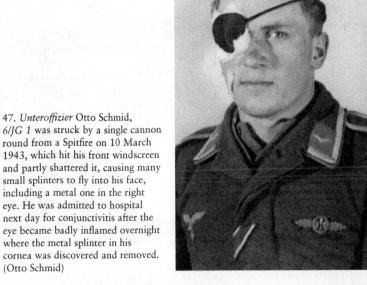

47. *Unteroffizier* Otto Schmid, 6/*JG 1* was struck by a single cannon round from a Spitfire on 10 March 1943, which hit his front windscreen and partly shattered it, causing many small splinters to fly into his face, including a metal one in the right eye. He was admitted to hospital next day for conjunctivitis after the eye became badly inflamed overnight where the metal splinter in his cornea was discovered and removed. (Otto Schmid)

48. *Unteroffizier* Otto Schmid, 6/ *JG 1*: 'My first wound', 10 March 1943; taken by a comrade just after he landed. Note the thickness of the armoured windscreen and its heavily damaged metal frame, and that the forward side window was destroyed and part of the back canopy plexiglass had gone too. Note two splinter wounds exactly between the eyes! All this damage from a single cannon round – a very lucky escape! (Otto Schmid)

49. Otto Schmid, *6/JG 1* (centre) with his first and second mechanics. In the *Luftwaffe*, all fighter pilots messed together irrespective of rank. Relations between flying crew and ground staff were also very good in the fighter units. (Otto Schmid)

50. *Major* Wilhelm-Friedrich 'Wutz' Galland, *Gruppenkommandeur II/JG 26* (left), returns the salute of *Oberleutnant* Otto Stammberger, *Staffelkapitän 4/JG 26*, 1943 in Vitry en Artois. 'Wutz' was the talented brother of the famous Adolf Galland, *General der Jagdflieger*, and was killed in action on 17 August 1943 with his score then at 55 claims. (Otto Stammberger, via Lothair Vanoverbeke)

*Right*: 51. *Oberfeldwebel* Ernst Heesen *5/JG 1*, a good mentor to Otto Schmid when he first joined *II/JG 1* in 1942. Heesen began his career with *I/JG 3* (became *II/JG 1* in mid-January 1942) where he downed a Spitfire in February 1941, followed by 14 Russian aircraft. In *II/JG 1* he claimed a further nine western victories before being killed in air combat with Spitfires when he crashed into the sea near Haarlem on 3 May 1943. (Otto Schmid)

*Below left*: 52. *Hauptmann* Hans-Ekkehard Bob, *Staffelkapitän 9/JG 54*, Home Defence, 1943. (Hans-Ekkehard Bob)

*Below right*: 53. *Feldwebel* Dr Felix Sauer, ex-*10/JG 53*, taken on 23 July 1943 while with a training unit; despite this he still saw some action over Germany. He was promoted to *Leutnant der Reserve* by the end of the war. (Dr Felix Sauer)

54a & 54b. *Hauptmann* Kurt Ruppert, *Gruppenkommandeur III/JG 26* since 7 April 1943 and who had joined the *Geschwader* in November 1940. He was killed in action on 13 June 1943, when he attacked a four-engined bomber formation from behind. He bailed out but opened the parachute too soon, plunging to the ground with a partly opened 'chute, dying half an hour after he landed without regaining consciousness. According to the *Geschwader Ehrenbuch* he had claimed 21 victories on 302 *Feindflüge*, and had been awarded the German Cross in Gold. The bottom photo shows him returning from a mission at either Wevelghem or Moorsele in Belgium in autumn 1942. (*JG 26* veteran via Lothair Vanoverbeke)

55. *Major* Priller, *Kommodore JG 26* (right foreground without helmet), at the funeral of *Hauptmann* Fritz Geisshardt, *Gruppenkommandeur III/JG 26* at Abbeville cemetery on 8 April 1943. Geisshardt, until January 1943 with *JG 77* (100 victory claims and awarded the *Eichenlaub zum Ritterkreuz*), attacked the flank of a B-17 formation on 5 April 1943 and was hit by return fire, being wounded in the stomach. He managed to belly-land at Ghent airfield but died the next day. (*JG 26* veteran via Lothair Vanoverbeke)

56. *Hauptmann* Johannes ('Hans') Naumann, who flew in 4th, 6th, 7th and 9th *Staffeln*, led the 6th and 7th as well as *II/JG 26*. A humorous pose, but putting the *Jagdflieger* on a pedestal is not so far-fetched given how they fought and what most went through, although with time there was ever less to laugh about. (*JG 26* veteran via Lothair Vanoverbeke)

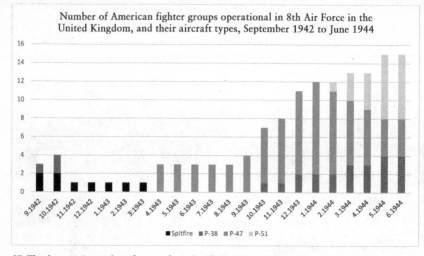

57. The decrease in number of groups from October to November 1942 was due to transfers to North Africa for Operation Torch. Total numbers rose steadily from September 1943 to June 1944, while at the same time P-38 groups increased in number gradually. Early in 1944, P-47s were increasingly replaced by P-51s which became dominant by May. P-38 = Lockheed Lightning; P-47 = Republican Thunderbolt; P-51 = North American Mustang.

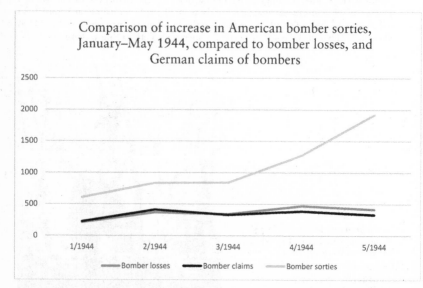

58. Shown also are bomber claims by German fighters which incorporate the total of bombers shot down and *Herausschüsse* (damaged and separated from formation); US bomber losses shown were to all operational causes, and exceeded German claims, implying also losses to German flak. In the last two months, growth in sorties vastly outpaced losses or perceived German victory claims.

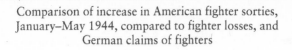

## Comparison of increase in American fighter sorties, January–May 1944, compared to fighter losses, and German claims of fighters

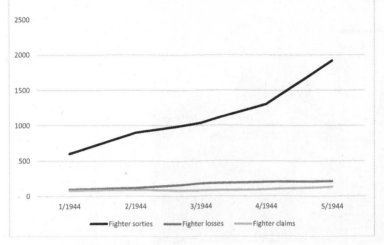

Fighter sorties ▬▬▬ Fighter losses ▬▬▬ Fighter claims

59. American fighter sorties, shown as one-tenth of real values for purposes of scale, vastly outpaced both US fighter losses and German fighter claims against them, for the period January to May 1944. US fighter losses to all operational causes.

60. *Feldwebel* Otto Schmid, *5/JG 1*: 'One can see the blue-grey underside of the wings, as well as the camouflage of the fuselage and tail well in this photo. The view from the cockpit of the FW 190 was very good, in all directions. Regarding the (white) spiral marking on the propeller hub, this was until *c.* 1944 up to the individual *Staffelführer*, whether the spiral was painted on or not. From 1944 onwards this spiral was painted on as a broad white stripe at the factory already, for the FW 190 A-6 and later models. The camouflage colour, or primer paint of the aircraft was a light blue-grey. The entire aircraft except for the underside, was sprayed with darker shadowing on top of this. The underside was kept in the primer blue-grey, and also the underside of the tail. On the sides of the fuselage as well as on the wings, on top and below, the *Balkenkreuz* (black cross) was added.' (Otto Schmid)

61. *Feldwebel* Fritz Buchholz, *II/ZG 26* with his senior mechanic *Unteroffizier* Barth. They are standing on the port wing of a Me 410; there is a Ju 52 in the background. (Fritz Buchholz)

62. *Leutnant* Gerhard Keppler, *2/JG 27* commented on some of his awards: 'The three silver wings on a blue background (just above the *EK 1*) was the badge for the glider C licence that I got before the war on the Teck. The plaque hanging next to it was some Italian award, I can no longer remember the name thereof.' The latter was probably the Italian Africa Service Medal. (Gerhard Keppler)

of the RAF against Holland and thus also against *JG 1*. From this it appeared that I had shot down the squadron leader; his name was Edney.' R. W. de Visser supplied further information to Otto Schmid on this action, specifically that it emanated from an attack on a German convoy off the Hook of Holland by 24 Beaufighters of Coastal Command who lost two aircraft to ships' flak and one (S/L Edney of 236 Squadron) to *Unteroffizier* Schmid of 4/JG 1.

Otto Schmid, now transferred to 6th *Staffel* of II/JG 1, was peripherally involved with the famous RAF raid on the Philips Works at Eindhoven in his last *Feindberührung* of the year. 'Mission on 6 December 1942: I had just landed with my *Rottenführer* at 12h04 after a scramble without any enemy aircraft being contacted, when we saw from the vantage of our dispersal area, about an hour later, at 13h04, a low flying Lockheed (Ventura) flying past our airfield. We, that is *Unteroffizier* Rauhaus and I, took off immediately and overtook this aircraft just before the island of Vlissingen. As soon as we were in range, we opened fire, taking turns to attack. On the last attack from directly behind, Rauhaus was able to set one engine alight, upon which the Lockheed belly-landed on Vlissingen. The victory was credited to him. The Philips Works in Eindhoven was heavily damaged in this raid. From 15h25 to 16h20 we flew the afternoon sea reconnaissance, but could see no ditched aircraft or crews in the Channel. The ditched crews from the raid had most likely been rescued by the English sea rescue service by then.'

Missions were also tied into a points system, detailed below, which was used as a means of fair judgement for an individual receiving decorations and, in the longer term, promotion. Otto Schmid commented that it was applied throughout the *Geschwader*. 'Regarding the points system in *JG 1*, I recall that this system was used in all units, so clear differentiation could be made for awards and even promotions.' For most mission types, if the flight was classified as a *Frontflug* then five points were awarded for *Alarmstart*, *Überwachungsflug* and *Seeaufklärung* operations, and one point if this condition was not met; for these same mission types and *Geleitflug* missions, if a full-length flight was made they also counted as five points, but if it was a short flight only one point was counted. A *Sperrflug* (terms all defined in caption to illustration 41) counted as one point only. When there was *Feindberührung*, 20 points were awarded, also when action was experienced against enemy ships, not just aircraft. It is important that this points system not be confused with that used by all *Geschwadern* for shooting down different types of Western aircraft, specifically applied to four-engined bombers, where full destruction counted three points, detaching it from its formation in a damaged state (*Herausschuss*) counted two points, and final destruction of such a detached bomber (*entgultige Vernichtung*) gave one point.[24] Analogously, full destruction of a twin-engined bomber earned two points, and that of a fighter one point. Both full destruction and *Herausschuss* also gave the pilot a victory, but a final destruction only counted as a victory in addition to its one point if the detachment from the bomber formation had been achieved by the flak.[25]

## Fighter-bombers over Southern England: March 1942–June 1943

As discussed in the chapter on the Battle of Britain, *Jabo* attacks had formed an intrinsic part of the later stages of this conflict, and their use continued on into about mid-1941. Full details of the *Jabo* campaign against Britain can be gleaned from a book written by aviation historian Chris Goss,[26] and it is from this book that the few details summarised here are taken. Thanks largely to the efforts of an already experienced fighter-bomber pilot, *Oberleutnant* Frank Liesendahl in JG 2, a dedicated *Jabostaffel*, 13/JG 2, renamed as 10/JG 2 in April 1942, was formed on 10 November 1941.[27] Following intensive training and trial attacks on southern England in late December 1941, 13/JG 2 was fully operational by March 1942, during which month JG 26 also formed a similar dedicated *Jabostaffel*, 10/JG 26, which became 10/JG 54 in March 1943. These low-level attacks by a combination of bombs and gunfire on southern English coastal towns targeted military and industrial assets on land and ships in harbour and at sea, and tended to be limited to small formations, mostly of *Rotte* and *Schwarm* strength, and occasionally up to *Staffel* numbers; the damage and casualties caused were disproportionately large, and anti-aircraft assets, supporting services and significant British fighter resources flying wasteful standing patrols had to be allocated to combating them. Due to their success, in February 1943 an entire *Jabogeschwader* was set up: *Schnellkampfgeschwader* 10, SKG 10, initially with *I* and *II Gruppen*, followed by IV/SKG 10, which absorbed the original two *Staffeln*, 10/JG 2 and 10/JG 54. As a result, from about March 1943, *Jabo* numbers increased and raids by 15 or 20 – even up to 40 aircraft in one case in January 1943 – became possible. Despite their success these raids were terminated abruptly in early June 1943 due to the crisis in the Mediterranean theatre[28] with the fall of Tunis and the expected invasion, somewhere, of southern Europe by the Allies, which duly fell on Sicily on 10 July 1943. Total *Jabo* losses in the period March 1942–June 1943 encompassed 62 aircraft and pilots, and while the British claimed 55 fighter-bombers falling to anti-aircraft fire and 51 to fighters, actual losses to these causes were 28 to each and one more shared between them, while five more *Jabos* fell to other causes, largely reflecting the hazards inimical to flying operations at very low levels.[29]

The *Jabo* operations also entailed additional inputs of JG 2 and 26 fighters to provide escorts and more remote supporting sweeps, and these of course led to additional losses to the units concerned. One of these was the youngest brother of former JG 26 *Kommodore* Adolf Galland, by then well established as the *General der Jagdflieger*. 22-year-old Paul Galland of 8/JG 26 was already a promising fighter pilot with 104 combat missions, an Iron Cross first class (*EK 1*), and 17 victories to his credit when the *Geschwader Ehrenbuch JG 26* recorded his loss.[30]

On the 31 October 1942, the day that *Leutnant* Galland died, in the afternoon he shot down a Boston near Diymuiden that had been using the protection of low clouds to intrude in over the coast of Flanders. In the evening the Third *Gruppe* took off, to provide escort for about 50 *Jabos* that were to carry out a retaliation (i.e. in relation to Bomber Command's raids on German cities) raid on Canterbury. Due to the poor visibility, low clouds and the many Fw 190s in the air, he lost contact with his *Gruppe*. On the return flight, about 15 km off Calais over the sea, he heard the message 'Contact with Spitfires' over the radio. He was flying close behind the *Jabos*. After making two curving sweeps he saw in the distance that a Spitfire at low level was behind and shooting at a Fw 190 [*Leutnant* Beese]. He flew towards them and attacked the Spitfire, whose pilot, however, saw him coming and pulled up into the clouds (at 400 m). *Leutnant* Galland had attacked in a left-hand turn from below and behind, and thus as he pulled up to follow, lost too much speed and hung below the clouds, almost motionless as he began to stall. He was thus forced to push the stick forward rapidly to gain speed, and at that the Spitfire popped out of the clouds and sat exactly behind him in firing position. *Leutnant* Galland plunged into the sea on fire.

At almost the same moment his wingman, *Feldwebel* Edmann, got behind the Spitfire and shot this down. The Spitfire caught fire immediately and dived vertically into the Channel.

## Some Leading Personalities in JG 26: Adolf Galland and Others

*Oberstleutnant* Adolf Galland led the *Geschwader* from 22 August 1940 at the height of the Battle of Britain until 5 December 1941,[31] when he was appointed *General der Jagdflieger* in place of Werner Mölders, who died in a crash in bad weather when flying back from the Russian front for *General* Udet's funeral. His place at the helm of *JG* 26 was taken by *Major* Gerhard Schöpfel who led it until 10 January 1943.[32] Galland was a leading ace in the West in his own right and had brought his score to 96 victories by November 1941, and held the highest decoration, *Ritterkreuz mit Eichenlaub, Schwerten und Brillanten* – Knights Cross with Oak Leaves, Swords, Diamonds.[33] *Oberleutnant* Otto Stammberger, *9/JG 26*, later *Staffelkapitän 4/JG 26*, recorded his memory of him in 1989:

We young and as yet unsuccessful pilots looked up to our *Kommodore* Galland as to an icon. That he was not an icon is perfectly obvious, but he was a fighter pilot with great successes, who hourly put his life on the line and was a wonderful example. Most of us were scared of him when we were detailed to accompany him in his hunting when bad weather prevented flying. Rotten shots like us missed all the time and he dropped geese, pheasants, partridges or laid out hares and rabbits with every shot. He hit everything with the first shot, he carried his Browning at the hip with his right hand and shot without aiming and from the hip everything that flew and ran, every shot was on target. And he shot the same way in the air, he was one with his machine and always shot at exactly the right moment – bull's eye! That a certain feeling of superiority to other people arose from these skills is understandable. This was particularly so against other people who were not fighter pilots. For clueless weaklings like us he also always had understanding, even though he really gave us hell and humiliated us in the next moment. He was very hard on himself and also expected the same from others. He always flew ahead and was the first to close with the enemy. In the air and so also on the ground, he made very rapid decisions; we had to obey and carry these out like lightning. Galland exactly conformed to someone who was a leader in heart and soul, without compromises. I honour him today still, we meet from time to time. Right now he is seriously ill. It must be really dreadful for such a keen hunter like him, not to be able to see anymore!!!

His successor at both *III/JG 26* and in the *Geschwader* command, Gerhard Schöpfel, had known Galland much longer. 'Adolf Galland was with me already in 1936 in the then-*Bernburger Jagdgruppe*. In 1940 he became my *Gruppenkommandeur* in *III/JG 26*, and later the *Kommodore* of *JG 26*. He was a very accomplished pilot, and was also technically gifted. On operations he was very hard on himself. As an officer and commander he kept his distance, he did not open up his heart. His father asked me in 1941 how we got on with his son. He told me that he did not always see eye to eye with him. These times are now long gone. Adolf Galland stood by to help me immediately when I experienced difficulties in my profession after the war. I kept some distance then, but today (writing in 1990) we have a good and comradely relationship.' All four Galland brothers were fighter pilots: the eldest, Dr Fritz Galland, served with *JG 3, 5*, reconnaissance units and training formations and scored a single victory; Adolf Galland was next eldest; his younger brother Wilhelm-Ferdinand ('Wutz') also served in *JG 26*, where he rose to *Gruppenkommandeur*, scored 55 victories and was awarded the *Ritterkreuz* before being killed over Germany on 17 August 1943; Paul Galland, whose demise over the Channel was recorded above, was the youngest.[34] One can only imagine the anxiety their parents must have suffered during the war, with the added burden of losing two of their sons in action. Otto Stammberger knew all the leading lights in *JG 26* and comments below on some of them.

I knew Priller (*Kommodore* 11 January 1943–27 January 1945),[35] Ruppert, Naumann and 'Wutz' Galland very well. After all, I was with them for almost five years. In 1941 I joined *9/JG 26* under *Oberleutnant* Kurt Ruppert, *Staffelkapitän* from 12 November 1940 to 6 April 1943, when he was killed in action with 21 victories to his name.[36] The *Kommandeur* of *III/JG 26* was *Major* Gerhard Schöpfel. Ruppert was a small, wiry officer, always calm, level-headed and serious. Hans (Johannes) Naumann, known as 'Häns'chen', was a jolly *Leutnant* in the 9th *Staffel* when I joined them. He was an outstanding pilot and we often flew together in the summer of 1941 against the Non-Stop Offensive, first in a *Rotte* together and then in a *Schwarm* where I led the second *Rotte*.

The 9th *Staffel* mostly operated as the top cover for the *Gruppe* or the entire *Geschwader*; after all we were the last *Staffel*. And in the *Staffel* I led the last *Rotte* that in its turn flew top cover for the *Staffel*. We were thus always 'on top, closest to The Lord'. However, this also meant that we were always the first to be attacked by the even higher-flying Spitfires, which explains the relatively few victories claimed by our *Staffel*. Häns'chen taught me how to avoid these attacks and how best to make it home again. Those were hard years of education; my friends who joined at the same time as me already had some victories to their names, but I despite many combat missions had not a single one! As examples were 'Paulchen' Galland, 17 victories, Robby Unzeitig, 19, etc. Häns'chen Naumann survived the war and now (1989) lives in Fürstenfeldbruck. Priller was strict but just, and this masked a good sense of humour. As the years of war passed by, we all tended to lose our sense of humour; there was nothing more to laugh about. That obviously affected our memories of specific comrades strongly. From my personal point of view, I never had serious or long-lasting differences with either a superior or someone of lesser rank. I was able to get on well with everyone and was well tolerated.

## The Aircraft

The views expressed below on the relative merits of the aircraft flying from both sides of the Channel make for interesting reading; it is often said that there was not that much to choose between them. Despite the better scoring of the German *Jagdgeschwader* along the Channel coasts, their British opponents remained respected and even feared opponents, as recalled by 'Häns'chen' Naumann, who led 6/JG 26 from 21 September 1942 to 17 August 1943 when he became *Gruppenkommandeur* of II/JG 26.[37]

From 1940 to autumn 1941 the Me 109 was superior to British fighters, particularly in rate of climb and level speed. From 1942 this situation changed through the introduction of more powerful engines in the Spitfire. The newly introduced Fw 190 changed little in this general situation. It was also inferior from 5,000 m upwards. The Fw 190 was marked by stability and very good and strong armament. In the beginning of its service there were very serious problems with the cooling system of the engine, it being inadequate for a fighter aircraft with the highly variable demands made on the engine during combat missions. Engine failures were an almost daily occurrence. In the beginning of its service life the average engine life was about eight hours. This certainly changed once a new cooling ring was installed on the radial engine, but long engine life such as that enjoyed by the English and US power plants remained mere dreams for us. This weakness of the Fw 190 weighed on us particularly during flights over the sea. In this respect I especially remember 12 February 1942, when the German capital ships broke through the Channel at which time we still had a lot of trouble with our engines.

*Leutnant* Otto Stammberger, *9/JG 26* painted a similar picture: 'In 1941 already, the Tommies with their Spitfire V achieved at least parity with our Me 109 F; the Spitfire engine was 100–150 horsepower stronger and this increased with time, and at heights from 8,000 m upwards she was effectively better, turned better generally and also climbed away upwards better than the Me 109 F. In summer and autumn 1941 our *Geschwader* re-equipped with the Focke-Wulf 190 and we were faster and more manoeuvrable up to *c.* 5,000 m; above that height, the Spitfire was again better, particularly the Spitfire IX, which had a new engine, new turbocharger, and new aerodynamics for the 1,700–1,800 horsepower it developed. Our radial engine on the Fw 190 developed 1,300–1,400 horsepower.'

*Unteroffizier* Otto Schmid of *5/JG 1* can report well on comparisons between the Me 109 and the Fw 190, having converted from the former to the latter at Rotenburg in Germany in May 1942. According to his logbook, he was given only one familiarisation flight and five circuits to do so, with a total flying time of a mere 38 minutes! This took place over two days, after which it was back to their base at Katwijk and a return to flying the Me 109 F-4. The actual switch to flying the Fw 190 on operations took place on 4 June 1942. There was much excitement in *II/JG 1* on receiving the new aircraft, and the various stages in preparing them for active operational flying were recorded in several photographs at the time, some included in the illustrations in this volume. 'On the quality of the Me 109 against that of the Fw 190, one can say that both were good aircraft, but the Fw 190 was significantly more robust. To balance this, the 109 gave one an elegant feel of flying. In the end it came down to the specific model of each aircraft which was flown. The two aircraft had more and more equipment and adaptations added over time, making them increasingly heavier and thus not faster either. However, if you could fly both aircraft properly, each could be used to achieve success. Unfortunately, the range of our aircraft was far too limited. When flying with combat performance, one had a total flying time of maximum 50 minutes (obviously not all at full combat power). One has to remember that, compared to this, the Thunderbolt and Mustang with drop tanks could stay in the air for four and a half hours.'

Adolf Glunz began his service on the Channel Front in the first half of 1941, where he gained two successes with *4/JG 52* (a logbook extract from this period is provided earlier in this chapter), followed by brief service on the Eastern Front, where three more successes came his way. He then joined *JG 26*. *Feldwebel* Glunz of *4/JG 26* became a major Channel Front ace who shot down 18 victories in this theatre during 1941–42.[38] By the end of the war he had raised his score to 72 claims and had been awarded the *Eichenlaub*.[39] This highly experienced pilot lays great stress on eyesight for success in combat, and underlines the fact that individual pilot ability coupled with technical knowledge of opponents' aircraft were more important than the relative merits of the opposing fighters. 'By and large the Spitfire was the equal of our Fw 190. The Spitfire was generally more manoeuvrable, but I was also able to shoot some of them down in turns while dogfighting. At the end of the day it really came down to the ability of the pilot, and especially in dogfights to the courage of the pilot. One cannot really talk about a specific tactic in pure fighter-*versus*-fighter combat. That depended inevitably on the different situations and attacking positions. Where possible I tried to climb above the enemy without being seen, to attack from above if at all possible and from the sun. That necessitated a particularly good long-range vision, as I had to see the enemy before he saw me, otherwise it was hardly possible to out-climb him. As in this regard I had exceptionally good eyesight, I was able to perform favourably in many combats. Not for nothing did we have the saying that "he who sees first, lives longer". In addition, it was also an advantage to have exact knowledge of the performance and flying characteristics of the various enemy aircraft, so as to adapt your own combat tactics to the situation.' The Fw 190 was a surprisingly advanced aircraft for its day, with a primitive, almost computer-like automated control system, known as the *Kommandogerät*; Otto Stammberger elaborates below.

Today one would describe this as a type of computer which controls all the engine functions. But in those days it was not yet electronic but rather mechanical-hydraulic in nature. Our basic starting point was to maintain a specific level of engine revolutions, i.e. revolutions per minute, which we could read off the rev-counter instrument. The *Kommandogerät* adjusted the pitch of the propeller blades, changing the angles thereof according to our speed, in either dive or climb situations, so as to keep a constant engine revolution value, i.e. this is a constant speed propeller unit. In addition, the *Kommandogerät* controlled the fuel injection system and provided the correct fuel-air mixture to the injection pump and the injection valves. And then the *Kommandogerät* controlled the point, or rather altitude, at which the turbocharger (a compressor) cut in, so that above 3,500 m the falling air pressure was compensated and the cylinders received enough air. While we took off from ground level at an air pressure value of one, and at 3,500 m this was reduced to 0.5–0.6, the turbocharger was activated mechanically, with a resultant jolt, and there was a loud noise in the aircraft, but the air pressure was restored to a value of one again, and the aircraft made an appreciable leap forwards. The Tommies soon worked this out, and then flew always beneath the altitude where the turbocharger cut in, thus handicapping us significantly. The air pressure fell off again markedly at 7,000 m, leaving us hanging like ripe plums in the air.

Later there was a secondary turbocharger which cut in at 6,000 m, ensuring an air pressure value of one at that height, but it took a lot of engine performance away to drive itself, so that in the end it gave us little advantage. The *Kommandogerät* also controlled the ignition timing for varying fuel-air mixtures and the temperature of the engine in summer and winter. I never experienced any fault with the *Kommandogerät*; one could also change the height at which the primary turbocharger kicked in, some pilots preferring normal air pressure to be restored from 4,000 m altitude, others already at 3,000 m. We ensured that, at least for a specific *Staffel*, a uniform altitude was selected. The *Kommandogerät* was only fitted to the BMW 801 radial engine, the Jumo 213 engine had other mechanical controls for every function, and also had a three level turbocharger!

Adolf Glunz, in his comments about the fighting over the Channel in 1941–42, stressed the importance of having knowledge of your enemy's aircraft. The high RAF casualties along the Channel coasts ensured a supply of enemy material for the German *Luftwaffe* technicians to study. I asked *Oberleutnant* Otto Stammberger, 9/JG 26, later *Staffelkapitän* 4/JG 26, to comment on these German investigations of enemy material: 'The enemy aircraft shot down in northern France were investigated by special salvage troops from the *Fliegerkorps*, and some were then transported to one of the experimental units at Rechlin or Berlin. We in the flying units and *Geschwader* had no influence on this at all, and anyway we had no salvage equipment or personnel. The different enemy types were studied at the experimental stations, and when they were still flyable (or could be repaired), they were then flown and the front-line units received reports on every element of new equipment found for every enemy aircraft type, be it new armament, new engines, new flying characteristics, climbing ability, etc. We were thus continually kept informed, but we ourselves did not investigate or fly these enemy aircraft.'

## Living Conditions on the Ground on the Channel Front and in Holland

JG 26 – and no doubt JG 2 also – lived well in northern France, as attested to by that excellent reporter, Otto Stammberger.

Our personal living conditions were, as elite soldiers, always good; we had adequate special food, and not food that made one feel full! – we always had [bean] coffee, and in the evenings cognac and wine. We hardly had any contact with the French population, we were after all on our field bases from first light, sited in the middle of the countryside and far away from large settlements, and then left the base in the evening after dusk had settled. Our quarters were in chateaux also in rural areas, or in requisitioned houses in small villages near the bases. How the French lived, we did not really see, but there was enough to eat in France, and on days when we were released from operations or standby we could drive to the nearest large town or city and enjoy a meal in a hotel, or enjoy coffee in a café where we could also order cognac. Our kitchen staff could buy eggs from the farmers and chickens as well as black market pork [meat was rationed].

The French civilian population, as in Germany, was allocated food in the markets, admittedly not generous amounts, because the

French agricultural sector also had to supply the occupying forces. The French, however, are inventive and there was thus always something available on the 'grey markets' that we could purchase for inflated Franc-based prices; with the black market exchange rate for our Reichsmark currency this was no problem to afford. As everywhere, he who has something can have everything, and he who had nothing had to survive on the minimum. In built-up areas and large cities, there were indeed great shortages of food; women and girls tried to use the oldest profession to keep the heads of their children and families above water. For our soldiers the utmost caution was ordered; not for nothing was the phrase 'the French sickness' used, and on infection there were rigorous punishments. Those who really had to satisfy their urges could do so in controlled establishments that were overseen by German doctors.

Relations with the Dutch people were also reasonably good and living conditions obviously pleasant, as attested to by *Unteroffizier* Otto Schmid of *II/JG 1*. 'Living conditions in Holland for us were very good. Relations with the people were proper. I can say that when the German soldiers behaved decently, then one had no problems with the Dutch. But as we have all experienced, there are always some bad apples. We have a saying: "when one shouts into the forest, then it echoes back again".'

## Conclusions

While the fighting over the Channel coast was intense, especially from 22 June 1941 onwards with the launch of the Non-Stop Offensive, it was still a relatively limited air war in this theatre till later in 1942. Numbers of bombers sent out with the sweeps were small, and penetration depths into enemy airspace were not significant given the limited range of the Spitfires. There was not yet any question of an effective challenge being made for air superiority, even over the Channel coast; only over the British Isles themselves could the RAF claim dominance. However, this was all to change during 1942, as the first harbingers of coming American might made themselves felt with the arrival of the 8th Air Force in this same theatre. Their first mission was flown on 4 July 1942, with a mere six Bostons borrowed from the RAF; on 17 August 1942 the first four-engined bomber raid went in, 12 out of 18 aircraft dispatched reaching their targets in Rouen.[40] By the end of that year more than 100 such bombers had been launched on three occasions, and raids by 50 to roughly 70 aircraft were not uncommon. By the end of the war raids well in excess of 1,000 – even close to 2,000 – four-engined bombers had become the norm,[41] and the *Luftwaffe* fighter arm in the West was to be consumed in this conflagration, such that by the time of the Normandy invasion in June 1944 undisputed air superiority had been gained above the Continent by the Allied air forces.

Fighter strength in the East was steadily denuded to feed the inferno in the West. It was this daylight onslaught – particularly involving the long-range, high-performance US fighters, especially the P-51 Mustang – that was responsible for neutralisation of the *Jagdflieger*. No longer were the clever and very effective fighter tactics of the *Jagdgeschwader* in the West of any great relevance, as most German fighter aircraft had to engage the massed American bomber formations, bristling with defensive armament of their own and escorted by swarms of long-range fighters of performance equal to and even superior to that of the improved Me 109s and Fw 190s. The experienced *Experten* began to fall in battle in large numbers alongside their unschooled colleagues, and the *Luftwaffe* fighter arm went into an unending decline, not even changed in any significant way by the advent of the German jets in late 1944. The Channel Front campaign of 1941–42 should be seen as the relatively small beginnings of this mighty Allied offensive, which was a war-winning weapon. The aerial Battle of Germany will be dealt with in the next chapter, from its advent in mid-1942 to its crowning achievement of air superiority over north-west Europe by the eve of the Normandy invasion on 6 June 1944.

# 7

# The Battle of Germany, August 1942–June 1944

The Battle of Germany (*Reichsverteidigung*, or Home Defence as it was also known) was one which became the central air battle of the war, and one of decisive importance as winning air superiority over the centre of the extended *Reich* would ensure the effective defeat of the German fighter arm, thereby secure the aerial dominance that was to be essential for the successful invasion of continental Europe on 6 June 1944. While the battle raged from the second half of 1942 already, with early small American daylight bomber raids on French, Belgian and Dutch targets, from January 1943 the US 8th Air Force began to attack German targets with ever increasing frequency and the battles became larger and more intense, and losses on both sides climbed dramatically.[1] In the autumn of 1943 the two great raids on Schweinfurt on 17 August (coupled to another on the Regensburg Messerschmitt factories) and 14 October signalled a climax of success of the German fighter forces against the four-engined bombers, which could not be escorted far into Germany due to existing fighters lacking range even with drop tanks.[2] Effectively, raids without escort all the way to and from targets deep within German territory were unsustainable – the *Luftwaffe* had the means and the methods to impose unacceptable losses on the bombers on the unescorted parts of their routes.[3] However, the cumulative price paid by the German fighter arm was also close to achieving success from an Allied perspective through the loss of experienced pilots, especially formation leaders at all levels, who were irreplaceable. Due to Germany's critical fuel situation, newly trained pilots were less and less prepared for battle of any kind, least of all the savage conflict raging in central European skies.

When *Hauptmann* Georg Schröder joined the high-altitude *Staffel 11/JG 2* (which was under command of *I/JG 2* at the time and was later renamed *4/JG 2*)[4] in July 1943, he was already an old man for a fighter pilot at 33; he was a very experienced instructor and became *Staffelkapitän* about a week later despite his total lack of operational experience! He had this to say about his operational life (which lasted over 17 months at a tough time of the war): 'It was a devilish time as the air was so full of iron; I regret this time extraordinarily – this time between Heaven and Earth was no walk in the park.' The pendulum of battle over Germany started to swing back to the Allies with the introduction of the Rolls-Royce Merlin-powered P-51 B Mustang, which could accompany the bombers all the way to their targets and back; the first P-51 escort took place on 13 December 1943, albeit in small numbers.[5] As more Mustangs became available, so the losses to American bombers of the 8th Air Force, based in the UK, and of the 15th Air Force, based in Italy, decreased to acceptable proportions, while the cumulative losses to the German fighters gradually led to their defeat.[6] The American daylight bombing also regularly targeted German airframe and aero-engine factories (including the 'Big Week' raids of February 1944), and as the American fighters gained ascendancy, so they began strafing *Luftwaffe* assets on the ground during 1944, further weakening *Luftwaffe* power.[7]

The Battle of Germany raged from its small beginnings on 17 August 1942 through to 5 June 1944, with the Invasion of Normandy the next day effectively leading to a fundamental change in German fighter assignments; now the vast majority of them were dispatched to Normandy, where they had no real effect on Allied air superiority and where their now mostly inexperienced pilots were slaughtered, even the experienced minority standing little chance of survival. Bombing of Germany naturally continued during the Normandy fighting from June to August, but with much-reduced German fighter defence. Thereafter massive daylight bombing continued for the rest of the year and into 1945 and up to the end of the war, the RAF bombers joining in late in 1944 sometimes as well. This second period of the Battle of Germany from the Invasion onwards and the Normandy battles will be dealt with in a subsequent volume. It was in this latter part of the great battle that the so-called German *Sturmgruppen*, of close formations of heavily armoured Fw 190s, protected by top cover of lighter and better-climbing Me 109s, made their appearance. The advent of highly advanced fighter aircraft such as the Fw 190 D, the Ta 152, the Me

109 K and finally the Me 262 jet fighters did little to change the reality of the *Luftwaffe*'s defeat over Germany; although tactical successes could still be achieved, strategically they were overwhelmed. The 1944–45 whirlwind had finally caught up with those who launched the 1939–41 wind.

The Home Defence campaign was thus a very long one, bitterly fought by both sides with enormous losses in machines and men; it was a battle where the incoming bomber formations would reach strengths in excess of 1,000 aircraft plus many hundreds of escorting fighters. A tragic aspect of the bitterness of this battle was the relatively common tendency among American fighter pilots to kill bailed-out German pilots on their 'chutes, or on the ground during and after a forced landing, as recounted by some of the witnesses below. Altitudes were significantly higher than in almost all other air battles of the war, as the American B-17s and B-24s could comfortably be flown well above 20,000 feet and American escorts also had very high ceilings. The Fw 190 had a performance envelope which rapidly shrunk above 20,000 feet; the other principle German fighter, the Me 109, had a good high-altitude performance but was outclassed mostly by the Mustang if not also by the Thunderbolt. The established German evasive manoeuvre of a half-roll and steep dive, which had been saving its pilots in the Battles of France and Britain in 1940, through all the fighting on the Eastern Front and around the Mediterranean, and which was virtual dogma amongst the *Jagdflieger*, was a fatal action against the American escort aircraft, with the Mustang being faster, diving and climbing better and also being very manoeuvrable. For the German pilots there were thus few prospects for survival and even fewer for racking up significant successes. However, some did survive and some even managed to accumulate very large scores against the Western Allies during 1943–45.[8]

Perhaps the most challenging new element which the Battle of Germany brought was in how to attack the large American four-engined bomber fleets, which flew close formations, carefully worked out to maximise use of their very heavy defensive armament. The *Jagdflieger* had tended to concentrate on fighter-*versus*-fighter combat throughout the war thus far, over France and England in 1940, over North Africa and in the East; though this gave them high scores, which was certainly *Luftwaffe* policy, it was strategically a war-losing approach as the Allied bombers were the targets that were the more dangerous in the bigger picture and which in the end destroyed much of the *Wehrmacht*'s fighting power, particularly in the East and North Africa. In the Home Defence there was no longer any choice for the *Jagdflieger*; initially the four-engined bombers were the only targets to attack, and later, with the increasing escorts, the bombers remained the critical element to be destroyed. Effectively attacking the American bomber formations set the German fighter pilots an almost insoluble problem and one which exercised their abilities and bravery to the utmost; it also led to many rather hare-brained ideas, mostly from the *Luftwaffe*'s upper echelons, as will be discussed in this chapter by the many eye-witnesses. It is thus fitting that the first extensive account be from an experienced *Reichsverteidigung* pilot, Otto Schmid, who flew as an *Unteroffizier* and later *Feldwebel* in all three *Staffeln* of II/JG 1 against the bombers for something like 13 months. In the end he was knocked down as well, losing a leg, and was very lucky to have survived at all; most did not. His account is really an excellent summary of the four-engined bomber problem and the actions taken to address it.

When the American Boeing B-17 became operational against us in the West, we realised very soon that with the conventional methods of attack no measurable success was to be achieved. Also, we were used to attacking out of the sun. However, with the size of the bomber formations this was also risky, as we were almost always shot at by other bombers in the formation who could aim at us from the side. Thus there was no other alternative but to attack from head-on and slightly above, which did work, as the bomber's gunners were given the least chance of replying with the chosen angle of attack, and the other advantage was that our high speed in a shallow dive gave us a stable gun platform, upon which again our aiming capacity depended – all of this provided, of course, that one did not open fire too soon. One could achieve successes with this tactic without being much bothered by being fired upon by other bombers in the formation. Also, with the high approach speeds in a head-on attack one passed very rapidly, and thus relatively safely, through the rest of the formation.

However, this all got much worse when, due to the losses of bombers, the escorting fighters suddenly appeared. These were made up of units of Mustangs and Thunderbolts, and sometimes Lightnings as well. But every time the numbers of these aircraft were frighteningly high. If we had enough advance warning we could reach the necessary height to be placed somewhat higher than the escorts. When we ourselves had enough fighters in this sort of position (which seldom occurred), a part of our fighters engaged the escorting American fighters in combat, while the other part could then concentrate on the bombers. Sadly, this seldom took place in reality; in practical terms we were forced to 'dance at two weddings'. The enemy escorting fighters adapted themselves to our new tactics and then flew ahead of the bomber formations and waited for us in almost all altitudes. Against this superior force we had nothing to counter with, as we lacked sufficient machines and well-trained pilots in the first place, and secondly the American and later also the English fighters were qualitatively and quantitatively superior. Our new pilots now had only a really shortened training. Mostly they could hardly even fly their own aircraft properly. Important to them was to get their aircraft into the air, and then if they survived, to get it down on the ground again after the mission was over. In most cases they were shot down after at most three to four missions, or crashed on their own. It was a tragedy how the German youth were wasted in this way. Our aircraft were continually improved, but unfortunately the power of our engines could not keep pace with the added weight imposed by the improvements. These disadvantages we had to try and equalize through flying ability. But 'many dogs are the death of the rabbit', as the old saying goes. The radius of action of our fighters over Germany was also very limited.

*Oberst* Gustav Rödel, who flew 980 combat missions from the beginning of the war until January 1945 (when appointed as commander of *Jagddivision 2* in the Home Defence), had seen it all on many different fronts, including even the Spanish Civil War; he went from *Staffelkapitän* in 1940 to *Kommodore* in 1943, all in *JG 27*, and managed to bring down 12 four-engined bombers among his 98 victory claims over the Balkans and the Home Defence. In correspondence sent to the author he recalls that of all his missions the attacks on the four-engined bomber formations remained nightmarish in his memory. Importantly, he also remembered that each individual attack on a different formation had a different pattern – there were many unknown factors that cropped up during the approach to a target formation, such as the weather, the actions of the fighter escort and the inherent difficulty of trying to manoeuvre a big formation of your own fighters. This is almost always the case in military actions – no matter how good the plan and the method, things tend to go wrong more often than they go right. Rödel stressed that the aim of the unit leader in the air was to get his formation into a suitable position to launch a head-on attack on a bomber formation, and also to fly in such a formation that each pilot therein got the opportunity to close up to the bombers and to fire on them – only one such run would be possible. After that it was basically every man for himself, and often you could not even look out for your wingman. The distances flown from the air bases to attack the bomber targets were far and fuel shortage remained a constant worry for the German pilots; after flying for a long while to make an interception, after the initial attack there would be precious little fuel left for dog fighting.

The difference between the Battle of Britain (where the wisdom of many attacks by small formations of defending fighters was proved correct with hindsight) and the Battle of Germany was in many ways one of scale. Over Germany the bombers themselves were much bigger, carrying many more defensive machine guns and with even larger escorts than those typically used over the United Kingdom, and the distances flown by both attackers and defenders were much greater than the cross-Channel and limited penetration raids flown over Britain. However, the *Luftwaffe* upper echelons persisted with launching *Gruppe-* and even *Geschwader*-scale attacks on the American bombers, despite there being enough senior pilots and even some of the commanders at higher levels still living who had seen the Battle of Britain and the successful British tactics with their own eyes.

Some pilots found themselves thrown into the Home Defence cauldron with little warning. One such was Georg Schröder, who ended up as *Hauptmann* and *Gruppenkommandeur II/JG 2*; his lengthy experience as a pilot, albeit not a combat pilot, no doubt helped to see him through a campaign that saw the death of many a highly successful ace.

After my schooling was over, as well as a succeeding practical training in an engineering works in Braunschweig, in April 1929 I began a course of technical study in aircraft construction. Thus the theory became one with the practical. In parallel to my studies I also flew, wherever and whenever possible, and naturally full-time during my holidays between semesters. In 1929 I flew gliders for two months at the Wasserkuppe/Rhön. In 1930 I switched immediately to powered aircraft. In September 1933 I completed my studies. At this time

I already had 350 flying hours to my name, and was also an assistant flying instructor. Regarding my professional activity, already more than a year before, I had concluded a binding agreement with two handshakes with the bosses, to join Focke-Wulf in Bremen in a fixed position in the industry as soon as my studies were complete. However, this did not take place, as with the new political direction the state guidelines for the future were still very unsure.

My membership of the *Ring der Flieger* (an association of various post-First World War flying clubs and organisations, changed forcibly in 1933 to the Nazi's *Deutschen Luftsportverband*) in Berlin made it immediately possible for me to become part of real, practical flying. That implies that I made an agreement with the German *Reich* as a flying instructor. Here my theoretical background provided me with a good understanding of the aviation world when taking my professional pilot licences in parallel with instructing. Thus I progressed from instructor to group flying instructor, chief instructor, and finally training leader of a flying school. This was not just an interesting time for me, but also a fulfilling one. Thus I was one of the very few civilians in a military field. However, I also had to enter myself into the career of a reserve officer and that went off without any problems. My transfer to a frontline unit followed in June 1943, once the fuel supply situation in the training schools had become very poor. After a short intermission learning to fly frontline aircraft types, I joined *Jagdgeschwader 2 Richthofen*. After about a week in this unit I was given the 11th *Staffel*.

This new environment, ever changing from minute to minute, required no small adaptability, not forgetting that the surrounding air was often devilishly iron-rich, and this necessitated also a very changed approach to life. 'War', one asked oneself immediately, 'just why?' Twice this curse had repeated itself in this century. People swore 'never a war again!', but soon there will have been a hundred more already, just think of the Balkans, and we are faced with nothing but doubt looking forwards. I was not spared scars either. Three times I had to use my parachute. Once was really stupid, as my own comrade cut off the fuselage 30 cm behind my cockpit hood with his propeller, and this was at a height of about 750 m above the ground. The second time was after a big dog fight with Spitfires who outnumbered us by at least three times; hit in the radiator, so once again I took to my 'chute but with a wind of ground speed of 70 km/h – three neck vertebrae separated and I was not allowed to fly for four weeks. The third bail-out will be detailed separately. My frontline successes encompassed: one Spitfire over Normandy, one at Monte Casino, three Boeing Fortress IIs, two Thunderbolts, six Mustangs and one Lightning. If I can apply a hunting analogy where the hunter shoots the Christmas hare in the company of his trusty dog, in my time high in the air the adage 'many dogs will be the death of the hare' applied!!!

Another pilot who survived the battles over Germany was *Oberleutnant* Hans Hartigs, who also had a lengthy period of flying experience before becoming a fighter pilot with *2/JG 26* in this deadly campaign. It is possible that having greater flying experience and being fully in control of a high-performance fighter aircraft, rather than having many victories as a successful fighter pilot in other theatres, may have been a better form of life insurance in the battles over Germany. 'After flying long-range reconnaissance over Poland–Russia–Mediterranean–Arctic areas, in 1943 I underwent fighter pilot training and then joined *JG 2* (where I claimed 10 *Abschüsse* – Spitfires, Marauders and Thunderbolts). In autumn 1943 I joined *2/JG 26* (claimed six four-engined bombers) and remained with them until I was shot down after my last victory and made POW on 26 December 1944.'

## A Complex Command and Organisational Setup

The higher command structure of the *Luftwaffe* fighter forces involved in this immense battle is briefly summarised below; it was complex and changed as the war went on.[9] In August 1942 there were two relevant commands: (1) *Luftwaffenbefehlshaber Mitte* (became *Luftflotte Reich* on 5 February 1944, till end of war) covered the *Reich* proper plus Holland (and the north-eastern half of Belgium) essentially; (2) *Luftflotte 3* (became *Luftwaffenkommando West* after 26 September 1944) covered France and the south-western half of Belgium, essentially.

*Luftwaffenbefehlshaber Mitte* (Air Force Commanding Officer Central) contained a single flying corps (*Fliegerkorps XII*), which in August 1942 comprised two night fighter divisions (*Nachtjagddivisions 1* and *2*, which on 1 October 1942 became, respectively, *Jagddivisions 1* and *2*) plus *Jagddivision 4*. *Luftflotte 3* had the subordinate *Jagddivision 3*, which was split into *Jagdfliegerführers* (shortened to *Jafü*) *2* (covering north-east France and south-western half of Belgium) and *3* (north-western France). Briefly, the *Jagddivisions* (fighter divisions) were situated as follows (renumbering as of 15 September 1943 in brackets):

*Jagddivision 1*: HQ at Deelen, central Holland; defence of Holland, north-east Belgium (*Jagddivision 3*).

*Jagddivision 2*: HQ at Stade, west of Hamburg; defence of central-northern Germany and German Bight (no renumbering, remained *Jagddivision 2*).

*Jagddivision 3*: HQ at Metz, eastern France, south of Luxembourg; defence of France and south-western Belgium (*Jagddivision 4*).

*Jagddivision 4*: HQ at Döberitz, just west of Berlin; defence of north-eastern Germany (*Jagddivision 1* from 15 September 1943).

In June 1943 *Jagddivision 5* (*Jagddivision 7* from 15 September 1943) was added, having been formed from *Jafü* South Germany (which itself had only existed from February to June 1943), HQ at Schleissheim, northern Munich; defence of southern Germany.[10]

Until mid-September 1943, while *General* Kammhuber commanded *Fliegerkorps XII* as a night fighter specialist, his headquarters controlled the night aerial activity within Germany and Holland, leaving day fighter direction and control to the *Jafüs*.[11] On 15 September 1943 a complete reorganisation of the higher commands took place, *Fliegerkorps XII* being replaced by *Jagdkorps I* (commanded by *General* 'Beppo' Schmid till 30 November 1944);[12] the renumbered *Jagddivisons* 1, 2, 3 and 7 fell under this new command structure, which lasted until 26 January 1945.[13] In parallel with this reorganisation, many of the *Jagdfliegerführers* were discontinued, tactical direction and control passing to the *Jagddivisions*, a process complete by year's end.[14] From August 1942, *Jafü Deutsche Bucht* had fulfilled the fighter control function for *Jagddivision 2*, being renamed *Jafü 2* in September 1943; similarly *Jafü Holland-Ruhrgebiet* served under *Jagddivision 1* and its new designation of *Jagddivision 3* from September 1943, and both these *Jafüs* were disbanded at the end of 1943.[15] *Jafü Berlin-Mitteldeutschland* served *Jagddivision 4* as its fighter control unit until September 1943, but once this was renamed as *Jagddivision 1* that month the *Jafü* was disbanded.[16] For the three north German *Jagddivisions* (numbers 1, 2 and 3, post-September 1943 numbering system), then, the *Jagdfliegerführern* had all disappeared by the end of 1943, the fighter control functions having been taken over by the parent *Divisions*. At the same time, also in September 1943, three new *Jafüs* were formed (!): *Jafü Schlesien* (Silesia; under *Jagddivision 1*, in the east thereof), *Jafü Ostmark* (Nazi name for Austria; under *Jagddivision 7*), and just for extra confusion *Jagdabschnittsführer Mittelrhein*, which despite the different title of sector-leader performed a full *Jafü* function and also fell under *Jagddivision 7*. In southern (and far-eastern) Germany, the *Jafüs* thus maintained and controlled fighter direction onto raids.

*Luftflotte 3* in France, led by the redoubtable Field Marshal Sperrle (from the fall of France till 23 August 1944), retained its single *Jagddivision* (the ex-Third, now renumbered *Jagddivision 4*, but still headquartered at Metz) and added a new one, *Jagddivision 5*, from 15 September 1943 with HQ in Paris; these two *Jagddivisions* were grouped together under *Jagdkorps II* (subordinate to *Luftflotte 3*), commanded by General Werner Junck.[17] The two *Jafüs*, 2 and 3, from September 1943 were renumbered, respectively, *Jafüs 4* and *5*, giving them the same numbers as their newly renamed parent *Jagddivisions*.[18] The designation *Jafü 4* had previously been used for the fighter direction centre in Rennes, Brittany (from 1 April 1943), and from 6 September 1943 this became *Jafü Bretagne* which existed till end August 1944.[19] A short-lived *Jafü Paris* was created in June 1943 only to be disbanded in September that same year.[20] Then there was an additional *Jafü Südfrankreich* (January 1943–August 1944) and another short-lived direction centre, *Jagdabschnittsführer Bordeaux* (April to July 1944), as well.[21] In typically German bureaucratic style there was a higher command unit encompassing the pre-September 1943 *Jafüs 2, 3, 4* as well as the short-lived *Jafü Paris*, but this also closed down in the big reorganisation of September 1943, with *Jagdkorps II* taking these over as well.[22] Finally, elsewhere, there was *Jagdabschnittsführer Ruhrgebiet* (in the new designation part of *Jagddivision 3*), created in April 1944 and terminated just four months later.[23]

All of the details of the many different *Jafüs* and their changes, renumbering and so on discussed in the preceding two paragraphs may be simplified by stating that, after the reorganisation of the Home Defence higher command units from September 1943 onwards, there were six *Jagddivisions* in the Home Defence;[24] one other *Division* was newly created from scratch in September 1943 and in 1944 one more *Jagddivision* would still be formed:

*Jagddivisions* 1, 2 and 3 covering northern Germany, Holland, north-east Belgium discontinued independent *Jafüs* (except for the new *Jafü Schlesien*), their functions being assumed by the parent *Divisions*;

In *Luftflotte 3* in France (and south-western Belgium) *Jagddivisions* 4 and 5 retained *Jafüs* of their own and there were others in southern France;

*Jagddivision 7* covering southern Germany actually created new fighter direction centres in *Jagdabschnittsführer Mittelrhein* and *Jafü Ostmark* (Austria and parts of Czechoslovakia);

*Jagddivision 30* was formed in September 1943 from *Oberst* Hajo Hermann's experimental *Kommando* to test using single-engine fighters at night in the so-called *Wilden Sau* night-fighting units (*JG's 300, 301, 302*) which later morphed into day fighters as well; disbanded 16 March 1944 and placed under *Jagdkorps I* from February 1944 only;[25]

*Jagddivision 8* was formed 15 June 1944 from *Jafü Ostmark*, which had itself been formed on 15 September 1943 in *Jagddivision 7*. It was split off from the southern German *Jagddivision* to cover the air war over Austria and adjacent territories (HQ at Vienna); part of *Jagdkorps I* until 26 January 1945.[26]

The *Jagddivisions* provide a useful means to divide the large Home Defence territory geographically, thereby avoiding excessive naming and locating of airfields, towns and cities in the following narrative. The post-September 1943 numbering of these *Divisions* will thus be applied to the entire Home Defence period covered in this chapter (August 1942–6 June 1944) as a means of simplification and rough location of the *Jagdgruppen*. There is a very noticeable increase in Home Defence single-engine fighter *Gruppen* which begins at the start of 1943 when the US 8th Air Force began raiding Germany proper, and then an even sharper step up in July–September 1943 when the southern defences had to be rapidly upgraded as the 15th US Air Force became operational from recently conquered Italian airfields, especially those around Foggia. The rapid strengthening of *Jagddivision 1* from March 1944 reflects the beginning of the US raids against Berlin.

    *Oberstleutnant* (later *Oberst*) Hanns Trübenbach was the commander of *Jagdabschnittsführer Mittelrhein* for a long time, and was effectively the fighter controller responsible for fighter direction in the Middle Rhein area of central Germany for a lengthy period. Below he provides an illuminating account of the command chaos that resulted from Göring's way of working, which became worse and more uncoordinated as the inevitability of defeat became more apparent. It is important in reading the account by Trübenbach to realise two points. First, confusion can easily result for the reader due to some aspects of the German language. A term such as *Jafü Mittelrhein* (cf. *Jagdabschnittsführer Mittelrhein*) can refer to the large unit which controls the fighters, or it can also refer to the person of its commander who carries a military title of exactly the same term, *Jafü Mittelrhein*. For example, when Trübenbach says that he commanded *Jafü Süddeutschland* from 15 September 1943 to 25 February 1944, this refers to his personal title as the *Jagdfliegerführer for Southern Germany*, which was his position within *Jagddivision 7*. At this time the unit *Jafü Süddeutschland* had long been subsumed into the command structure of *Jagddivision 7* and no longer existed officially, as already discussed above. Secondly, Hanns Trübenbach was already involved in the setting up of the *Mittelrhein Jafü* headquarters (Dachs) at Darmstadt from early 1943, many months before the unit, *Jagdabschnittsführer Mittelrhein*, officially existed; official status only came once it had been created and organised. One therefore cannot assume that personnel appointments and transfers will tie in perfectly with the official dates of the existence of *Luftwaffe* command and control units.

The air war of our enemies led relatively quickly to an encirclement manoeuvre, and in defence against this the already very early organisation and setting up of the *Jagddivisions* with their insufficient ground organisations, especially of flight reporting systems, were no longer adequate. I had not been *Kommodore* of the training *Jagdgeschwader JG 104* in Fürth near Nuremberg for even a year when I was ordered to get myself to Vienna and Wiener-Neustadt in order to lead discussions for setting up an Industry-*Staffel* for the large aircraft factory at the latter place. The order for this was given on 13 October 1942 and my *JG 104* was determined as the unit to provide the flying personnel of the factory with the necessary tactical instruction. The Industry *Staffel* pilots were to be instructed in shooting skills by suitable officers with Western Front experience. On 14 October 1942 I travelled on further to Regensburg to the

Messerschmitt factories for initial talks on a similar arrangement, but only for an Industry *Kette* (a vic of three aircraft). However, this should have entailed a special application to *Jagddivision 5* in Munich (later, after 15 September 1943, renumbered to *Jagddivision 7*). However, they had the time to delay the setting up of this factory defence *Kette*, as I established when I telephoned back to the factory director in Regensburg on 20 October 1942. These two sidelights are only related here to show that we had far too few pilots and also no relevant ground organisation to be able to create such units out of nothing.

But from now on began a wild time, bit by bit, to blow steam into a *Reichsverteidigung* organisation and to change the existing headquarters into large battle headquarters. The Home Defence now had priority! At this time *Jagddivision 5* was still titled the Higher Command of the Fighter and *Zerstörer* Schools. With the increasing attacks of the Allied bomber formations this *Kommando* was changed into a *Jagddivision* (from June 1943) and the large north–south defensive region was expanded through the addition of *Jagdfliegerführer (Jafü) Mittelrhein* (in the north-west of the *Jagddivision 7* area, centred on Darmstadt).[27] My authority (as *Jafü Mittelrhein*) now equated to that of a brigade commander and included also an affiliated court-martial unit. My headquarters was sighted on the Marienhöhe immediately on the outskirts of Darmstadt. With about 4,000 female communications helpers in the flight reporting systems and a large alternate headquarters my command corresponded to all that was needed for the control of the night fighter and day fighter *Geschwadern*. A few hundred metres below the Marienhöhe and its high lookout tower was the Ludwigshöhe, where the *Flak Division* had situated themselves. The divisional commander and his deputy were generals well known to me, and with whom I worked outstandingly well the whole time. During the building up of this large headquarters on the Marienhöhe and all its necessary component organisations, on 16 August 1943 I was commanded to go to Vienna for the setting up of *Jafü Ostmark*. On 15 September this headquarters on the Kobenzel was operational. During this time *Oberst* Handrick was brought in as *Jafü* South Germany in the now renamed *Jagddivision 7* (Handrik was thus the *Jagdfliegerführer* or chief fighter controller for *Jagddivision 7* and his title should not be confused with that of the earlier direction unit *Jafü Süddeutschland*). Handrik had been the gold medal winner in the decathlon event at the 1936 Olympics and was married to a distant relative of Göring, who lived just nearby in Murnau. This didn't suit Göring and he transferred me to Munich on 10 September 1943 and Handrik to Vienna. I noted on 9 September 1943, while in Vienna, that Italy capitulated on 8 September 1943.

The personal whims and prejudices of Göring are well illustrated above. For Trübenbach the chaotic set of ever-changing tasks and responsibilities continued apace. He even became involved in countering a mass POW escape, that from *Oflag XXI B* at Schubin in western Poland; 33 RAF (and Fleet Air Arm) officers got out through a tunnel, two drowned while trying to cross from Denmark to Sweden in a canoe and the rest were all recaptured.[28] The fact that many prisoners travelled rapidly by train meant that escape counter-activity had to be initiated across a huge area, including southern Germany. The loss of Tunisia in May and the Allied invasion of Sicily in July 1943, followed by landings in Italy from September onwards, led to something of a panic also as the southern parts of the *Reich* became vulnerable. Göring also began to issue ever more strident requirements for his fighter pilots as the battle of Germany and the overall war situation became more and more serious. Hanns Trübenbach's account thus continues below.

Thus with effect from 15 September 1943 I was *Jafü* South Germany in the large headquarters of Minotaurus in Munich/Schleissheim in *Jagddivision 7*. Up till 6 October 1943 I was inducted into the secrets of day and night fighter controlling with *Oberst* Grabmann in Deelen/Holland. Grabmann was already commanding this *Division* (*Jagddivision 1*) and had a lot of experience. I lived with him in his villa, in which as a passionate interpreter of Chopin he organised a wonderful piano concert one day. On 15 October 1943 in the hurly-burly of this already totally mad time *Jagddivision 5* in Munich became *Jagddivision 7*. We can glance back briefly to the time of mid-1943 when the decisive measures of the highest air war leadership were taken in which Göring personally had a hand. Already in early 1943, on the night of 5–6 March, 47 (*sic*) English officers made a mass escape from the Hohensalza POW camp, which led to special measures for the purpose of investigation and triggered defensive measures. I had to report at 03h40 at night that for my command I had set all relevant measures in place! I never heard anything about whether this group of officers was ever caught.

On 28 June 1943 the following message went to the fighter units: 'The changed and more drastic situation of the bomber war against the Reich must be immediately taken account of. The dangers that bombardment of the Obersalzberg, and the cities of Munich, Augsburg and Nuremberg could take place from Tunis has risen considerably.' Thus immediate measures for their aerial defence were needed! In an ensuing command discussion the following personnel decisions were made known: *Oberstleutnant* Oesau became *Tagjagdführer Rennes* (part of *Jafü Bretagne*); *Major* Gollob to be *Jafü Paris*; *General* Osterkamp to be *Jafü* Sicily; *Oberst* von Maltzahn to be *Jafü* Greece; *Oberst* Trautloft to be Fighter Inspector East; and *Oberst* Lützow to be Fighter Inspector South. Thereafter it soon became apparent that the Italian flight reporting organisation could not perform to the high standards expected, so that signals units became reliant on expanded radio traffic. Apart from this the enemy bomber formations were from now on to be accompanied at a distance by German observation aircraft who were to report their courses and targets. This in turn required outstanding crews in multi-engined fast aircraft, but who first had to be trained. Under great urgency *Fernflugmeldekommando* (long-range reporting command) *Verona* and the *Funkverbindungstrupp* (radio communications squad) *Mailand* were set up. From 15 October 1943 the *Frontflugmeldewelle Süd* (front aircraft reporting wavelength south) was additionally made available for use. *Reichsminister der Luftwaffe and Oberbefehlshaber der Luftwaffe* (i.e. Göring, somewhat sarcastically!) ordered also on 15 October 1943 that after each enemy attack that *Jafüs* had to obtain from the *Jagdgruppen* and *Zerstörergruppen* an accounting of the battle and their successes!

On the same day came the order for *Jagddivision 5* in Munich to transform into *Jagddivision 7*. There was a special order to accompany the change in the command staff of the now *7th Jagddivision*. Our headquarters were situated in a large bunker, the Minotaurus. Göring felt deeply hurt by the lack of success in the whole conduct of the war. Already on 9 October 1943 all commanders, including *Jafü Ostmark* (Austria) had to be made aware of the *Reichsmarschall*-order, that said that all fighter and *Zerstörer* units had to fly, even under bad weather conditions, and to the last drop of their fuel. This order was broadened by the *Reichsmarschall* on 16 October 1943: 'Only the toughest leaders are to be used in action in the flying units. Pertinent reviews of incumbents and suggestions for the relevant filling of these posts are to be submitted!' At the headquarters of the *Jagddivisions* of the Home Defence the messages, the tactical instructions, the battle reports of the fighter units followed close upon each other. Continuously, new weapons were tried out on the fighter aircraft. The successes of these against the four-engined bombers were quite substantial, as long as there were no losses and as long as the weapons technicians could begin the necessary conversions at the production stages already. But here also the new means reached the frontline squadrons too late. The air war over Italy and southern Germany became ever tougher. The need for Ju 88 crews for tracking and following bomber formations became ever greater. They were also supposed to guide the fighter units to the enemy formations when the weather was bad. Hitler and Göring had long decided, that next to the day fighters, the night fighter arm (including the *Wilden Sau* with Me 109s and Fw 190s) were to be brought to perfection. But neither defensive arm was in a position any longer to cause such losses to the enemy's massed formations that would provide the German leadership with a long enough breather to organise massive opposition by day and night. In this regard the high *Abschuss* – victory claim – figures of a few heroes no longer helped either. The year 1944 thus began with enormous losses on all fronts. The book by Heinz Knoke gives the best example of the fight against the four-engined bomber formations, better than any other book from this time; it is worth reading.

The English edition of this recommended book, titled *I Flew for the Führer*,[29] is an appropriate one as Knoke was something of an unrepentant Nazi even after the war; it should be noted that Hanns Trübenbach was nothing of the kind and the recommendation is thus only for the realities of the aerial combat over Germany and the living conditions of the *Luftwaffe* fighter pilots on the ground, as related well in this book. As 1944 dawned it had become clear to senior officers in the Home Defence like Trübenbach, and indeed across the entire *Luftwaffe*, that the war could no longer be won. Göring's reactions and requirements became more and more strident and Nazi Party organisations became involved also, the entire complex mess becoming ever more like a disturbed ants nest. The increased fighter defences of the southern German and Austrian region brought in additional complications in that fighting now often took place over the Alpine mountains, and retrieving bailed-out German aircrew in such terrain brought with it a host of unexpected problems. *Oberst* (promoted 1 June 1944) Hanns Trübenbach's account of how a senior officer such as himself (he was officially *Jafü Mittelrhein* from early 1943 to the end of November 1944, excluding the period 15 September 1943 to 25 February 1944, when he acted as *Jafü* Southern Germany) was expected to perform multiple miracles with few resources continues below.

If the question is asked of me how I saw the situation from my perspective as a *Jafü* in the Home Defence, then this judgement can only be from a purely personal experience point of view. Thus the year 1944 was characterised by the death battle of a nation, whose leadership in total and immoderate over-estimation of all military and political realities led them to continue a war that could no longer be won. And thus all the new developments of weapons and aircraft were sacrificed to the enemy's overwhelming superiority even though the many attempts had produced excellent results in defence against the bomber streams. But these attempts, and the operational use of the Me 262 must also be seen as part thereof, could never lead to mass destruction of the bomber streams that by now were coming in masses of up to 1,000 four-engined bombers which in practical terms were able to hit their targets fatally. On 4 January 1944 at our *Jagddivision* headquarters in Munich I met with the Inspector of *In16*, who till then was (and remained) responsible for the entire air-sea rescue service.

Now, and very urgently, an Alpine rescue service had to be created to find and rescue shot-down crews in the mountains. Thus the pilots were to receive in place of their dinghies an Alpine tent bag to prevent them freezing to death in the impassable mountain massif. The parachute canopy had to be red-coloured to make them more visible from the air. Heinkel He 45 aircraft towing gliders were equipped with rocket charges, and were to watch over the battle areas. Fighter crews were to receive additional equipment such as emergency signal lights, red flares, colour staining bags, etc. Included in this was also a flare pistol that could shoot off exploding smoke and loud-bang cartridges. The men of the mountain watch, who had to be stationed all over the mountains, were to be able to answer with the same signals to provide encouragement to the shot down crews. One can imagine what a task this was for the *In16*, to cover the enormous Alpine region with such an emergency service.

With the testing of the newly developed radio apparatus FuG120, which I performed myself from Munich in many crossings of the Alps, I could sing a song of praise, especially when one even thought of having to force-land there in a Me 109. This radio was a self-locating direction finder with 32 frequencies to determine your own position, especially useful when one had had to fly for a long time without sight of the earth! Fieseler Storchs and Ju 88s carrying the so-called 'Alps' drop-pack were converted as Alpine rescue aircraft in *In16*. In addition there was a so-called small conversion pack whose contents I personally did not get to know. Then the use of flying doctors in helicopters was considered for emergency missions. Paratroop units had to be issued with emergency ration packs; the fighter pilots or the bomber-tracking aircraft etc. had to carry a small but important sanitary pack with anti-frost cream, analgesic medicine, bandages etc. It had also been shown that bailed out pilots generally lost their flying boots with the jerk of the opening 'chute, and came down with freezing legs where they would meet further freezing Alpine conditions. Thus the order went out to all flying units: when bailing out, hang on to your fur-lined flying boots!

On 18 January 1944, *In16* ordered the placement of mountain hut emergency equipment to be able to launch help from such bases. The mountain troops' medical orderly school in St Johann in Kitzbühel was urgently asked to watch for parachutists jumping over the Alpine area on all their training missions there, as the enemy incursions increased. In the middle of January a further *Reichsmarschall*-order went out to all units that the training of fighter bomber crews in dropping bombs be enforced. Through this one wanted to destroy the close-flying bomber formations. But all these new measures needed time and personnel for their effect to be felt. Transfers and assignments rained down as never before! The *Reich* was thus in an uproar as never before during this war. The fronts were crumbling everywhere. The command of the naval war as well as the upper echelons of the army were also hit by all this. Now the Party also entered the lists and tried to inculcate backbone into the people, while the already demented party bosses prattled on about the imminent final victory of the *Führer*. By using highly decorated frontline soldiers to give talks at factories one believed that even higher achievements could be made. In the army units in the West the most amazing rumours of the new wonder weapons of the *Führer* circulated, who was already preparing a total final victory. Even so there were in reality still a large number of military and party-aligned leaders who believed this nonsense.

From 21 February till 7 March 1944, with my wife and the two little girls, as well as Götz, I began to enjoy a lovely holiday in Bad Kohlgrub, close to Oberammergau. But the family was scarcely together than I was called back from leave by *Generaloberst* Stumpf of the *Luftflotte* (*Luftflotte Reich*) on 25 February. I had to go to Darmstadt immediately (*Mittelrhein* area) where I was to take over the command and controlling of the day fighters (i.e. to become *Jagdfliegerführer Mittelrhein*). Until 10 March 1944 there followed extensive preparations in Darmstadt for the planned large headquarters Dachs (*Jagdabschnittsführer Mittelrhein*) that was especially to be prepared for command of the day and night fighters through communications technology. On 11 March I was allowed to go back on leave and made my way back to my wife and children in Bad Kohlgrub. However, on 18 March I was again called back from leave. On the orders of Göring, I was transferred with immediate effect to Insterburg in East Prussia as *Jafü* there. Not commanded but displaced! The position went with the authority of a brigade commander. So I packed up and took off in a Me 108, landing at Posen on the way, intending to fly on to Insterburg the next day. However while still in Posen I received a message not to fly on to East Prussia. Imagine such theatricals!

To sum it up briefly, on 23 March 1944 under a new Corps command with headquarters near Berlin (*Jagdkorps I*), I found myself in Darmstadt again where I was to take over the further building-up of the brigade staff Dachs and was with immediate effect saddled with leading the day and night fighter activities. The responsible signals commander had done marvels in the few days of my absence. And my two most important officers, the Ia day and Ia night, were in place (the Ia in the German system was the senior staff officer, assigned as operations officer). I had at my disposal a marvellously equipped ground organisation and from my headquarters post I could speak directly to Hitler, Göring and further high commands, that is without any intermediary agencies. The same applied for direct contact with my immediate superior, the Corps staff in Jüterbog near Berlin. The glass wall map in my headquarters, measuring 9 m by 9 m, could show all flight movements so that a perfect command and controlling of all units was guaranteed. On the night of 30/31 March 1944 I was able to achieve my first success during the mass raid on Nuremberg. When this target was recognised, all the night fighter units available were subordinated to me tactically. I was lucky to be able to lead the night fighters quickly enough into the approaching bomber stream, so that 31 enemy bombers could be destroyed on that leg of their journey. In the following months there followed an unimaginable concentration of units of the night fighters and the day fighters in the central German region, where the most important targets of the enemy bombers lay. My headquarters was already overburdened from a command perspective and required additional personnel.

On 14 May 1944 I was ordered to Jüterbog to the *Jagddivision* Commanders conference at *Jagdkorps 1*. We were informed about the developing situation by the commanding general. I flew back in my Me 109 before lunch already, in order to prepare the necessary orders to be sent out to the flying units. The threat of the Invasion hung over everything! On 17 May I had to fly to Biblis urgently. With my second aircraft, a Me 109 G 5 I took off in Darmstadt. Just as my undercarriage retracted my engine jerked to a stop and from a few metres height I was forced to belly-land on earth again. Despite the low speed at take-off I only just managed to stop before hitting the trees by tramping heavily on my elevator controls. The vertebrae in the small of my back were compressed and the flight surgeon hung me immediately in a harness to stretch the vertebrae. What had happened? The gear from the main drive of the camshaft had broken right through; a material failure that I had never experienced in my career before. The two headquarters on the Marienhöhe and the lower Ludwigshöhe (where the flak division was located) were only a few kilometres from Darmstadt. For me this was a reason to seek an alternate headquarters somewhere else in the south in an already existing signals and tracking station and to prepare it. We called this Dachs-Mitte. From there we could accommodate all our personnel and undertake our command functions, in case Darmstadt was ever to be bombed. On the 6 June 1944 at 03h00 I received the report of the beginning of the Invasion, initially with landings between Cherbourg and Le Havre.

## 1942: The Bombing Offensive Begins; the Head-on Attack Method Is Born

On 17 August 1942 the first American four-engined bomber mission was flown, against the railway yards at Rouen-Sotteville, France, with 12 B-17s.[30] Until the end of the year another 26 raids would be flown, with numbers of bombers increasing gradually, and on three occasions just over 100 were dispatched.[31] Escort was given by RAF Spitfires, augmented by small numbers of US Spitfire squadrons, and a few P-38 sorties, and often involved complex sweep missions in direct and indirect support of the bombers.[32] On the first raid the German fighter pilots did not identify the bombers as something new and thought they were British Halifaxes and Stirlings, and the first US four-engined bomber was not claimed until 6 September 1942.[33] By then the *Luftwaffe* fully realised they faced a new and formidable foe and it had taken some time and experience before they figured out how to attack them successfully and shoot some of these large, relatively fast and well-armed bombers down.

The first major step forward in fighting against the bombers came along the Atlantic coast of south-western Brittany and Western France where the major U-boat bases lay, at Brest, Lorient, St Nazaire and La Pallice. Here distances were too great to allow any Spitfire escorts and German fighter pilots could concentrate on dealing with the bombers alone. These ports were poorly defended at the time, a single *Staffel*, namely 8/JG 2, at Brest being the only fighters available until 22 November when the rest of *III/JG* 2 returned to the area, based at Vannes-Meucon.[34] *Hauptmann* Egon Mayer had just been appointed the new *Kommandeur* of III/JG 2 at the beginning of the month[35] and it was he who first mooted the head-on attack on four-engined bomber formations after careful perusal of combat reports[36] and no doubt also examinations and/or reports made of the first force-landed and crashed bombers in northern France. The first such frontal attack took place on 23 November 1942 when the bombers went for St Nazaire where cloud cover led many to abort, leaving two very small groups of B-17s in two formations of four and five aircraft.[37] Mayer led his *Gruppe* in the first head-on attack ever on the group of four bombers, using successive *Kette* (vic) formations of three fighters to attack in a single devastating onslaught which immediately knocked down two of them and seriously damaged the other two, one crashing and being destroyed in the UK as a result.[38] The other formation of five aircraft was also attacked, as were some other small groups and another bomber was lost from one of the latter.[39] Interestingly, the famous 'finger four' fighter formation was abandoned by Mayer in launching his head-on attack, but the inherent wisdom of only using a small formation head-on against a large bomber formation, as was the norm later, was born here already. Leading anything larger than at most a *Staffel* in a frontal attack prevented many of the pilots from opening fire for fear of hitting their own comrades; generally most leaders preferred to attack using one *Schwarm* at a time in rapid succession, as will be seen by further accounts later in this chapter. And thus a famous technique was born from very small beginnings – only four bombers in the formation and an attack by successive *Ketten* of an entire fighter *Gruppe*; such favourable numerical conditions would seldom occur in the future! In addition, one of the attacking Fw 190s and its pilot were lost to defensive fire and two more damaged as they pulled up above the small bomber formation. This would also remain a perennial question, whether to pull up over the bomber formation to enable a quick turn and dive on the formation from the rear (and also to finish off damaged stragglers from the head-on attack), or to dive away, which was safer in terms of return fire but generally led to one losing the chance of attacking stragglers or even getting back to that particular formation at all.

In time the head-on method pioneered by Egon Mayer would be used by many more pilots from a large number of *Jagdgruppen*, and an adaptation of attacking from slightly above at a shallow angle was added in to the frontal assault method, as is described by many of the veterans involved in the Home Defence in this chapter. However, not all were agreed on this – certainly coming from slightly above and head-on gave one greater speed and thus safety also, but return fire if the attackers were spotted in time would also be greater than coming in head-on at the same level, as discussed below by Otto Stammberger of 9/JG 26. A highly experienced and very successful Home Defence pilot, *Hauptmann* Alfred Grislawski, *Staffelkapitän 1/JG 1* and later of *8/JG 1*, and who was credited with 17 four-engined bomber victories over Germany,[40] believed in coming in head-on at the same level as the target bomber and then pulling up over them very closely. 'Attack made exactly from head-on at the same height firing with all weapons, from a distance of 200 m, then pass over the bombers at 2–3 m above them. In my *Staffel* three comrades were shot hanging on their parachutes by Americans. I never heard of anything like this being done by the English or the Russians.' American fighter pilots shooting at helpless bailed-out German pilots is an oft-repeated reality of this brutal and decisive air battle over the German homeland.

The head-on attack method does not seem to have been universally adopted in *JG 2*, where it was first invented, and there also appear to have been at least some pilots who had little regard for Egon Mayer as a four-engined bomber combatant (however, some professional jealousy may also have been an influence here!). *Hauptmann* Erich Rudorffer flew in *JG 2* against the American four-engined bombers right from the beginning of their raids in 1942 until August 1943, when he was transferred to the Russian front; he was acting *Gruppenkommandeur* of *II/JG 2* from January to May 1943, and then confirmed in that post until August of the same year.[41] 'Egon Mayer was hardly a major player to me. The four-engined killer in *JG 2* then was Georg Eder; those who saw him making attacks on bomber formations always considered it a miracle that he survived; however, he was one of our fighter pilots who was wounded most often and most seriously. I did not myself fly head-on attacks on the bombers in 1943, only with the Me 262 later in the Home Defence.' While *JG 2* might not have been so enamoured of the frontal attack method, it appears to have been more popularly adopted in their sister Channel Front *Geschwader* of *JG 26*, and early on as well. *Oberleutnant* Otto Stammberger, *4* and *9/JG 26* recalls: 'On 20 December 1942 the USAAF attacked the aircraft works at Romilly sur Seine near Paris. I shot my second Boeing down in this raid, from head-on; six men of the crew bailed out, and the machine crashed west of Meaux, about 40 km west of Paris, on a large road intersection. I know nothing about the fate of its pilot.'

In fact, while Egon Mayer might have actually flown the first head-on attack against the four-engined bombers, this method might also have been thought of and applied in several different units at about the same time and for the same obvious reasons, as discussed here by Otto Stammberger; this could also explain at least partially what Erich Rudorffer said about his colleague *Hauptmann* Egon Mayer. Otto Stammberger also discusses the disadvantages of attacking these powerful bomber formations from the rear.

The head-on attack method actually resulted automatically: the four-engined bombers had only glass in front without any armour, and their forward defence comprised one MG in the cabin, a double gun turret above the cabin and another one below the cabin (this was actually a later innovation in more advanced B-17 models). The upper turret could not shoot downwards and the lower one could not shoot upwards. Thus when we attacked from in front at the most we had three MGs firing at us. When attacking from behind there were six to eight MGs when one approached slightly from the quarter rather than directly behind; this was always the case anyway, as the bombers had time during our long run-up of 10 to 20 seconds to fly some avoiding manoeuvres. They already started shooting at distances of about

1,500 m, to give themselves courage and to let loose like in the Wild West. Now a four-engined bomber did not fly alone, and there were always 20 to 23 machines in a formation and they produced a very fine spread of fire! And then we had to fly for 10 to 20 seconds in our approach with tracers going past our cockpits to left and right – when we were lucky. In addition the bombers were armoured against rear attack, the rear gunner in his turret, the fuel tanks, the pilots' cabin, were all protected at the back by sheets of armoured plate. Thus it was logical that one rather attacked one from head-on and as one was flying in *Staffel* formation or in a *Gruppe*, you always tried to attack with at least a *Schwarm* at a time, thus four aircraft in a line next to each other, to spread the return fire. The rear attack was comparable to one standing under a shower, turning the tap on and expecting not to get wet – for 20 seconds! Is that at all possible? But we had to carry the attack through. That our young and inexperienced pilots got frightened when confronted with this massive defensive fire and turned away early is no surprise, nor is it any wonder that only three or four bombers were shot down on a mission. And these were always shot down by the old hands, thus Priller got 11 four-engined bombers, Glunz 21 including five in one day, Hermichen 26 of them, Staiger 19, Naumann 7, Wiegand also 7, Radener 10 four-engined bombers and Hackl 32 of them. These were all pilots in our *Geschwader JG 26*.

The view of *Oberst* Gustav Rödel given earlier in this chapter is also pertinent here, namely that each attack on a four-engined bomber formation was different and unique and many unpredictable factors played a role; over-emphasis of attack methods and a particular favourite method should thus not be stressed too much either. During August to December 1942 there were only three fighter *Geschwader* in place to oppose the new bomber threat. *JG 2* was in the *Jagddivision 5* area of northern France, but on 8 November *I/JG 2* transferred to southern France and on the 17 November *II/JG 2* was sent to Tunisia,[42] both these moves related to the Allied invasion of North Africa, Operation Torch. Just before this *II/JG 2* had spent a week in south-west France (20–26 October 1942), and in November (9–22 November) *III/JG 2* was in central France, before moving to defence of the U-boat bases on the latter date for the rest of the year. *JG 26* with three *Gruppen* was stationed in north-east France and south-west Belgium, the *Jagddivision 4* region.[43] Thirdly, there was *JG 1*, with *II* and *IV Gruppen* in *Jagddivision 3* (north-west Germany/Ruhr and Holland)

and *I/JG 1* in *Jagddivision 2* (northern Germany and German bight, including Hamburg).[44] *III/JG 1* only came into being early in 1943.[45] It was these nine *Jagdgruppen* (reduced to seven by November) that opposed the 27 American bomber raids made on France and the Low Countries in 1942; targets were spread amongst the U-boat bases, the fighters' own airfields, railway, shipyard and fewer industry targets.[46]

Some relevant statistics of claims and losses to both sides appear in the tables below. What is immediately obvious is the great accuracy of German claims against fighters, while those against bombers showed some exaggeration, hardly surprising considering that such large and well-defended aircraft would very often require more than one attack before fatal damage was inflicted; also descending aircraft already unable to get home might be attacked again by an inexperienced pilot who would understandably claim it as his own exclusive victory. Of course one cannot discriminate the proportions of American bomber losses due to flak and those by German fighters, implying that the exaggerated bomber claims by the fighter pilots were almost certainly higher than shown. Throughout the Battle of Germany (and by day and night also) the German flak defences remained dangerous and effective, and as the power of the fighter arm gradually waned as it lost the battle of attrition, so was the flak arm boosted and increased in its fighting power.[47] In fact, it is estimated that the *Luftwaffe*'s flak arm was responsible for at least half of American aircraft lost in combat over Europe.[48] Also, an estimated 66,000 US four-engined bombers were damaged by flak.[49] These features of claims data against the bombers would endure throughout the battle over Germany, as would the ludicrously high claims of German fighters shot down by the bomber crews: in the table below 211 fighters were claimed by bomber gunners which would effectively have wiped out around six *Jagdgruppen*! Once again, German fighters lost to Allied bombers and fighters are impossible to discriminate, and there would appear to be some exaggeration of Allied fighter claims also, but not significantly large. German fighter losses amounted to about a *Gruppe* in aircraft terms, which for roughly six months was not excessive; however, the 20 dead pilots were much harder to replace, and as time went by replacements were ever poorer prepared as the German fuel shortage began to bite with very negative consequences in the training schools. The attrition of personnel – and, in due course, of critical and irreplaceable fighting leaders – had begun, and it was never to cease, right up to the Normandy invasion and beyond, to the end of the war.

German fighter claims versus Allied losses, north-west Europe, August 1942 – end of year[50]

| Luftwaffe claims | JG 2 | JG 26 | JG 1 | Real losses | Real damaged aircraft |
|---|---|---|---|---|---|
| Spitfire | 11 | 34 | 0 | 46 | 12 |
| B-17 & B-24 | 25 + 1 HSS | 16 + 1 HSS | 2 | 35 | 248 |
| P-38 | 0 | 1 | 0 | 1 | 1 |

German fighter casualties versus Allied claims[51]

| Luftwaffe losses | JG 2 | JG 26 | JG 1 | Allied fighter claims | US bomber claims |
|---|---|---|---|---|---|
| Aircraft lost | 19 | 13 | 2 | 31 German fighters | 211 German fighters |
| Aircraft damaged | 1 | 12 | 1 | | |
| Pilots lost | 14 | 4 | 2 | | |
| Pilots wounded | 4 | 0 | 0 | | |

One additional German fighter lost in action, to *Ergänzungsjagdgruppe West.*[52]
HSS = *Herausschuss,* i.e. a four-engined bomber separated from its formation and in a damaged state.

A glimpse into the daily life of a fighting pilot in *9/JG 26* over about five weeks during September–October 1942 is provided by the summary in the previous chapter from the logbook of *Leutnant* Otto Stammberger. Interestingly, operations were still aimed at the United Kingdom and RAF activity over the Channel, with American bomber incursions still relatively rare events. What is really fascinating in the logbook excerpt is his self-criticism for having made four attacks on the bomber he managed to shoot down on 9 October – this was strong motivation for the head-on attack method, which would have suggested itself as a potential (or at least partial) solution to most pilots who had already been exposed to the inevitable consequences of an attack on the large American bombers from behind. This time Stammberger was lucky, with only one hit in his cabin, but then again it only takes one bullet to have a fatal effect; as always, luck was the fighter pilot's greatest asset.

*JG 26*, the famous *Schlageter Geschwader*, was led throughout 1942 by *Kommodore* Gerhard Schöpfel, who recalls below the very useful data obtained from eavesdropping on Allied radio traffic after raids and actions over northern France and the Channel. This information was made even more useful by British and American claims being transmitted in separate messages. One can only guess at the amusement that the American bomber crew claims brought to the *Jagdflieger*, at this stage and later, although as Otto Stammberger notably commented, later in the war there was less and less to laugh about! 'In my time as *Kommodore* of *JG 26* (6 December 1941–10 January 1943),[53] when this *Geschwader* was serving as the only operational such unit in the Pas-de-Calais, after combats we listened in on British radio transmissions and could often ascertain, that more losses had occurred than the number of *Abschüsse* (victories) we had claimed. It could be assumed that some enemy aircraft on their return flights had crashed due to the effects of damage sustained in combat. I remember one of the first attacks on the American four-engined bombers with American and British fighter escort, I think it was 1942 and against Eindhoven. When we monitored the British radio reports, we found out for the first time, that the victory claims of the Americans and the British were given separately. The American claims exceeded the number of aircraft we had scrambled. It was significant for us that on the next day a British formation approached Northern France, leading to my *Geschwader* scrambling, and then after reaching the coast they turned away; in our view this was to show the Americans how many German fighters there were still operational. In reality we had lost perhaps three aircraft, and claimed around nine enemies shot down. The US bomber boys reported 150 victories.'

## 1943: The Slugging match; the Luftwaffe Appears to Be Winning

The *Jagdgruppen* involved in the Home Defence and their *Jagddivision* assignments during 1943 are summarised in the table below. Due to American bomber formations not yet penetrating to Berlin and surrounds, the *Jagddivision 1* area was poorly defended, and *Jagddivision 7* and *Jafü Ostmark* only received *Jagdgruppen* in the second half of 1943, once the 15th Air Force raids from Italy into southern Germany and Austria (plus the Balkans) began. Quite clearly the bulk of available fighter forces were in *Jagddivisions 2, 3* and *4* where 8th Air Force incursions were at their maximum during 1943; this geographic weighting of the all-too-few *Jagdgruppen* to hand would change in 1944.

*Jagdgruppen* assigned to different *Jagddivisions* (with dates) for year of 1943[54]

| Jagdgruppe | Jagddivision 1 | Jagddivision 2 | Jagddivision 3 |
|---|---|---|---|
| I/JG1 | | 1 January–1 April | 1 April–31 December |
| II/JG 1 | | | 1 January–31 December |
| III/JG 1 | | | 1 April–31 December |
| IV/JG 1 | | | 1 January–31 March |
| I/JG 2 | | | |
| II/JG 2 | | | |
| III/JG 2 | | | |
| I/JG 3 | February–April | | April–21 October |
| II/JG 3 | | 12 August–31 December | |
| III/JG 3 | | | 3–23 August |
| IV/JG 3 | | | 24–31 December |
| I/JG 11 | | 1 April–31 December | |
| II/JG 11 | | 1 April–17 November & 18–31 December | 17 November– 18 December |
| III/JG 11 | | May–31 December | |
| 10/JG 11 | | 7 July–31 December | |
| I/JG 26 | | | 7–10 June & 23 June–25 November |
| II/JG 26 | | | 28 July–15 August |
| III/JG 26 | | June–August | August–September & November–31 December |
| I/JG 27 | | | 29 July–13 August |
| II/JG 27 | | | |
| III/JG 27 | | | |
| II/JG 51 | | | |
| II/JG 53 | | | |
| III/JG 54 | 15 August–31 December | 27 March–23 June | 23 June–15 August |
| I/JG 300 | | | 10 October–31 December |

| Jagddivision 4 | Jagddivision 5 | Jagddivision 7 | Jafü Ostmark |
|---|---|---|---|
| | | | |
| | | | |
| | | | |
| | | | |
| | 25 January–31 December | | |
| | 15 March–31 December | | |
| | October–31 December | | |
| 21 October–31 December | | | |
| | | | |
| | | 23 August–31 December | |
| | | 1–30 June & September–24 December | |
| | | | |
| | | | |
| | | | |
| | | | |
| 1–22 January & 10–23 June, & 25 November–31 December | | | |
| 1 January–28 July & 15 August–31 December | | | |
| 1 January–June & September–November | | | |
| 14 April–June | January–14 April | 14–22 August | 22 August–31 December |
| 12 September–18 November | | 1 August–12 September & 18 November–31 December | |
| | | | July–23 September |
| | | 18 August–December | |
| | | | 16 October–31 December |
| 12 February–27 March | | | |
| | | | |

Other assignments not shown above: (1) *Southern France: I/JG 2* – 1–25 January; (2) *U-boat bases: III/JG 2* – 1 January–October; *South-west France: I/JG 27* – June–28 July. *Jagddivision* numbering as from mid-September 1943.

During 1943 the Me 110 heavy fighters had been withdrawn from the Russian and Mediterranean fronts and were concentrated in the Home Defence region, as they were seen as having good potential for attacking large formations of tightly packed American four-engined bombers with longer-range rockets and heavy cannons to try and break them up, but at the same time being kept further inland and away from Allied escort fighters. Thus *Jagddivision 1* had *I/ZG 26* (December; Me 110s) and *II/ZG 26* (October–31 December; Me 410s); *Jagddivision 3* had *III/ZG 26* (31 July–October; Me 110s) which in October moved back to *Jagddivision 2* till the end of the year; *Jagddivision 7* had *I* and *II/ZG 76* (August–31 December; Me 110s) as well as *II/ZG 1* (November–31 December; Me 110s).[55] Prior to joining *Jagddivision 7*, *II/ZG 1* was based on the Atlantic coast from 5 August till November 1943, where it operated over the Bay of Biscay in company with Ju 88 heavy fighters from *I* and *III/ZG 1* (October–31 December).[56]

*Unteroffizier* Heinz Ludwig flew in Russia from May 1942 to July 1943 as a rear gunner/radio operator, and his unit (*I/ZG 1*), by then renamed *I/ZG 26*, was moved to the Home Defence in August 1943. Before seeing action *I/ZG 26* needed time to build up again and especially to absorb new crews fresh from the training schools. Ludwig was teamed up with such a new pilot and was involved in a collision during a training flight, thrown out of the aircraft and fractured his skull on 2 September 1943:

> When we left Russia in mid-1943 and joined the Home Defence at Wunstorf-Hannover, experienced crewmen were assigned to new pilots just arrived from the training schools, and so we radio operators were switched; I was crewed up with *Leutnant* Lux. He was very inexperienced in everything and on our last training flight before being declared operational, when the entire *Staffel* (*3/ZG 26*) took off with 16 aircraft, we collided with our wingman at 1,000 m; I was the only survivor. And our *Staffelkapitän*, *Oberleutnant* Stratmann was to blame for this, as to begin the assembly after the take-off, he made a steep turn to the right too soon. The pilots following behind him jerked their aircraft away to the right, and we who were still catching up with them were still in a gentle left hand turn and my pilot pulled the crate away to the right and below the others, to avoid crashing into the aircraft in front of us.

Our *Kaczmarek* came roaring in to join up with us, black smoke coming out of his exhausts. I reported his position continually to my pilot and saw then how he disappeared below our right wing. I called to my pilot 'right, below us'; and then there was a loud bang. As quick as lightning I removed my seatbelt, seized the red cabin roof handle, pulled it and I was out, pulled the ripcord of my 'chute, and then it was all calm and quiet. When I looked down, the blood ran down my face, I threw my goggles away, so that I could see properly. I saw both aircraft hit the ground diagonally below me with two enormous balls of fire. The other pilot managed to bail out, but died later of his injuries. Those at the airfield were able to follow the drama from the ground, and saw how I was shot out like a rocket 100 m vertically up above the fireball. I had suffered a fracture of the base of the skull, was badly concussed and had been burned in the face. But I was not even in hospital for a week – I wanted to rejoin my gang. For over a quarter of a year I was forbidden to fly. Once again I had been lucky!!!! *Unteroffizier* Baumeister (his old pilot in Russia) received a new radio operator in Wunstorf, with whom he was shot down (21 February 1944). I was no longer flying missions at the time.

A highly experienced Me 110 pilot (who flew in the Battle of Britain already), *Oberstleutnant* Georg Christl was a staff officer by the time of the Home Defence *Zerstörer* missions, but his comments are nevertheless valuable. 'On the operations of the Me 110 against the four-engined bombers I cannot say much – at this time I was on the Staff of *General* Galland. When the *Zerstörers* were able to reach a bomber formation where no escort was present, then they achieved good successes. As soon as the American fighters appeared on the scene, there was nothing that could be done – then there were very heavy losses. The Me 110 gave sterling service as a night fighter.' This succinctly says it all about the *Zerstörer* missions in the Home Defence; where the *Luftwaffe* high command had high hopes of what they might achieve, they could not conceive of American fighters with high performance ever being able to penetrate deep into the *Reich* and thus upset the Me 110s and 410s in their envisaged job of breaking up the four-engined bomber formations. Alas, the P-51 Mustang was to make nonsense of this misconception by late 1943 to early 1944.

Someone directly involved in testing new methods and new technology to oppose the four-engined bomber menace was *Hauptmann* Horst

Geyer, whom the author was privileged to meet in 1990. Horst Geyer was appointed to lead a special test unit, *Erprobungskommando 25* in about June 1943, which he did for a year; this unit's job was to develop and test under operational conditions new weapons against these large bombers. His unit consisted of four *Staffeln*, including one equipped with fighters, one with *Zerstörers* and one with bombers including the He 177. They were based at Parchim, north-west of Berlin in *Jagddivision 1*, but also operated out of Achmer (south-west of Hamburg) and Wittmundhafen (west of Wilhelmshaven). One of the rather more bizarre weapons they tried out was 107 kg rockets which measured 21 cm in diameter; 33 launcher tubes were mounted on a He 177 to fire vertically, the idea being to fly beneath the four-engined bomber formation and then discharge the tubes up into them. It was never tried in action due to the dangers from enemy fighters. Tests of this weapon were also carried out on Me 110s and Ju 88s. Another weapon, if possible even more awkward than the airborne rocket barrages, comprised 200 m-long cables with an explosive charge at the end; these were supposed to be released from canisters on the attacking fighter when flying against enemy bombers and the very sharp cables were then meant to cut the bombers' wings. The cables would theoretically be automatically released from the fighter once they contacted a bomber. This idea was tried out on the wing of a four-engined bomber sitting on high supports on the ground. While approaching this target the oncoming fighter had to make small course corrections and the resultant movement at the ends of the 200 m cables was much larger, making a successful attack on the target very difficult. This idea was tried in action but without success. Another weapon proposed was to spray a chemical substance which rendered plexiglass opaque, thus blinding the bomber crews. The experiments were a great success but it was never used in practice because the Allies installed a replacement glass type in their aircraft which was not vulnerable to the chemicals. Horst Geyer's unit also carried out experiments with Henschel flying bombs, including the Hs 193 remote control bomb. While Horst Geyer did not tell me exactly what he thought of all these rather bizarre ideas, his actions suggested that he was not that enthusiastic about using them himself. During his year with *Erprobungskommando 25* he flew many missions against the four-engined bombers in conventional fighters, claiming six victories with them, including a B-24 on 8 October 1943, a Mosquito on 6 November 1943 as well as a P-51, two P-38s and a B-17 during the first half of 1944. His Mosquito victory in November 1943 was the first to fall to a fighter over Germany; he shot it down at 14,000 m and it dived vertically to destruction. Unfortunately his wingman, *Unteroffizier* Herzog, dived down after it into huge cumulus clouds, where his aircraft became iced up and he dived to his death in the sea out of control. For this feat, Geyer was awarded the German Cross in Gold, presented by none other than *Oberstleutnant* Georg Christl.

To complete this discussion of the methods proposed, tested and even used repeatedly against the four-engined bomber formations, two more need to be added: attacks using under-wing rocket launchers, and attempts to drop bombs onto the bomber formations. Their trials and use go beyond just 1943 and include also 1944, and the views of veteran Home Defence pilot Otto Schmid below put them into some sort of context, including how some writers have exaggerated their importance. When he rejoined *II/JG 1* in early 1944, *Feldwebel* Otto Schmid had to also do some training flights with practice bombs:

The bombing was done for practice purposes using 50 kg cement bombs. The bombing range lay north of our base at Rheine in Emsland. This area was sparsely populated as it had been a pasture and moorland area and was well suited to this usage. We flew these practice flights when no enemy incursions had been reported. Only one aircraft flew to the bombing range at a time, so that the operational readiness of the *Staffel* was not affected. At the time it was purely training; we had also practiced this at the training schools with the Me 109 E and the 50 kg cement bombs. Presumably this was done in case we should need to use the training at some future time. We were certainly not thinking of an invasion or operations in Russia at all. The experiments to attack the four-engined bomber formations with bombs were not successful as our machines carrying the bombs were too slow in the approach. In addition the escort fighters very rapidly adapted themselves to this technique and concentrated on attacking these clumsy Fw 190s so that the bombs they were carrying mostly had to be dropped before they reached their target formations. It did not work out much better with the rockets. Some of the Fw 190s were equipped with two rockets, each weighing 100 kg, but only very seldom were they able to get into the correct position for launching them, from about 800 m range, as they were also troubled by the escort fighters and had to shoot off the rockets too fast and hope for the best. Naturally, when the range was correct and they were aimed it could happen that at least two bombers went down due to their explosions. However, having said that, these were essentially the dreams of our higher command, but these gentlemen had forgotten that these special aircraft needed an enormous escort of their own and such resources we did not possess. Thus these things were put back into the mothball cupboard of our Mr 'Meier' (Hermann Göring). These experiments were not carried out by the 5th *Staffel* of *JG 1* but by the 2nd *Staffel*.

Otto Schmid continues his comments on the use of bombs and rockets against the four-engined bomber formations, with some rather scathing remarks on how some post-war authors have twisted the truth. 'As far as using bombs and rockets against the four-engined bombers are concerned, quite a few "scribblers" have most likely tried to make their accounts interesting. What quite often came out in such publications makes one's hair stand on end; some authors told tales based on such ignorance resulting in absolute nonsense instead of the truth, that it makes you want to cry. And such "authoritative writers" are most probably responsible for sending out spurious accounts of attack methods that amount to fairy tales. As I already said, these attack methods (bombs, rockets, etc.) would most likely have had good success, when everything worked out perfectly: improved engine power of the carrying aircraft, and the necessary own fighter escort. However, in practice none of these things were possible.'

*Leutnant* Gerhard Keppler had been one of the old hands in the Western Desert, and from the beginning of 1943 flew in the Home Defence as a member of 2/*JG* 27; he spent some months during mid-1943 as an instructor but then returned to the fray. He thus had wide experience of fighting the bomber formations over Germany; of his seven victories during the war, six were four-engined bombers claimed from the second half of 1943 to April 1944. Like Otto Schmid he saw little real potential in the use of rockets to attack the bomber formations, despite having some success with them. He used a different method to attack the bombers, obliquely from behind. 'I attacked the four-engined bombers which I managed to shoot down always from behind, this meant that I approached them from behind but obliquely so and then only just before opening fire did I turn sharply in directly behind them. The first one that I shot down was with the "Dödel", the two rockets that we carried in open launching tubes one under each wing, which we could fire from a greater range than the guns.

However the operations of the aircraft so equipped did not prove a success, and soon after we received aircraft with a large calibre cannon firing through the propeller hub and using very effective incendiary ammunition.'

While 1943 began relatively quietly for the German Home Defence, as the Americans began raiding Germany proper, there was a very substantial increase in the weight of the American attack, with US escort fighters finally becoming active in the second quarter of the year. By year's end an enormous change in fighting intensity had taken place, as demonstrated by the relevant statistics.

Statistical data for German fighters in Home Defence for 1943[57]

| 1943 | Serviceable Me 109s | Serviceable Fw 190s | Combat losses Me 109s | Combat losses Fw 190s | Pilot losses (+ and M) Me 109s | Pilot losses (+ and M) Fw 190s |
|---|---|---|---|---|---|---|
| Quarter 1 | 126 | 221 | 19 | 23 | 7 | 10 |
| Quarter 2 | 289 | 263 | 65 | 56 | 22 | 26 |
| Quarter 3 | 408 | 184 | 147 | 148 | 52 | 58 |
| Quarter 4 | 378 | 179 | 274 | 147 | 116 | 73 |
| Total 1943 | - | - | 505 | 374 | 197 | 167 |

Numbers of serviceable aircraft are for end of third month in each quarter.[58]
Losses are total for *Reichs* Home Defence daylight losses; two aircraft lost by *Luftflotte 2*[59] in Italy are excluded as that theatre forms part of a separate volume.
+ and M = killed and missing.

It can be seen in the above table that serviceable Fw 190 numbers decreased significantly in the third quarter of the year. Demand for the Fw 190s was very high across all fronts, and from August 1943 they began to replace the Stukas in the ground-attack *Schlachtgeschwadern* also.[60] The more numerous Me 109 thus replaced the Fw 190s of several Home Defence *Gruppen* during the course of 1943: *III/JG 1* relinquished them from 1 April 1943, *III/JG 26* from 14 May 1943, and *II/JG 2* from August 1943.[61]

If the aircraft losses are calculated as a percentage of serviceable aircraft available at the end of each quarter, then for Me 109s these were between 15 and 23 per cent for quarters one and two, rose to 36 per cent for quarter three and then dramatically to just over 72 per cent in the final quarter of the year. Interestingly, for the Fw 190, similar calculations show a very similar trend with one noticeable exception, that relatively low losses for the first two quarters (10–21 per cent) suddenly jump to 80–82 per cent for the second half of the year. This might reflect the significant increase in American escort fighter sorties and claims for the 8th Air Force from quarter three onwards (see next table below), as these fighters (P-38s and P-47s, plus a few P-51s) were all supercharged, high-altitude aircraft and the Fw 190 struggled in fighter-*versus*-fighter combat above about 20,000 ft. Looking at survivability of the two German fighters (expressed through percentage of pilot fatalities of fighters lost), the Me 109s give figures between 33 and 42 per cent against 39–49 per cent for the Fw 190 – logically, the Fw 190 was a bit more dangerous to its pilots when damaged fatally.

However, the German fighter pilots liked their Fw 190s very much and many preferred this machine to the Me 109; one of these was *Oberleutnant* Otto Stammberger, 4 and 9/JG 26:

> The Fw 190 was a wonderful aircraft that we pilots all really loved. She had outstanding flying characteristics, was completely tame at take-off and landing, was fast, very manoeuvrable, and in the dive even faster while staying controllable up to 700 or even 800 km/h. One had to know how to fly an aircraft, i.e. one had to already have a feel for the machine, and then she was grateful and did everything you asked of her. She was incredibly stable for shooting and was very tough. And then there was the weaponry: four 20 mm cannons and two MGs, which was exactly what was needed against the four-engined bombers. Some details: when taking off one only had to keep the stick steady, there was no torque effect, and one didn't have to push the stick to lift the tail, she took off on her own and flew straight. Forward view was poor and one saw nothing due to the big BMW radial engine; in the beginning this made one somewhat uncertain, but you could lightly move the tail side to side to see, and the aircraft still stayed on a straight course. In contrast the Me 109 easily broke away on take-off and when it did it could not be stopped turning, and a crash was inevitable. With the Me 109 in the take-off one had to keep the tail down and use opposite rudder to the torque, but only until a specific speed had been reached, until the airflow became linear on the tail, and no longer loaded on the one side due to the torque effect of the propeller and powerful engine. Determining this moment was purely a matter of feel, one that gave many a young pilot sleepless nights. And some never learnt this!

In tests of the early P-47 against a captured Fw 190, the latter was superior below 15,000 ft and the former above 20,000 ft; specifically, the Fw at the lower altitudes had better climb and acceleration, but the P-47 could counter with a superior dive and zoom climb, and the Thunderbolt could easily out-dive both German fighters,[62] which would kill many a *Luftwaffe* pilot as this had always been their favourite and most effective escape manoeuvre.

Some use was also made of night fighters to oppose the American incursions, 10 being lost in such missions in the first half of 1943, and this climbed to 36 in the second half.[63] The *Zerstörer* units came into operation over Germany in the second half of 1943, 207 being serviceable in quarter three and 139 in quarter four, with respective losses of six climbing radically to 108 aircraft in the final three months of the year.[64] With only a single *Gruppe* of the new Me 410s, the majority were the old Me 110, which was terribly vulnerable to fighter attack; as the American escorts increased markedly in the fourth quarter of 1943, operation of the heavy fighters thus became untenable except in areas far removed from potential US fighter escort activity.

Some more statistical data in the table below shows very clearly how American bomber sorties climbed during the year, as did those of their escorts; the losses of both and the claims of both are also given.

Statistical data for American four-engined bomber and fighter operations of the 8th Air Force against the German Home Defence for 1943[65]

| 1943 | Bomber sorties | Fighter sorties | Operational losses (all causes) of bombers | Operational losses (all causes) of fighters | Fighter claims against German fighters | Bomber claims against German fighters |
|---|---|---|---|---|---|---|
| Quarter 1 | 1,467 | 0 | 75 | 0 | 0 | 251 |
| Quarter 2 | 3,667 | 861 | 194 | 13 | 17 | 764 |
| Quarter 3 | 8,015 | 3,618 | 366 | 36 | 130 | 1,170 |
| Quarter 4 | 10,906 | 8,059 | 517 | 123 | 267 | 1,068 |

Operational losses included those due to fighter action, flak, operational accidents (such as collisions). Excludes all American losses related to tactical operations over Europe – i.e. operations of light bombers. 8th Air Force fighter arm only became active in quarter 2. Sortie totals reflect aircraft taking off at the start of a mission, not aircraft over target, which was always a lower figure.[66]

In the fourth quarter of 1943, the 15th US Air Force, based in Italy, also began flying missions against the Home Defence, starting in a small way with 432 bomber sorties, 112 by fighters, with 33 bombers lost but no escort fighters missing (nor any claims by them), and in excess of 56 bomber claims of German fighters shot down.[67] In 1944 the contribution of the 15th Air Force would also grow by leaps and bounds. In sum, then, the second half of 1943 brought some radical changes to the Battle of Germany: vastly increased American aircraft numbers, significant fighter escorts of increasing range, and the launch of an entire new air force in Italy. To counter this, the Germans reacted by pulling fighters from the Eastern and Mediterranean theatres back to Germany, re-establishing the heavy fighter groups as interceptors rather than the ground-attack role they had largely been performing in the south and east prior to this, and totally reorganising the *Jagddivisions* and their *Jafüs* in September 1943, as already discussed.

The very first fighter group of the 8th Air Force was the 4th, formed from the three American-manned Eagle Squadrons of the RAF. Formally constituted on 29 September 1942, the 4th Fighter Group flew its first mission on 2 October 1942.[68] Used to the small, light and sleek Spitfires they had flown till then, the 4th Group were re-equipped with the massive P-47 early in 1943, flying their first mission in the new mount on 10 March.[69] The equally famous 56th Fighter Group (an elite unit which had already flown the P-47 for quite some time and had mastered it),[70] eventual top scorers of the 8th Air Force, arrived in the UK in January 1943, and flew its first full group mission on 13 April 1943, the same day that the 78th Fighter Group also debuted.[71] The latter had arrived in the UK equipped with the P-38 in December 1942, but lost most of its pilots and all the aircraft to the North African theatre and was also re-equipped with the P-47.[72] Towards the end of the year, several more fighter groups arrived (all equipped with P-47s except for two that flew P-38s) and began operations over the Reich and conquered territories: 353rd Fighter Group flew its first operation on 9 August 1943, 352nd Fighter Group on 9 September 1943, the 355th on 14 September 1943, the 55th (P-38) and 356th Groups on 15 October 1943, 359th Group on 13 December 1943 and 358th Group a week later, and finally the 20th Group (P-38) flew its first group operation on 28 December 1943.[73] Having begun the year with a single fighter group, the 8th Air Force had 11 in operation already by the end of the year. One more fighter group merits special mention here: the 354th, equipped with the new Merlin-engined P-51 B Mustang, was part of the tactical 9th Air Force, but was loaned to the 8th Fighter Command; it flew its first operation on 1 December 1943 and first bomber escort four days later.[74] Without any drop tanks the P-51 B could reach Stuttgart, with two 75-gallon tanks it could reach Berlin, and with the use of two tanks of 108 gallons each it could even reach Vienna.[75] This made almost all of the Home Defence airspace vulnerable to the Mustang's deadly presence, except for the far-eastern reaches of the Reich. Now suddenly even *Jagddivision 1* fighters were vulnerable to attack by these escorts, and basing P-51 Bs in Italy meant the same for those of *Jagddivision 7*.

Some insight into the advent of the American escort fighters into the airspace of the Home Defence can be gleaned from the recollections of a very successful pilot in the battle, Adolf Glunz of *II/JG 26*. Glunz led 5th and 6th *Staffeln* and ended the war as an *Oberleutnant* with 72 victory claims, including 20 four-engined bombers.[76] Being directly along the Channel coast, where many of the bomber formations crossed into German territory on their way to more distant targets, *JG 26* were among the first *Jagdgeschwaders* to feel the weight of the American escort fighters.

> We mostly attacked formations of four-engined bombers in small groups (about six to eight aircraft) from head-on. To lead a large fighter unit direct from head-on was hard to achieve due to its poor manoeuvrability, and in addition the bombers often changed course when they saw what we were getting up to. With just two or four machines, or when I was alone, I mostly attacked from about 45° above and from ahead but in the quarter, to hit the unarmoured pilot's cabin if possible. In this way due to my high diving speed, the chance of my getting hit was smaller, as our attacks in this fashion were often only noticed at the last minute. We avoided attacks from behind a formation if at all possible, as the combined defensive fire of a close formation of bombers was so strong, that one had little chance to get away with it in one piece. Straggling lone bombers I naturally did attack from behind also. It became difficult when the bombers approached with fighter escort that was normally greatly superior to us in numbers also. A well-carried-out attack so that as many as possible of us were able to fire, became almost impossible then. In such cases a

part of our fighters attempted to tie up the escorting fighters in dog fights, in order to give the others an opportunity to attack the bombers. Otherwise we tried to cut through the fighter escort from above with high speed, and then to get at the bombers in the dive, from head-on, as already described. This of course needed an accurate estimation of the approach path to the bombers and also the deflection angle, as well as very accurate shooting, as only a short burst was possible due to the high closing speed. In addition one had to get so close to the bombers to ensure that this short burst was concentrated and on target that the bomber fell right away. A second attack on the same bomber was mostly impossible due to the escorts.

Perhaps even more important than the increasing numbers of the highly motivated and aggressive American fighters was the extension of their range. Initially the early Spitfires (280 km range) and then the P-47 Thunderbolt replacements (370 km) only allowed escort to just past Antwerp or the middle of the Zuider Zee in Holland.[77] The American air force as a stopgap measure experimented with use of the 200-gallon ferry tanks which they had in large enough quantities; due to altitude-pressure problems they could only be filled up to 75 to 100 gallons for operations but allowed an additional 120 km of penetration, and were first used on 28 July 1943.[78] Operational units, by judicious use of throttle and by taking some risks in keeping the drop tanks on past the enemy coast, could squeeze the range by another 24 km, giving a total penetration of around 530 km, which equated to almost being able to reach Bremen on the German North Sea coast.[79] Then at the end of August 1943, US-made 85-gallon tanks arrived in numbers quickly followed by quantities of the British-manufactured 108 gallon tanks in early September.[80] With this new adaptation the American fighters were for the very first time able to provide a P-47 escort all the way in and out for a raid on Emden on 27 September 1943.[81] Once again the pilots were courageous enough on operations to keep their (108 gallon) drop tanks on till they sighted the enemy or until empty, extending their range to 600 km (penetration potential now past Bremen, covering the operational area of *Jagddivision* 3 well). Thus on 4 October 1943, the 56th Fighter Group were able to surprise a formation of Me 110s and cause drastic casualties, claiming 15.[82]

Another innovation, from September 1943, was the so-called relay escort system where US fighters did not waste precious fuel and range by flying continuously with slower bombers, forcing inefficient use of engine power, but rather using a number of groups to fly to predetermined rendezvous points with the bomber formation to then dominate the airspace around it for their fuel duration time, before being replaced by another unit.[83] The *Luftwaffe* fighter arm soon worked out the counter to this tactical innovation, which was to attack the escorting fighters at coastal landfall (with the help of radar and their controllers), which was tried on 14 October but with little success, as the American fighters were happy to dogfight and were then still able to continue in some numbers on their original mission for some time.[84] By November 1943 the P-38 was added to the equation, with a range of around 725 km with two drop tanks which could get them to approximately Hamburg or Frankfurt.[85] However, this aircraft had severe technical problems, particularly with its engines at the high altitudes typical of the Battle of Germany, and this lowered their effective use and increased losses significantly as crippled fighters on one engine became easy prey to the *Luftwaffe* Experten.[86]

*Oberleutnant* Otto Stammberger, although wounded in the Home Defence and no longer able to fly combat missions from May 1943, remained with his *Geschwader* and was able to see what the effect of the escort fighters was on their operations and on his friends. 'I did not experience meeting the American fighters Thunderbolt, Lightning, Mustang in my operational time up to 13 May 1943; they only came later. From reports of my friends I knew that the Thunderbolt and particularly the Mustang were greatly feared; the Lightning although very manoeuvrable was slow and very vulnerable to being fired upon – in the beginning it was used for long-range escorts but soon replaced by the Mustang due to losses. The two fighters Thunderbolt and Mustang had excellent engines with superchargers (driven by exhaust gasses), flew at 11,000 and even 12,000 m still with practically full power, while the pressure in our mechanical superchargers fell to one-third or even a quarter of its normal pressure. We did not have any of the high temperature-bearing special steel that could tolerate the exhaust gas temperatures of an advanced supercharger. The Thunderbolt was more manoeuvrable, the Mustang was faster, and with drop tanks could fly for three and a half to four hours. The Thunderbolt was faster in the dive than both the Me 109 and Fw 190, so that anyone who tried to dive away to escape pursuit was lost. Many of our young pilots met their end in this way.'

'Stotto' Stammberger emphasized that *JG 26* lay directly in the path of many of the major raids against the Reich and was thus often the first to make contact with the American formations and their escorts. He paints a sombre picture of what it was like to be a fighter pilot on the Channel Front operating against the British and opposing the Americans with their four-engined bombers from August 1942 onwards.

In the fight against the four-engined bombers we always had to first climb up slowly to their altitude of about 8,000 m which took 20 minutes, before we were able to start looking for them at *c.* 480 km/h. The US air force formations flew at about 380–400 km/h and we never knew where they were flying to. For the fighter pilots on the Channel coast it was always a case of luck if we actually intercepted them. For us it was always a matter of life and death fighting against the four-engined bombers. We did not get leave any more, the experienced pilots became ever fewer, and young, incompletely trained pilots arrived in the operational *Staffeln* and were scared of their own aircraft. We had enough aircraft, and thus the young folk, 19 to 20 years old, had to fly with us. They would be shot down within three to four missions and that was, in practical terms, within two, three days. Many of our older pilots suffered from stomach cramps; they hardly ate any more, just chocolate, coffee and cigarettes. When the loudspeakers blared out 'scramble' they often threw up.

This also happened to me; I was shot down by a Spitfire at 8,000 m on 13 May 1943 by a Norwegian pilot. My aircraft exploded, but I fell free, badly burnt, my parachute also partly burnt, so that I fell to earth like a stone and the Spitfire pilot left me. I did, however, survive – other comrades were not so lucky. Our *Geschwader JG 26 Schlageter* suffered 600 per cent losses during the war, we only operated against the Anglo-Americans in the West. My own tactic against the four-engined bomber streams was the attack from the front. The bombers were not armoured in front, they only had glass/perspex cabin windows. Our effective shooting time was generally only one to two seconds, as we rushed at each other with a closing speed of about 900 km/h and then our salvo from four cannons of 20 mm calibre and two MGs of 17 mm calibre had to be on target, on the cabin.

It was very difficult to be able to attack the formations from head-on, and luck was always part of it when I was able to get to the bomber stream from exactly ahead with my *Staffel*, and also with the fighter escort on your neck – up till summer 1943 they were Spitfires that could only fly as far as Antwerp – later came the Thunderbolt and Mustang, the latter could fly with to Berlin! Often I could only get at the enemy with four aircraft, each formation having 30 four-engined bombers in it, and one formation after the other; we always had directed on our fighters the massed return fire of the bombers' machine guns, irrespective of the position from which we attacked them. An attack from the rear of a formation exposed us to this defensive fire for many seconds and we lost the most pilots with such attacks; attacks from the sides were also only successful for experienced pilots due to the high deflection angle. With head-on attacks from early 1943 onwards, the closed-up bomber formations turned either right or left into our attack direction, at about 25 degrees, and then our direct attack from dead ahead was impossible, and we had to try and follow their direction change and our attack went past the formation. That's what the escorting fighters were waiting for and they then dived on us. It was not at all pleasant!!!

The head-on attacks were forbidden by the *Reichsmarschall* later in 1943 due to insufficient successes. The bomber formations began to shoot at us at a distance of 1,500 m, our effective firing range began at 400 m. Our young pilots got frightened with all the visible muzzle flashes and themselves started to shoot as well, naturally all of it going below the bomber formations. They also tended to turn away at a distance of 300–400 m from the bombers, found themselves alone then and were an easy prey for the escort fighters. In a head-on attack the bombers rapidly grew as big as barns in our sights in a few seconds and the young pilots became scared they would ram them and broke off their attacks much too early. No preaching would help in such cases, those who lacked nerve were lost. Up till my getting shot down by the Spitfires in May 1943 I had a total of 10 combats against the four-engined bombers and in these shot down six of them, four of them in head-on attacks. I can state that in my time, to the end of May 1943, that I was always able to get at the bombers on the Channel coast when no escort fighters were there, and then mostly I also was able to shoot a bomber down. When escort fighters were present (at that time only Spitfires), we were kept away and could not get to the bombers. In this the Spitfires were outstanding protectors! After having been wounded in May I was no longer able to fly and performed staff duty in my *Geschwader* till the end of the war.

Despite the steadily increasing weight of American four-engined bomber formations and soon enough also of their increasingly long-legged escorts, early in 1943 combat with medium bombers of the RAF and their escorts remained an important facet of the lives of the German fighter pilots stationed along the Channel coast and in Holland. As an example, on 22 January 1943 off the coast north-west of Antwerp, 10 Fw 190s of *II/JG 1* accompanied by two more from the 11th *Staffel* intercepted a formation of 15–20 Mitchells (reported by the fighter pilots as Hudsons) escorted by Mustangs and Spitfires.[87] The German fighters claimed three of the bombers, four Mustangs and two Spitfires, with British losses exactly equal to these claims except for the two Spitfires.[88] *Unteroffizier* Otto Schmid of *5/JG 1* was one of the successful pilots against the Mustangs, shooting one down: 'The first P-51s (P-51 A model) were not as elegant in their shape as those that came later; this early model was still quite angular. Despite this they were still very fast and manoeuvrable.' The early Mustangs, with their Allison engines and somewhat limited performance, gave the German pilots a false security about fighting this aircraft. The transformation of its fighting power and range that came with the P-51 B model, fitted with a Merlin engine, was significant; the next time Otto Schmid saw a Mustang they were the later model so feared by the *Luftwaffe* fighter pilots. By then he was an instructor in *Ergänzungsjagdgruppe West*. 'My second meeting with the P-51, this time with the outstanding Rolls-Royce Merlin engine (actually a licence-built Packard Merlin), I experienced in autumn 1943 at the airfield at St Trond in Belgium. We had to land there on the way to another destination while flying in a Me 108 as the fuel tank was leaky, and so I got to admire the new Mustang from safe cover as some flew over this field at a distance of about 50 m from us. There were four of them. Luckily they had not seen us, otherwise our 108 would have been finished and we would have had to take the train back to Cazaux.'

On 4 February 1943 the Americans bombed Emden (as Hamm, the primary target, was not found due to cloud).[89] The bombers had claimed 25 German fighters shot down against real *Luftwaffe* losses of nine aircraft, three pilots lost and four wounded; five B-17s were lost, one apparently to a ramming.[90] Once again, Otto Schmid flying in *6/JG 1* was involved in this interception and was witness both to the apparent ramming as well as the excessive bomber claims:

> If the Americans really had shot down as many German fighters as they claimed in every attack, then by the end of 1943 there would have been no Fw 190s and Me 109s left in the skies. In the air battle with the four-engined bombers on 4 February 1943 the *Staffelkapitän* of the 6th *Staffel*, *Oberleutnant* Leonhardt, probably rammed a bomber after he saw that there was no longer any chance to free himself from destroying this aircraft; he was in all likelihood seriously wounded so that he could no longer avoid a collision. Our then friends from the other side were fortunate that our leadership did not know what they should concentrate on. The one wanted bombers, despite the fact that the time of the German bomber was long gone due to too little defensive armament and a lack of escort fighters, the other wanted Stukas and yet again others wanted long range bombers. Our leaders overlooked the most important aspects; instead of frittering away the aircraft production, they should have concentrated on one or two fighter types. Unfortunately the training of the pilots for this same purpose was never driven with the necessary intensiveness that we needed. I read once in a book about the production of the American Mustang and Thunderbolt fighters. There the industry had to produce the fighters that the air force wanted. With us it was exactly the opposite. We were equipped with what resulted from the conflict of interest between industry and politicians.

In the war diary of *II/JG 1* (copy via Otto Schmid) for this action on 4 February, there was a report of great frustration in 6th *Staffel* as despite their seven Fw 190s each making three to four attacks on the bomber formation, the only effect they could observe was two right-hand engines and one left-hand engine being put out of action. *Oberleutnant* Leonhardt was seen to follow a Boeing out to sea and on his second attack was hit by return fire.

This Emden raid also marked the first use of night fighters against American bomber formations, with eight Me 110s of *IV/NJG 1* making close attacks from the rear of the bombers, claiming three but resulting in all the Me 110s being damaged and two crash-landing.[91] *Oberleutnant* Martin Drewes, a very successful night fighter pilot from *IV/NJG 1*, comments below on the use of these specialised and highly trained crews and aircraft in such situations. 'Day operations of the night fighters against the American four-engined bombers were seen as a means of reinforcing the German attack, especially when the weather was bad. The problem was that our aircraft were not suited to this. When such a night fighter aircraft, with its expensive radar and communications and navigation equipment, was hit by defensive fire, then it was lost to night operations, at least for some time. Thus the successes achieved through these means were in no way proportional to the costs of these operations. I once received 72 holes in my aircraft on such a mission. It could no longer be flown. Of course, due to our slow speed, which was only a bit greater than that of the Boeings, we could only attack them from behind. And because we could shoot well, we achieved many hits on them and shot down several of them. However, in the larger scheme of things this was not a decisive contribution. The Me 262 came much too late. But the sabotage within our own ranks was much greater than we thought. But these are themes that cannot be gone into here.' One more idea from high command on economy of force and effective application of available aircraft and crews (available perhaps, but not trained, equipped or rested for day missions) which did not pan out in practice.

In March 1943 *Unteroffizier* Otto Schmid, *6/JG 1* had a very lucky escape:

On 10 March 1943 the 5th and 6th *Staffeln* took off for an operation over northern Belgium. Due to confused leadership by our *Staffelkapitän Hauptmann* Wickop, despite having been warned by *Oberfeldwebels* Heesen and Bach that there was a large Spitfire unit flying up sun from us, we were immediately attacked by them at a disadvantage. We had to thus break up our close formation straight away, to avoid the machines diving vertically down at us. Fortunately in this I only received one hit. Unfortunately I received many small splinters. One of them ended up in the cornea of my right eye. At first I thought these were only small wounds in my face, as can be seen on the photographs (illustrations 47 and 48). Unfortunately overnight I developed a very bad conjunctivitis inflammation; I could hardly see any more. In the naval hospital in Bergen op Zoom I was examined carefully, and then they also found the splinter in my eye. The eye was also very inflamed from the slipstream coming through the broken windscreen. This splinter was then removed with a magnet. I had to remain in hospital for about 14 days, until 22 March by which time everything had healed up. After that I was given permission by the chief doctor and also at his wish, even though it was strictly forbidden, to do a low level flypast over the hospital, as I flew back from my first operation, after leaving them on 24 March. The doctors were very excited, as they assured me later by telephone!

*II/JG 1*'s war diary for 10 March 1943 (copy supplied by Otto Schmid, via Dutch air historian R. W. de Visser) does not even note Otto's wounds. He elaborated further on the leadership of *6/JG 1* on this (for him at least) momentous day. 'That *Hauptmann* Wickop possessed operational experience is without doubt, otherwise he would not have been flying as *Staffelkapitän*. In any case things were covered up so that his mistake on this mission was not made known further up the chain. From 1 April to 11 May 1943 I was very 'generously' given a recovery period at Ospedaletti on the Italian Riviera. From 1 June 1943 I was ordered to Cazaux as an instructor in the *Jagdergänzungsgruppe West*. When I returned to the 6th *Staffel* on 31 January 1944, Wickop was no longer with the unit.'

Just back from leave after his facial wounds on 11 May 1943, Otto Schmid flew an escort mission the very next day for fighter-bombers (*Jabos*) across the Channel. 'This mission was to protect the *Jabos* against English fighters. The *Jabos* did not belong to *JG 1*; as far as I remember they belonged to *JG 26*. On 12 May 1943 it was planned to attack a large convoy coming from the north and steaming towards the Thames Estuary, in *Planquadrat* (grid square) 1365, with *Jabos* carrying 250 kg bombs. But as Spitfires were already approaching, most of the bombs were dropped in the water prematurely. From what we could see no ship was damaged or even sunk. We busied ourselves for a while with the English fighters and then broke off the dogfights due to fuel shortage. Neither side could show any *Abschüsse*.' The pressure from 8th Air Force attacks was obviously not yet enough to stop activity of the *Jagdflieger* aimed across the Channel at their old enemies in the RAF. However, illustration 41 summarises Otto Schmid's combat career from his first joining *II/JG 1* in early 1942 until he left them at the end of May 1943 and is based on his detailed logbook entries for this entire time period. What is noticeable for the period of January–May 1943 is that his missions became dominated by scrambles as the US 8th Air Force began to raid Germany proper and particularly northern Germany in the first half of 1943.

Otto Schmid also comments on the good accommodation he and his fellow pilots enjoyed, as well as the fact that all ranks enjoyed the officers' mess together. 'We had very good accommodations, even if these were sometimes of the barracks type. In Katwijk and Woensdrecht (*II/JG 1*'s base August 1942–4 March 1943) there were well-equipped barracks, in Schipol (4 March–1 April 1943; thereafter returned to Woensdrecht) and Rheine, all in small buildings. Mostly we were two to a room, but sometimes also with single rooms. It all depended on the size of the barracks or house. The accommodations were never in the immediate vicinity of the airfield, as this was too risky in case of any air attacks on the bases. Mostly they were 0.5–1 km away, in Schipol 3 km from the field. We could thus sleep peacefully. We were always accommodated in the officers' mess together with the officers, in contrast to the bomber units. In the fighter units in this regard there were no differences or exceptions; thus when there was occasion to celebrate something we could do so together. At the end of the day, when we were in the air we were dependent on each other. There was thus an outstanding comradeship amongst us, which was of the greatest importance in our missions against numerically superior enemies. After all, we were all young boys between 20 and 25 years old and had no time for such nonsense.'

A few weeks after Otto Schmid had been wounded in the face, another Otto, *Oberleutnant* Stammberger of *4/JG 26*, was once more able to down a four-engined bomber, this time by an unusual attack tactic from the beam; once more *Luftwaffe* monitoring of Allied signals traffic was able to confirm his *Abschuss* as a victory. 'On 31 March 1943, 93rd *Feindflug*, shot down one Liberator, as my 4th *Abschuss*. My notes in addition to my logbook entry: 100 km north of Ostende out into the North Sea. One attack from the beam, second attack from behind, achieved hits in the fuselage and right wing and he descended in a right turn into the clouds; formation was on the return flight, the Liberator was straggling a bit, and I was alone after the preceding action. I could not follow the Liberator any more, as I had no more fuel for this. In the evening at 22h00 the Technical Watch Officer of the Monitoring Unit, who listened to enemy radio and voice communication, confirmed my combat as an *Abschuss*: the crew had bailed out, as the machine could only be held in a descending right hand spiral and they could no longer get back to their base. Thus through listening in on the enemy's radio traffic my *Abschuss* was confirmed; as I was alone and had no witnesses the victory would not otherwise have been counted, as had happened to me more than once.' An excerpt from Otto Stammberger's logbook for March–April 1943, below, shows that his combats and missions with enemy contact were now dominated by the American four-engined bomber formations rather than the RAF.

Example of a fighter pilot's operational life, Home Defence, March–April 1943, based on flying logbook, 24 March–5 April 1943: *Oberleutnant* Otto Stammberger, *Staffelkapitän 4/JG 26*, flying Fw 190 (based at Vitry, France the entire time, but sometimes landing at Wevelghem in Belgium) (Source: Otto Stammberger)

MARCH
24: Fighter patrol, 09h47–10h36
25: Mission, 15h24–16h02
28: Mission, 11h50–12h20
    *Feindflug* (#92), 12h47–13h50; met enemy, 60 four-engined bombers, 10 km off the coast at Eastbourne
31: *Feindflug* (#93), 12h07–13h08; one Liberator shot down (4th victory)

APRIL
 1: Patrol over sea, 17h18–18h15
 2: Patrol over sea, 20h03–20h43
 3: *Feindflug* (#94), 15h41–16h26; met enemy, 10–15 Spitfires, over Le Touquet
    Patrol over sea, 20h10–20h45
 4: Patrol over sea, 12h07–12h47
    Mission, 19h01–19h58
 5: *Feindflug* (#95), 14h44–15h46; one Boeing shot down (5th victory), landed Wevelghem

Otto Stammberger described the mission against the American bombers on 5 April 1943 in detail, as related below.

Mid-day at 12h00 many echoes were picked up over south-east England by the Freya radars; the Americans were climbing and assembling in a large circle. We fighters then went to readiness in our aircraft (*Sitzbereitschaft*) and waited. The bomber formation then turned onto a southerly course, probable target Paris. The First *Gruppe* received take-off orders, about 40 Fw 190s in St Omer with instructions to climb in the Amiens area. The Third *Gruppe* in Abbeville was then also let loose, the Second *Gruppe* in Wevelghem remained in reserve. Thus about 80 aircraft were launched. Then at Calais the four-engined formation made a left-hand turn and flew to the south-east in the direction of Ostende. Now the Second *Gruppe* in Wevelghem took off with instructions to climb south of the mouth of the Scheldt. The First and Third *Gruppen* were directed towards Antwerp, but they were now 100 km away. In the meantime a four-engined bomber formation had crossed the coast at Ostende, about 60 bombers with strong fighter escort being reported, flying in three groups (60 in each), probable target Antwerp. The Second *Gruppe* had in the meantime sighted the enemy, who was still flying 2,000 m higher than them and about 30–40 km ahead of them, the *I* and *III Gruppen* not seeing anything yet, as they were still about 60 km away.

While the Second *Gruppe* was manoeuvring into attack position from the right rear quarter, the formation had reached Antwerp and bombed the ERLA aircraft factories in Antwerp-Mortsel. The formation then turned around to the left and flew over the mouth of the Scheldt again and homewards on a westerly course. The Second *Gruppe* now caught up with the bomber formation on their return flight and shot down several four-engined bombers (four aircraft out of 180!!) and then landed themselves in among the newly arrived English fighter escort that had just relieved the old one and taken up their bomber charges over the coast. I shot down a Boeing from ahead, hits seen in the cabin, three men bailed out, and it glided down to the right; impact near Woensdrecht, and own aircraft hit in left wing.

Of the four *Abschüsse* of our *Geschwader* on 5 April, our *Kommandeur* of the *II Gruppe*, *Hauptmann* W-F. Galland, achieved the first one at 15h25 at Hobboken/Belgium; its pilot, Lieutenant

Fisher, was killed. At 15h28 our *Kommodore Major* Josef Priller got the second bomber, which crashed at Zandvliet/Belgium; its pilot, Lieutenant Kelly, was also killed. My victory followed at 15h35 at Dinteloord/Holland; the pilot, Lieutenant William Parker, bailed out but died. At 15h38 the fourth bomber was shot down by *Oberfeldwebel* Roth of my *Staffel*, at Kalmhout/Belgium, its pilot, Lieutenant Robert Seelos, bailing out and surviving. I have corresponded with Seelos, and we have met twice, when he was in Germany on business. His father had been born in Munich and as a young man went to America with his own father. 'Wutz' Galland was my *Gruppenkommandeur* in II/JG 26 when I took over the 4th *Staffel* as *Staffelkapitän* in February 1943. 'Wutz' was a straightforward and strict officer who was an outstanding shot. He only joined us in the *Geschwader* in 1942 and up till 17 August 1943 he achieved 55 *Abschüsse*, including many four-engined bombers. Too many Thunderbolts were the cause of his death. He was fair and friendly, but beware of him if you had messed up. *I* and *III Gruppen* did not catch up with the formation and flew home again. The Second *Gruppe* lost two aircraft to the bombers' defences. This was the description of a mission in April 1943; later, after the American long-range fighters, Mustangs and Thunderbolts, had become operational, attacks on the bombers became almost impossible. The wide-ranging escort and those flying in advance of the bombers almost always were able to turn us away and caused grievous losses to our shrinking fighter units.

For other units lying along the Channel and Dutch coastal areas, combat with British formations remained more prominent. Even before Otto Schmid had left *6/JG 1* to become an instructor, while he was still recovering from his wounds on the Riviera, on 3 May 1943 a combat against British Ventura bombers and their Spitfire escort cost the lives of two experienced pilots, *Oberfeldwebel* Heesen of 5th *Staffel* and *Feldwebel* Pfeiffer of *4/JG 1*, who were shot down by the escort.[92] 11 Venturas escorted by three squadrons of Spitfires had been dispatched by the RAF against a power station just to the north of Amsterdam, but they were caught at low level on the way in, losing nine bombers, and one badly damaged (which nevertheless made it home), while the last one pressed on and bombed, only to be shot down immediately thereafter.[93] Squadron Leader Trent and his navigator were the only two crew members to survive, the former earning a Victoria Cross for his bravery.[94] Nine of the Venturas fell to *II/JG 1*, who also claimed two of the Spitfires;[95] the German side of this combat can be illustrated through the combat report of the *Gruppenführer* of *II/JG 1, Hauptmann* Dietrich Wickop:[96] 'On 3 May 1943 at 17h20 I took off with the *Gruppe* after an alarm from *Jafü Holland/Ruhrgebiet*. Through the Y-system I was directed at 7,000 m to *c*. 20 km west of Den-Haag, where we sighted at 17h40 an incoming enemy formation comprising two bunches of 12 to 15 Lockheed-Venturas accompanied by 40 Spitfires. The formation was flying on an approximate course for Amsterdam. I sent the 5th *Staffel* to tie up the escort and attacked with the *Stabsschwarm*, the front bomber formation of six Venturas. I dived from above and to the right on the left-outside Ventura and opened fire from slightly below and to the left from 50–80 m range. From the same position immediately thereafter, from a distance of about 20–30 m, I fired at a second Ventura flying to the right and saw hits in the fuselage and left wing. Shortly afterwards long, bright flames came out of the left engine. The Ventura dived away to the north. I pulled away and watched the Ventura and then made a second attack from above and the left, upon which fragments of the aircraft broke away and the fire spread to both wings. I pulled up and saw that the Ventura exploded in the air at *c*. 1,200–1,500 m. Fragments of the aircraft fell to the ground 1 km north-west of Oostzaan Station in swampy ground.' Otto Schmid had learned much from his senior comrades, including Heesen, when he first joined his *Gruppe* and paid this tribute to two of them: 'The *Oberfeldwebeln* Heesen and Lüth were first-class comrades and for new pilots at the front were outstanding teachers and examples to follow. When I first joined *JG 1* I flew with both of them as *Rottenflieger* and later as *Rottenführer* in their *Schwarms*. One simply felt safe flying with them, as during operations they flew very carefully in order to always keep an eye on their "chicks". Sadly, *Oberfeldwebel* Heesen was shot down in combat with Spitfires on 3 May 1943 in a combat near Haarlem, Holland and crashed into the sea. Despite intensive searches by the air-sea rescue services, nothing of him was found. *Oberfeldwebel* Lüth was shot down and killed on 6 March 1944 in aerial combat with Boeing B-17s.'

Despite the American escort fighters having just got started, due to their as-yet limited range most German targets remained well beyond their reach.[97] Such was the case also on 17 April 1943, when the 8th Air Force sent out the then-record number of 115 aircraft assigned to a single target, namely the Focke Wulf works in Bremen; 16 bombers were lost and 39 damaged.[98] *III/JG 54* claimed four of the bombers, one of which was destroyed in very unique fashion by *Hauptmann* Hans-Ekkehard Bob, *Staffelkapitän 9/JG 54*: 'The high point of the Second World War was the missions in the Home Defence of Germany. This was also the high point of my own operations, with the destruction of a four-engined bomber, a Flying Fortress B-17 (17 April 1943) through ramming at an altitude of 8,000 m, that led to the crash of both aircraft. I saved myself through bailing out.' Bob had led *9/JG 54* at the rear of the *Gruppe*'s formation into a head-on attack but the bombers turned away at the right moment and ruined this attempted attack, so Bob made a second one from dead ahead again, diving below the bomber formation a fraction of a second too late and hitting the wing of the B-17.[99] He was basically thrown out of the disintegrating Me 109 after he undid his straps, and landed among the bailed-out crew of his victim.[100] While this was a somewhat extreme way to confirm a victory, this day also saw the first officially recognised *Herausschüsse*,[101] whereby a German pilot managed to separate a four-engined bomber from its formation due to it having been hit and damaged; these also counted as full victories.[102]

In early April 1943, while unescorted bombers were penetrating into French airspace, the *Luftwaffe* high command decided to also make use of their advanced training units, assigning experienced instructors and their best students to tackle such formations, which were already making incursions into the previously peaceful airspace where training schools had been concentrated.[103] One such student was *Obergefreiter* Horst Petzschler. 'Here (at *Jagdfliegerschule* in Paris-Villacoublay, *1/JG 105*) in April 1943 I met up with seven other young pilots and one experienced instructor and on 1 May we were sent to tackle 200 B-17 Flying Fortresses bombing the radar centre in Guyancourt. We finished only one of them, because we were far too excited!! The *Kommandeur* wanted to lock us all up for having been so stupid! He said that soon they would come with fighter escorts and then the good time for shooting them down would be past, and he was right!'

June 1943 saw the formation of *IV/JG 3* (later a famous *Sturmgruppe*) as well as *JG 25* and *JG 50*, neither of which exceeded a *Gruppe* in strength.[104] The latter two units were commanded by two top Eastern

Front aces, *Oberstleutnant* Herbert Ihlefeld and *Major* Hermann Graf, and were to tackle the fast, high-flying Mosquitoes that came and went almost with impunity across the Homeland much to Göring's discomfort.[105] They became operational in July but had little success and were disbanded in October (*JG 50*) and December (*JG 25*) 1943.[106] Graf's favoured situation in the *Luftwaffe* (as a major propaganda figure and leading light in the NSFK – National Socialist Flying Corps) was underlined by his being able to set up his own private soccer team from existing air force personnel which was attached to *JG 50* and, somewhat ironically, called the 'Red Fighters';[107] one has to wonder whether this was not at least part of the reason for *JG 50*'s lack of success against the Mosquitoes. Both units also became involved in the more general Home Defence in their brief existence.[108] Another prominent National Socialist believer, *Oberstleutnant* Hajo Herrmann, a highly decorated bomber pilot, in April 1943 initiated the idea of the *Wilden Sau* ('Wild Boar'), a single-engined, non-radar-equipped night fighter, with an experimental *Kommando*, the idea being that these would operate over cities attacked at night, with the searchlight defences, flares and ground fires providing enough illumination to allow something akin to conventional fighter attacks over major targets.[109]

*Jagdgeschwader Herrmann* was formally set up on 26 June 1943 and by late August had been renamed *JG 300*.[110] Initially they had no aircraft of their own and utilised those of *JG 1* and *JG 11*, certainly not an ideal situation especially as regards maintenance or pilot satisfaction in the parent units. While Otto Schmid was away on instructing duties, *II/JG 1* had to share their aircraft with one of the newly formed *Wilden Sau* single-engined night fighter groups, namely *II/JG 300*.[111] Like most good ideas it had its drawbacks, as detailed by *Feldwebel* Otto Schmid: '*Oberst* Herrmann was the initiator of the "*Wilden Sau*". For this our day fighter aircraft were taken over by this concern after our daily duty was done and night sorties flown with them against attacking British bombers. When in the evening 10 serviceable Fw 190s were taken over from our *Staffel*, then we could count on only three or four of them still being there the next morning. All the rest had either been shot down or wrecked in forced landings. As effective as this bunch were announced as being, they clandestinely disappeared again after a while.' From 10 October 1943, *I/JG 300* would increasingly fly day missions as part of the mainstream Home Defence, and in 1944 all three of the *Wilden Sau*

*Geschwader* became day fighters as well.[112] Going back to June 1943, with only three American fighter groups operational, all on the P-47, the belief in the bomber being able to fight its way through to targets and back home again still prevailed in the 8th Air Force; in that month (22 June) a new concept within this philosophy was launched with the YB-40, a B-17 fitted out with extra guns, more ammunition and additional armour.[113] The concomitant extra weight they carried made them slower than the mainstream bombers once those had unloaded, not only making them isolated targets themselves[114] but also rather dampening their use as escorts on the return flights. Their only useful innovation was the so-called 'chin turrets', powered twin-gun turrets fitted in the lower nose of the B-17s[115] (and later B-24s also) to counter the head-on attacks. This worked to a point, but almost inevitably Göring tried to stop the successful head-on tactic himself, as already recounted by *Oberleutnant* Otto Stammberger of *JG 26*. This is also evident in the account that follows; once again, Göring often acted in what might be described as the interest of the enemy. *Hauptmann* Georg Schröder, *Staffelkapitän 4/JG 2* and later *Gruppenkommandeur II/JG 2*, who flew in the Home Defence for almost a year from July 1943, was a firm believer in the frontal attack method on the American bomber formations and an experienced practitioner of this art:

> From the First World War and thereafter, it had become doctrine that fighter attacks were made from behind the enemy aircraft. I also heard this personally from veterans themselves who practised this as their standard method. In the early days this was also the practice in the Home Defence. When the four-engined 'furniture vans' with their own defence rearwards made attacking them there much less attractive, then the attack from head-on became the alternative, and in fact, in my opinion, this was necessary also. As a result in our *Geschwadern* the attack from the front was common, and I can even say today it was the surest possible way to attack so long as there was no fighter escort, and through this method the bomber losses became unpleasant for the enemy. With an attack from behind a bomber formation, the slogan was 'dead man'! With an attack from the front one naturally had to make the approach carefully. In this approach the bombers even also had a small blind spot at a certain angle. The approach from head-on implied an enormous time pressure. The combined speeds of the two sets of converging aircraft

of 750 to 850 km/h was no board game. Even a schoolchild could work out what view the approach speed gave. In addition, those being attacked in the bomber formations could not manoeuvre out of the way as the possibilities for colliding when moving sideways in tight formations would soon become too great.

Another point for reflection is – and this question must remain – how did the gunners in the noses of the 'furniture vans' react? Are all people in such a moment all going to be pronounced heroes? I would suggest that even long rows of question marks would not suffice for this question. On the relative merits of attacking from ahead or behind one could write volumes! For an attacker from head-on it is naturally critical if he wishes to survive, and also important of itself, how he dives beneath the bombers and departs from the scene. This is another topic of endless discussion. There is only a fraction of a second available for this decision. In this tiny fraction of time no gunner from the rest of the bomber formation would be able to aim his guns accurately. These things were all aspects of life insurance. One day in France in 1943 (probably 20 October),[116] when we were stationed in Evreux, one morning we were instructed that we should fly an escort with my entire *Staffel* from Paris to Marseilles. All necessary data on times, places etc were prescribed and were to be adhered to in our orders; in addition total radio silence. Within this planning our return flight was to be made only in the late afternoon. Once we had got back home perfectly, then only did we hear about what happened during the day; a four-engined bomber interception was ordered for the *Geschwader – Stab* and all three *Gruppen* – with direct orders 'attack from behind'. This could only have come from some chair-borne genius sitting in a staff position. The result was perplexing; successes – nil, two pilots killed, three more aircraft lost after their pilots had to bail out! This event was a typical example that a lovely theory can be proven totally wrong. In my opinion no further thought or words need be wasted.

Georg Schröder of *II/JG 2*, in describing what life was like as a *Luftwaffe* fighter pilot in France during July 1943–May 1944, also emphasised that there was ongoing combat with light bombers, both RAF and American, their escorts, and also Allied fighter patrols.

It was thus not only the four-engined bomber raids that had to be repelled but a whole system of assaults, within which the B-17 and B-24 formations played a leading role. 'From the beginning of July 1943, when I came to the front, the two-engined bomber missions decreased. Most bombers leaving England now went towards Germany, not only against industry, but also already markedly against the large cities. Personally I only had one contretemps with a small formation of Marauders north of Rennes, when two of us in a *Rotte* returned from a coastal patrol. Thus only one quick attack was possible. My target immediately showed a strong smoke trail, and immediately flew away to the north. I could not bother myself any more about him, albeit for the single reason that I only had enough fuel to make it to my own airfield. For us, within the general course of events, this was the time when *Rotten* continually relieved each other in flying coastal patrols. Enemy *Rotten* came often at low level. As far as I remember our tasks were dominated by flying reconnaissance missions. Astonishingly, the enemy pairs flying in from the north always reached the coast at the same point, and at the same time. One of my *Feldwebels* soon got into the swing of this system, and collected 16 *Abschüsse*. In this summer and late summer we also had various high-altitude missions in different areas. Thus our missions were also directed against the four-engined bombers – B-17s. In the middle of September on one such mission I was able to force one of these birds to belly land near Beaumont-le-Roger. With the four-engined bomber incursions, it often happened that a base transfer would take place when the assembly of the formations over England was recognised, as well as which course they would take up on departure. In this way we were also quite often able to refuel our tanks. There were not any serious interferences by the enemy of our take-offs and landings.'

On 17 August 1943, the 8th Air Force launched a complex and major operation to coincide with their first anniversary of bombing the Germans in Europe. The plan was for 146 B-17s to bomb the Messerschmitt factories at Regensburg, with a second full-strength formation of 230 B-17s close behind aimed at the ball-bearing plants concentrated in Schweinfurt; both targets represented deep-penetration raids where unescorted bombers would inevitably be exposed to German fighter attack for long periods.[117] While the Schweinfurt raid was to return to the United Kingdom, that on Regensburg was to fly south and land on bases in Tunisia; the plan was sound and should have split the German defences on the vulnerable return legs, but as so often in western Europe the weather had its own plan, resulting in a four-hour delay to the departure of the Schweinfurt raid.[118] As a result, an envisaged B-26 light bomber mission to attack airfields in northern France, both as a diversion and also to tie up at least some German fighters was split into two separate raids to coincide with each of the major incursions, and these were accompanied by RAF Spitfires.[119] For George Schröder's unit, *II/JG 2*, the diversion worked for the Regensburg raid and they claimed one Spitfire for two damaged Me 109s; in the afternoon, against the returning Schweinfurt raid, American escorts ensured they had no success.[120] The Regensburg raid was escorted in by an initial group of P-47s as far as just south-east of Diest, which was then replaced by the famous 56th Fighter Group, who would take them almost to Aachen before having to turn back.[121] The German fighters directed by *Jafü Holland-Ruhr* had already begun their attacks before the Thunderbolts had to leave, and continued them south of Koblenz as the bomber stream headed deep into Germany to the south-east.[122] Four of the available seven *Luftwaffe* day fighter *Gruppen* made contact along with one of two night fighter *Gruppen*, in all claiming seven B-17s shot down and four *Herausschüsse* for the loss of seven day fighters.[123]

As the bombers progressed past Koblenz and entered the region covered by *Jagddivision 7* (then still numbered 5 in the pre-September 1943 system), the Germans only had Hermann Graf's *JG 50* and multiple training and night fighter units as well as the *Industrieschutzstaffel* of the Messerschmitt works itself with which to oppose the incursion. Despite this they did well for the loss of a single fighter, *JG 50* claiming six bombers, two falling to training units, two to night fighters and one to the Regensburg factory defence unit.[124] It may be recalled that the latter actually only comprised a *Kette* of three Me 109s, set up reluctantly on the prodding of *Oberstleutnant* Hanns Trübenbach. Trübenbach had been sent to Vienna on 16 August to help set up *Jafü Ostmark* and must have been pretty upset at thus missing the Schweinfurt raid the very next day; as *Jafü Mittelrhein* he would have been responsible for directing the fighter resources of *Jagddivision 7*, but in the event his deputy seems to have done an adequate job! In all, 24 of the Regensburg raiders were lost and another written off in

North Africa, but the bombing had been good and substantial damage was done at the Messerschmitt factories.[125] Less impressive was the fact that only 197 of the 404 fighters directed on to the Regensburg bombers actually made contact.[126]

This would improve in the afternoon battle against the Schweinfurt raiders, when 244 of 468 fighters scrambled made contact.[127] This was an altogether much tougher battle, partly due to the fact that *Luftwaffe* fighters assembled at lunchtime to intercept the expected return of the Regensburg bombers were still in place when the second incursion took place along a very similar route.[128] This was not bad planning, as without the weather intervening the two formations were to have been following one another closely.[129] Against the incoming Schweinfurt raid, *Jafü Holland-Ruhr* was able to direct eight day fighter *Gruppen* plus one and a *Staffel* of night fighters (which claimed 21 bombers and three *Herausschüsse*; lost 15 day fighters, five night fighters); *Jafü 2* put one night fighter *Gruppe* onto the raid (lost two aircraft); *Jagddivision 7* (reinforced by two *Gruppen* of *JG 1* from further north by this stage in the day) directed three *Jagdgruppen* plus training units onto the raid (claimed 10 bombers, one *Herausschuss*; losses were three day fighters).[130] For the outgoing raid, *Jafü Holland-Ruhr* led five day and one night fighter *Gruppen* to contact and combats (claimed eight bombers, three P-47s; lost three day and seven night fighters); *Jagddivision 7* directed one night fighter *Gruppe* and a training unit onto the retreating bombers (two B-17s claimed for four night fighters lost); *Jafüs 2* and *3* in *Luftflotte 3*'s Channel coast region directed many of their fighters onto the outgoing raid and its escorts (claimed five bombers, one *Herausschuss*, one P-47 and a Spitfire; lost three of its own fighters).[131] Among the latter three losses was *Major* 'Wutz' Galland, *Gruppenkommandeur* of *II/JG 26*, and former commanding officer of Otto Stamberger of *4/JG 26*. According to the relevant entry in the *Geschwader Ehrenbuch* of *JG 26*,[132] the *Gruppe* had taken off at 16h52 on the 17 August 1943, from Lille-North, to intercept the outgoing bombers from Schweinfurt, which they did in the area of Lüttich. *Major* Galland led his *Gruppe* in a mass head-on attack having approached the retreating bombers on a reciprocal course,[133] but after the attack the *Stabskette* (Staff vic of three aircraft) was attacked from behind and below by several Thunderbolts from close range, while the *Stabskette* was overtaking the bomber formation, presumably to perform a second head-on attack. Galland was not seen again,[134] and his remains were only found a couple of months later near Maastricht, buried deep in the wreckage of his aircraft in soft ground.[135]

The Germans had been outfoxed by the 56th Fighter Group, led by the redoubtable Colonel 'Hub' Zemke; they had met the outgoing bombers at the correct rendezvous but had flown on a way and then turned back, coming in from the direction of Germany, which the German fighters would not have suspected.[136] And thus the attrition of German fighter leaders continued – it was these losses that ripped the guts out of their fighter force in the end and by June 1944 made the Invasion possible – the fighter force still existed but by then it was dominated by young and inexperienced replacement pilots with few experienced leaders left any more. This was the critical aspect of the Battle over Germany. The Schweinfurt raid lost a total of 36 bombers plus three more written off in the United Kingdom, for a total during the day of 64 B-17s, plus three P-47s for the 8th Air Force; another 168 bombers were damaged.[137] These were losses the 8th Air Force could not afford, and the victory pendulum over the *Reich* now swung well towards the German side. However, there were still problems in the German defence to iron out, among them the absence of a central control[138] which would help to address fighter units moving from one *Jagddivision* (and then also to another *Jafü*'s control) to another during an American incursion. The size of the Home Defence territory, and the choices open to the Americans to make multiple raids and complex routing with feints made movement of fighter units across the territory to be defended almost mandatory. Many aspects of this type of shortcoming were to be addressed in the major reorganisation of the Home Defence in September 1943, but this still excluded *Luftflotte 3*.[139] Another cause for concern should have been the continuing use of training units in the battle; any battle of attrition rests in the first place on a basis of pilot/crew training programmes and aircraft production that provide the reserves necessary to achieve victory in extended fighting.

*Unteroffizier* Otto Schmid, flying as an instructor in *Ergänzungsjagdgruppe West*, stationed in Cazaux near Bordeaux, was far removed from the centre of the action over the Homeland, but would also become embroiled in that battle late in 1943 as all available fighters and pilots, fully trained or not, became involved in the titanic struggle taking place over central Europe. Here in south-western France, Schmid was also witness to the tribulations of the aircraft supporting the German U-boats in their patrols far out into the Atlantic over the Bay of Biscay. 'The He 177 (known as the "*Reichs* firelighter" due to its propensity to catch fire) was a pure faulty concept. Heinkel wanted four engine nacelles for this aircraft, but unfortunately two engines were coupled together in a single nacelle on each wing (for the absolutely ludicrous purpose of making this large aircraft capable of dive-bombing); that led to perennial over-heating of the engines. When I was in Cazaux as an instructor we escorted the He 177s stationed in Bordeaux-Merignac when they left on long-range reconnaissance missions, often following them out to sea for a while for fun. On the next day we would learn that they had not returned.'

While Schweinfurt, with its five ball-bearing factories, had been hit hard in the raid of 17 August 1943, much of the manufacturing equipment could be salvaged; in fact, high explosive had little large-scale effect on the ball-bearing-manufacturing machinery – the great danger was fire, as the manufacturing process generally used a lot of oil and if this could be ignited through a major incendiary attack then the machinery would generally be damaged beyond repair.[140] Dispersal of this industry, which was critical to arms manufacture, had been considered long before this initial raid, but in one of the many anomalies typical of Nazi Germany, moving portions of an industry likely to attract bombing into different locations went against the views and desires of many *Gauleiters*, the regional Nazi leaders, most of whom were members of the party of very long standing and thus had the ear of Hitler.[141] With the Americans realising that another attack was needed and with much of this vulnerable target still concentrated in Schweinfurt, the stage was thus set for the second crisis and turning point in the daylight bombardment of Germany: the second Schweinfurt raid, on 14 October 1943.

Following the shock of the losses in the first Schweinfurt raid, the 8th Air Force bombed only targets in France, Belgium and Holland until 6 September 1943, when a raid on aircraft manufacturing capacity in Stuttgart underlined the point once again: heavy raids penetrating far into the *Reich* beyond effective escort would almost inevitably suffer unsupportable losses – in this case of 55 four-engined bombers.[142] Then there was another lull before the bombers went back to a German target again, hitting Emden on 27 September – this time the losses were much reduced (eight bombers all told) due to an escort of six full fighter groups all the way due to adequate supplies of suitable drop tanks.[143] These 262 Thunderbolt sorties (and bearing in mind that the escort comprised relays of aircraft replacing each other) only lost two aircraft and one pilot; in return they claimed 21 German fighters – in reality, 28 out of the 388 that sortied against this raid were lost to the P-47s and the bombers' gunners, 18 *Luftwaffe* crew members perishing with them.[144] Despite rather poor bombing results,[145] this was the sort of attrition that the *Jagdgruppen* could ill afford. The lesson was clear: effectively escorted bombing raids was the only answer. And the lesson was repeated twice almost immediately: on 2 October, when Emden was hit again, only one bomber and no P-47s fell to German fighters, who themselves lost 11 aircraft and six pilots; and on 4 October, when Frankfurt and various other targets were bombed, they and a diversion force lost 16 bombers and one P-47 to the *Luftwaffe*'s 23 aircraft and 17 crewmen.[146] Three more raids before 14 October gave the defenders better successes, but the attrition of the *Jagdgruppen* continued nonetheless.

On 14 October 1943, the second Schweinfurt raid was launched. The plan was to dispatch two formations of B-17s and a third, weaker one of B-24s, all on an almost straight course to Schweinfurt due to range restrictions of the one B-17 formation.[147] In addition, weather forecasts, while good for the target area, were likely to be problematic over the United Kingdom.[148] Due to the poor weather over the UK the B-24 formation was unable to form up and was reduced to a mere diversion over the North Sea.[149] Escort fighters were similarly badly affected by the weather: of the six American fighter groups available, one was wasted on the B-24 fiasco, two were largely restricted by the weather and one was recalled when it could not find the bombers.[150] Only the 56th and the 353rd Groups were thus able to provide penetration support for the two B-17 formations.[151] With the centralisation of fighter control for the three northern *Jagddivisions* (numbers 1, 2 and 3) now in place, about 672 of 882 German fighter sorties made contact with the bombers, mostly after their small escorts had turned back, and a slaughter followed:[152] of the 320 B-17s dispatched, 229 got to the target, and losses encompassed 60 bombers missing, seven more written off in the UK and 138 damaged; five P-47s were lost and two pilots.[153] This time German fighters from all six *Jagddivisions* (numbers 1, 2, 3, 4, 5, 7, the latter including also *Jafü Ostmark*) were successfully guided to the bomber streams.[154] By the time the mauled bomber formations returned to the positions where their escorts should have picked them up again, none appeared as the weather had by now negated all American and RAF fighter take-offs from southern England.[155] Even more catastrophic bomber losses were largely avoided due to the poor weather advancing onto the Continent.[156] German fighter claims have been tabulated for all the participating units to give a total of 96½ B-17s shot down (the half claim would reflect one shared with the flak arm), 11 *Herausschüsse*, and four P-47s shot down.[157] A primary post-war source written by two of the relevant German fighter commanders in 1954 gives a total claim of 124 aircraft destroyed of which 42 were credited to the flak arm, leaving 82 for crediting to the Jagdgruppen.[158] Comparing this with the just-mentioned tabulation would suggest that only 82 of the tabulated 96½ victory claims were in fact confirmed by the *Reichsluftfahrtministerium*. German fighter losses totalled 53 aircraft and 29 crewmen lost.[159] This time Schweinfurt was very heavily hit, but emergency measures and dispersal in the coming months managed to keep the German arms industry going.[160]

On 14 October, training units were brought into the combat equation once more. Among those involved was *Feldwebel* Dr Felix Sauer, now an instructor in *JG 104*, stationed near Fürth. At least this turned out to be a reasonably happy story in the midst of a hard-fought and often ruthless struggle over Germany: 'I recall an American bomber shot down by myself in Germany, on 14 October 1943. The bomber having been hit, was going to prepare for a forced-landing – when I noticed this, I immediately stopped firing, drew near the rear gunner and waved. He, too, had stopped firing. Then I set myself in front of the bomber and waggled my wings – signalling him to follow me – which he did. Then I led them to the airport of Kitzingen (near Würzburg) – where, due to a fatal misunderstanding of the ground defences, they were shot at and burst into flames. This made me furious and I regretted it very much. Only four members of their crew managed to survive by parachuting, among them the rear gunner Sergeant Will C. Tench from Allentown, Pennsylvania. When, next day, I went to see him to offer my apology for the wrong interference by the flak, I asked him if he had noticed that I had stopped shooting after them releasing their landing gear, he hugged me and said, "Oh yes, you are a very fair fighter." To me, this was my best war experience. We shook hands and promised to meet again after the war – which is going to happen next year (writing in 1990); I hope for a reunion and reconciliation with the four survivors.'

*JG 3 Udet* was one of the major fighter units withdrawn from the Eastern Front during 1943 to reinforce the Home Defence; while *I/JG 3* was transferred in February already, *III* and *II/JG 3* left in August and were almost immediately placed within the Home Defence line-up.[161] The *II Gruppe* was placed within *Jagddivision 2*, where they remained for the rest of the year.[162] *Oberfeldwebel* Helmut Notemann, *5/JG 3*, a veteran of Stalingrad, recalled the change in their situation. 'In August 1943 we were withdrawn from the Eastern Front and transferred to Ütersen, where we were re-equipped, and thereafter we moved to Schipol at Amsterdam in the west. From there our missions were largely against incoming bomber formations, mostly defending against their accompanying fighter escorts. In the time until December 1943 we lost 18 comrades, among them *Major* Brändle, *Hauptmann* Lucas and *Hauptmann* Stolte. At the end of December 1943 I was transferred to *JG 103* as an instructor.' *Oberleutnant* Walter Bohatsch, also of *5/JG 3* (and later *Staffelführer 1/JG 3*, *Staffelkapitän 2/JG 3*), detailed the chaos of their withdrawal from Russia, with an almost immediate flight back to that front again. What he also emphasizes is that there was no attempt to instruct the *Gruppe* in the realities and methodology prevalent in the west and the Home Defence; though expected to make use of it, they were given no induction in the Y-system (essentially a friend-not-foe transmitter fitted to German fighters, and part of the complex fighter control system used in the Home Defence) either. This is a prime example of the poor high command so often typical of the *Luftwaffe*. When you lack resources one should then at least make the best possible use of those you have!

From the Mius front (Kuteinikowo) in Russia the *II Udet* moved to Ütersen in about mid-August 1943 to help defend the northern part of Germany. One *Staffel* at a time, the *Gruppe* flew to Uman in Russia where 'Papa Dralle' (supply officer of the *Geschwader*) received us like royalty. Chairs were filled, there was fresh fruit and warm Kirsch. From there we flew back further via Lemberg, Liegnitz to Ütersen. For the first time in many months the unit was once again in a civilised area. In the evenings and nights particularly all the pilots flew 'free chases' in and around Ütersen. The big disappointment came some days later, when the *Kommandeur*, *Major* Brändle, told us of the order that all 40 of our machines had to be flown back to the Eastern Front, to Lemberg. Despite the great shortage of fuel that was already noticeable, the high command thus managed to burn off many thousand litres of fuel in the air at the cost of the Home Defence. In Ütersen many of the old hands from the 5th *Staffel* were still there. Kirschner was awarded the *Eichenlaub* and was temporarily not with the *Staffel*. As acting *Staffelkapitän* in his place I led the gang. This was still the case with the move to Schipol. The rain for *II Gruppe* now came to an end, and with giant steps we moved into the drought.

Poorly prepared for operations in the west, we were now required to perform tasks that we were not capable of. For *II Gruppe* there was no introduction to the Y-process and no practice missions with it were flown. One could not shake off the feeling that the high command considered that such a successful 'eastern' *Gruppe* would also be able to achieve the same in the west. But no time was left to prepare us for the equipment and tactics of the western air war. The old hands thus either died or became exhausted (no longer mentally capable of handling the situation) and were transferred (the *Luftwaffe* does not seem to have used that terrible designation 'LMF – lack of moral fibre' so prevalent a cause of fear in the RAF, whereby aircrew that could not go on were demoted and disgraced).

The first few western operations were, to put it mildly, a fiasco. I remember one of our first western operations (18 October 1943).[163] The *Gruppe* (35 aircraft) took off from Schipol in the late afternoon to intercept four-engined bombers and just after dropping our external fuel tanks we met the enemy over the North Sea and attacked the bomber formation, scoring a few successes. After difficult dog fights with escorting fighters and Fortress IIs our unit was completely scattered. In small groups and alone we flew back towards base, but it soon became obvious that in the meantime mist had rolled in and it was no longer possible to land anywhere in Holland. I flew as far eastwards as my fuel would allow and at Rheine I saw the ground through a gap and managed to land deadstick with my propeller standing. As far as I remember, the *Gruppe* lost 16 aircraft and several total losses, including *Hauptmann* Stolte and *Feldwebel* Klohs (14 Me 109s were in fact lost or damaged, eight being total write-offs).[164] A few days later *Oberst* Lützow (their old *Kommodore*) visited us in Schipol and raised our morale; he promised that *II Gruppe* would be the first fighter unit to convert to the Me 262.

Along with many other pilots the *II Gruppe* while in Holland lost *Kommandeur Major* Brändle, *Kommandeur Hauptmann* Lemke, *Staffelkapitäne* Lucas (killed in the Leiden area after a mission over the Scheldt River mouth) and Stolte. Kirschner (had been *Staffelkapitän 5/JG 3*) was transferred to *JG 27*. Soon after we received a report that Kirschner had been shot down over Yugoslavia, bailed out and was murdered on the ground by partisans. 'Poldi' Münster took over the 5th *Staffel*. Jupp Schütte, Klohs and Trapan were all killed, while Brinkmann, Mohn and Notemann were transferred. 'Specker' (*Oberfeldwebel* Grünberg) and I were the only two oldies left in the 5th *Staffel*. The *Gruppe* often flew from Volkel, after the airfield at Schipol was no longer safe due to rising water levels in the canals. The Tommies were always trying to bomb the dykes with Blenheims (*sic*, more modern twin-engined bombers) to flood the airfield. On one such attack we had a scramble (3 November 1943)[165] but only met the retreating enemy formation over the sea. Over the radio I heard that Brändle was having difficulties with his *Katschmarek* or wingman (who was not able to become involved in the fight; I no longer recall his name) and was involved in a dogfight with Spitfires. Immediately after this he sent a radio message that he could not get away from the 'Indians'. *Major* Brändle did not return from this mission. His successor was *Hauptmann* Lemke, who only flew a few missions with the *Gruppe* before the same fate befell him (killed 4 December 1943).[166] Temporarily *Hauptmann* Sannemann (6th *Staffel*) took over the *Gruppe*.

I also remember the missions escorting convoys at sea, such as the one with the freighter *Weissenberg*, and others, sailing from the mouth of the River Scheldt to the West Frisian Islands. There was always a *Rotte* of Me 109s over these convoys and with these missions (this one was on 23 November 1943)[167] we had an uncomfortable feeling in the pits of our stomachs that the Tommies would certainly not miss the opportunity to attack the convoy. And so it was. Off Den Helder the convoy was attacked by a squadron of Beaufighter torpedo carriers with strong fighter escort (Spitfires) and the *Weissenberg* was hit on the beam and sunk. My *Katschmarek* and I did not have the least chance to get at the torpedo aircraft with the strong fighter escort. I have also not forgotten the big tirade against the fighter pilots of all three of our *Gruppen* delivered by Hermann Göring in Arnhem (Galland, Trautloft and Lützow were also present).

It is also clear from his reminiscence above that the RAF, bombers and fighters, plus of course American medium bombers and escorts, pursued an ongoing and deadly campaign against the German fighter arm in parallel with the latter's main task of fighting the four-engined bombers. In the months from September to December, *II/JG 3 Udet* lost a total of 22 pilots in action in the Home Defence: these included two *Gruppenkommandeure*, *Major* Kurt Brändle (172 victories) and *Hauptmann* Wilhelm Lemke (killed 4 December 1943; 131 victories); two *Staffelkapitäne*, *Hauptmann* Paul Stolte (*6/JG 3*, 18 October 1943; 43 victories) and *Hauptmann* Werner Lucas (*4/JG 3*, 24 October 1943; 106 victories); three veteran senior NCOs, Josef Schütte (*5/JG 3*, 4 December 1943; 40 victories), Werner Klohs (*5/JG 3*, 18 October 1943; 18 victories) and Walter Stienhans (*6/JG 3*, 3 November 1943; 10 victories); four pilots with between one and four victories apiece and 11 without any at all.[168] All of the leaders and the experienced NCOs were irreplaceable – all the Home Defence units were experiencing similar bloodletting, and by this stage in the war things were not any better in either the east or south.

During 1943, the Home Defence units (*Jagddivisions 1, 2, 3, 4, 5, 7, Jafü Ostmark*) lost one *Geschwader Kommodore*, eight *Gruppenkommandeure*, 29 *Staffelkapitäne* and six *Staffelführer*.[169] Among them was *Hauptmann* Dietrich Wickop, *Gruppenführer II/JG 1*, whose combat report was given earlier in this chapter; *Hauptmann* Rudolf Germeroth, *Staffelkapitän* of *3/JG 3*, who had led the *Platzschutzstaffel Pitomnik* in the Stalingrad pocket; and *Kommodore* Hans Philipp of *JG 1*, who had felt bad about killing Russian aircrew in the east, where he was a major ace with *JG 54*. Then there were also the *Schwarmführern* and the *Rottenführern* – normally in the *Luftwaffe* a pilot would only get to start leading a *Rotte* after several months of combat and 40–50 *Feindflüge*, and the leadership of a *Schwarm* would usually require much more than those norms. As an example, below Otto Schmid describes a mission in December 1943 as an instructor leading a student in a *Rotte* into action; despite even his experience, he was not yet a *Schwarm* leader.

But over Germany, the Low Countries and Austria these critical leaders were perishing and their places would have to be taken by less experienced men, less able to defend themselves, never mind look after comrades of minimal experience. An overall lowering of quality of *Jagdgruppen* had thus begun, and would continue into the first part of 1944. By the time of the invasion in June 1944, the subsequent rapid destruction of most fighter units sent to Normandy took only a few weeks, and during the rest of 1944 over the German Reich's shrinking extent it had become an absolute slaughter of very large proportions.

The same story of high attrition, especially of irreplaceable experienced pilots and leaders, can be told of any Home Defence unit in the second half of 1943. *Oberleutnant* Rudolf Engleder flew two tours in *JG 1*, the first from 1 April to 16 December 1943 when he was in 1st and 2nd *Staffeln*, and the second from 10 March 1944 to 15 April 1944 when he was once again in 2/*JG 1*, now as a *Hauptmann* (high casualties bring rapid promotion, typical of the Home Defence). Due to having been an instructor, as well as having gained a full instrument rating, he was already an experienced pilot by the time he joined I/*JG 1* in April 1943. He became *Staffelführer* (i.e. leading the *Staffel* but not yet formally appointed as *Staffelkapitän*) 2/*JG 1* on 17 August 1943, *Staffelkapitän* 1/*JG 1* on 1 October 1943 and then *Staffelkapitän* 2/*JG 1* on 10 November 1943, but not for long, as he himself relates: 'On 16 December 1943 I was shot down at an altitude of 8,000 m over Northern Holland in combat with a B-17; in hospital from 18 December till 20 February 1944.' Nor were the training units spared the loss of experienced leaders. Despite being in apparent safety while instructing at Cazaux, *Feldwebel* Otto Schmid on several occasions found himself back in action, as described below.

On 5 December 1943 we flew an operation against 200 B-17s that were coming to attack the U-boat bases on the French Atlantic coast. The same thing repeated itself on 31 December and on 5 January 1944. The bombers flew out from England with a southerly course until they reached the northern Spanish coast, and then took an easterly course to the Biscay coast north of Biarritz, and finally flew over the land northwards towards Bordeaux–St Nazaire (actually on 31 December 1943, the bombers attacked various training school airfields in the Bordeaux region, the very bases from which

*Ergänzungsjagdgruppen West* and *Ost* operated);[170] by doing so they also flew exactly over our flying exercise zone. We had been put on three-minute readiness very early and were able to await their approach at leisure. The instructors of *Ergänzungsjagdgruppe West* flew against the bombers with their best students.

On 31 December we took off with the most suitable students to attack the bomber formation, which was flying at *c.* 6,000 m. As the most operationally experienced instructor, together with one of my students I flew the so-called *Holzaugenrotte* (the covering *Rotte* above and behind the rest) and could see how our *Staffelkapitän Oberleutnant* Strohal suddenly made strange movements slipping to the left and the right as we approached within *c.* 2 km of the bombers. This made his *Rottenflieger* nervous and he began to make the same movements, but to the consternation of them both in the opposite directions, so that one did not have to wait long before they collided. Both machines exploded and dived to destruction in flames. Nothing was ever found of them as they had crashed into a marshy area. I saw the entire thing from my position about 1,000 m above our own formation. Just before the bombers flew over Lake Biscaross (*c.* 50 km south-west of Bordeaux) I attacked the Boeing flying closest to me from ahead and slightly above, aimed carefully at the cabin and let the machine fly through my fire. The result was that it dived down vertically. I must have hit the pilots with a full burst.

After I had overhauled the formation again, I attempted the same manoeuvre once more, but this time the machine exploded after a short burst of fire. By chance I must have hit the oxygen system or one of the bombs the aircraft was carrying. The time interval between the two *Abschüsse* was about 15 minutes. No crew member got out of either of these aircraft. Hopefully in future we will be spared from wars. On the third approach to the bombers unfortunately both cannons jammed, so that I had to break off the mission. One was able to fly these attacks absolutely according to the book as there were no escorting fighters. Of course, one could not completely ignore the massed return fire of the bombers. On 5 December 1943 and 5 January 1944 the course of events was similar, but I did not have the luck to score two victories on those missions.

Actually, on each of these two missions he did shoot down one B-17 – still a very impressive performance. His relevant logbook entries are summarised below.

Example of a fighter pilot instructor's episodic operational life, south-western France, based on flying logbook, 5 December 1943–5 January 1944: *Feldwebel* Otto Schmid, *Ergänzungsjagdgruppe West*, flying Fw 190 (based at Cazaux, about 50 km south-west of Bordeaux, where they fell under the direction of *Jafü Bretagne*).[171] (Source: Otto Schmid)

DECEMBER
  5: Scramble, 12h15–13h05 (48th *Feindflug*); contact with *c.* 200 Boeing F-IIs, 12h48 shot down one B-17
 31: Scramble, 11h40–12h40 (49th *Feindflug*); contact with 200 Boeing B17-F-IIs, shot down two B-17s, at 11h57 and 12h20

JANUARY
  5: Scramble, 10h20–11h15 (50th *Feindflug*); contact with 33 Boeing B17-F-IIs, 10h40 shot down one B-17

## *1944: 8th and 15th Air Forces Win the Battle of Attrition; the Mustang*

An excellent overview of how the Battle of Germany wore down the German fighter arm is provided by *Hauptmann* Johannes 'Hans or Häns'chen' Naumann, someone who saw action in the West from 1939 till the end of the war (9 and 4/JG 26, *Staffelkapitän* 6 and 7/JG 26, *Gruppenkommandeur* II/JG 26). The long-lived battle of attrition in the West was something the *Luftwaffe* was not prepared for at all; they never organised an adequate pilot training scheme, and were overtaken by Allied productive capacity and technical advances.

As the war progressed (beyond 1942) the superiority of the enemy fighters increased ever more towards the end of the conflict, particularly at heights above 5,000 m. This made the battle against the US four-engined bombers much harder, as they always flew very high, and in very large numbers. Thus, month by month and year by year we lost our technical superiority faster and faster, so that the combat against the American four-engined bomber formations had to be taken on under very unfavourable conditions for us. Just the number and effectiveness of the defensive weapons of the Boeing and Liberator formations changed the picture decisively. Added to that was their elevated operating altitudes up to 7–9,000 m, also on long-distance missions. Even our preferred fighter flown in action later in the war, the Fw 190 D-9, achieved its maximum engine power at 4,800 m, which means that above that height the engine steadily lost power.

Above 8,000 m almost no performance remained. The chances of an effective combat against a bomber or even escort fighter was thus reduced to a minimum. In fact it became a lucky exception! In my experience, for example the engine in the Fw no longer functioned at 8,500 m due to lack of oxygen. One can just imagine the implications of this in a combat situation. The Thunderbolt and Mustang pilots flying above us probably laughed themselves half to death when we could not follow them. That was very frustrating for us and we looked back longingly to the years 1940 and 1941.

The losses in our battles with the four-engined bombers and their escorts increased against steadily decreasing *Abschuss* successes on our part to the point of no longer being acceptable. Even the old hands (*alte Hasen*) found it increasingly difficult, and their ranks thinned drastically. In the end I can say that we were beaten by technology. Then the abilities and experience of the individual pilot hardly counted any more. Of course the numerical superiority ranged against us was very important also. But when the two combine, inferior numbers and inferior quality, then the result can only be a sudden end. And that's what happened. The two *Geschwadern* – JG 2 and JG 26 – that fought exclusively in the West all throughout – provide an opportunity through their histories and reading the balances of their minutiae to see how and with what equipment the *Luftwaffe* was beaten in the west, and how they had to accept a hopeless degradation.

The number of American fighter groups by late 1943 was already high at 11, and then grew even more, with 15 by May 1944 (illustration 57).[172] While numbers of fighters were static at three groups from April to August 1943, from September until June the following year they rose steadily. Numbers of P-38s increased gradually from November 1943, while P-47s were increasingly replaced by P-51s in the first half of 1944, the P-51s becoming dominant by May (illustration 57).[173] Even more important than mere numbers, though, was the effective range of the fighters over German territory: in February 1944 the use of 150-gallon belly-mounted drop tanks and then two 108-gallon external wing tanks increased the range of the P-47s to 683 and 764 km (past Hamburg) respectively.[174] In the same month, by fitting two 108-gallon drop tanks to the P-38 Berlin was in comfortable range. But it was the P-51 that was to lead the charge – from December 1943 to January 1944, without any external tanks, it could fly up to 764 km; in March that went up to 1,045 km (using two 75-gallon wing tanks; well past Berlin and almost to Prague) and in the same month by carrying two 108 gallon tanks the

Mustang could fly to Vienna and back from the United Kingdom.[175] Initial Mustang numbers were very limited, the 354th Fighter Group (on loan to 8th Air Force from the 9th Air Force) being the only one available in December 1943,[176] and even by February 1944 only one more group had been added to the battle, this time as part of the 8th Air Force.[177] However, the increased range and numbers of all three fighter types did the job together in defeating the *Luftwaffe* before the Invasion.[178] Unescorted bomber raids were no longer part of the equation, and the German fighters were faced with the very difficult task of trying to get at the large four-engined bomber formations, and manoeuvring their own units at *Gruppen* strengths into favourable attack positions, while hoping not to be disturbed in this and indeed trying to avoid being intercepted by the escort fighters. With time, and with increasing losses of experienced pilots and leaders, and the aggressive American fighters becoming almost omnipresent, the task became impossible. Exactly what this meant even for the veterans is well expressed by *Feldwebel* Otto Schmid, who found a very different intensity and stress related to the Home Defence when he returned to *II/JG 1* on 31 January 1944 after an absence as an instructor for the previous eight months:

Between the missions of 1942 and 1943 and those of 1944 there was a very big difference. One could hardly concentrate to try and perform an accurate attack, as the enemy fighter cover was too large. One could say the relative strength was in a ratio of one to ten. These missions were thus a pure *Himmelfahrtkommando* (trip to Heaven!), and we were regularly burned. Of the old experienced pilots, most had been killed, and from the new, inexperienced pilots one could no longer expect efficient cover. These new pilots were happy even just to get their aircraft safely back on the ground. There could no longer be any question of their having mastered their aircraft. When one reads the combat reports from that time, there were already many aircraft which fell out on take-off due to flying errors. The same happened also with the landings. I can still very clearly remember the fear that gripped myself and the other pilots in the morning when we drove out to the airfield. Everything revolved around just one thing: hopefully this evening I will still be here healthy and sound. It was a terrible prospect – hundreds of bombers and double as many fighters. And we were a sad little band of 30–40 aircraft.

From the break of dawn every day till it got dark we were at readiness beside our machines at our dispersals. We had some accommodation there with a sitting room and a sleeping area, that we made use of when nothing exciting was happening. Otherwise when the weather was good we stayed close to our machines so that we could climb right in if there was a scramble. We only had *Sitzbereitschaft* (sitting in the cockpits) when enemy formations were assembling on the English east coast, before flying towards their targets in Germany. It also happened that we would be deceived and the massed aircraft took an entirely different course towards Germany. Apart from these occasions we seldom had *Sitzbereitschaft* in my time. Much more often we were at five minutes or three minutes readiness. With the latter we had only three minutes from climbing in till lifting off from the field. But with good mechanics this was easily achieved; for example, the second mechanic helped to do up the straps while the first mechanic started the engine. Then all one had to do was open the throttle. The bombers were not so dangerous when they flew without fighter escort. The danger lay in the escorts, and they were murderous. One had hardly concentrated on a bomber, and there they came two, three or even a complete *Schwarm* of Thunderbolts or Mustangs interfering with us. After having shaken these off you had to set up the attack on the bombers once more. And then one had to go back through the fighter escort once again. But every now and then we were able to achieve a really properly led attack.

The Home Defence was reinforced by a total of eight *Jagdgruppen* during the first part of 1944 up till the invasion (6 June 1944): two were from JG 5 on the Ice Sea Front and Norway; the other six were from the *Wilden Sau* single-engined night fighter groups who changed to day fighting, and who by now had their own aircraft rather than using those of day fighter *Gruppen* as had been the case in 1943. One *Gruppe* had left the Home Defence for the Balkans so the net gain was seven Gruppen.[180] The *Wilden Sau* generally lacked training and experience in day fighting and were to suffer particularly high losses as a result.[181] While *Jagddivisions* 1, 2 and 3 were roughly equal in their strengths of *Jagdgruppen*, *Jagddivisions* 4 and 5 of *Luftflotte* 3 were essentially restricted to a single *Geschwader* each, and compared to 1943, *Jagddivision* 7 and *Jafü Ostmark* had been considerably reinforced as the raids from the 15th Air Force in Italy gained rapidly in strength and impact. The *Zerstörergruppen* had not been reinforced but ZG 26 became re-equipped with the Me 410, an improvement on the Me 110 but still very vulnerable to US escort fighter attack. As can be seen in the table below, most of these heavy fighters were kept in *Jagddivisions* 1 and 7 further away from where significant escort fighter activity was expected.

*Jagdgruppen* assigned to different *Jagddivisions* (with dates) for the period
1 January 1944–6 June 1944 (Invasion of Normandy on latter date)[179]

| Jagdgruppe | Jagddivision 1 | Jagddivision 2 | Jagddivision 3 |
|---|---|---|---|
| I/JG1 | | 5 April–Invasion | 1 January–18 March & 24 March–5 April |
| II/JG 1 | | | 1 January–18 March & 23 March–Invasion |
| III/JG 1 | | 7 April–Invasion | 1 January–7 April |
| I/JG 2 | | | |
| II/JG 2 | | | |
| III/JG 2 | | | |
| I/JG 3 | 28 February–Invasion | | 9 January–28 February |
| II/JG 3 | 26 February–Invasion | 1 January–26 February | |
| III/JG 3 | | | |
| IV/JG 3 | 26 February–Invasion | | 1 January–26 February |
| I/JG 5 | | | |
| II/JG 5 | 31 May–Invasion | | |
| I/JG 11 | | 1 January–Invasion | |
| II/JG 11 | | 1 January–Invasion | |
| III/JG 11 | | 1 January–Invasion | |
| 10/JG 11 | | 1 January–Invasion | |
| I/JG 26 | | | |
| II/JG 26 | | | |
| III/JG 26 | | | 1–8 January |
| I/JG 27 | | | |
| II/JG 27 | | | |
| III/JG 27 | April–May | | |
| II/JG 53 | | | |
| III/JG 54 | 1 January–20 April | | |
| I/JG 300 | | | 1 January–Invasion |
| II/JG 300 | | | 8 March–Invasion |
| I/JG 301 | | | |
| III/JG 301 | 29 March–5 April | | |
| I/JG 302 | 11 January–9 May | | |
| II/JG 302 | 9 April–Invasion | | |
| III/JG 302 | 3 May–Invasion | 8 April–3 May | |

| Jagddivision 4 | Jagddivision 5 | Jagddivision 7 | Jafü Ostmark |
|---|---|---|---|
|  |  | 18–24 March |  |
|  |  | 18–23 March |  |
|  |  |  |  |
|  | 12 May–Invasion |  |  |
|  | 1 January–Invasion |  |  |
|  | 1 January–15 May |  |  |
| 1–9 January |  |  |  |
|  |  |  |  |
|  |  | 1 January–Invasion |  |
|  |  |  |  |
|  |  | February–Invasion |  |
|  |  |  |  |
|  |  |  |  |
|  |  |  |  |
|  |  |  |  |
|  |  |  |  |
| 1 January–Invasion |  |  |  |
| 1 January–17 April & 25 April–17 May |  |  |  |
| 8 January–18 April and 26 April–Invasion |  | 18–26 April |  |
|  |  |  | 1 January–Invasion |
|  |  | 1 January–3 June | 3 June–Invasion |
|  |  | May–Invasion | March–April |
|  |  | 3 March–Invasion | 1 January–3 March |
|  |  | 20 April–Invasion |  |
|  |  |  |  |
|  |  |  |  |
|  |  | 5 January–Invasion |  |
|  |  | 13 April–Invasion | 5–13 April |
|  |  |  | 9 May–Invasion |
|  |  |  |  |
|  |  |  |  |

Other stations not shown above: (1) Southern France: *I/JG 2* – January–20 February and 8 April–12 May; *II/JG 26* – 17–25 April; (2) U-boat bases: *III/JG 2* – 15 May–Invasion; south-west France: *II/JG 26* – 17 May–Invasion.

Zerstörergruppen assigned to different *Jagddivisions* (with dates) for the period 1 January 1944–6 June 1944[182]

| Zerstörergruppe | Jagddiv. 1 | Jagddiv. 2 | Jagddiv. 3 | Jagddiv. 4 | Jagddiv. 5 | Jagddiv. 7 | Jafü Ostmark |
|---|---|---|---|---|---|---|---|
| II/ZG 1 | | | | | | | 1 January–Invasion |
| I/ZG 76 | | | | | | 1 January–25 April | |
| II/ZG 76 | | | | | | January–25 April | |
| III/ZG 76 | | | | | | 1 January–2 April | |
| I/ZG 26 | 1 January–1 April & 29 April–Invasion | 1–29 April | | | | | |
| II/ZG 26 | 1 January–February & 24 March–Invasion | | | | | February–24 March | |
| III/ZG 26 | 22 March–11 May | 1 January–22 March | | | | 11 May–Invasion | |

6/ZG 26 (II/ZG 26) stayed on in *Jagddivision 7* until 10 April and then to *Jagddivision 1.* 7/ZG 26 (III/ZG 26) was in *Jafü Ostmark* from 13 May–Invasion. All units equipped with Me 110 except for those units which flew Me 410 (times when equipped with those aircraft shown in bold).

Following his terrible in-flight accident while training in September 1943, and a long period of convalescence thereafter before he could fly again, in about mid-December 1943, Me 110 gunner *Unteroffizier* Heinz Ludwig returned to active duty with *I/ZG 26*. Alas his old pilot from the Russian Front had been teamed up with a new gunner, and both were killed early in 1944; Ludwig had to crew up with a new pilot on his return. 'My old pilot (*Unteroffizier* Bruno Baumeister) had been a barman in civilian life and I was a barber; we were a happy team in Russia, where we flew over 100 *Feindflüge*. He was killed in the Home Defence (on 21 February 1944, with *3/ZG 26* and his then-gunner *Unteroffizier* Dowo). Our radio call-sign in *3/ZG 26* was Simba, and I survived while 52 other crews did not. I was wounded in an attack at 7,800 m, made from head-on on a Fortress formation with four rockets which we called *Dödel*, and which had an effect like a Stalin organ. I had two non-confirmed B-17 victories. The remains of *ZG 26* were partly re-equipped with Me 410s in 1944 until their dissolution in August 1944. After that I became a fighter controller in the headquarters of *Jagddivision 1* (*Daedelus* control centre) at Döberitz near Berlin, and in January 1945 we moved to the castle of the von Ribbecks near Nauen.' The losses suffered by the *Zerstörerflieger* in the Home Defence were very high, as can be seen from the example of a single *Gruppe*, *I/ZG 26*, in the table below. Accidental losses in the new Me 410s were also quite high, as was often the case for new aircraft in all air forces:

Flying personnel losses, *I/ZG 26*, Home Defence, October 1943–May 1944 (data: Heinz Ludwig) (+ = killed)

|  | Pilot + in action | Gunner + in action | Pilot wounded in action | Gunner wounded in action | Pilot + accident | Gunner + accident |
|---|---|---|---|---|---|---|
| October 1943 | 1 | 1 | 1 | 1 | 1 | 1 |
| November 1943 | 1 | 0 | 1 | 2 | 2 | 2 |
| December 1943 | 5 | 6 | 2 | 0 | 0 | 0 |
| January 1944 | 3 | 2 | 3 | 2 | 1 | 1 |
| February 1944 | 10 | 4 | 7 | 6 | 0 | 0 |
| April 1944 | 0 | 0 | 1 | 0 | 1 | 1 |
| May 1944 | 2 | 1 | 2 | 1 | 2 | 1 |

One other *Zerstörergruppe*, stationed on the Atlantic coast of France to support the U-boats operating from the bases there and in southern Brittany, appears to have been largely spared the action of their Home Defence colleagues. *Oberfeldwebel* Joachim Robel flew as a gunner/ radio operator in the Ju 88s of *I/ZG 1*. 'In 1943 we were transferred from Italy to Brest (October 1943–12 June 1944).[183] We took over the coastal protection as well as escorting the incoming and outgoing U-boats. The U-boats were continually attacked by British flying boats, and our job was to shoot these down. We flew with drop tanks; without these we had an effective range of only 500 km. In 1944 I was transferred again, as an instructor to the *Zerstörer*-School in Memmingen. In December 1944 flying ended for us; there was no more fuel. I was sent to join the paratroopers in Austria.'

Statistical data for German fighters in Home Defence for January-May 1944[184]

| 1944 | German fighter sorties | US bombers claimed shot down | *Herausschüsse* | US fighters claimed shot down | Combat losses all German aircraft | Crew losses (+ and M) |
|---|---|---|---|---|---|---|
| January | 4,156 | 195 | 27 | 80 | 266 | 185 |
| February | 4,707 | 373 | 36 | 88 | 471 | 251 |
| March | 3,752 | 311 | 17 | 80 | 436 | 253 |
| April | 5,262 | 372 | 14 | 94 | 519 | 293 |
| May | 5,863 | 310 | 22 | 131 | 577 | 276 |

All statistics relate to opposing strategic four-engined bomber raids and exclude fighting against light bomber activity and that of their escort fighters; German fighter sorties an estimate for Me 109s, Fw 190s, Me 110s, night fighters operating by day, Me 410s.[185] Losses are total for *Reichs* Home Defence daylight losses (includes also night fighters lost in day sorties, plus a few bombers involved in supporting day fighter operations); 68 aircraft lost by *Luftflotte 2*[186] opposing 15th Air Force raids, mainly over Italy, are excluded as that theatre forms part of a separate book. Victory claims reflect all six *Jagddivisions* and *Jafü Ostmark*.[187] + and M = killed and missing. A small portion of Home Defence operations would have opposed raids in south-eastern Europe and these are included in the above statistics.[188]

In addition to the data in the table above, which particularly impacts on comparing German fighter claims with American losses (see next table below) is that during January–May 1944 the flak arm of the Home Defence put in claims for 654 American aircraft shot down, the vast majority of them four-engined bombers.[189] Noticeable in the data above is that German fighter sorties only rose a small amount when compared to incoming American sorties from the 8th and 15th Air Forces (compare with table below); also, German claims against bombers remained about the same, month to month (excluding January 1944), but those against American fighters increased in April–May. Losses of German defending aircraft climbed almost every month and from March onwards exceeded their own claims by increasing numbers. Clearly, the battle of attrition was being lost.

Statistical data for American four-engined bomber and fighter operations of the 8th and 15th Air Forces against the German Home Defence for January-May 1944[190]

| 1944 | US bomber sorties | US fighter sorties | Operational losses (all causes) of US bombers | Operational losses (all causes) of US fighters | US fighter claims of German fighters | US bomber claims of German fighters |
|---|---|---|---|---|---|---|
| January | 6,066 | 6,005 | 211 | 95 | 230 | 497 |
| February | 8,332 | 8,956 | 366 | 115 | 372 | 465 |
| March | 8,429 | 10,348 | 341 | 181 | 437 | 369 |
| April | 12,749 | 13,042 | 472 | 203 | 530 | 524 |
| May | 19,190 | 19,171 | 418 | 213 | 643 | 181 |

Operational losses include those due to fighter action, flak, operational accidents (such as collisions). Excludes all American losses/claims related to tactical operations over Europe – i.e. operations of light bombers and their escorts. Sortie totals reflect aircraft taking off at the start of a mission, not aircraft over target which was always a lower figure.[191]

From the above table it can be seen that the increase in American bomber sorties was massive, and this greatly exceeded the much smaller overall increase rate in American bomber losses (illustration 58) – bomber losses per sortie were thus going down fast; this translates very simply into a rapid victory in the battle of attrition for the two American air forces. German claims against bombers were also going down from February onwards, again signalling their steady erosion of effectiveness (illustration 58).[192] A similar type of chart for the American fighters shows an analogous result (illustration 59).[193] Once again, the increase in sorties vastly exceeds slowly climbing fighter losses, while German claims do not keep pace with the American fighters lost. More American fighters were therefore being lost to other causes, most likely flak defences, as they increasingly attacked German fighter airfields in strafing runs on the way home.[194] Once again the Germans were losing the battle of attrition, and fast at that.

Comparing the two data tables above, by examining total German claims by their fighter arm as against total German fighters lost we can see that from March onwards, and by increasing amounts, German losses exceeded their claims; once again, the attrition was clearly going the way of the Allies, hardly a surprise in view of the vast increase in American sorties of both fighters and bombers (the latter remained dangerous for the German fighters). One point to also note here is that despite American fighter sorties increasing by over three times from January to May 1944 while those for German fighters (all types) went up by just over 40 per cent for the same period, American fighter numbers were never really larger than German fighter numbers. Serviceable single-engined Me 109s and Fw 190s numbered 671 at the end of March 1944,[195] as compared to 576 (January 1944) and 720 (May 1944) American fighters on the establishment of the groups then in operation (12 groups in January and 15 in May;[196] assume 48 aircraft per group).[197] In fact, bearing in mind that there were also the twin-engined German fighters, and that serviceable American fighter numbers would always have been lower than establishment, there was no superiority in numbers for the American fighters. But they were using their forces more effectively (many more sorties per aircraft), and they were clearly dominating the airspace and winning the battle of attrition. Their effect on the German pilots was obviously out of some proportion to their numbers, as can be seen in the recollection below of *Oberleutnant* Otto Stammberger of *JG 26*, who although no longer flying operations after May 1943 saw the battle up close for its duration:

> Everything changed abruptly with the introduction of the American escort fighters, Mustang and Thunderbolt, in 1943 and 1944. Huge superiority in numbers, powerful engines, more weaponry than us, better flying characteristics, especially in the dive, which up till then had always been our saving grace. Suddenly we were being shot down in the dive, and now had to take our chances in dog fights, which only a few could achieve. Our green pilots achieved, if any, three to four missions, then they were dead. It was pure murder, there was no way out; we tried as unit leaders to avoid combat with enemy fighters. But that only very seldom succeeded as the enemy was everywhere. That was how things looked during our desperate

situation in 1944. With the introduction of the Fw 190 D-9 with its in-line Junkers engine at the end of 1944 things improved; we were technically superior, but still numerically very inferior, and still only a few experienced pilots led a *Staffel* made up of young and even too-young comrades, who like all of them were shot down very soon.

The twin problem of protecting themselves against escort fighters and also successfully attacking large bomber formations was quite clearly never solved. Although always arguable, a comparison to the same problem confronting Fighter Command of the RAF during the Battle of Britain, where the British fighters were outnumbered by the attacking fighters (on the combat front at least), might be revealing. High command leadership of the first order on the British side applied small attacking formations of British fighters virtually universally (except for mostly ineffective wing-strength interceptions of 12 Group), the squadron of 12 aircraft being the norm. Perhaps smaller formations, and thus many more attacks in more dispersed places and times in the Battle of Germany, may have helped? But then again, comparisons of a Commander-in-Chief like Göring with the likes of Fighter Command's Air Chief Marshal Dowding and his right-hand man Air Vice-Marshal Keith Park verge on the far-fetched.

The standard formation size over Germany had long been the *Gruppe*, but as American numbers grew this became gradually enlarged to *Geschwader*-sized formations, and in early 1944 the *Gefechtsverband* (ad hoc groups to be led by experienced and aggressive senior officers) which on occasion exceeded even the *Geschwader*-sized groupings.[198] This response, of meeting force with force, was one typical of the German military way of thinking and actually in line with military orthodoxy, and it smacks of the rather abortive attempts at three- and five-squadron wings in the Battle of Britain, led by Air Vice-Marshal Leigh-Mallory, commander of RAF 12 Group. Just as over England the Luftwaffe would have welcomed large fighter-*versus*-fighter combats, so too would the Americans over Germany, and these often occurred because of the large size of the German defenders' formations. They could easily be seen in the air, and were clumsy and very hard to place correctly for the desired tactic of attack on a moving bomber formation. Many *Jagdflieger* leaders repeatedly stressed that the ideal unit for a head-on attack (the best method) on a bomber formation was a *Schwarm* of four aircraft up to a *Staffel* of around eight aircraft, as already established by accounts in the previous section of this chapter, dealing with 1943. Such smaller formations could be manoeuvred around the sky with ease, were harder to spot from a distance by escort fighters, and could disappear below an assaulted bomber formation more quickly and effectively. However, such an approach was hardly in accord with Göring's personality, his desire to smash the American incursions and his need to impress a Führer increasingly disillusioned with the *Luftwaffe*; the big formation approach also fitted in with orthodox military thinking and most high-ranking German air officers stemmed originally from an army background. The large *Jagdgeschwader* grouping idea stemmed from the First World War already, and Göring was steeped in the thinking of that era.

It was also Göring who strongly favoured ever heavier armament for the German fighters (large cannon, rockets, etc.) and an attack from behind the bomber formations, as he envisaged large numbers could be shot down by strong formations of determined and heavily armed German fighters. This was an approach which also easily accommodated the *Sturmangriff* ('storm attack'; another term very reminiscent of ground combat and army ways of thinking) of a massed rear attack at close range by specially armoured fighters. Such *Sturm* attacks could also be carried out by relatively inexperienced pilots – the flying skills needed were not exceptional at all, what was really required was the right National Socialist spirit to push through such attacks irrespective of return fire. All of this allied to the heavier weaponry of the *Sturm* fighters would also have appealed to Hitler. The idea of the *Sturmangriff* came from *Major* Hans-Günther von Kornatzki and might (inadvertently) have been part of a wider-spread radical way of thinking in the German armed forces, especially the idea of possible suicide attacks on naval targets.[199] While von Kornatzki's envisaged *Sturm* unit was to approach a bomber formation from behind, in a closely spaced arrow-head formation, flying in to close range in order to ensure success, it was never in fact or concept a suicide outfit at all.[200] However, that said, the concept of ramming a bomber as a final measure and doing your best to bail out shortly before the actual impact was part of the *Sturm* philosophy.[201] *Sturmstaffel 1* was set up in late 1943 under von Kornatzki as an experimental unit to evaluate the method in combat and began operations in January 1944.[202] The success achieved by this unit of volunteers (which operated under the wing of *I/JG 1* in *Jagddivision 2* until April) led to the creation of three eventual *Sturmgruppen* in the Home Defence starting in May 1944, which absorbed the experimental *Staffel*.[203] Their major operations and successes mostly post-dated the Invasion and will be explored in more detail in a subsequent volume.

In line with these developments, the head-on attack became more and more discouraged from the top down in the Home Defence. The prescribed method was a formation attack from behind, from slightly higher than the bombers; this did not require the highly skilled leadership and highly developed flying skills of the individual pilot inherent in the head-on attacks. The latter could be very effective, but normally only with experienced and highly skilled pilots and would not be a practical method for the green and poorly trained pilots now dominating the *Jagdwaffe*. The head-on method inherently never really produced the large bomber casualties, more likely in a massed attack from behind (with also large German fighter casualties due to much longer exposure to return fire). *Oberleutnant* Alfred Hammer, *Staffelkapitän* 6/JG 53 recalled the new orthodoxy: 'One tried to approach the bomber formations from above and behind, and then to shoot them down from a range of *c.* 200 m.'

*Hauptmann* Wolfgang Späte, who played the leading role in bringing the Me 163 rocket-powered fighter up to operational standard and into action against the American bomber formations (and also commanded *JG 400*), was also for a short period the *Kommandeur* of a 'normal' Home Defence *Jagdgruppe*, *IV/JG 54*. As such he was privy to the accepted method for attacking the large and tightly flown four-engined bomber formations. 'Against American bomber formations, if possible, attacks were to be made in closed-up formations of *Gruppen* strength or even *Geschwader* strength. The approach was made at about 500–1,000 m above the bomber formation. Finally, a formation dive of the fighter formation was made from behind and above, to cover the final distance to opening fire, when the enemy defences were at their most effective, as quickly as possible. Our fighter formations attacked thus against the full width of the bomber formation, to spread the enemy's return fire on as many targets as possible.' What he is describing here was the ideal and approved method for attacks on four-engined bomber formations, as prescribed for *Luftwaffe Jagdgruppen* in the Home Defence in 1944; he was only stationed in the Home Defence as commander of *IV/JG 54* for a brief period (29 May 1944–invasion), during which the *Gruppe* was busy converting onto the Fw 190.[204] His own experience and five successes against these bombers came only later, when he was flying jets in *I/JG 7* as *Kommandeur*.

However, some units, normally with experienced leaders, disregarded the recommended method and stuck to the head-on assault. *JG 1* was fortunate in having some of the best remaining leaders in the *Luftwaffe* in the Home Defence, but their casualties were very high, not even the most capable and experienced being spared in this remorseless struggle. On 10 March 1944 *Hauptmann* Rudolf Engleder re-joined *2/JG 1* as *Staffelkapitän* once more (after recovery from wounds), a post he held only until 15 April, when he was given a rest as an instructor in *Jagdergänzungsgruppe West*; he commented on the *JG 1* leadership. 'Basically we attacked the four-engined bombers head-on. *Oberstleutnant* Hans Philipp was a strong personality and an excellent *Kommodore* (1 April 1943–8 October 1943) and formation leader. The same can be said of his successor, *Oberst* Walter Oesau, who led the *Geschwader* from 10 October 1943 till 11 May 1944. *Oberst* Oesau was killed in air combat on 11 May. One of the best formation leaders in the air was *Oberstleutnant* Heinz Bär, who led *II/JG 1* as *Gruppenkommandeur* from 9 March till 12 May 1944.'

The treatment meted out to Heinz Bär by Göring was typical of his personality and reflected also a very wasteful use of an outstanding combat leader. Having fallen foul of the *Reichsmarschall* following his exhausting time in the Mediterranean theatre in mid-1943, Bär had then served as *Kommandeur* of *Jagdergänzungsgruppe Süd* until the end of 1943, whereupon he was transferred to *6/JG 1* in the Home Defence as a *kommissarischen Staffelführer* (difficult to translate but approximating to an acting *Staffel* leader though not formally appointed as *Kapitän*).[205] For an experienced *Gruppenkommandeur* holding the rank of *Major*, this was a deliberate demotion and purposeful insult towards Bär by Göring. *Feldwebel* Otto Schmid, *5/JG 1* also remembers Bär as an outstanding combat leader in the air, and an unconventional officer unpopular with high commanders. 'Bär was in all ways a first-class person and officer. Perhaps it was his mistake that he was very unconventional in several things. Perhaps this upset some of the gentlemen of the upper echelons. As a pilot and as a leader of his unit in the air he was outstanding!!! Bär was just such a man as people like Göring did not want around him. He was an uncomfortable man for these folk and not at all an unconditional "yes-man". When I rejoined *5/JG 1* at the end of January 1944, *Major* Bär was there as *Kommandeur* of *II/JG 1*.' He was mistaken about Bär already being *Gruppenkommandeur* of *II/JG 1* at the end of January 1944; what he probably meant was that Bär already often led the *Gruppe* in the air. In formal terms, Heinz Bär was *Staffelkapitän 6/JG 1* from 19 February till 15 March when he was promoted to *Gruppenkommandeur*.[206] For Bär himself, this sort of nonsense was not a major factor; as long as he could fly, fight and lead in the air, he was perfectly happy (based on personal memories of Bär related to me by Professor Paul Skawran, who knew him well). That the *Luftwaffe* leadership could indulge themselves in such stupidities during the middle of the worst air battle of the war, when experienced and capable leaders were very rare birds, borders on the insane.

Rudolf Engleder was one of the very top 'four-engine killers' in the *Luftwaffe*. He sent me an *Abchuss* list comprising 30 victories in all on roughly 70 *Feindflüge*, 29 scored during his time in *JG 1* in the Home Defence between 22 June 1943 and 10 April 1944; 25 of these were four-engined bombers. However, in the unit history volumes of *JG 1/JG 11*, only 20 victories are listed for him;[207] another unit history, of *JG 1*, gives him 27 victories by the time he was wounded on 16 December 1943,[208] which is only one less than in his own list (note however that his list includes one un-numbered victory, making the comparison, in fact, perfect). Just to complicate things further, Engleder quoted 38 *Abschüsse* in his correspondence with the author, credited to him by the *Kriegswissenschaftliches Institut*, University of Freiburg. This illustrates one of the realities of working with German fighter pilots and their victory totals. Most pilots based their personal score on what they reported as shot down to their units, generally at the *Staffel* level, unless they were part of the staff of a higher unit. Not all of these victories were passed on to higher authority for possible final confirmation and issuing of the requisite official *Abschussanerkennung* slip by the *Reichsluftfahrtministerium* (RLM), generally delayed by several months. Victory claims were checked at the *Gruppen* and *Geschwader* levels (and sometimes also by higher headquarters such as *Jagdkorps*, *Jagddivision*, etc.) before finding their way to the RLM; for many if not most pilots, their personal score ignored any that were eventually not confirmed at a higher level, and in many cases were also displayed on the aircraft's tails under the same reasoning. It is thus likely that the smaller total of 20 victories given in the one case[209] reflects the final confirmed score *versus* a higher tally reflected in the other unit history,[210] which would appear to have used his own personal count. This is a highly complex subject which will be treated in detail in a separate volume.

Despite the larger share of the action and the casualties being experienced in the Home Defence, the ongoing and extensive operations of lighter twin-engined bombers and their escorts (U.S. 9th Air Force and the RAF) within a more tactical role along the Channel coast and Holland continued throughout. They also had a continuous effect on the *Luftwaffe* fighter arm and caused serious casualties, in parallel with those suffered in the strategic-scale Battle of Germany against the four-engined bombers. Those units lying closer to the UK thus had to do battle with both Allied attacking forces, as *Obergefreiter* Pay Kleber, 7/JG 2 remembered. 'I was operational with 7/JG 2 from late 1943 until January 1944 at Creil (France), situated north of Paris. On my nineteenth operational flight I was shot down over the Channel and wounded by a Spitfire at a height of 9,000 m; my radiator was hit. The aircraft later caught fire and I managed to make a belly-landing on the coast. Frenchmen helped me out of my aircraft. I was taken by a doctor at a V-1 launching site to hospital in Rouen. Living conditions on the ground were satisfactory for both accommodation and rations, also for the ground crews. Tactics against the four-engined bomber formations: attack from the front. From the middle of 1944, they were usually attacked from above, out of the sun.'

But the crews with the hardest job of all over Germany were the poor devils in the *Zerstörergruppen*. Still flying the vulnerable and venerable Me 110s, I/ZG 26 would only be re-equipped with the more modern and faster Me 410 in April 1944. Their only hope was to avoid the American escort fighters if at all possible, which was never going to be achievable all the time, as related here by *Unteroffizier* Heinz Ludwig, gunner/radio operator in one of 3/ZG 26's aircraft. 'In the Home Defence it was only very seldom that we could catch a formation of big bombers (*dicke Autos*) without fighter escort (*Indianer*). Several times we were vectored onto a formation by the ground headquarters, and when we found them at 8,000 m, it was the time of the relief of one set of escort fighters by another. In such situations it was a case of "stop and every man save yourself", and then always some of our comrades did not return home. With the operations with the four *Dödeln* (underwing rocket tubes) in autumn 1943, we had unbelievable problems in this regard! Sometimes when we reached bomber formations, there was a pause until the escorting fighters had been drawn off, and then we went for the bombers from head-on.' Interestingly, in their much weaker aircraft they still stuck to head-on attacks when they had the opportunity, as described by Heinz Ludwig:

On 11 January 1944 we were 16 machines and we assembled at 8,200 m as usual over the Müritzsee. Then we received the order: fly course 250 degrees, incursion of *dicke Autos* flying east in the area of Braunschweig-Hannover in the direction of Berlin. We took up our fighting formation, that is in *Schwarms* of four machines, the four aircraft almost at the same height and about 50 m apart, the three other Schwarms behind us and stacked upwards with about 200 m between them. After flying for a short distance we saw ahead of us and to the right the condensation trails of the bomber formations, with two or three following the first. We were flying as the third aircraft in the leading *Schwarm*, thus as *Rottenführer*. Our *Staffelkapitän* Stratmann called out on the radio: 'all Simba aircraft Pauke, Pauke', that is: attack.

About 5 kilometres ahead of the formation we turned right onto an exact opposite course, and were a bit higher than them, then descended and now everything happened with lightning speed. I looked forwards, past the 'turn-over bar' (like the roll bar on an open vehicle) and the armour plate and saw that three escorting Mustangs protecting the leading Fortress II were all firing at us. Just before this came the call from the *Kapitän*: 'fire'. The rockets swept forwards trailing smoke into the bomber formation, wings and fuselages were hurled through the air with the explosions, and then we were hit in our crate. I felt a strong blow in the right shoulder, saw that the right hand side of the cabin was gone, also the 'turn-over bar', and of my oxygen supply system only a piece was still hanging in my mouth, the rest was gone. I noticed also that my pilot had pulled the machine up over the formation, and then I was gone – no more oxygen! I came to at about 4,000 m, the aircraft was diving vertically, the right engine was smoking, blood was flowing across my face, then I ripped the oxygen mask and goggles down and asked my pilot, if I should get out. As we pulled out into horizontal flight he said that we had reached a speed of 850 km/h, and I waited a moment. He was able to extinguish the fire in the right hand engine. I determined immediately where we were, as that was also part of the job of the radio operator, and we dragged ourselves by the one remaining engine to Hannover-Langenhagen. As we approached I shot off a red Very light from the flare gun, then we rolled up to the headquarters building, engine off, I opened my cabin roof, many ground crew ran up to us, I called 'I'm wounded', climbed out and went to the cabin roof of my pilot; he pulled open the release lever and we hugged each other on the wing and then clambered down. I then received immediate medical attention; they pulled 17 splinters out of my right shoulder with tweezers.

The aircraft looked terrible on its right-hand side. Up to where the seat of the pilot was, externally, all the paint had been stripped off to the bare metal, the panelling and side window were gone; we had been hit by 2 cm explosive shells, and apart from that we had some machine gun hits in the tail. Some of our comrades had been killed, how many Fortresses had been shot down I no longer remember exactly, I think it was seven (actual losses to the *Gruppe* had been six aircraft destroyed, five damaged with six crewmen dead and four wounded; they claimed five B-17s shot down).[211] After letting our headquarters in Braunschweig-Völkenrode know of our emergency landing, we took the train, with parachutes and my bandaged head, to our old home. There we received a welcome in the old fliers' tradition. My pilot had only light wounds. We had been lucky once again. We had both climbed out of the aircraft sopping wet with sweat.

When Otto Schmid, now promoted to *Feldwebel*, returned to 5/JG 1 on 31 January 1944 after eight months of instructing at *Ergänzungsjagdgruppe West* (Fighter Operational Training Unit West) he found things much changed. One difference was that although aircraft production had been greatly stepped up this did not always equate to each machine having the best equipment:

We were very happy with the work of the *Jafü* (*Jafü Holland-Ruhr*) in Holland in 1942–43. With the aircraft equipped with the Y-device in every machine we could be very accurately directed on to the enemy formations. We received the Y-device in September 1942, which was really good for guiding the fighters in the air. In the beginning it was installed in every machine so that the *Jafü* who was headquartered in Deelen close to Arnhem, knew all the time where his lambs were and at what height. Also, at all times the location of an *Abschuss* and the height at which it was made could be established; similarly, it was also possible when one of our machines went down to determine accurately where this happened. Unfortunately all this was only in the beginning, and later the responsible industry claimed delays in deliveries due to the effects of the war, and then only the *Staffelführer*'s aircraft was so equipped and perhaps also that of the *Schwarmführern*.

When I returned to my *Staffel* in February 1944, only two aircraft in the unit were equipped with the Y-device. One had to thus orientate yourself in the air on your own devices. Unfortunately this was a problem when flying over solid cloud cover, but one always found a gap somewhere in the clouds. The main thing was to find your own base again. Naturally the English and American radar control systems were greatly superior to ours. It could thus occur that we could be superbly guided on to an enemy formation, only to find them pre-warned by their own radar controllers, awaiting us in a favourable position. Despite this we always made the best of the situation. This all changed when the enemy's superior numbers became so large that we could practically fight only to survive (from 1944 onwards). Fortunately I only took part in this time period for a short while. Of my old *Staffel* comrades there was soon nobody left.

However, the armament of the Fw 190s had improved while he was away at the training school. During his time in *II/JG 1* in 1942–43 the Focke Wulf had been lighter-armed, but this had now all changed. 'The Fw 190 was equipped with two MG 17s, as well as four MG 151/20 cannons. The first model (A-2) had only the two MG 17s and two MG 151 cannons. The MG 151s were placed in the wing roots. In the A-4 two additional MG 151s were added in the wings. All MG 151s had 20 mm calibre. The weapons were built in by the factories and were coarsely adjusted there already. Neither the pilot nor his commanding officer were allowed to interfere in the arrangement of the weapons. Only the *Staffel* armourer was allowed to do the fine adjustment. In this the machine was jacked up at the back to place it in an orientation equivalent to high speed level flight and the aircraft was then clamped solidly. Then the weapons were aligned on a point at 500–800 m distance and with the engine running the weapons were tested with live ammunition. When everything had been correctly adjusted, it was only the pilot who could ensure hitting the target or not. I watched when my new Fw had its weapons adjusted out of sheer interest; we had an outstanding *Waffenmeister, Oberfeldwebel* Wilk.' It is interesting that *Luftwaffe* pilots at all levels were not allowed to influence the harmonisation of their guns, and that solely the *Waffenmeister* had control of this. In the RAF and US Army Air Force this was certainly not the case and the more experienced pilots tended to harmonise the guns as they wished, often at much closer range than 500 m.

Just over a week after re-joining *II/JG 1*, Otto Schmid had his first meeting with the enemy, now much more formidable than he had been in May 1943; he was shot down almost immediately. 'On 8 February 1944 we flew a mission against incoming American formations. We had contact with Lightnings, Thunderbolts and Boeing B-17 units. In the ensuing dog fight with the fighters I received one or more hits in the engine, which seized as a result. After a short time it began to burn as well. It was high time to get out. As I got rid of the cockpit canopy and simultaneously pushed myself away from the aircraft a flame licked at my left sleeve, which was no loss. If I had delayed pushing away at all, this flame (caused by the enormous slipstream of the now open cockpit) would have been directly in my face. One has to have luck. The aircraft crashed into a factory building that collapsed entirely. Thankfully the workers had just gone on their lunch break, so that none were injured. Most likely they had been watching the air combat, or had gone to the bomb shelters.'

At least Otto Schmid had the good fortune to belong to a single-engined fighter unit and had considerable combat experience behind him, improving his chances of survival. *Feldwebel* Fritz Buchholz was a newly joined member of *II/ZG 26* in early 1944 with no combat experience at all (but lots of flying experience, which probably helped save his life several times), and flew his first operation in the hard school of the Home Defence three days after Otto Schmid's lucky escape from his burning Fw 190. Fritz Buchholz flew the Me 410, which was a considerable improvement on the by now obsolete Me 110, but this was soon offset by its ridiculous armament of a 5 cm cannon: 'The Me 410 was no problem to fly at all, and she was also very fast. However, by the later addition of the 5 cm cannon she became very cumbersome and no longer turned well.' Fritz Buchholz sent me a copy of a published article (source not given; in *Jägerblatt*?) he wrote on his experiences during the war in the *Luftwaffe*, on which the following account is based. He joined the ground staff of *III/JG 26* before the war and after the French campaign volunteered for pilot training and was successful in this. After attaining an instrument rating he was retained as an instructor for a long time, but eventually was posted to *ZG 76* in the Home Defence but almost immediately thereafter was transferred to *Zerstörerschule* for an abbreviated but necessary training in his new role. Having been posted to *II/ZG 26* at Hildesheim (*Jagddivision 1*) led by *Hauptmann* Tratt, he flew his first mission on 11 February 1944 on a single-seat Me 410 but suffered an engine failure and had to force-land at another airfield for repairs; that same evening in bad weather he flew back to base to learn that his *Kommandeur* had claimed two or three P-38s and his wingman had made a belly-landing (three Lightning claims and this single damaged Me 410 were the sum total of recorded claims and losses for the *Gruppe* on this mission).[212] After some more operations with and without rocket launchers, in March 1944 they were re-equipped with two-seater Me 410s with a 5 cm cannon added which made the aircraft very poor in manoeuvring; they were moved to Königsberg (north-east of Berlin), relatively far removed from the activities of American escort fighters, which would have been deadly for their now very clumsy aircraft. The 5 cm cannon was perhaps the high point of the up-gunning of the Home Defence fighters, and certainly reflected a point way beyond practical common sense; one can imagine that Hitler, with his penchant for heavier guns on increasingly larger tanks, bigger battleships and so on, must have thoroughly approved of the 5 cm aircraft cannon.

II/ZG 26 were now sent into action against incoming four-engined bombers in the eastern parts of Germany from the Baltic coast right down into Bavaria, and were sometimes given single-seat fighter escorts of their own. Although the 5 cm cannon could be very effective, leading to bombers literally exploding with one hit, its longer range led to pilots firing too soon and it often jammed after one or two rounds (only 21 carried) and its successes did not meet expectations. It led also to the loss of their *Gruppenkommandeur*, *Hauptmann* Tratt, who was shot down in a very risky lone attack on a bomber formation on 22 February 1944 and killed with his gunner; he was the leading *Zerstörer* ace at the time on 38 victories.[213] *Oberleutnant* Prokopp, who had been the sole eyewitness to Tratt's demise, was himself rammed by a P-47 and killed, next to Fritz Buchholz's Me 410. *Leutnant* Dassow, another ace in II/ZG 26 who was very dissatisfied with the poor performance of the 5 cm cannon, had eight 2 cm cannons added below the nose of his Me 410, with which he was successful. With the Americans starting to bomb successfully through cloud cover and *Zerstörer* pilots generally lacking instrument training, Buchholz, as an experienced instructor, was roped in to teach *Schwarm* leaders these skills in between flying missions. A few times he was also made to lead their Me 410 formation through total overcasts before handing over to the leader once they were in the clear; however, when they were attacked by American escort fighters the pilots dived eastwards, avoiding cloud cover. Such tactics led to severe losses, and Buchholz could not help his flaming comrades, but with his well-developed blind-flying skills he was able to escape in the clouds and successfully navigate homewards. This was not much appreciated by many of his comrades. On 13 May 1944 they were vectored onto a B-24 formation flying south-east over the Baltic heading for Posen, where they later bombed aircraft works, and followed the bombers in a parallel course to east of Frankfurt/Oder, when they were bounced by roughly 20 Mustangs. Buchholz was shot down, bailing out safely; II/ZG 26 losses totalled six Me 410s, seven crewmen killed and two wounded.[214] The clocks in their aircraft were very valuable and were thus fastened onto the dashboard with a single hinge held by one fastener, the idea being that pilots bailing out should grab the clock and jam it in their pocket as they went – Fritz Buchholz recalls that on 13 May not a single clock was thus saved!

The excerpt below from *Feldwebel* Fritz Buchholz's logbook makes for interesting reading. Notably, they flew many missions over long distances without meeting the enemy. This was inevitable in view of their being stationed far to the east in the German theatre, as far from the dangers of American escort fighters as possible, and being expected to cover this far-eastern airspace from the Baltic Sea right down to southern Germany.

Example of a *Zerstörer* pilot's operational life, Home Defence, April–May 1944, based on flying logbook, 11 April–30 May 1944: *Feldwebel* Fritz Buchholz II/ZG 26, flying Me 410 (based at Königsberg, north-east of Berlin, the entire time, but sometimes landing elsewhere after a combat) (Source: Fritz Buchholz)

APRIL

13: Mission, 13h25–15h40; landed at Neuburg/Donau (returned to Königsberg that evening)
26: Mission, 09h50–10h30
29: Mission, 10h40–12h45

MAY

7: Mission, 10h10–12h15
9: Mission, 09h30–12h00
12: Mission, 13h05–15h20 (*Feindflug*); combat in Dresden area, 5 cm cannon jammed after second round; landed Erfurt-Bindersleb (returned to Königsberg that afternoon)

13: Mission, 13h15–15h00 (*Feindflug*); attacked by 20 Mustangs, shot down, Buchholz bailed out north-east of Reppen

19: Mission, 13h15–15h20

22: Mission, 13h00–14h55

24: Mission, 10h20–12h22

28: Mission, 13h35–15h15

29: Mission, 11h20–13h07 (*Feindflug*); shot down 1 Consolidated Liberator north of Warnemünde (Baltic Sea), combat north of Stettin

30: Mission, 10h37–12h08

On 20 and 21 February, Otto Schmid flew his last operations of the war. By this time the pace of operations of the frontline *Staffeln* had become very fast, and multiple operations on the same day were no longer a rarity. The chances of even an experienced pilot lasting long under such circumstances were even further reduced. 'Talking of the operations on 20 and 21 February 1944: it was definitely hard to fly multiple missions on each of these days. Unfortunately on my last two days of the war I had no more luck hunting anymore. After such strenuous operational days we were completely exhausted by the evenings. But despite this we still allowed ourselves to have a few glasses from the sheer joy that we had survived the day. On the second operation (his last) on 21 February we again met the enemy and fought hard against Liberators and Thunderbolts. If one can imagine the proportions of the aircraft involved in this air battle, then it was easily in a ratio of 1:10 in favour of the enemy. It was swarming with American fighters. One had to try and "cheat" your way through them directly to get at the bombers. The Liberator that I was attacking had begun to burn in one engine, but unfortunately I could not watch any more, as I was then hit myself and had to break off the combat. On 21 February 1994 I celebrated my second 50th birthday; on this day 50 years ago at about 14h40 I was seriously wounded during my second operational sortie of the day, during an attack on B-24 Liberators. Despite my shattered leg (3 explosive bullets) I was able to crash-land at our base and with that the war was ended for me. Unfortunately my left leg had to be amputated. Despite this I have never lost the joy of life.' Below is an excerpt from Otto Schmid's logbook detailing his last month of active operations in *Jagddivision 3*, where meeting the enemy was a distinct likelihood as many incursions came in over the Dutch coast and proceeded south-eastwards into Germany.

Example of a fighter pilot's operational life, Home Defence, based on flying logbook, 4 February–21 February 1944: *Feldwebel* Otto Schmid, *5/JG 1*, flying Fw 190 (based at Rheine, north-west Germany where they belonged to *Jagddivision* 3) (Source: Otto Schmid)

FEBRUARY

5: *Rotten* mission, 13h17–14h00

6: *Schwarm* mission, 14h10–15h10

8: Scramble, 11h20–12h35 (51st *Feindflug*); contact with Lightnings, Thunderbolts and Boeings. Due to hit in engine *ausgeflogen* ('flew out' – i.e. bailed out!), engine on fire

12: *Gruppen* mission, 16h15–17h07

14: *Staffel* mission, 14h00–15h00

17: flew four practice bomb drop flights to bombing range

19: *Gruppen* mission, 14h05–14h55
*Gruppen* mission, 17h40–18h35

20: Scramble, 10h45–12h00 (52nd *Feindflug*); contact with 50–60 Thunderbolts
Landed Oldenburg, about 100 km north-east of Rheine, in *Jagddivision* 2
Scramble from Oldenburg, 12h57–13h26 (53rd *Feindflug*); contact with Boeings, Liberators and Thunderbolts. Landed back at base, Rheine

21: Scramble, 12h55–14h00 (54th *Feindflug*); contact with Liberators and Thunderbolts
Scramble, 14h20–14h55 (55th *Feindflug*); contact with Liberators and Thunderbolts. Due to being hit, crash-landed. Leg wounded due to being hit by three explosive bullets. Left leg amputated up to thigh

From Otto Schmid's logbook excerpt above, one can see that he flew 11 missions within the space of 17 days, meeting the enemy on five of these missions, and being shot down on one of them and very seriously wounded on another. He was heavily involved in the missions against the American assaults (and associated RAF night raids) over 'Big Week', designed to smash the *Luftwaffe* defenders in the air and their aircraft production on the ground in the factories, between Sunday 20 February and Friday 25 February 1944.[215] Despite heavy damage, the German aviation industry survived and continued to pump out more than enough aircraft; it was pilots, experienced leaders and fuel that was their Achilles heel, not aircraft. While Big Week cost the 8th Air Force 157 bombers, the 15th Air Force 90 bombers and the RAF 131 night bombers, American fighters claimed 231 German fighters shot down (most by 8th Air Force, the 15th claiming only 14) against German losses of 326 fighter aircraft and, much worse, 170 dead and 112 wounded aircrew.[216] As a percentage of sorties, bomber losses were still worryingly high in the 15th Air Force, which lacked adequate long-range escorts.[217] On 20 February 1944 Otto Schmid's *Gruppe* (*II/JG 1*) took off from their base at Rheine, had a combat with P-47s then landed far away at Oldenburg, refuelled and within the hour were scrambled a second time, from Oldenburg, and had a second combat against American bombers and fighters. On 21 February 1944 he again flew two scrambles, with the second take-off within 20 minutes of landing from the first. Indeed, very intensive and stressful fighting, and with little chance of coming through it for long without injury or worse.

Despite many of the *Jagdgruppen* following high command's recommended method of attacking four-engined bomber formations en masse from behind during 1944, *II/JG 3* became an exception as they changed from the rear attack to the head-on method early in 1944. Another innovation which came in during 1944 was the concept of the *Höhengruppe*, to oppose enemy escort fighters and which normally comprised Me 109s with better high-altitude performance and lighter armament than the Fw 190s concentrating on the bombers. *I/JG 3* was such a *Gruppe*. *Oberleutnant* Walter Bohatsch, a veteran of the Russian Front, flew in both *I* and *II/JG 3* in the first few months of 1944 and details his experiences here. 'On the attack method used by the *Udet Geschwader*, one can say that in the beginning of our time in the Home Defence (autumn 1943) all attacks on American bomber formations were made from behind and above. The losses were very heavy, and one then changed to flying the attacks from ahead, and this required good flying skills and iron nerves were also part of it. When this tactic was brought in I was already with the 1st *Staffel* (joined *1/JG 3* in March 1944), and then *Staffelkapitän* of *2/JG 3* (from April 1944).[218] *I Gruppe* flew exclusively high-altitude missions as escorts for the heavy fighters which attacked the bombers; thus we mostly had to do with the American escorts of the four-engined bombers, the Mustangs and Thunderbolts. The superior numbers of the enemy were depressing. At this time, April 1944, I mostly led the *I Gruppe* in the air. When we could launch 25 Me 109s into the air then that was a lot. In air combat one then had to take on 150 to

200 Mustangs – an occupation with a very poor prognosis. The losses were correspondingly large. In three months my pilots changed three times.' At the end of 1943 Bohatsch had still been with his old unit, *5/JG 3*, and was very unhappy at first on having to leave a *Staffel* he had served with for so long and to leave his great friend *Oberfeldwebel* Hans Grünberg (nicknamed 'Specker') behind, as described below.

*Hauptmann* Sannemann (acting *Gruppenkommandeur*) moved *II/JG 3* to Rothenburg a.d. Würm on Christmas Day 1943; *Oberfeldwebel* Notemann an old hand of the 5th *Staffel* was transferred to *Luftkriegsschule I*. While re-equipping at Rothenburg some of our pilots flew in a Me 108 to the Erla factory to test fly their new Me 109s as the factory had too few pilots of their own to do the job. From Rothenburg Home Defence missions were flown and the losses of old and young pilots continued. It was considered a positive if one was only shot down and able to bail out, and that this was lucky. On one of the missions (20 February 1944)[219] flown against the 'Big Week' raids, during an attack on Liberators, I was shot down by Thunderbolts and had to bail out and suffered serious burns; wingman *Unteroffizier* Scheibe also had to bail out. The *Gruppe* later moved to Gardelegen (1 March 1944, stayed there up till the invasion)[220] and *Hauptmann* Rohwer became *Kommandeur* in March but was soon killed (30 March 1944).[221] At this time my transfer to the *I Gruppe* took place, as *Staffelkapitän* of the 1st *Staffel*; this closed a circle for me, as I received command of the *Staffel* once led by my brother Heinz.

The departure from 5th *Staffel* and from 'Specker' was very hard for me. We had survived through all these hard times and had become a sworn brotherhood, and 'Specker' and I were the last remaining pilots from Russia. There now began a new part of my time as a fighter pilot. The *I Gruppe* was a purely high-altitude unit and flew escort for the *II* and *IV Gruppen*. This *Hohenjagd* was the hardest task for any fighter unit and we had the highest losses in the *Geschwader*. Where I previously referred to rain and drought, so the *Höhenjagd* was the super-drought. The blessings from above in the form of Mustangs, Thunderbolts and Lightnings came down so richly that the changing of the guard of *I Gruppe* pilots occurred at a fast pace. Now we received very young replacement pilots with very limited flying experience of any kind. Five *Feindflüge* for a new pilot was already a proud achievement. I will always remember the last mission of 'Poldi' Münster (*Ritterkreuzträger* and *Staffelkapitän 5/JG 3*, killed when he collided with a B-24 on 8 May 1944),[222] which I was able to see clearly from higher altitude and hear over the radio; after he was able to shoot down two B-17s he appears to have rammed a third bomber. He was awarded a posthumous *Eichenlaub*. *Leutnant* Grünberg took over 5th *Staffel* after him. On this mission Münster was leading the *II Gruppe* and I led the *I Gruppe*. From this time I also recall pilots of the *I Gruppe* whom I would like to mention: *Oberleutnant* Schleef (*Staffelkapitän 3/JG 3*),[223] who alternated with me in leading the *Gruppe* in the air; *Leutnant* Fritz (killed 13 April 1944);[224] *Feldwebel* Petzschler; and *Feldwebel* Bilek. The *Kommandeur* then was *Hauptmann* Mertens (from 14 April till past the invasion)[225] and thereafter *Hauptmann* Laube; the Adjutant was *Leutnant* Lösch.

One of Walter Bohatsch's newly arrived pilots in *2/JG 3* in 1944 was *Feldwebel* Horst Petzschler, who came fresh from the Eastern Front. 'On 14 April 1944 I was transferred from *JG 51* on the Eastern Front to the Home Defence; up to the invasion I was able to shoot down four American aircraft, but had to bail out myself once and also made a belly-landing in a potato field near Peenemünde! Then it was back to *Stabstaffel/JG 51* in Russia.' His four Home Defence claims encompassed one B-17 and one P-51 on 12 May 1944, one B-24 two days later, and one P-51 on 28 May. His return to the east was hardly an improvement as he was immediately caught up in the massive Russian *Bagration* offensive, which utterly destroyed the German Army Group Centre.

Far to the south of where *II/JG 1* and *II/JG 3* had been flying against the 'Big Week' raids of the 8th Air Force, units in *Jagddivision 7* in southern Germany and from its subordinate *Jafü Ostmark* in Austria fought against the incursions of the 15th Air Force from Italy, who were bombing the southern German aircraft factories during this week.[226] *Leutnant* Gerhard Keppler, *2/JG 27* flew against three of these raids (see logbook excerpt below) and recalled his later adventures thereafter. 'I only flew in the Home Defence (*Reichsverteidigung*) until 1 April 1944. On this day I had to "climb out" and injured my head in bailing out. Through this my balance abilities were largely lost and I could no longer fly operationally. From that time forward I was Company Chief (C/O of the ground crew echelon) and Technical Officer of the unit leader school (*Verbandsführerschule*) of the *General der Jagdflieger*. Living conditions on the ground in the Home Defence were always good, we only had problems with the increasing losses and the replacement thereof with improperly trained pilots and especially in the quality of the technical material.'

Example of a fighter pilot's operational life, Home Defence, based on flying logbook, 22 February 1944–1 April 1944: *Leutnant* Gerhard Keppler, 2/JG 27, flying Me 109 (based at Fels am Wagram, Austria, under *Jafü Ostmark*, itself under *Jagddivision 7*) (Source: Gerhard Keppler)

## FEBRUARY
22: Scramble, 12h20–14h20; air combat at 6,000 m above clouds, with Liberator, one *Abschuss* near Graz
23: Scramble, 11h10–12h30; shot down one Boeing at Wels
24: Scramble, 12h00–13h20 (263rd *Feindflug*); shot down one Boeing near Traunsee, bailed out over Fels

## APRIL
1: Local flight, 08h00–08h10; bailed out and injured

*Oberleutnant* Fritz Engau, an experienced night fighter pilot who had to re-muster to the day fighters due to losing his night vision after being wounded, joined 2/JG 11 in *Jagddivision 2* in January 1944. Despite initially being a *Staffelführer* and later *Staffelkapitän*, he was tasked with leading the entire *Gruppe* quite often and even on occasion the entire *Geschwader*, and on one memorable sortie flew at the head of a massive *Gefechtsverband*! These were the realities of the Home Defence for junior leaders in the first half of 1944, when losses of more senior leaders forced such duties on to them, as related below.

I was part of the night fighters in Belgium (St Trond) during 1943. In January 1944 I had to leave due to loss of night vision after having been wounded and changed over to day fighting, where I took over leadership of 2/JG 11 as *Staffelführer*. I thus got to be part of the terrible first half of 1944 in the Home Defence. I also acted in the air as leader of the entire *I Gruppe* at times, or even the entire *Geschwader* (when no more senior or experienced unit leader was available). Once I even led the *Gefechtsverband* of *Jagddivisions* 1 and 2 in the air north of Berlin. In *I/JG 11* we had already lost leaders like Hermichen (wounded), with König and Zwernemann killed, which is why I ended up in leadership positions in the air. The successful *Oberleutnant* König just like me lost his night vision when he lost one eye, and also moved from night fighters to day fighters.

This was a half year of very high losses in the *Luftwaffe* day fighters over Germany. Our base was at Husum and then Rotenburg/Hannover. *I/JG 11* (and the entire *JG 11*) had terrible losses; in north-west and north Germany insiders talked of the 'grave of *JG 11*' in these regions. There were hardly any survivors from the battles against vastly superior numbers. On 26 May 1944 *Hauptmann* Simsch arrived in our *Gruppe* as the new *Kommandeur*. All my records and documents were destroyed in the heavy bombing raid on our airfield at Rotenburg at the end of May 1944. Until the invasion I moved with my 2nd *Staffel* to Lüneburg, as our base at Rotenburg had been largely destroyed by eight waves of bombers. *I/JG 11* attacked the large four-engined bomber formations in 1943/1944 always and exclusively from the front (often with only four to six aircraft). The frontal attack was thus the standard method of the *I Gruppe*. Combat against the Mustangs mostly occurred after the head-on attack had been made, but sometimes before we could carry them out. With these situations there were many possibilities for us. I had three confirmed victories over Mustangs that were really very hard to achieve. The Fw 190 had better climbing abilities at all heights than the Mustang 1B. A zoom climb after a dive showed itself only after a long time as an advantage for the FW190. The '190' was also more manoeuvrable than the Mustang, but the turning circle of the Mustang was definitely smaller. The Mustangs thus performed many tight turns in combat. The acceleration capabilities of the Fw 190 were, however, better than those of the Mustang. A Mustang flying at full throttle in level flight, which then went straight into a steep dive, could not be caught by the 190. But a Mustang that went into a dive without full throttle could be caught by the 190.

I was credited with seven confirmed victories in all. I was also involved in 10–15 *Herausschüsse* of bombers from their formations in the head-on attacks of *I Gruppe*; these were mostly credited to me as I was normally flying at the head of the attacking formation and could thus aim accurately at the nearest bomber. *Herausschüsse* are not victories as such, but are bombers that have been damaged, had engines hit, etc., that are forced from the formations as a result and limp away. As we had to stay with the formations and attack them again, we were not able to follow these lame ducks and finish them off.

In actual fact, in the *Luftwaffe* victory accreditation system a *Herausschuss* did count as a victory, being awarded with two points as opposed to the three points given for a full destruction of a four-engined bomber; final destruction (*endgültige Vernichtung*) of a '*Herausschuss*' was not counted a victory and got just one point, but quite a few appear in pilots' victory lists and some were in fact confirmed as victories also.[227]

While Fritz Engau and his fellow pilots of *I/JG 11* were ignoring *Luftwaffe* higher command instructions on how to attack the bomber formations by deliberately flying head-on attacks in their heavily armed Fw 190s, *II/JG 11* was equipped with the more lightly armed Me 109 G with a good high-altitude performance; they thus served as the *Höhenjäger* in protecting their comrades in *I/JG 11*. Among these high-altitude pilots was Ernst Richter, previously wingman to the famous Walter Nowotny of *I/JG 54* on the Russian Front. 'After having been promoted to *Feldwebel* (while in Russia with *I/JG 54*) at the beginning of April 1944 I was transferred to *JG 11* at Wunstorf near Hannover. In this *Geschwader* I flew a total of 23 *Feindflüge* in the Home Defence and on the Invasion Front and had eight Abschüsse confirmed (two of them in the Home Defence, both Mustangs). *II/JG 11* were high-altitude fighters (*Höhenjäger*) that were only to attack the escorting fighters of the bomber streams. There we flew the Me 109 G, with which we could climb as high as 14,000 m. As the machine did not have a pressurised cabin, the time above 12,000 m was very unpleasant, one was exposed to the so-called altitude sickness that after a maximum of 20 minutes was fatal! Well, we never lasted that long at those heights. But only by diving from these great heights did we stand any chance against the at least ten-times superior numbers of the enemy. The four-engined bombers were attacked from head-on by heavy fighters in closed-up formations. These heavy fighters were Fw 190s that were better armoured also. Of those I had no experience directly.'

On the second abortive 8th Air Force raid on Berlin on 4 March 1944 (largely disrupted by the inclement weather, as had been the first attempted raid on this target the previous day)[228] a total of six P-38 Lightnings was lost;[229] two crashed in England and four were missing, three of the latter from the 20th Fighter Group. One of these three was flown by Lieutenant Harry E. Bisher,[230] whose damaged aircraft had lost an engine. However, he was lucky this day to meet an opponent who was not cold-bloodedly out to destroy every enemy machine he could find, especially a lame duck on one engine. *Leutnant* Gerd Wiegand of *4/JG 26* recounts what happened when they met in his 'Easter Story of 4 March 1944'.

I don't know what motivated me to tell this story; was it the third letter request from Dominique van den Broucke, or was it the Easter sermon today, with its message of resurrection that served to remind me of the event in the first part of the story on 4 March 1944 and its second part that I was able to experience in October 1988? It is the story of two young lieutenants, one American and one German. The one sat in a Lightning, had a trip as part of the fighter escort to Berlin behind him, and after having been hit was flying – without a compass or any real idea of where he was – back to England. The other was myself, then in the second year of my membership of *4/JG 26 – Schlageter*, equipped with the much loved Focke Wulf 190. That 4 March 1944 was a day of exceptionally bad weather. Due to this fact the pilots, as also in the past eight days, had more enthusiasm for winning a round of drinks than in performing any heroic deeds. In the last combat on 24 February 1944 – it was my 92nd *Feindflug* – I had been able to shoot down one B-17 and two Thunderbolts. That was the high point of my then still young fighter pilot career – *Abschüsse* numbers 23 to 25. Thinking back, I could not have guessed that four days after Easter, on 8 March, I would find myself in the greatest peril, trying to free myself from my burning Fw 190 and return safely to earth on my parachute with serious burns to my face.

The bad weather of the past eight days had made all of us pilots a bit nervous. I can remember very well that we really and truly appreciated this weather situation out of idleness or fear. But I also remember that such a feeling of the urge to perform again would grow in us after a few days, a bit like sailors on a sailing ship who after an over-long time in the doldrums wished for a really stiff breeze again. However, even 4 March did not promise to deliver this stiff breeze. After all, the church tower of Wevelghem – west of our airfield – was temporarily not visible from the dispersal of the 4th *Staffel* on the eastern end of the field due to hail. Then a white wall came past north of the field again, so that an immediate operation was not to be expected. The air was damp and cold and one felt that a black frost could occur any minute. We knew that bomber formations were on their way to Berlin and that the first fighter escort squadrons were already on their way back. I still love this cold, damp air even today.

Just to escape the tobacco cloud of our dispersal hut I splashed out to my number '10'. Theo, my mechanic, was telling me about a possible improvement to our newly acquired external fuel tank dropping mechanism. A few weeks before, as the *Staffel*'s TO (Technical Officer), I had had racks built on wheels that we could place underneath our tanks and which were capable of turning 90° in a 4-metre radius when one pulled them. They worked excellently. If we were sent off on a short-range mission as fighters, then we dropped the tanks before switching the engine on and they could easily be wheeled out of the way. If we had a long mission ahead of us, then the racks were merely pulled away before we switched on and we took off with the tanks on. Previously we had to drop the tanks after taking off when enemy contact threatened. That way, of course, a lot of precious fuel was wasted. In the middle of our discussion suddenly came the alarm for enemy aircraft. Theo and I looked at each other in confusion. Aircraft alarm without scramble orders? Now it got lively on the field. I saw how our armourer suddenly sat upright in his machine gun emplacement and got ready to fire his twin guns. Others jumped with curses into the prepared air raid trenches and holes that were still half full of water – those were standing orders. But still no combat alarm, no orders to sit in our aircraft (*Sitzbereitschaft*) and no take-off orders – what was going on? The answer came from above in the form of engine noise that soon resolved itself into a Lightning that became visible at 1,000 m over the airfield. We were astounded. There was a Lightning flying happily at 1,000 m over a German fighter base and then disappearing behind the next rain cloud.

No combat alarm? No take-off orders? Most likely the *Jafü* wanted to spare the health of the fighters in view of the weather. As I was trying to gather my thoughts, another Lightning appeared over the field at the same height – but this time on a northerly course. It wasn't difficult to deduce that it must have been the same aircraft, and someone had binoculars and called out, 'One of his engines has failed!' Then it became clear to me that the *Indian* up there possibly thought he was over England and was looking for a place to land. Why was he flying backwards and forwards? My thoughts raced. Something must be done; at the end of the day, it was my turn to lead the scramble *Rotte*. Then I got an idea: he is looking for a landing place, you can show him one – take off! The thought is the father of the deed. I moved into my seat, the external tank dropped off, Theo understood immediately and removed it to the side and then it seemed to take an age before the starter handle was up to its revolutions. My trusty '10' took straight away, with blue exhaust smoke. I did up my seatbelt, closed the cabin, switched on the radio and off I went directly out of the camouflaged box at full throttle.

The church tower of Wevelghem was easily visible and was soon underneath me. Apparently there was a large hole in between the rain clouds, in which I now found myself. My mind was still racing. Where would he now be? How would I get close to him without shooting? How can I bring him to the airfield without him shooting me down? An inner voice now articulated itself to me that I should behave nobly. Yes, I wanted to do so, I wanted to land with him at our airfield. Hopefully Beckmann, my wingman, would not shoot him down. The idea fascinated me, an *Indian* with a Lightning in Wevelghem – that would really be something! But where was he? In the meantime my altimeter showed 500 m. I lowered my rate of climb to have enough speed as a precaution. In the meantime I had naturally reached the boundary of my opening in the clouds and had to turn round. Another turn and then the decision to stay below him, otherwise I would most likely not see him at all. After some seconds flying east I then had to cross his north–south course and then turn south myself, in the hope of seeing him somewhere. My idea worked perfectly, he came flying over me exactly 300 m higher. I saw his stationary engine. Now a short climb, a half roll and already I was sitting behind him and a bit higher. As he was flying slowly I also had to cut back the throttle to stay obliquely behind him.

He got ever bigger – now I could see the rivets on his fuselage. Never before had I seen a Lightning from so close. The pilot was looking ahead and below; he hadn't noticed me yet. Now was the critical moment. He turned around, I saw his shocked face and straightaway he pulled his Lightning into a defensive turn that forced me to also turn. So my dream bubble burst that I could direct him to our airfield with hand signals. I could not fly ahead of him, as then he would certainly have shot me down – but now it was getting dangerous. Thank God I had reduced my throttle in time, so that I could turn with him. Any question of giving signals or other such games was no longer to be considered. Where was my nobility not to want to shoot down a crippled enemy? I told myself to stick close to him and force him to bail out and aimed at his wing that was right in front of me big as a plank. I pressed the firing button but no shot came out. I had not yet switched on the weapons. Right, another turn and now with switched on weapons, I aimed carefully directly at the wing, but it didn't work out as I was too close. The flying debris would have hit me. So, one more turn and now in the other wing, I pressed the buttons and the wing flew off. The Lightning sliced down and at last he bailed out. One more turn and I saw the parachute, I saw the man, and he waved and did not appear to be wounded. And now I panicked, because the hole in the clouds had moved on to the West. Wevelghem was now disappearing behind a thick wall of hail. Only now did it occur to me in what a stupid undertaking I had landed myself and I had to think about bailing out myself. I could already see myself before the court martial due to deliberate wrongdoing and then I saw the walls of my hole in the cloud flying open. There was also a chance to climb up and with hopefully better vision at 4,000 m to get to the coast and to find one of the many fields there. Then suddenly a pronounced triangular railway pattern, a well-known church tower and already the field at Lille North was coming out of the clouds and I was saved.

After a smooth landing I had a happy reunion with old friends. Lille North had been our base only a few weeks before. I reported my landing and the *Abschuss* telephonically to the *Geschwader*. They had no news yet about the parachutist. An unusual happiness gripped me. I can still remember this feeling very well at having nobly performed my duty and was at peace with God and the world. Our old quarters were nearby in a villa belonging to nobility. Key staff were still there to keep the house in order. I let myself be brought there to enjoy a nice evening with old friends, but this did not happen. My enquiries about the fate of the American who had bailed out ended in the report of the duty officer that he had fallen into the Leie River and drowned. His body had not yet been found. In those times we were not subtle, seeing as the air war had cost us many of our best friends. But I remember after this report that I had no joy in the *Abschuss* and I made off unhappily to my quarters. Four days later I myself was hanging on my parachute and found myself in hospital with serious facial burns. Since then 44 years have passed and I had kept the damned war in the past. In early 1988 Dominique van den Broucke managed to find me, to tell me that the parachutist from all that time ago did not drown after all, rather surviving the jump well and with the help of the Résistance he was able to get back to England and eventually the USA. He was Lieutenant Colonel Bisher, now a grandfather just like me. This was one of the very few good stories out of this appalling war. It is my Easter story of this year (1988).

A wonderful and happy story in the midst of the continuing carnage over the Homeland. Two combat reports from April 1944 serve as examples of what it was more typically like to fly in action against the overwhelming superiority of the Allied air power. The first report of *Oberfeldwebel* Otto Bach, *5/JG 1* is that of an experienced pilot, whose 13th victory claim this was.[231] 'On 11 April 1944 at 10h02, I took off as *Rottenführer* within the *II/JG 1* after a scramble alarm. We were directed with the Y-system. At 10h59 we contacted the enemy, consisting of 15–18 Boeing F-IIs and 30–40 Thunderbolts and Mustangs in grid square GB-FB at 6,000 m. The enemy formation was flying an easterly course. The *Gruppe* attacked a somewhat separated unit (15–18 aircraft) from ahead and slightly below, in closed-up *Gruppe* formation. In this attack I fired at one Boeing that was flying right at the outside end of the left flank, so effectively that parts of the cabin flew off immediately and the Boeing dived down steeply. Three crew members bailed out with their parachutes. The aircraft was destroyed when it crashed in flames in square FB – north of Fallersleben. I saw the impact.'[232] Flying right next to Bach in this attack was his *Rottenflieger*, *Flieger* Blech, who in a portion of his report recorded: 'In this attack flying next to my *Rottenführer* I shot up the second Boeing from the left so effectively that the left-hand lower part of the fuselage and the inner part of the left wing immediately caught fire. Fragments were blown off the belly of the aircraft. The aircraft turned steeply to the left, diving away. I could not see the impact with the ground that must have been in grid square FB at about 11h00 due to the subsequent combat with the enemy fighters.'[233] This was Blech's very first victory claim.[234] Poor Georg Blech had been demoted to *Flieger* (the lowest *Luftwaffe* rank), presumably during training, for having visited his relations (most likely without permission – i.e. AWOL), and went on to shoot down three more four-engined bombers and a P-51; one of the bombers he rammed and then bailed out, wounded.[235] He would be shot down and bail out another four times and was promoted to the grand rank of *Gefreiter* by late in 1944, only to be killed in action by P-51s on 26 November 1944.[236]

Despite strafing attacks on German airfields becoming more common as the first half of 1944 went by,[237] some German pilots recall that they did not observe much hindrance of their activities at their bases. *Hauptmann* Georg Schröder, *Gruppenkommandeur II/JG 2* remembered: 'There were not any serious interferences by the enemy of our take-offs and landings. I only experienced this once, at the airfield at Creil, in May 1944, already very early in the morning, before the first dawn light when 25–30 Thunderbolts at a height of 2,500–3,000 m wanted to provide us with "cover"! In the event we did not take off. At the end of the day we were not exactly beginners in our trade either! We had been well informed of the possibility of such interferences. Whether and how other plans were advantaged through these enemy actions, we would never have known.'

## A Battle of Attrition Lost; No End in Sight

The long, slow death of an effective *Luftwaffe* fighter arm, achieved by May 1944, enabled the Allied invasion of Normandy to proceed successfully, which in time would put an end to Hitler's Third Reich, along with the advancing Russian armies from the east. The defeat of the *Jagdflieger* was a sad burden for the few survivors to bear. *JG 2*'s ex-*Kommodore*, *Oberst* Walter Oesau, who had been banned from further operational flying after bringing his score to 100 victories, did later return to active operations, as *Kommodore JG1* (from 12 November 1943).[238] He led this *Geschwader* until his death on 11 May 1944 in a heroic yet hopeless dogfight against several P-38s, by then also exhausted from months of difficult combat against the American raids.[239] By this time his score had reached 118 victories (plus a further nine from the Spanish Civil War);[240] another of the great fighter pilots and outstanding leaders was gone – men like Oesau were simply irreplaceable. Otto Schmid, *II/JG 1* remembers him. 'I got to know our *Kommodore* Walter Oesau in Deelen, Holland. He was a very interesting man.'

Some experienced pilots almost made it only to die just before the war ended. When *Feldwebel* Otto Schmid returned to 5/*JG 1* on 31 January 1944 after an eight-month break of instructing at *Ergänzungsjagdgruppe West*, hardly anyone he had known previously in the *Gruppe* was still alive. 'It is a tragedy when one reads (in the *JG 1* unit histories)[241] how one's comrades, with whom you had so much fun, were killed one after the other. When I follow their fates in this way, I am completely happy with my wooden leg. My very good friend from those days Günther Kirschner at the end crashed on take-off with the He-162 – just 10 days before the war's end! This damned madness! He had been my *Rottenführer* in my early days at the front. After our conversion in late summer 1942 onto the Fw 190, I was assigned more to fly reconnaissance missions over the sea as *Rottenführer*. He had become the *Staffelführer* of 5/*JG 1* after *Leutnant* Tschira, the incumbent, had crashed fatally after returning from a mission (21 June 1943).[242] I was then transferred to the *Ergänzungsjagdgruppe* at Cazaux as instructor and saw Kirschner again only in February 1944 in the 5th *Staffel*. He briefly visited me in the hospital after I lost my leg, before the *Gruppe* moved to the area of Paderborn. Since then I have never had contact again with any *Staffel* member – a pity. His grave is in the cemetery at Leck/ North Friesland.'

Even though he was no longer able to fly active operations after being shot down and wounded in May 1943, *Oberleutnant* Otto Stammberger continued to serve in *JG 26* on their staff. As a result, he was aware of what was happening and was also in constant contact with the pilots, many of whom were his friends. He thus provides the impartial viewpoint of someone who understood exactly what the issues were for the ordinary line pilots. His brief account below makes it clear that once the Battle of Germany got going, there was no way out for the *Luftwaffe* nor for the vast majority of its fighter pilots either; basically, things would only get worse. His comments on the approach of the controllers to directing the fighters are very interesting and reflect also the 'doctrine' that attack from the rear was to be pushed at all costs:

In 1944 the American bomber streams flew almost always on the same course into Germany, from which they broke away in different directions to attack a variety of targets. Our aircraft received a built-in apparatus (Y system) that sent back a recognisable signal when radar waves hit the aircraft, so that the controller always knew where his own fighters were. Then the pilots received orders to fly specific courses and were continuously directed further. This was necessary as the USAAF also flew above cloud cover, so that we no longer had any view of the earth anymore to orientate ourselves. However as in the control centres they only monitored bomber formations and not the enemy fighters, we were always vulnerable to the US fighters – after all, we were mostly vectored along a generally long curved line from behind the bomber formations! After we had suffered large losses due to this idiotic controlling approach, our air leaders refused to obey the directions any more in 1945. In the final days directing of our fighters onto the bomber streams was abandoned by the high command and we merely flew cover over the airfields for the jet fighters, again with high losses!

# 8

# Conclusions

This volume attempts to provide an overview of the Second World War experiences and memories of *Luftwaffe* fighter pilot veterans who flew in the west from September 1939 to June 1944 within a framework of factual data derived from original records and post-war research. Any examination of the *Luftwaffe*, or the German armed forces as a whole, is coloured by the stain of association with the Nazi regime and its xenophobia, its industrial-scale campaign of slave labour and murder, and its philosophy of ethnic cleansing. The vast majority of the members of the German armed forces were well aware of the Holocaust and the atrocities. Whatever any individual fighter pilot may have known, witnessed directly or denied knowing vehemently, he was serving an evil regime even if fighting for his country as a 'pure patriot'. However, this being said, the German pilots were very brave, fought as hard as they could for their country, and in the end were defeated by an overpowering superiority. Hitler and his high commanders had prepared only for a short war; they had to win early on or basically not at all. In this context, the relevance of the Battle of Britain is enhanced – if it had been lost, all of Hitler's aims might have been fulfilled.

The *Luftwaffe* experienced its peak operational strength at the opening of the assault on France and the Low Countries in May 1940, and the importance of German aircrew and aircraft combat losses there should not be forgotten. While RAF losses were also heavy, they were replaced much faster as the Air Staff had always envisaged a long war and heavy attrition. The British economy, unlike its German counterpart, was running on a war footing already, reserves of aircraft were in place, and the repair system was much better organised, flexible and efficient than that of the *Luftwaffe*.[1]

The decline of German air strength was exacerbated in the Battle of Britain when they were defeated in a planned and prepared battle of attrition, led by the inimitable Air Chief Marshal Sir Hugh Dowding of Fighter Command and his most important subordinate, Air Vice-Marshal Keith Park; both were fired within weeks of achieving this crucial and historic victory. It was particularly the loss of peacetime-trained aircrew and unit leaders over England that was to prove critical for the *Luftwaffe* in the future. Dowding and Park's focus on stopping and breaking up bomber formations rather than aiming for fighter-*versus*-fighter combat forced the German Me 109s to fight regularly, and not just when they were in an ideal position for their favoured tactics of bouncing and zoom-climbing. By early September 1940 the cumulative Me 109 losses had become very serious, and by the middle of the month bomber sorties were limited by the smaller number of serviceable escort fighters available. Ironically, then, it was shortage of fighters that led to the cessation of the *Luftwaffe*'s daytime bomber attacks. German production of Me 109s lagged British fighter production, and was lower than losses. The outnumbered RAF fighters tended to fare better when employed in smaller and more nimble attacking formations which were often harder to spot. This also minimised their overall casualties, even though individual squadrons would be badly mauled on occasion. The flawed and arrogant 'short war' concept of the German political leadership, plus incompetence in higher *Luftwaffe* leadership, had ensured a shock defeat.

The German obsession with aces and numbers of enemy aircraft shot down, with all decorations graded and tightly correlated with scores, meant that it became the *Jagdwaffe* norm to aim for a successful bounce from higher altitude, to shoot accurately at close range (preferably from just below and behind your victim) and then to zoom-climb back to the protection offered by your comrades, who had stayed above as an umbrella. This method favoured the leaders of the units at all scales, whose hapless wingmen were there to be shot at, protect your tail and confirm the almost inevitable victory.

Incompetent air force leadership, however was not a German preserve. While the invasion of Russia in 1941 absorbed most German fighter strength, in the west along the Channel coast, two *Geschwadern* held the fort against a resurgent RAF Fighter Command in 1941–42. Now led by prominent detractors of their two victorious predecessors, an offensive 'Trenchardian' RAF philosophy ensured that the two western *Geschwadern* were faced with plentiful targets, obligingly flying in large, unwieldy fighter formations to protect minimal numbers of mostly light bombers attacking targets of minor importance. The *Jagdflieger* exacted a high price in British casualties for their own fairly limited losses. In many ways it was the Battle of Britain in reverse. As their enemy's bombers were not a real factor in this ridiculous RAF campaign, the *Jagdwaffe* achieved a true tactical and strategic victory over the Channel coast. As the US four-engined bomber incursions began, this comfortable Channel war began to fall apart. Interestingly, the German fighters during 1941–42 applied Keith Park's successful defensive dictum of attacking large and unwieldy RAF formations with smaller formations of their own.

The American daylight bombing offensive over northern France, from small beginnings in August 1942, moved to attacks on Germany itself in 1943 and rapidly expanded into the major air battle of the war, absorbing most of the *Jagdgruppen* from other theatres into defending the 'centre', or the Home Front as it became known. The *Experten*, whether from the western (Channel), southern or Eastern Fronts, were faced by a new dilemma with the large and tight formations of well-armed and relatively fast and high-flying four-engined bombers. There was no point trying to bounce them, and only by getting in close and firing hard and long could they be damaged or dispatched. Attacks from the rear, previously effective against almost all bombers met, were too costly. A new tactic soon emerged: attacking from head-on, where the bombers were much more vulnerable. However, it required a great deal of skill as the firing time was minimal due to the high closing speeds, and the breakaway, normally down beneath the formation, had to be timed very carefully. It was also soon realised that head-on attacks were only effective when between four and eight aircraft (shades of Keith Park again!) attacked – using any more was senseless, as they could not fire effectively. A peak in *Luftwaffe* effectiveness was reached on two raids against the Schweinfurt ball-bearing industry, on 17 August and 14 October 1943, when application of all available single-engined fighters, and even the vulnerable *Zerstörer* and some night fighters, plus ever heavier guns and also rockets, together caused unbearable losses to the American bombers. The only solution was long-range escort, where the available P-47 Thunderbolts and longer-ranged but mechanically less reliable P-38 Lightnings were not adequate for deep-penetration raids. It was the upgraded Merlin-engined P-51 Mustang, a superb aircraft with the necessary range, that changed everything.

The cumulative effects of this long battle of attrition, from August 1942 through to the invasion of Normandy in June 1944, wore down the *Jagdwaffe*; casualties to its irreplaceable leaders at all levels were the real problem, as supplies of machines and poorly trained youngsters were well enough maintained. Over the period from late 1943 to May 1944, air superiority over Germany and France passed to the Americans. This was the critical factor that allowed the invasion on 6 June 1944. The *Jagdflieger* did achieve many successes against the bombers, but never enough in the end, and at too great a cost to themselves. The air war in the west had been irretrievably lost.

# Notes

## Preface

1. Nowarra, Heinz J., *The Messerschmitt 109: A famous German fighter* (Letchworth: Harleyford Publications Ltd., 1966), p. 12.
2. ibid.
3. Braatz, Kurt, *Gott oder ein Flugzeug* (Moosburg, Germany: NeunundzwanzigSechs Verlag, 2005), pp. 265–7.
4. Read, Anthony, *The Devil's Disciples* (London: Pimlico, Random House, 2004).
5. Suchenwirth, Richard, *Historical turning points in the German Air Force war effort* (Maxwell Air Force Base, Alabama: USAF Historical Division, Research Studies Institute, Air University, 1959). USAF Historical Studies No. 189 (13 introductory pages and 143; translated from the original German). Accessed via webpage of the Air Force Historical Research Agency: www.afhra.af.mil/studies/numberedusafhistoricalstudies151-200. asp. p. 14 details Nazi influence in the *Luftwaffe*; Kesselring, Albert, *The memoirs of Field-Marshal Kesselring* (Stroud: The History Press, 2015). A reprint of the original, published first in 1953; see p. 26 for influence of National Socialism in the *Luftwaffe*.
6. Rosenbaum, Ron, *Explaining Hitler: the search for the origins of his evil* (London: Macmillan, 1998).
7. Segev, Tom, *Soldiers of Evil* (New York: Berkely Books, 1991).
8. Evans, Richard, *The Third Reich at War* (London: Penguin, 2009).
9. Rall, Günther, *Mein Flugbuch* (Moosburg: NeunundzwanzigSechs Verlag, 2004). p. 222 details the ignorance in question.
10. Gilbert, Martin, *Second World War* (London: Weidenfeld and Nicolson, 1989).

## 1 Poland

1. Bekker, Cajus, *Angriffshöhe 4000. Die deutsche Luftwaffe im Zweiten Weltkrieg* (Munich: Wilhelm Heyne Verlag, 1967).

2. Dierich, Wolfgang, *Die Verbände der Luftwaffe 1935–1945* (Stuttgart: Motorbuch Verlag, 1976).

3. Bekker, Cajus, *op. cit.*

4. Bob, Hans-Ekkehard, *Betrayed Ideals. Memoirs of a Luftwaffe fighter ace* (Bristol: Cerberus Publishing, 2004).

5. Möbius, Ingo, *Am Himmel Europas. Der Jagdflieger Günther Scholz erinnert sich* (Chemnitz: Eigenverlag Ingo Möbius, 2009).

6. Bekker, Cajus, *op. cit.*

7. Throughout the book data for German losses are derived essentially from the *Luftwaffe* Quartermaster General Loss Returns, and for confirmed victory claims mostly from the lists first published on the web by Tony Wood: *Tony Wood's Combat Claims and Casualties Lists;* accessed via Don Caldwell's website: don-caldwell.we.bs/claims/tonywood.htm (with many succeeding repeats and relatively minor edits by fellow historians).

8. Kesselring, Albert, *The memoirs of Field-Marshal Kesselring* (Stroud: The History Press, 2015); a reprint of the original, published first in 1953. The event is detailed on p. 47.

9. Stargardt, Nicholas, *The German War* (London: The Bodley Head, 2015).

10. *ibid.*

11. *ibid.*

12. *ibid.*

13. Bekker, Cajus, *op. cit.*

## 2 Denmark and Norway

1. McKinstry, Leo, *Hurricane. Victor of the Battle of Britain* (London: John Murray, 2011).

2. McKinstry, Leo, *op. cit*; Prien, Jochen, *Geschichte des Jagdgeschwaders 77, Teil 1, 1934–1941* (Eutin: Struve-Druck, 1992).

3. Prien, Jochen, *op. cit*; Dierich, Wolfgang, *Die Verbände der Luftwaffe 1935–1945* (Stuttgart: Motorbuch Verlag, 1976); Bekker, Cajus, *Angriffshöhe 4000: Die deutsche Luftwaffe im Zweiten Weltkrieg* (Munich: Wilhelm Heyne Verlag, 1967).

4. www.raf.mod.uk/history/rafhistorytimeline1940.cfm

5. Bekker, Cajus, *op. cit.*

6. *ibid.*

7. ww2db.com/battle_spec.php?battle_id=93

8. *ibid.*

9. McKinstry, Leo, *op. cit.*

10. www.epibreren.com/ww2/raf/index.html (46 Squadron history accessed).

11. McKinstry, Leo, *op. cit*; www.epibreren.com/ww2/raf/index.html

12. Prien, Jochen, *op. cit.*

13. Middlebrook, Martin and Everitt, Chris, *The Bomber Command War Diaries* (Harmondsworth: Viking, Penguin, 1985).

14. Prien, Jochen, *op. cit.*

15. *ibid.*

16. *ibid.*

17. *ibid.*
18. *ibid.*
19. *ibid.*
20. Prien, Jochen and Rodeike, Peter, *Jagdgeschwader 1 und 11. Einsatz in der Reichsverteidigung von 1939 bis 1945, Teil 1, 1939–1943* (Eutin: Struve Druck, 1993).
21. Prien, Jochen, *Geschichte des Jagdgeschwaders 77, Teil 2, 1941–1942* (Eutin: Struve-Druck, 1993).
22. Prien, Jochen, 1992, *op. cit.*
23. *ibid.*
24. *ibid.*
25. *ibid.*

## 3 The Phoney War

1. Cornwell, Peter, *The Battle of France: then and now* (Old Harlow: Battle of Britain International Ltd., 2007).
2. Middlebrook, Martin and Everitt, Chris, *The Bomber Command War Diaries* (Harmondsworth: Viking, Penguin, 1985).
3. *ibid.*
4. British Wellington bombers were not armed with cannons, only with 0.303 inch machine guns.
5. Throughout the book data for German losses are derived essentially from the *Luftwaffe* Quartermaster General Loss Returns, and for confirmed victory claims mostly from the lists first published on the web by Tony Wood: *Tony Wood's Combat Claims and Casualties Lists;* accessed via Don Caldwell's website: don-caldwell.we.bs/claims/tonywood.htm (with many succeeding repeats and relatively minor edits by fellow historians).
6. Middlebrook, Martin, *op. cit.*
7. Cornwell, Peter, *op. cit.*
8. *ibid.*
9. *ibid.*
10. *ibid.*
11. *ibid.*
12. *ibid.*
13. *ibid.*

## 4 Invasion of France and the Low Countries

1. Cornwell, Peter, *The Battle of France then and now* (Old Harlow: Battle of Britain International Ltd., 2007); Cull, Brian, Lander, Bruce and Weiss, Heinrich, *Twelve Days in May* (London: Grub Street, 1999); Wood, Derek and Dempster, Derek, *The Narrow Margin* (London: Arrow Books, 1969); Jackson, Robert, *Air War over France May-June 1940* (London: Ian Allan, 1974).
2. Cull, Brian, *op. cit.*
3. *ibid.*
4. Cornwell, Peter, *op. cit*; Cull, Brian, *op. cit.*

5. Wood, Derek, *op. cit.*

6. Cornwell, Peter, *op. cit*; Cull, Brian, *op. cit.*

7. Cull, Brian, *op. cit.*

8. Jackson, Robert, *op. cit.*

9. Cull, Brian, *op. cit.*

10. *ibid.*

11. Cornwell, Peter, *op. cit*; Prien, Jochen, *Geschichte des Jagdgeschwaders 77, Teil 1, 1934–1941* (Eutin: Struve-Druck, 1992); Weal, John, *Jagdgeschwader 2 'Richthofen'* (Oxford: Osprey Publishing, 2000); Aders, Gebhard and Held, Werner, *Jagdgeschwader 51 'Mölders'* (Stuttgart: Motorbuch Verlag, 1985); Prien, Jochen and Stemmer, Gerhard, *Messerschmitt Bf 109 im Einsatz bei der II./Jagdgeschwader 3* (Eutin: Struve-Druck, 1996).

12. Cornwell, Peter, *op. cit.*

13. *ibid.*

14. *ibid.*

15. *ibid.*

16. *ibid.*

17. *ibid.*

18. Young, Peter (ed.), *The World Almanac Book of World War II* (New York: World Almanac Publications, 1981).

19. Cornwell, Peter, *op. cit.*

20. Jackson, Robert, *op. cit.*

21. *ibid.*

22. *ibid.*

23. *ibid.*

24. *ibid.*

25. Cornwell, Peter, *op. cit.*

26. *ibid.*

27. *ibid.*

28. Terraine, John, *The Right of the Line* (Ware: Wordsworth Editions Ltd., 1997).

29. Cornwell, Peter, *op. cit.*

30. *ibid.*

31. *ibid.*

32. Data for confirmed victory claims mostly from the lists first published on the web by Tony Wood: *Tony Wood's Combat Claims and Casualties Lists;* accessed via Don Caldwell's website: don-caldwell.we.bs/claims/tonywood. htm (with many succeeding repeats and relatively minor edits by fellow historians). These claims lists are not complete and contain gaps, some large also, especially for certain Me 110 units in 1940; however, they do reflect accredited victory claims and not just submitted and unverified claims.

33. *ibid.*

34. Obermaier, Ernst, *Die Ritterkreuzträger der Luftwaffe* (Mainz: Verlag Dieter Hoffmann, 1966).

35. *ibid.*

36. *ibid.*

37. *ibid.*
38. Note 32, *op. cit.*


## 5 The Battle Of Britain

1. Klee, Karl, *Operation SEA LION and the role of the Luftwaffe in the planned invasion of England* (Maxwell Air Force Base, Alabama: USAF Historical Division, Research Studies Institute, Air University, 1955). USAF Historical Studies No. 157 (translated from the original German). Accessed via webpage of the Air Force Historical Research Agency: www.afhra.af.mil/studies/numberedusafhistoricalstudies151-200.asp.
2. *ibid.*
3. *ibid.*
4. *ibid.*
5. *ibid.*
6. *ibid.*
7. Wood, Derek and Dempster, Derek, *The Narrow Margin* (London: Arrow Books, 1967).
8. *ibid.*
9. Wood, Derek, *op. cit*; Mason, Francis K., *Battle over Britain* (London: McWhirter Twins, 1969); Orange, Vincent, *Dowding of Fighter Command* (London: Grub Street, 2011); Dowding, Air Chief Marshal Sir Hugh C.T., Air Officer Commanding-in-Chief, Fighter Command, RAF, *The Battle of Britain* (London: HMSO, 1946). Supplement to the *London Gazette* of 10 September 1946, pp. 4543–4571, published on 11 September 1946 as a Despatch by Dowding.
10. Orange, Vincent, *Park: the biography of Air Chief Marshal Sir Keith Park* (London: Grub Street, 2013).
11. Orange, Vincent, 2011, *op. cit*; Orange, Vincent, 2013, *op. cit*; Dowding, Air Chief Marshal Sir Hugh, *op. cit.*
12. Wood, Derek, *op. cit*; Mason, Francis K., *op. cit*; Orange, Vincent, 2011, *op. cit*; Orange, Vincent, 2013, *op. cit.*
13. Wood, Derek, *op. cit*; Mason, Francis K., *op. cit*; Orange, Vincent, 2011, *op. cit*; Orange, Vincent, 2013, *op. cit*; Dowding, Air Chief Marshal Sir Hugh, *op. cit.*
14. Wood, Derek, *op. cit.*
15. Mason, Francis K., *op. cit.*
16. Dye, Air Commodore Peter, *The Royal Air Force Air Power Review* (3/4 Winter 2000). *Logistics in the Battle of Britain*, vol. 3/no. 4, pp. 15–36.
17. Klee, Karl, *op. cit*; Wood, Derek, *op. cit*; Mason, Francis K., *op. cit*; Orange, Vincent, 2011, *op. cit*; Orange, Vincent, 2013, *op. cit*; Dowding, Air Chief Marshal Sir Hugh, *op. cit.*
18. Mitcham, Samuel, *Eagles of the Third Reich* (Manchester: Crécy Publishing, 2010).
19. *ibid.*
20. *ibid.*

21. Cornwell, Peter D., *The Battle of France then and now* (Old Harlow: Battle of Britain International, 2007); Cull, Brian, Lander, Bruce and Weiss, Heinrich, *Twelve Days in May* (London: Grub Street, 1999).

22. Cornwell, Peter D., *op. cit.*

23. Cull, Brian, *op. cit.*

24. Suchenwirth, Richard, *Historical turning points in the German Air Force war effort* (Maxwell Air Force Base, Alabama: USAF Historical Division, Research Studies Institute, Air University, 1959). USAF Historical Studies No. 189 (13 introductory pages and 143; translated from the original German). Accessed via webpage of the Air Force Historical Research Agency: www.afhra.af.mil/studies/numberedusafhistoricalstudies151-200.asp

25. *ibid.*

26. Dye, Air Commodore Peter, *op. cit.*

27. Mason, Francis K., *op. cit.*

28. Holm, Michael, webpage, *The Luftwaffe, 1933–1945*; www.ww2.dk

29. Barbas, Bernd, *Die Geschichte der III. Gruppe des Jagdgeschwaders 52* (Überlingen: self-published, undated). (Official edition of the *Traditionsgemeinschaft JG 52*).

30. Barbas, Bernd, *Die Geschichte der II. Gruppe des Jagdgeschwaders 52* (Überlingen: self-published, undated). (Official edition of the *Traditionsgemeinschaft JG 52*).

31. Holm, Michael, *op. cit.*

32. Prien, Jochen and Stemmer, Gerhard, *Messerschmitt Bf 109 im Einsatz bei der III./Jagdgeschwader 3* (Eutin: Struve-Druck, 1995).

33. Prien, Jochen and Stemmer, Gerhard, *Messerschmitt Bf 109 im Einsatz bei der II./Jagdgeschwader 3, 1940–1945* (Eutin: Struve-Druck, 1996).

34. *ibid.*

35. Prien, Jochen, *Geschichte des Jagdgeschwaders 77, Teil 1, 1934–1941* (Eutin, Germany: Struve-Druck, 1992).

36. Mason, Francis K., *op. cit*; Holm, Michael, *op. cit.*

37. Mason, Francis K., *op. cit.*

38. Holm, Michael, *op. cit.*

39. *ibid.*

40. Ramsey, Winston. G. (ed.), *The Battle of Britain: then and now* (London: Battle of Britain Prints International Ltd., 1982).

41. Orange, Vincent, 2011, *op. cit.*

42. Ramsey, Winston. G., *op. cit.*

43. Holm, Michael, *op. cit.*

44. Ramsey, Winston. G., *op. cit.*

45. Mason, Francis K., *op. cit.*

46. Data for confirmed victory claims mostly from the lists first published on the web by Tony Wood: *Tony Wood's Combat Claims and Casualties Lists;* accessed via Don Caldwell's website: don-caldwell.we.bs/claims/tonywood.htm (with many succeeding repeats and relatively minor edits by fellow historians). These claims lists are not complete and contain

gaps, some large also, especially for certain Me 110 units in 1940; however, they do reflect accredited victory claims and not just submitted and unverified claims.

47. *ibid.*

48. Prien, Jochen, 1995, *op. cit.*

49. Steinhilper, Ulrich and Osborne, Peter, *Spitfire on my tail* (Bromley: Independent Books, 2009).

50. Klee, Karl, *op. cit.*

51. Mason, Francis K., *op. cit.*

52. Wood, Derek, *op. cit*; Mason, Francis K., *op. cit*; Ramsey, Winston. G., *op. cit*; Parker, Nigel, *Luftwaffe Crash Archive,* Vol. 1 (Walton on Thames: Red Kite Books, Air Research Publications, 2013); Parker, Nigel, *Luftwaffe Crash Archive,* Vol. 2 (Walton on Thames: Red Kite Books, Air Research Publications, 2013).

53. Wood, Derek, *op. cit*; Mason, Francis K., *op. cit.*

54. Mason, Francis K., *op. cit*; Ramsey, Winston. G., *op. cit*; Parker, Nigel, Vol. 1, *op. cit*; Parker, Nigel, Vol. 2, *op. cit*; Parker, Nigel, *Luftwaffe Crash Archive,* Vol. 3 (Walton on Thames: Red Kite Books, Air Research Publications, 2013); Parker, Nigel, *Luftwaffe Crash Archive,* Vol. 4 (Walton on Thames: Red Kite Books, Air Research Publications, 2014).

55. Mason, Francis K., *op. cit.*

56. Holm, Michael, *op. cit.*

57. Bekker, Cajus, *Angriffshöhe 4000. Die deutsche Luftwaffe im Zweiten Weltkrieg* (Munich: Wilhelm Heyne Verlag, 1967).

58. *ibid.*

59. Ramsey, Winston. G., *op. cit.*

60. Wood, Derek, *op. cit*; Mason, Francis K., *op. cit*; Ramsey, Winston. G., *op. cit.*

61. Ramsey, Winston. G., *op. cit*; Parker, Nigel, Vol. 3, *op. cit.*

62. *ibid.*

63. *ibid.*

64. Orange, Vincent, 2013, *op. cit.*

65. Price, Alfred, *The Hardest Day; the Battle of Britain 18 August 1940* (London: Arrow Books, 1990).

66. Price, Alfred, *Battle of Britain Day; 15 September 1940* (London: Sidgwick and Jackson, 1990).

67. Suchenwirth, Richard, *op. cit.*

68. Prien, Jochen, 1992, *op. cit.*

69. Suchenwirth, Richard, *op. cit.*

70. *ibid.*

71. Dye, Air Commodore Peter, *op. cit.*

72. Ramsey, Winston. G., *op. cit*; Parker, Nigel, Vol. 3, *op. cit*; Parker, Nigel, Vol. 4, *op. cit.*

73. Bungay, Stephen, *The Most Dangerous Enemy* (London: Aurum Press, 2009).

74. Orange, Vincent, 2011, *op. cit*; Orange, Vincent, 2013, *op. cit*; Dowding, Air Chief Marshal Sir Hugh, *op. cit.*
75. Mason, Francis K., *op. cit.*
76. Mason, Francis K., *op. cit*; Orange, Vincent, 2011, *op. cit.*
77. Mason, Francis K., *op. cit.*
78. Barbas, Bernd, *Die Geschichte der I. Gruppe des Jagdgeschwaders 52* (Überlingen: self-published, undated). (Official edition of the *Traditionsgemeinschaft JG 52*).
79. Steinhilper, Ulrich, *op. cit.*
80. Ramsey, Winston. G., *op. cit.*
81. Barbas, Bernd, *III. Gruppe, op. cit.*
82. Ramsey, Winston. G., *op. cit.*
83. Parker, Nigel, Vol. 4, *op. cit.*
84. Holm, Michael, *op. cit.*
85. Note 46, *op. cit.*
86. Dowding, Air Chief Marshal Sir Hugh, *op. cit.*
87. Parker, Nigel, *Luftwaffe Crash Archive*, Vol. 6 (Walton on Thames: Red Kite Books, Air Research Publications, 2014).
88. *ibid.*
89. Mason, Francis K., *op. cit.*
90. Dowding, Air Chief Marshal Sir Hugh, *op. cit.*
91. Note 46, *op. cit.*
92. *ibid.*
93. Weal, John, *Jagdgeschwader 2 'Richthofen'* (Oxford: Osprey Publishing, 2000).
94. Mason, Francis K., *op. cit.*
95. Bungay, Stephen, *op. cit.*
96. *ibid.*
97. *ibid.*
98. *ibid.*
99. *ibid.*
100. Weal, John, *op. cit*; Federl, Christian, *Jagdgeschwader 2 "Richthofen"* (Zweibrücken: VDM Heinz Nickel, 2006).
101. Prien, Jochen, 1995, *op. cit*; Prien, Jochen, 1996, *op. cit*; Prien, Jochen and Stemmer, Gerhard, *Messerschmitt Bf 109 im Einsatz bei Stab und I./Jagdgeschwader 3* (Eutin: Struve-Druck, 1997).
102. Caldwell, Donald L., *JG 26: top guns of the Luftwaffe* (New York: Orion Books, 1991); Caldwell, Donald L., *JG 26 Luftwaffe Fighter Wing Diary, 1939–1942*, Vol. 1 (Mechanicsburg: Stackpole Books, 2012); Caldwell, Donald L., *JG 26 Luftwaffe Fighter Wing Diary, 1943–1945*, Vol. 2 (Mechanicsburg: Stackpole Books, 2012).
103. Ring, Hans and Girbig, Werner, *Jagdgeschwader 27, Die Dokumentation über den Einsatz an allen Fronten 1939–1945* (Stuttgart: Motorbuch Verlag, 1975).
104. Prien, Jochen, 1992, *op. cit*; Aders, Gebhard and Held, Werner *Jagdgeschwader 51 'Mölders'* (Stuttgart: Motorbuch Verlag, 1985); Prien,

Jochen, *Geschichte des Jagdgeschwaders 77, Teil 4, 1944–1945* (Eutin: Struve-Druck, 1995).

105. Barbas, Bernd, *III. Gruppe, op. cit*; Barbas, Bernd, *II. Gruppe, op. cit*; Barbas, Bernd, *I. Gruppe, op. cit.*

106. Prien, Jochen, 1992, *op. cit*; Prien, Jochen, 1995, *JG 77, Teil 4, op. cit.*

107. Prien, Jochen, 1992, *op. cit.*

108. Prien, Jochen, *Pik-As: Geschichte des Jagdgeschwaders 53, Teil 1* (Illertissen: Flugzeug Publikations, 1989); Prien, Jochen, *Pik-As: Geschichte des Jagdgeschwaders 53, Teil 3* (Eutin: Struve-Druck, 1991).

109. Held, Werner, Trautloft, Hannes and Bob, Ekkehard, *Die Grünherzjäger: Bildchronik des Jagdgeschwaders 54* (Friedberg: Podzun-Pallas-Verlag, 1985).

110. Federl, Christian, *op. cit.*

111. Prien, Jochen, 1995, *III/JG 3, op. cit*; Prien, Jochen, 1996, *op. cit*; Prien, Jochen, 1997, *op. cit.*

112. Caldwell, Donald L., 1991, *op. cit*; Caldwell, Donald L., 2012, Vol. 1, *op. cit*; Caldwell, Donald L., 2012, Vol. 2, *op. cit.*

113. Ring, Hans, *op. cit.*

114. Aders, Gebhard, *op. cit.*

115. Barbas, Bernd, *III. Gruppe, op. cit*; Barbas, Bernd, *II. Gruppe, op. cit*; Barbas, Bernd, *I. Gruppe, op. cit.*

116. Prien, Jochen, 1992, *op. cit.*

117. Prien, Jochen, 1989, *op. cit.*

118. Rosipal, Gunther, *JG 54* loss list. Downloaded from www.jps-net/wartburg/ LossList htm on 03.07.2000 (homepage of *JG 54*, Bob Wartburg).

119. Prien, Jochen, 1992, *op. cit.*

120. Note 46, *op. cit.*

121. *ibid.*

122. Bungay, Stephen, *op. cit.*

123. Note 46, *op. cit.*

124. Bungay, Stephen, *op. cit.*

# 6 The Channel Front, 1941–42

1. Data for confirmed (by the German Air Ministry) victory claims mostly from the lists first published on the web by Tony Wood: *Tony Wood's Combat Claims and Casualties Lists;* accessed via Don Caldwell's website: don-caldwell.we.bs/claims/tonywood.htm (with many succeeding repeats and relatively minor edits by fellow historians). These claims lists are not complete and contain gaps, some large also, especially for certain Me 110 units in 1940; however, they do reflect accredited victory claims and not just submitted and unverified claims which were sent in by the individual fighter units. The statistics for 1941 claims in the relevant table were mainly derived from unit histories (submitted rather than confirmed claims).

2. Caldwell, Donald L., *JG 26 Luftwaffe Fighter Wing Diary, 1939–1942*, Vol. 1 (Mechanicsburg: Stackpole Books, 2012); Prien, Jochen and Rodeike, Peter, *Jagdgeschwader 1 und 11. Einsatz in der Reichsverteidigung von*

*1939 bis 1945, Teil 1, 1939–1943* (Eutin: Struve Druck, 1993); Weal, John, *Jagdgeschwader 2 'Richthofen'* (Oxford: Osprey Publishing, 2000); Prien, Jochen, *Pik-As: Geschichte des Jagdgeschwaders 53, Teil 1* (Illertissen: Flugzeug Publikations, 1989); Caldwell, Donald L., *JG 26 Luftwaffe Fighter Wing Diary, 1943–1945,* Vol. 2 (Mechanicsburg: Stackpole Books, 2012); Federl, Christian, *Jagdgeschwader 2 "Richthofen"* (Zweibrücken: VDM Heinz Nickel, 2006).

3. Sims, Edward H., *The Fighter Pilots* (London: Cassell, 1968).
4. *ibid.*
5. Weal, John, *op. cit.*
6. Copy of combat report (*Gefechtsbericht*) held by Bundesarchiv-Militärarchiv Freiburg, Germany, via Otto Schmid.
7. Prien, Jochen, *Pik-As: Geschichte des Jagdgeschwaders 53, Teil 3* (Eutin: Struve-Druck, 1991).
8. Mitcham, Samuel, *Eagles of the Third Reich* (Manchester: Crécy Publishing, 2010).
9. Extract from the diary of *Oberfähnrich* Hans Strelow, 5/JG 51; Prof. P. R. Skawran who was a *Luftwaffe* psychologist spent time with various fighter units. While with JG 51 he copied several diary entries from Strelow's private effects after his death in action. Some of these he provided to the author.
10. Caldwell, Donald L., 2012, Vol. 1, *op. cit*; Caldwell, Donald L., 2012, Vol. 2, *op. cit.*
11. *Geschwader Ehrenbuch JG 26,* multiple volumes, held by the Bundesarchiv-Militärarchiv in Freiburg Germany (reference: 10/265–275); copies of some individual reports supplied via Lothair Vanoverbeke.
12. *ibid.*
13. Caldwell, Donald L., 2012, Vol. 1, *op. cit.*
14. Prien, Jochen, 1989, *op. cit.*
15. *ibid.*
16. Franks, Norman, *The Greatest Air Battle: Dieppe, 19th August 1942* (London: William Kimber, 1979).
17. Caldwell, Donald L., 2012, Vol. 1, *op. cit*; Franks, Norman, *op. cit.*
18. Caldwell, Donald L., 2012, Vol. 1, *op. cit.*
19. Franks, Norman, *op. cit.*
20. Note 11, *op. cit.*
21. Caldwell, Donald L., 2012, Vol. 1, *op. cit.*
22. Vaittinen, Juha, *The lengths of the RAF operational tours,* article on his webpage: juhansotahistoriasivut.weebly.com.
23. Prien, Jochen, 1993, *op. cit.*
24. Prien, Jochen, 1993, *op. cit*; Obermaier, Ernst, *Die Ritterkreuzträger der Luftwaffe* (Mainz: Verlag Dieter Hoffmann, 1966).
25. *ibid.*
26. Goss, Chris, *Luftwaffe Fighter-Bombers over Britain* (Manchester: Crécy Publishing, 2013).
27. *ibid.*
28. *ibid.*

29. *ibid.*
30. Note 11, *op. cit.*
31. Caldwell, Donald L., 2012, Vol. 1, *op. cit.*
32. Caldwell, Donald L., 2012, Vol. 1, *op. cit*; Caldwell, Donald L., 2012, Vol. 2, *op. cit.*
33. Caldwell, Donald L., 2012, Vol. 1, *op. cit*; Obermaier, Ernst, *op. cit.*
34. de Zeng, Henry L. IV and Stankey, Douglas G., *Luftwaffe Officer Career Summaries* (2014 updated version). Accessed via Michael Holm's website, *The Luftwaffe 1933–1945*: www.ww2.dk; this source at www.ww2.dk/lwoffz.html.
35. Caldwell, Donald L., 2012, Vol. 2, *op. cit.*
36. Caldwell, Donald L., 2012, Vol. 1, *op. cit*; Caldwell, Donald L., 2012, Vol. 2, *op. cit.*
37. *ibid.*
38. *ibid.*
39. de Zeng, Henry, *op. cit.*
40. Freeman, Roger A., *Mighty Eighth War Diary* (London: Jane's, 1981).
41. *ibid.*

## 7 The Battle of Germany, August 1942–June 1944

1. Caldwell, Donald L., *Day Fighters in Defence of the Reich; a War Diary, 1942-45* (Barnsley: Frontline Books, 2011).
2. *ibid.*
3. Freeman, Roger A., *Mighty Eighth War Diary* (London: Jane's, 1981).
4. Holm, Michael, webpage, *The Luftwaffe, 1933-1945*; www.ww2.dk
5. Caldwell, Donald L., *op. cit.*
6. *ibid.*
7. Freeman, Roger A., *op. cit.*
8. Reschke, Willi, *Jagdgeschwader 301/302 "Wilde Sau"* (Atglen: Schiffer Publishing, 2005).
9. Holm, Michael, *op. cit*; Lexikon der Wehrmach webpage, Kommandobehörden der Luftwaffe (Luft); www.lexikon-der-Wehrmacht.de/Gliederungen/KommandoLwL.htm; Caldwell, Donald L., *op. cit.*
10. *ibid.*
11. Caldwell, Donald L., *op. cit.*
12. Holm, Michael, *op. cit.*
13. Holm, Michael, *op. cit*; Lexikon, *op. cit*; Caldwell, Donald L., *op. cit.*
14. Caldwell, Donald L., *op. cit.*
15. Holm, Michael, *op. cit.*
16. Holm, Michael, *op. cit*; Lexikon, *op. cit*; Caldwell, Donald L., *op. cit.*
17. *ibid.*
18. Holm, Michael, *op. cit.*
19. *ibid.*
20. *ibid.*
21. *ibid.*
22. *ibid.*

23. *ibid.*
24. *ibid.*
25. Holm, Michael, *op. cit*; Lexikon, *op. cit*; Caldwell, Donald L., *op. cit.*
26. *ibid.*
27. Caldwell, Donald L., *op. cit.*
28. Crawley, Aidan, *Escape from Germany* (London: Corgi Books, 1968).
29. Knoke, Heinz, *I flew for the Führer* (London: Corgi Books, 1966).
30. Freeman, Roger A., *The Mighty Eighth; a history of the U.S. 8th Army Air Force* (London: Macdonald and Jane's, 1976).
31. Caldwell, Donald L., *op. cit*; Freeman, Roger A., 1981, *op. cit.*
32. Caldwell, Donald L., *op. cit.*
33. *ibid.*
34. Holm, Michael, *op. cit.*
35. *ibid.*
36. Weal, John, *Jagdgeschwader 2 'Richthofen'* (Oxford: Osprey Publishing, 2000).
37. Weal, John, *op. cit*; Freeman, Roger A., 1981, *op. cit*; Freeman, Roger A., 1976, *op. cit.*
38. Weal, John, *op. cit*; Freeman, Roger A., 1976, *op. cit.*
39. Freeman, Roger A., 1976, *op. cit.*
40. Bergström, Christer with Antipov, Vlad and Sundin, Claes, *Graf and Grislawski: A pair of aces* (Hamilton: Eagle Editions, 2003).
41. Weal, John, *op. cit.*
42. Holm, Michael, *op. cit*; Caldwell, Donald L., *op. cit.*
43. *ibid.*
44. *ibid.*
45. Holm, Michael, *op. cit.*
46. Caldwell, Donald L., *op. cit*; Freeman, Roger A., 1981, *op. cit*; Freeman, Roger A., 1976, *op. cit.*
47. Price, Alfred, *Battle over the Reich* (Shepperton: Ian Allan, 1973).
48. Westermann, Edward B., *Defending Hitler's Reich: German ground-based air defences, 1914–1945* (University of North Carolina: PhD dissertation, 2000). Issued as Report No. FY00–259 by the Department of the (US) Air Force; 380 pp.
49. *ibid.*
50. Caldwell, Donald L., *op. cit*; Freeman, Roger A., 1981, *op. cit*; Freeman, Roger A., 1976, *op. cit.*
51. *ibid.*
52. Caldwell, Donald L., *op. cit.*
53. Priller, Josef, *J.G. 26: Geschichte eines Jagdgeschwaders* (Stuttgart: Motorbuch Verlag, 1980).
54. Holm, Michael, *op. cit*; Caldwell, Donald L., *op. cit.*
55. Holm, Michael, *op. cit*; Dierich, Wolfgang, *Die Verbände der Luftwaffe 1935–1945* (Stuttgart: Motorbuch Verlag, 1976).
56. Holm, Michael, *op. cit.*
57. Caldwell, Donald L., *op. cit.*

58. Holm, Michael, *op. cit*; Caldwell, Donald L., *op. cit.*

59. Caldwell, Donald L., *op. cit.*

60. Holm, Michael, *op. cit.*

61. Holm, Michael, *op. cit*; Weal, John, *op. cit.*

62. Freeman, Roger A., 1976, *op. cit.*

63. Caldwell, Donald L., *op. cit.*

64. *ibid.*

65. *ibid.*

66. *ibid.*

67. *ibid.*

68. Morris, Danny, *Aces and Wingmen; the men and machines of the USAAF Eighth Fighter Command 1943–45* (London: Neville Spearman, 1972).

69. Freeman, Roger A., 1976, *op. cit.*

70. *ibid.*

71. Morris, Danny, *op. cit.*

72. Freeman, Roger A., 1976, *op. cit.*

73. Freeman, Roger A., 1976, *op. cit*; Morris, Danny, *op. cit.*

74. Freeman, Roger A., 1976, *op. cit.*

75. Overy, Richard, *The Bombing War; Europe 1939–1945* (London: Allen Lane, Penguin Books, 2013).

76. Caldwell, Donald L., *JG 26 Luftwaffe Fighter Wing Diary, 1943–1945*, Vol. 2 (Mechanicsburg: Stackpole Books, 2012); Priller, Josef, *op. cit*; Obermaier, Ernst, *Die Ritterkreuzträger der Luftwaffe* (Mainz: Verlag Dieter Hoffmann, 1966).

77. Overy, Richard, *op. cit.*

78. Freeman, Roger A., 1976, *op. cit.*

79. *ibid.*

80. *ibid.*

81. *ibid.*

82. *ibid.*

83. *ibid.*

84. *ibid.*

85. Freeman, Roger A., 1976, *op. cit*; Overy, Richard, *op. cit.*

86. Freeman, Roger A., 1976, *op. cit.*

87. Prien, Jochen and Rodeike, Peter, *Jagdgeschwader 1 und 11. Einsatz in der Reichsverteidigung von 1939 bis 1945, Teil 1, 1939–1943* (Eutin: Struve Druck, 1993).

88. *ibid.*

89. Caldwell, Donald L., 2011, *op. cit.*

90. *ibid.*

91. *ibid.*

92. Prien, Jochen, *op. cit.*

93. Middlebrook, Martin and Everitt, Chris, *The Bomber Command War Diaries* (Harmondsworth: Viking, Penguin, 1985).

94. *ibid.*

95. Prien, Jochen, *op. cit.*

96. Copy of combat report (*Gefechtsbericht*) held by Bundesarchiv-Militärarchiv Freiburg, Germany, via Otto Schmid.
97. Caldwell, Donald L., 2011, *op. cit*; Freeman, Roger A., 1976, *op. cit*; Overy, Richard, *op. cit.*
98. Caldwell, Donald L., 2011, *op. cit.*
99. Bob, Hans-Ekkehard, *Betrayed Ideals; memoirs of a Luftwaffe fighter ace* (Bristol: Cerberus Publishing, 2004).
100. *ibid.*
101. Caldwell, Donald L., 2011, *op. cit.*
102. Obermaier, Ernst, *op. cit.*
103. Caldwell, Donald L., 2011, *op. cit.*
104. Caldwell, Donald L., 2011, *op. cit*; Bergström, Christer, *op. cit.*
105. *ibid.*
106. Holm, Michael, *op. cit*; Caldwell, Donald L., 2011, *op. cit*; Bergström, Christer, *op. cit.*
107. Bergström, Christer, *op. cit.*
108. Caldwell, Donald L., 2011, *op. cit.*
109. Lorant, Jean-Yves and Goyat, Richard, *Jagdgeschwader 300 "Wilde Sau"*, *Vol. 1, June 1943–September 1944* (Hamilton: Eagle Editions, 2005).
110. *ibid.*
111. Holm, Michael, *op. cit.*
112. *ibid.*
113. Caldwell, Donald L., 2011, *op. cit.*
114. *ibid.*
115. *ibid.*
116. *ibid.*
117. *ibid.*
118. Freeman, Roger A., 1976, *op. cit.*
119. Freeman, Roger A., 1981, *op. cit.*
120. Caldwell, Donald L., 2011, *op. cit.*
121. Coffey, Thomas M., *Decision over Schweinfurt* (London: Robert Hale, 1978).
122. Caldwell, Donald L., 2011, *op. cit.*
123. *ibid.*
124. *ibid.*
125. Caldwell, Donald L., 2011, *op. cit*; Freeman, Roger A., 1976, *op. cit.*
126. Caldwell, Donald L., 2011, *op. cit.*
127. *ibid.*
128. *ibid.*
129. Coffey, Thomas M., *op. cit.*
130. Caldwell, Donald L., 2011, *op. cit.*
131. *ibid.*
132. *Geschwader Ehrenbuch JG 26*, multiple volumes, held by the Bundesarchiv-Militärarchiv in Freiburg Germany (reference: 10/265–275); copies of some individual reports supplied via Lothair Vanoverbeke.
133. Caldwell, Donald L., 2012, *op. cit.*

134. *Geschwader Ehrenbuch*, *op. cit.*
135. Caldwell, Donald L., 2012, *op. cit.*
136. *ibid.*
137. Caldwell, Donald L., 2011, *op. cit*; Freeman, Roger A., 1981, *op. cit*; Freeman, Roger A., 1976, *op. cit.*
138. Caldwell, Donald L., 2011, *op. cit.*
139. *ibid.*
140. Coffey, Thomas M., *op. cit.*
141. *ibid.*
142. Caldwell, Donald L., 2011, *op. cit.*
143. *ibid.*
144. Caldwell, Donald L., 2011, *op. cit*; Freeman, Roger A., 1981, *op. cit.*
145. Caldwell, Donald L., 2011, *op. cit.*
146. Caldwell, Donald L., 2011, *op. cit*; Freeman, Roger A., 1981, *op. cit.*
147. Caldwell, Donald L., 2011, *op. cit.*
148. *ibid.*
149. Freeman, Roger A., 1981, *op. cit.*
150. *ibid.*
151. *ibid.*
152. Caldwell, Donald L., 2011, *op. cit.*
153. Freeman, Roger A., 1981, *op. cit.*
154. Caldwell, Donald L., 2011, *op. cit.*
155. *ibid.*
156. *ibid.*
157. *ibid.*
158. Schmid, Josef and Grabmann, Walter, *The German Air Force versus the Allies in the West, the Air War in the West (Part I, The Air War over Reich territory by Day and Night, 15 September 1943 to 31 December 1943)* (Maxwell Air Force Base, Alabama: USAF Historical Division, Research Studies Institute, Air University, 1954). USAF Historical Studies No. 158 (109 pp.; translated from the original German). Accessed via webpage of the Air Force Historical Research Agency: www.afhra.af.mil/studies/numberedusafhistoricalstudies151-200.asp
159. Caldwell, Donald L., 2011, *op. cit.*
160. Coffey, Thomas M., *op. cit.*
161. Holm, Michael, *op. cit.*
162. Holm, Michael, *op. cit*; Caldwell, Donald L., 2011, *op. cit*; Prien, Jochen and Stemmer, Gerhard, *Messerschmitt Bf 109 im Einsatz bei der II./Jagdgeschwader 3, 1940–1945* (Eutin: Struve-Druck, 1996).
163. Prien, Jochen, 1996, *op. cit.*
164. *ibid.*
165. *ibid.*
166. *ibid.*
167. *ibid.*
168. *ibid.*

169. Lorant, Jean-Yves, *op. cit*; Prien, Jochen, 1993, *op. cit*; Weal, John, *op. cit*;
     Prien, Jochen and Stemmer, Gerhard, *Messerschmitt Bf 109 im Einsatz bei
     Stab und I./Jagdgeschwader 3* (Eutin: Struve-Druck, 1997); Prien, Jochen,
     1996, *op. cit*; Caldwell, Donald L., 2012, *op. cit*; Priller, Josef, *op. cit*;
     Aders, Gebhard and Held, Werner *Jagdgeschwader 51 'Mölders'* (Stuttgart:
     Motorbuch Verlag, 1985); Rosipal, Gunther, *JG 54 loss list*. Downloaded
     from www.jps-net/wartburg/LossList htm on 03.07.2000 (homepage of
     *JG 54*, Bob Wartburg); Prien, Jochen and Stemmer, Gerhard, *Messerschmitt
     Bf 109 im Einsatz bei der III./Jagdgeschwader 3* (Eutin: Struve-Druck, 1995);
     Prien, Jochen, *Pik-As: Geschichte des Jagdgeschwaders 53, Teil 3* (Eutin:
     Struve-Druck, 1991); Ring, Hans and Girbig, Werner, *Jagdgeschwader
     27, Die Dokumentation über den Einsatz an allen Fronten 1939–1945*
     (Stuttgart: Motorbuch Verlag, 1975).
170. Caldwell, Donald L., 2011, *op. cit*.
171. Holm, Michael, *op. cit*; Caldwell, Donald L., 2011, *op. cit*.
172. Freeman, Roger A., 1981, *op. cit*; Freeman, Roger A., 1976, *op. cit*.
173. *ibid*.
174. Overy, Richard, *op. cit*.
175. *ibid*.
176. Freeman, Roger A., 1981, *op. cit*; Overy, Richard, *op. cit*.
177. Freeman, Roger A., 1981, *op. cit*.
178. Overy, Richard, *op. cit*.
179. Holm, Michael, *op. cit*; Caldwell, Donald L., 2011, *op. cit*.
180. Holm, Michael, *op. cit*; Lorant, Jean-Yves, *op. cit*; Reschke, Willi, *op. cit*;
     Aders, Gebhard, *op. cit*.
181. Lorant, Jean-Yves, *op. cit*; Reschke, Willi, *op. cit*.
182. Holm, Michael, *op. cit*; Caldwell, Donald L., 2011, *op. cit*.
183. Holm, Michael, *op. cit*.
184. Caldwell, Donald L., 2011, *op. cit*.
185. *ibid*.
186. *ibid*.
187. *ibid*.
188. *ibid*.
189. Price, Alfred, *op. cit*.
190. Caldwell, Donald L., 2011, *op. cit*.
191. *ibid*.
192. *ibid*.
193. *ibid*.
194. Morris, Danny, *op. cit*.
195. Caldwell, Donald L., 2011, *op. cit*.
196. Freeman, Roger A., 1981, *op. cit*; Freeman, Roger A., 1976, *op. cit*.
197. Fry, Garry L. and Ethell, Jeffrey L., *Escort to Berlin; the 4th Fighter Group
     in World War II* (New York: Arco Publishing, 1980).
198. Caldwell, Donald L., 2011, *op. cit*.
199. Neitzel, Sönke and Welzer, Harald, *Soldaten: on fighting, killing and dying*
     (London: Simon and Schuster, 2012).

200. Prien, Jochen and Rodeike, Peter, *Jagdgeschwader 1 und 11. Einsatz in der Reichsverteidigung von 1939 bis 1945, Teil 2, 1944* (Eutin: Struve Druck, undated).

201. Prien, Jochen, undated, *op. cit*; Neitzel, Sönke, *op. cit*.

202. Caldwell, Donald L., 2011, *op. cit*; Prien, Jochen, undated, *op. cit*.

203. Neitzel, Sönke, *op. cit*; Caldwell, Donald L., 2011, *op. cit*; Prien, Jochen, undated, *op. cit*.

204. Holm, Michael, *op. cit*.

205. Prien, Jochen, 1993, *op. cit*; Prien, Jochen, undated, *op. cit*.

206. Holm, Michael, *op. cit*; Prien, Jochen, undated, *op. cit*.

207. Prien, Jochen, 1993, *op. cit*; Prien, Jochen, undated, *op. cit*.

208. Mombeek, Eric, *Defending the Reich; the history of Jagdgeschwader 1 "Oesau"* (Drayton: JAC Publications, 1992).

209. Prien, Jochen, 1993, *op. cit*; Prien, Jochen, undated, *op. cit*.

210. Mombeek, Eric, *op. cit*.

211. Caldwell, Donald L., 2011, *op. cit*.

212. *ibid.*

213. Caldwell, Donald L., 2011, *op. cit*; Obermaier, Ernst, *op. cit*.

214. Caldwell, Donald L., 2011, *op. cit*.

215. Yenne, Bill, *Big Week; six days that changed the course of World War II* (New York: Berkley Caliber, 2013).

216. Caldwell, Donald L., 2011, *op. cit*.

217. *ibid.*

218. Prien, Jochen, 1997, *op. cit*.

219. Prien, Jochen, 1996, *op. cit*.

220. Holm, Michael, *op. cit*.

221. Prien, Jochen, 1996, *op. cit*.

222. *ibid.*

223. Prien, Jochen, 1997, *op. cit*.

224. *ibid.*

225. *ibid.*

226. Caldwell, Donald L., 2011, *op. cit*; Freeman, Roger A., 1981, *op. cit*; Freeman, Roger A., 1976, *op. cit*.

227. Prien, Jochen, 1993, *op. cit*; Prien, Jochen, undated, *op. cit*; Data for confirmed (by the German Air Ministry) victory claims mostly from the lists first published on the web by Tony Wood: *Tony Wood's Combat Claims and Casualties Lists;* accessed via Don Caldwell's website: don-caldwell. we.bs/claims/tonywood.htm (with many succeeding repeats and relatively minor edits by fellow historians). These claims lists are not complete and contain gaps, some large also, especially for certain Me 110 units in 1940 and later; however, they do reflect accredited victory claims and not just submitted and unverified claims which were sent in by the individual fighter units. See also many other unit histories in the bibliography to support this point.

228. Caldwell, Donald L., 2011, *op. cit*.

229. Freeman, Roger A., 1981, *op. cit*.

230. 8th Air Force Historical Society website: www.8thafhs.com; 20th Fighter Group page on this website.
231. Prien, Jochen, 1993, *op. cit*; Prien, Jochen, undated, *op. cit.*
232. Copy of combat report (*Gefechtsbericht*) held by Bundesarchiv-Militärarchiv Freiburg, Germany, via Otto Schmid.
233. *ibid.*
234. Prien, Jochen, undated, *op. cit.*
235. *ibid.*
236. *ibid.*
237. Freeman, Roger A., 1976, *op. cit*; Morris, Danny, *op. cit.*
238. Mombeek, Eric, *op. cit*; Weal, John, *op. cit.*
239. *ibid.*
240. Obermaier, Ernst, *op. cit.*
241. Prien, Jochen, 1993, *op. cit*; Prien, Jochen, undated, *op. cit*; Mombeek, Eric, *op. cit.*
242. Caldwell, Donald L., 2011, *op. cit*; Prien, Jochen, 1993, *op. cit.*

## 8 Conclusions

1. Dye, Air Commodore Peter, *The Royal Air Force Air Power Review* (3/4 Winter 2000). *Logistics in the Battle of Britain*, vol. 3/no. 4, pp. 15–36.

# Bibliography

Aders, Gebhard and Held, Werner, *Jagdgeschwader 51 'Mölders'* (Stuttgart: Motorbuch Verlag, 1985)

Barbas, Bernd, *Die Geschichte der I. Gruppe des Jagdgeschwaders 52* (Überlingen: self-published, undated)

Barbas, Bernd, *Die Geschichte der II. Gruppe des Jagdgeschwaders 52* (Überlingen: self-published, undated)

Barbas, Bernd, *Die Geschichte der III. Gruppe des Jagdgeschwaders 52* (Überlingen: self-published, undated)

Bekker, Cajus, *Angriffshöhe 4000. Die deutsche Luftwaffe im Zweiten Weltkrieg* (Munich: Wilhelm Heyne Verlag, 1967)

Bergström, Christer with Antipov, Vlad and Sundin, Claes, *Graf and Grislawski: A pair of aces* (Hamilton: Eagle Editions, 2003)

Bob, Hans-Ekkehard, *Betrayed Ideals. Memoirs of a Luftwaffe fighter ace* (Bristol: Cerberus Publishing, 2004)

Braatz, Kurt, *Gott oder ein Flugzeug* (Moosburg, Germany: NeunundzwanzigSechs Verlag, 2005)

Bungay, Stephen, *The Most Dangerous Enemy* (London: Aurum Press, 2009)

Caldwell, Donald L., *JG 26: Top guns of the Luftwaffe* (New York: Orion Books, 1991)

Caldwell, Donald L., *Day Fighters in Defence of the Reich; a War Diary, 1942–45* (Barnsley: Frontline Books, 2011)

Caldwell, Donald L., *JG 26 Luftwaffe Fighter Wing Diary, 1939–1942*, Vol. 1 (Mechanicsburg: Stackpole Books, 2012)

Caldwell, Donald L., *JG 26 Luftwaffe Fighter Wing Diary, 1943–1945*, Vol. 2 (Mechanicsburg: Stackpole Books, 2012)

Coffey, Thomas M., *Decision over Schweinfurt* (London: Robert Hale, 1978)

Cornwell, Peter, *The Battle of France: then and now* (Old Harlow: Battle of Britain International Ltd., 2007)

Crawley, Aidan, *Escape from Germany* (London: Corgi Books, 1968)

Cull, Brian, Lander, Bruce and Weiss, Heinrich, *Twelve Days in May* (London: Grub Street, 1999)

Dierich, Wolfgang, *Die Verbände der Luftwaffe 1935–1945* (Stuttgart: Motorbuch Verlag, 1976)

Dowding, Air Chief Marshal Sir Hugh C. T., *The Battle of Britain* (London: HMSO, 1946)

Dye, Air Commodore Peter, *The Royal Air Force Air Power Review* (3/4 Winter 2000)

Evans, Richard, *The Third Reich at War* (London: Penguin, 2009)

Federl, Christian, *Jagdgeschwader 2 "Richthofen"* (Zweibrücken: VDM Heinz Nickel, 2006)

Franks, Norman, *The Greatest Air Battle: Dieppe, 19th August 1942* (London: William Kimber, 1979)

Freeman, Roger A., *The Mighty Eighth; a history of the U.S. 8th Army Air Force* (London: Macdonald and Jane's, 1976)

Freeman, Roger A., *Mighty Eighth War Diary* (London: Jane's, 1981)

Fry, Garry L. and Ethell, Jeffrey L., *Escort to Berlin; the 4th Fighter Group in World War II* (New York: Arco Publishing, 1980)

Gilbert, Martin, *Second World War* (London: Weidenfeld and Nicolson, 1989)

Goss, Chris, *Luftwaffe Fighter-Bombers over Britain* (Manchester: Crécy Publishing, 2013)

Held, Werner, Trautloft, Hannes and Bob, Ekkehard, *Die Grünherzjäger: Bildchronik des Jagdgeschwaders 54* (Friedberg: Podzun-Pallas-Verlag, 1985)

Jackson, Robert, *Air War over France May–June 1940* (London: Ian Allan, 1974)

Kesselring, Albert, *The Memoirs of Field-Marshal Kesselring* (Stroud: The History Press, 2015)

Klee, Karl, *Operation SEA LION and the role of the Luftwaffe in the planned invasion of England* (Maxwell Air Force Base, Alabama: USAF Historical Division, Research Studies Institute, Air University, 1955)

Knoke, Heinz, *I flew for the Führer* (London: Corgi Books, 1966)

Lorant, Jean-Yves and Goyat, Richard, *Jagdgeschwader 300 "Wilde Sau", Volume One, June 1943–September 1944* (Hamilton: Eagle Editions, 2005)

Mason, Francis K., *Battle over Britain* (London: McWhirter Twins, 1969)

McKinstry, Leo, *Hurricane. Victor of the Battle of Britain* (London: John Murray, 2011)

Middlebrook, Martin and Everitt, Chris, *The Bomber Command War Diaries* (Harmondsworth: Viking, Penguin, 1985)

Mitcham, Samuel, *Eagles of the Third Reich* (Manchester: Crécy Publishing, 2010)

Möbius, Ingo, *Am Himmel Europas. Der Jagdflieger Günther Scholz erinnert sich* (Chemnitz: Eigenverlag Ingo Möbius, 2009)

Mombeek, Eric, *Defending the Reich; the history of Jagdgeschwader 1 "Oesau"* (Drayton: JAC Publications, 1992)

Morris, Danny, *Aces and Wingmen; the men and machines of the USAAF Eighth Fighter Command 1943–45* (London: Neville Spearman, 1972)

Neitzel, Sönke and Welzer, Harald, *Soldaten: on fighting, killing and dying* (London: Simon and Schuster, 2012)

Obermaier, Ernst, *Die Ritterkreuzträger der Luftwaffe* (Mainz: Verlag Dieter Hoffmann, 1966)

Orange, Vincent, *Dowding of Fighter Command* (London: Grub Street, 2011)

Orange, Vincent, *Park; the biography of Air Chief Marshal Sir Keith Park* (London: Grub Street, 2013)

Overy, Richard, *The Bombing War; Europe 1939–1945* (London: Allen Lane, Penguin Books, 2013)

Parker, Nigel, *Luftwaffe Crash Archive*, Vol. 1 (Walton on Thames: Red Kite Books, Air Research Publications, 2013)

Parker, Nigel, *Luftwaffe Crash Archive*, Vol. 2 (Walton on Thames: Red Kite Books, Air Research Publications, 2013)

Parker, Nigel, *Luftwaffe Crash Archive*, Vol. 3 (Walton on Thames: Red Kite Books, Air Research Publications, 2013)

Parker, Nigel, *Luftwaffe Crash Archive*, Vol. 4 (Walton on Thames: Red Kite Books, Air Research Publications, 2014)

Parker, Nigel, *Luftwaffe Crash Archive*, Vol. 6 (Walton on Thames: Red Kite Books, Air Research Publications, 2014)

Price, Alfred, *Battle over the Reich* (Shepperton: Ian Allan, 1973)

Price, Alfred, *The Hardest Day; the Battle of Britain 18 August 1940* (London: Arrow Books, 1990)

Price, Alfred, *Battle of Britain Day; 15 September 1940* (London: Sidgwick and Jackson, 1990)

Prien, Jochen, *Pik-As: Geschichte des Jagdgeschwaders 53, Teil 1* (Illertissen: Flugzeug Publikations, 1989)

Prien, Jochen, *Pik-As: Geschichte des Jagdgeschwaders 53, Teil 3* (Eutin: Struve-Druck, 1991)

Prien, Jochen, *Geschichte des Jagdgeschwaders 77, Teil 1, 1934–1941* (Eutin: Struve-Druck, 1992)

Prien, Jochen, *Geschichte des Jagdgeschwaders 77, Teil 2, 1941–1942* (Eutin: Struve-Druck, 1993)

Prien, Jochen, *Geschichte des Jagdgeschwaders 77, Teil 4, 1944–1945* (Eutin: Struve-Druck, 1995)

Prien, Jochen and Rodeike, Peter, *Jagdgeschwader 1 und 11. Einsatz in der Reichsverteidigung von 1939 bis 1945, Teil 1, 1939–1943* (Eutin: Struve Druck, 1993)

Prien, Jochen and Rodeike, Peter, *Jagdgeschwader 1 und 11. Einsatz in der Reichsverteidigung von 1939 bis 1945, Teil 2, 1944* (Eutin: Struve Druck, undated)

Prien, Jochen and Stemmer, Gerhard, *Messerschmitt Bf 109 im Einsatz bei der III./Jagdgeschwader 3* (Eutin: Struve-Druck, 1995)

Prien, Jochen and Stemmer, Gerhard, *Messerschmitt Bf 109 im Einsatz bei der II./Jagdgeschwader 3* (Eutin: Struve-Druck, 1996)

Prien, Jochen and Stemmer, Gerhard, *Messerschmitt Bf 109 im Einsatz bei Stab und I./Jagdgeschwader 3* (Eutin: Struve-Druck, 1997)

Priller, Josef, *J. G. 26: Geschichte eines Jagdgeschwaders* (Stuttgart: Motorbuch Verlag, 1980)

Rall, Günther, *Mein Flugbuch* (Moosburg, Germany: NeunundzwanzigSechs Verlag, 2004)

Ramsey, Winston. G. (ed.), *The Battle of Britain: then and now* (London: Battle of Britain Prints International Ltd, 1982)

Read, Anthony, *The Devil's Disciples* (London: Pimlico, Random House, 2004)

Reschke, Willi, *Jagdgeschwader 301/302 "Wilde Sau"* (Atglen: Schiffer Publishing, 2005)

Ring, Hans and Girbig, Werner, *Jagdgeschwader 27, Die Dokumentation über den Einsatz an allen Fronten 1939–1945* (Stuttgart: Motorbuch Verlag, 1975)

Rosenbaum, Ron, *Explaining Hitler: the search for the origins of his evil* (London: Macmillan, 1998)

Schmid, Josef and Grabmann, Walter, *The German Air Force versus the Allies in the West, the Air War in the West (Part I, The Air War over Reich territory by Day and Night, 15 September 1943 to 31 December 1943)* (Maxwell Air Force Base, Alabama: USAF Historical Division, Research Studies Institute, Air University, 1954)

Segev, Tom, *Soldiers of Evil* (New York: Berkely Books, 1991)

Sims, Edward H., *The Fighter Pilots* (London: Cassell, 1968)

Stargardt, Nicholas, *The German War* (London: The Bodley Head, 2015)

Steinhilper, Ulrich and Osborne, Peter, *Spitfire on my tail* (Bromley: Independent Books, 2009)

Suchenwirth, Richard, *Historical turning points in the German Air Force war effort* (Maxwell Air Force Base, Alabama: USAF Historical Division, Research Studies Institute, Air University, 1959)

Terraine, John, *The Right of the Line* (Ware: Wordsworth Editions Ltd, 1997)

Weal, John, *Jagdgeschwader 2 'Richthofen'* (Oxford: Osprey Publishing, 2000)

Westermann, Edward B., *Defending Hitler's Reich: German ground-based air defences, 1914–1945* (Chapel Hill: University of North Carolina, PhD dissertation, 2000)

Wood, Derek and Dempster, Derek, *The Narrow Margin* (London: Arrow Books, 1969)

Yenne, Bill, *Big Week; six days that changed the course of World War II* (New York: Berkley Caliber, 2013)

Young, Peter (ed.), *The World Almanac Book of World War II* (New York: World Almanac Publications, 1981)

## Web Pages

deZeng, Henry L. IV and Stankey, Douglas G., *Luftwaffe Officer Career Summaries* (2014 updated version); www.ww2.dk/lwoffz.html

Eighth Air Force Historical Society; www.8thafhs.com (20th Fighter Group page on this website)

Holm, Michael, *The Luftwaffe, 1933–1945*; www.ww2.dk

Lexikon der Wehrmacht; www.lexikon-der-Wehrmacht.de/Gliederungen/KommandoLwL.htm (Kommandobehörden der Luftwaffe (Luft) page on this website)

Rosipal, Gunther, *JG 54 loss list* (downloaded 3 July 2000); www.jps-net/wartburg/LossList htm (homepage of *JG 54*, Bob Wartburg)

Royal Air Force, Ministry of Defence; www.raf.mod.uk/history/rafhistorytimeline1940.cfm

Traces of World War 2; www.epibreren.com/ww2/raf/index.html; (webpage of Bart F. M. Droog)

Vaittinen, Juha, *The lengths of the RAF operational tours;* juhansotahistoriasivut.weebly.com.

Wood, Tony, *Tony Wood's Combat Claims and Casualties Lists;* don-caldwell.we.bs/claims/tonywood.htm

World War II Database; ww2db.com/battle_spec.php?battle_id=93

# Acknowledgements

*Oberst* Hanns Trübenbach, erstwhile *Kommodore* of *JG 52* and senior controller in charge of *Jafu-Mittelrhein*, a key part of the defence of Germany from 1943 to 1944, was a true old-world gentleman who provided me with a wealth of fact and opinion, and kindly gave me his own copies of several important books, long out of print. *Feldwebel* Otto Schmid of *II/JG 1* served along the Channel and over Germany before losing a leg in combat; he described his experiences in great detail, with copies from his logbooks, official combat reports of his *Gruppe* and documents from colleagues. *Oberleutnant* Otto Stammberger, *II* and *III/JG 26*, veteran of fighting over the Channel and Germany, was another generous source of information, photographs and documents. Three other treasured witnesses were *Oberfeldwebel* Artur Dau, *7/JG 51*, *Oberstleutnant* Günther Scholz and *Leutnant* Dr Max Clerico both of *7/JG 54*, who all provided detailed insights into operations over France in 1940 and the Battle of Britain. I consider myself extremely fortunate to have gotten to know these men well, and to have become friends with them. They were special people and together with the other witnesses made this book possible.

Many of the Luftwaffe veterans went out of their way to answer my innumerable questions and supplied me with honest and forthright opinions on many aspects of their war experiences. This is no easy thing for most veterans of any conflict to do, as it tends to reactivate long-dormant memories they have no wish to recall. Those not already mentioned are listed and thanked below. *Oberleutnant* Franz Achleitner, *III/JG 3*; *Major* Hans-Ekkehard Bob, *III/JG 54*;

*Oberleutnant* Walter Bohatsch, *I* and *II/JG* 3; *Major* Erhard Braune, *III/JG* 27; *Feldwebel* Fritz Buchholz, *II/ZG* 76; *Hauptmann* Josef Bürschgens, *I* and *III/JG* 26; *Oberleutnant* Günter Büsgen, *I/JG* 52; *Oberstleutnant* Georg Christl, *ZG* 2, *III/ZG* 26; *Hauptmann* Emil Clade, *III/JG* 27; *Unteroffizier* Alois Dierkes, *V/LG* 1; *Oberleutnant* Fritz Engau, *I/JG* 11; *Hauptmann* Rudolf Engleder, *I/JG* 1; *Oberst* Wolfgang Falck, *I/ZG* 76, *I/ZG* 1; *Major* Horst Geyer, *Stab/JG* 51, *EKdo* 25; *Oberleutnant* Adolf Glunz, *II/JG* 26; *Oberleutnant* Gerhard Granz, *I/ZG* 2; *Oberleutnant* Hans-Theodor Grisebach, *I/JG* 2; *Hauptmann* Alfred Grislawski, *JG* 50, *I* and *III/JG* 1; *Oberleutnant* Hans Grünberg, *II/JG* 3; *Hauptmann* Alfred Hammer, *II/JG* 53; *Hauptmann* Hans-R. Hartigs, *JG* 2, *I/JG* 26; *Oberleutnant* Alfred Heckmann, *II/JG* 3, *I/JG* 26; *Unteroffizier* Johann Heinrich, *II/ZG* 76; *Oberstleutnant* Hans-Joachim Jabs, *II/ZG* 76, night fighters; *Leutnant* Gerhard Keppler, *I/JG* 27; *Obergefreiter* Pay Kleber, *III/JG* 2; *Major* Dr Heinz Lange, *III/JG* 54; *Hauptmann* Theodor Lindemann, *III/JG* 26; *Unteroffizier* Heinz Ludwig, *I/ZG* 26; *Oberleutnant* Werner Ludwig, *III/ZG* 26; *Gefreiter* Rudolf Miese, *II/JG* 2; *Oberleutnant* Victor Mölders, *I/ZG* 1, *I/JG* 51; *Hauptmann* Johannes Naumann, *II* and *III/JG* 26; *Leutnant* Josef Neuhaus, *II/ZG* 26; *Oberfeldwebel* Helmut Notemann, *II/JG* 3; *Feldwebel* Fritz Oeltjen, *III/JG* 54; *Oberfeldwebel* Georg Pavenzinger, *I/JG* 51; *Unteroffizier* Rudolf Petzold, *I/ZG* 76; *Feldwebel* Horst Petzschler, *I/JG* 3; *Hauptmann* Werner Pichon-Kalau vom Hofe, *III/JG* 51; *Hauptmann* Rolf Pingel, *I* and *III/JG* 53, *I/JG* 26; *Oberleutnant* Alfons Raich, *III/JG* 3; *Leutnant* Alfred Rauch, *II/JG* 51; *Oberfeldwebel* Ernst Richter, *II/JG* 11; *Oberfeldwebel* Joachim Robel, *II/ZG* 76, *I/ZG* 1; *Oberst* Gustav Rödel, *Stab/JG* 27; *Major* Erich Rudorffer, *I* and *II/JG* 2; *Leutnant* Dr Felix Sauer, *II/JG* 53; *Major* Gerhard Schöpfel, *III* and *Stab/JG* 26; *Hauptmann* Georg Schröder, *I* and *II/JG* 2; *Leutnant* Jochen Schröder, *II/ZG* 1, *III/ZG* 76; *Unteroffizier* Karl Siedenbiedel, *II/JG* 2; *Major* Wolfgang Späte, *IV/JG* 54; Hauptmann Ulrich Steinhilper, *I/JG* 52; *Oberstleutnant* Hennig Strümpel, *I/JG* 2; *Hauptmann* Paul Temme, *I/JG* 2; *Leutnant* Gerhard Wiegand, *II/JG* 26.

Two other people meriting special mention and thanks are Juha Vaittinen, a Finnish air historian who supplied documents from Finnish archives for both Finnish and German air forces, and Lothair Vanoverbeke, Belgian air historian and well-published author who kindly sent me much material and many photographs from his own extensive *Luftwaffe* contacts and researches, particularly for *JG* 26.

I owe both of them a large debt of gratitude. Donald Caldwell, noted historian and author of an excellent study of the Battle of Germany, helped with material and advice. My final individual acknowledgement is to Professor Paul Robert Skawran, a psychologist in the *Luftwaffe*. He had spent a large part of the war with diverse units and famous pilots, and being an experienced psychologist was able to provide insights into their characters, achievements and failings in great depth. He also had considerable documentary material with which he was exceptionally generous.

Shaun Barrington and Alex Bennett of Amberley Publishing are thanked sincerely for their encouragement and ongoing support. I also offer my heartfelt thanks to my wife, Mariánne, who is a talented writer and illustrator of her own series of children's books, and provided not only great support but also much inspiration, being much the better writer. My appreciation as well to my brother, Dr Andrew Eriksson, who helped considerably in many ways: storing back-ups, reading several chapters and scratching the surface of my ignorance of computers. A final thanks to my parents, who bought me many books when I was young and let me fly solo at age 15.

# Index

Achleitner, *Leutnant* Franz   101
air battles, specific raids
  Big Week   174, 266–7, 268,
    269–70
  Channel dash   153–4
  Dieppe landing   155–6
  Dunkirk   52–6
  Non-Stop Offensive   137, 141,
    143, 148, 166, 171
  Schweinfurt   173, 229–32,
    233, 234–5, 283
*Armée de l'Air* (French Air
  Force)   40, 63–4

Bader, Squadron Leader
  Douglas   112
Bär, *Oberstleutnant*
  Heinz   256–7
Blech, *Flieger* Georg   277
Bob, *Hauptmann*
  Hans-Ekkehard   23, 225, pl. 52
Bohatsch, *Oberleutnant*
  Walter   236, 267, 268–9
Brändle, *Major* Kurt   236, 238,
  239

Braune, *Oberleutnant*
  Erhard   24, 26, 63, 86, pl. 18
Buchholz, *Feldwebel* Fritz   262,
  263–5, pl. 61
Bürschgens, *Oberleutnant*
  Josef   33, 56, 77, 101–2, pl.
  7, 25
Büsgen, *Oberleutnant*
  Günter   111, 113

Christl, *Oberstleutnant*
  Georg   105, 203, 205, 310
Clade, *Feldwebel* Emil   54, 78, 310
Clerico, *Leutnant* Dr Max   7,
  23, 24–5, 40–1, 75–7, 102,
  309, pl. 13, 14, 26

Dau, *Oberfeldwebel* Artur   32,
  43–4, 56, 89, 91–2, 92–3,
  97–9, 309, pl. 20, 22
Dierkes, *Unteroffizier* Alois   24,
  31, 49, 115, 310
Dowding, Air Chief Marshal Sir
  Hugh   69–71, 110–11, 253,
  282

Ederer, *Oberfeldwebel*
Josef  143, 153
Eggers, *Oberleutnant* Leo  78
Engau, *Oberleutnant* Fritz  270,
272, 310
Engleder, *Hauptmann*
Rudolf  240, 256, 257, 310

Falck, *Hauptmann* Wolfgang  8,
26, 27, 49, 54, 310

Galland, *Generalmajor*
Adolf  13, 66, 76, 78, 81,
83, 86, 130–1, 147, 154, 163,
164–5, 203, 239, pl. 28
Galland, *Leutnant* Paul  154,
163–4, 166
Galland, *Major* Wilhelm-
Ferdinand 'Wutz'  165,
222–3, 231–2, pl. 50
*General der Jagdflieger* (General
of Fighters)  13, 66, 92, 163,
164, 269
Gentzen, *Hauptmann*
Johannes  24, 48
Geyer, *Hauptmann*
Horst  144–5, 204–5, 310
*Glorious,* HMS  27, 29
Glunz, *Oberleutnant* Adolf  144,
151–2, 168, 169–70, 196, 211,
310, pl. 45
Goebbels, Dr Josef  12
Gollob, *Oberst* Gordon  13, 187
Göring, *Reichsmarschall*
Hermann  12, 13, 23, 33,
41, 58–9, 71, 77, 79, 83, 85,
88, 121, 122, 123, 131, 143,
147–8, 184, 186–8, 191, 206,
226–9, 239, 253, 254, 256

Grabmann, *Oberst* Walter  72,
116, 186
Graf, *Major* Hermann  226, 230
Granz, *Oberleutnant*
Gerhard  23, 25, 48, 112,
310, pl. 28
Gray, Pilot Officer Colin  102
Grisebach, *Oberleutnant*
Hans-Theodor  32, 50, 95,
106, 310
Grislawski, *Hauptmann*
Alfred  194, 310
Grünberg, *Leutnant* Hans
'Specker'  238, 268, 269, 310

Hahn, *Oberleutnant* Hans
'Assi'  100, 120, pl. 30
Hammer, *Oberleutnant*
Alfred  255, 310
Handrick, *Oberst* Gotthard  72,
185–6
Hartigs, *Oberleutnant*
Hans  180, 310
Heckmann, *Unteroffizier*
Alfred  64, 79, 310
Heesen, *Oberfeldwebel*
Ernst  218, 223, 224, pl. 51
Heinrich, *Gefreiter* Johan  104,
116–17, 310, pl. 29
Herrmann, *Oberst* Hajo  226
Heydrich, *Obergruppenführer*
Reinhard  25, 29–30
Himmler, *Reichsführer*
Heinrich  12, 25
Hitler, Adolf  8, 13, 14, 24–5,
55, 62, 69, 77, 81, 188, 191,
233, 254, 263, 278, 281, pl.
3, 4
Holocaust (genocide)  14–15,
25–6

Ihlefeld, *Oberstleutnant*
  Herbert   60, 118, 130, 131,
  147, 226
Italian Air Force   129

Jabs, *Oberleutnant*
  Hans-Joachim   47, 67, 89,
  116, 310
*Jagdfliegerführer (Jafü)* (Fighter
  Leader/Controller)   11, 41–2,
  43, 72–3, 82, 88, 92, 108, 143,
  180–7, 189, 191, 199, 201,
  210, 224, 230–1, 232, 234,
  239, 242, 245, 247–8, 250,
  260, 269, 270, 274, 309

Kain, Flying Officer
  'Cobber'   39
Keppler, *Leutnant*
  Gerhard   206–7, 269–70, 310,
  pl. 62
Kesselring, *Generalfeldmarschall*
  Albert   25, 71, 72, 76, 85, 88,
  122
Kleber, *Obergefreiter* Pay   14,
  258, 310
Kornatzki, *Major* Hans-Günther
  von   254

Lange, *Oberleutnant* Dr
  Heinz   23–4, 49, 79, 102, 310
Leigh-Mallory, Air Vice-Marshal
  Trafford   70, 253
Leykauf, *Oberfeldwebel*
  Erwin   48, 102–103
Lindemann, *Oberleutnant*
  Theodor   153, 310
Ludwig, *Unteroffizier*
  Heinz   202–3, 249, 258–60,
  310

Ludwig, *Unteroffizier*
  Werner   100, 310, pl. 24
*Luftwaffe* (German Air Force)
  fighters
  attacks on US bombers
    use of night fighters   218
    use of training units   225,
    235, 240–2
  Battle of Germany, command
  structure   180–8, 190–2
  casualties
    Poland   26
    Phoney War   38
    Invasion of France   44–5,
    46–47, 57–8, 65
    Dunkirk   53
    Battle of Britain   109–10,
  113, 115, 132–4
    Sweeps 1941   139
    Dieppe   115–6
    *Jabo* attacks UK
  (1942–3)   163
    Germany   197–8, 207–8,
  233–4, 239–40, 249, 250–2
  comparison with enemy
  aircraft   48–9, 51, 54–5,
  89–90, 108, 113, 124, 166–9,
  174, 202–3, 209, 213–14, 249,
  258–60, 262–5, 272
  drop tanks   78, 85
  orders of battle
    Poland   22–3
    Denmark, Norway   27
    Invasion of France   41–3
    Battle of Britain   72–4,
  109
    Germany 1943   199–202
    Germany 1944   245–8
  *Sturmgruppen*   174, 225,
  254

tactics
  against RAF sweeps  137–9,
141, 149–50, 150–1
  against US bombers  175–8,
193–6, 203–7, 211–12,
214–16, 220–1, 227–8, 242–3,
244–5, 253–6, 267, 270–2
  bomber escorts over
Britain  83–5, 95, 102–4, 111,
114–15
  fighter-bombers (*Jabos*) over
Britain (1940)  121, 123–4,
124–5; (1942–3)  162–4
  victory claims, credits
    Poland  24
    Norway  28–30
    Phoney War  38
    Dunkirk  53
    Invasion of France  65–7
    Battle of Britain  130–1,
133, 135–6
    Sweeps 1941  139–40
    Dieppe  156
    Germany  197–8, 233–4,
250–1
    over-claiming  38–9, 136,
140, 257
  *Wilden Sau*  183, 188, 226,
245
  Y-system  224, 236–7, 260–1,
276, 279
Lützow, *Oberst* Günther  13, 82,
95, 187, 237, 239

Maltzahn, *Oberst* Günther
  Freiherr von  82, 187, pl. 16
Marseille, *Hauptmann*
  Hans-Joachim  90
Meimberg, *Leutnant* Julius  100,
120, 123

Messerschmitt fighter aircraft,
  designation Bf 109/Me
  109  11–12
Messerschmitt, Professor
  Willy  11–12, 77, 85
Miese, *Gefreiter* Rudolf  99–100,
119–21, 122–3, 128–9, 310,
pl. 23, 30
Milch, *Generalfeldmarschall*
  Erhard  41, 71, 79, 110
mission types, definitions
  (*Einsatz, Feindflug*)  159–60
Mölders, *Oberleutnant*
  Victor  22, 25, 46, 58–9, 92,
124, 310
Mölders, *Oberst* Werner  13, 22,
33, 38, 39, 66, 72, 82–3, 92,
97, 118, 124, 130, 131, 144–5,
164

Nacke, *Hauptmann* Heinz  67,
104, 116
National Socialist Flying Corps
  (NSFK)  14, 226
Naumann, *Hauptmann* Johannes
  'Hans'  8, 150–1, 165–6,
166–7, 196, 242–3, 310, pl. 56
Neuhaus, *Unteroffizier* Josef  79,
143, 310
Notemann, *Oberfeldwebel*
  Helmut  236, 238, 268, 310

Oeltjen, *Feldwebel* Fritz  32, 80,
310
Oesau, *Oberst* Walter  93,
130–1, 187, 256, 278
Osterkamp, *Generalmajor*
  Theodor  72, 82, 83, 88, 92,
187

Page, Pilot Officer Geoffrey 92

Park, Air Vice-Marshal
Keith 69–71, 109, 110, 253,
282, 283

Pavenzinger, *Oberfeldwebel*
Georg 34, 92, 97, 119,
124–6, 130, 310, pl. 21

Petzold, *Unteroffizier*
Rudolf 35–7, 310

Petzschler, *Feldwebel* Horst 225,
269, 310

Philipp, *Oberstleutnant*
Hans 239, 256

Pichon-Kalau vom Hofe,
*Leutnant* Werner 92, 310

Pingel, *Hauptmann* Rolf 48, 80,
310

points system, victories 161–2,
272

Priller, *Oberstleutnant* Josef
'Pips' 165–6, 196, 223, pl. 55

Raich, *Leutnant* Alfons 95–7,
310

Rauch, *Unteroffizier* Alfred 89,
310

Richter, *Feldwebel* Ernst 272,
310

Robel, *Oberfeldwebel*
Joachim 104–5, 143, 154–5,
250, 310

Rödel, *Oberst* Gustav 177–8,
196, 310

Rudorffer, *Hauptmann* Erich 89,
132, 142, 194–5, 310

Ruppert, *Hauptmann* Kurt 158,
165, pl. 1, 46, 54

Sauer, *Feldwebel* Dr Felix 121,
235, 310, pl. 53

*Scharnhorst*, battleship 27, 29

Schmid *Generalleutnant* Josef
'Beppo' 181

Schmid, *Feldwebel*
Otto 158–61, 167–8, 171,
176–7, 205–6, 216–17,
218–20, 223, 224, 226, 232–3,
239–42, 244–5, 256–7, 260–2,
265–7, 278, 309, pl. 35, 37,
40, 41, 47, 48, 49

Schnell, *Oberfeldwebel*
Siegfried 100, 131, pl. 30

Scholz, *Oberleutnant*
Günther 23, 48, 78–9, 80,
102, 143, 309, pl. 3, 14, 15,
26

Schöpfel, *Major* Gerhard 15,
54, 77, 103, 131, 141–2, 149,
155, 164–5, 199, 310, pl. 27,
44

Schröder, *Hauptmann*
Georg 174, 178–80, 227–9,
230, 278, 310

Schröder, *Leutnant* Jochen 45,
52, 59–60, 93–4

Skawran, *Professor* Paul
Robert 257, 294 n.9, 311

Smythe, Sergeant George 99

Späte, *Hauptmann*
Wolfgang 255, 310

Sperrle, *Generalfeldmarschall*
Hugo 34, 71, 73, 182

Stammberger, *Oberleutnant*
Otto 7–8, 87, 137–9, 140–1,
148–50, 153–4, 157–8, 160,
164–6, 167, 168–9, 170–1,
194, 195–6, 198, 199, 208,
213–16, 220–3, 227, 252–3,
279–80, 309, pl. 1, 34, 46, 50

Steinhilper, *Oberleutnant*
 Ulrich   90, 103–4, 113–14,
 123–4, 310
Strelow, *Oberfähnrich*
 Hans   145
Strümpel, *Hauptmann*
 Hennig   64, 80–1, 107,
 131–2, 310
Stumpf, *Generaloberst*
 Hans-Jürgen   74, 191

Tratt, *Major* Eduard   262, 263
Trautloft, *Oberst* Hannes   80,
 81, 91, 93, 187, 239
Trübenbach, *Oberst* Hanns   7,
 32–3, 55, 60–3, 73, 81–6,
 88–9, 90–1, 114–15, 117–19,
 122, 126–8, 129, 130, 147–8,
 183–192, 230, 309, pl. 17

Udet, *Generaloberst* Ernst   144,
 145, 164
USAAF (US Army Air Force)
 fighters
 aircraft types and
 numbers   210–11, 243,
 drop tanks   168, 173, 211–13,
 234, 243, 250
 range   212–13, 243–4

Wenke, *Unteroffizier* Paul   116,
 117, pl. 29
Wick, *Major* Helmut   66, 82,
 130–2
Wickop, *Hauptmann*
 Dietrich   218–19, 224, 239
Wiegand, *Leutnant* Gerhard   9,
 196, 273–7, 310
Wiggers, *Hauptmann* Ernst   97,
 119, 126